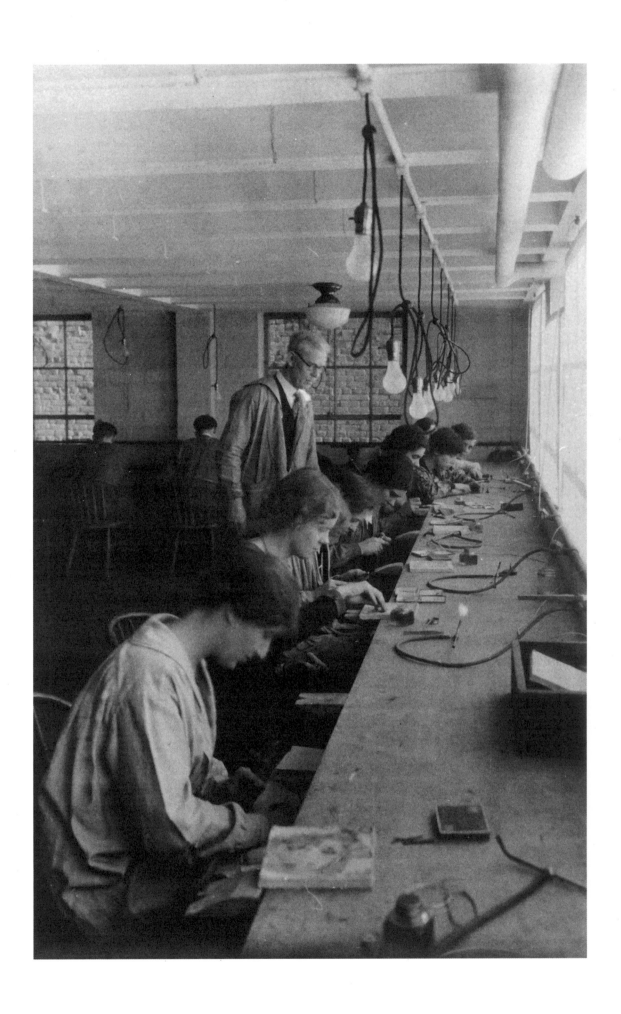

INSPIRING

BOSTON'S
ARTS AND CRAFTS
MOVEMENT

REFORM

MARILEE BOYD MEYER
CONSULTING CURATOR

Essays by
DAVID ACTON ✴ BEVERLY K. BRANDT
EDWARD S. COOKE, JR. ✴ JEANNINE FALINO
NANCY FINLAY ✴ ANNE E. HAVINGA
MARILEE BOYD MEYER ✴ SUSAN J. MONTGOMERY
NICOLA J. SHILLIAM

DAVIS MUSEUM AND CULTURAL CENTER
DISTRIBUTED BY HARRY N. ABRAMS, INC., PUBLISHERS

THIS CATALOGUE, INSPIRING REFORM: BOSTON'S ARTS AND CRAFTS MOVEMENT, IS PRODUCED BY THE DAVIS MUSEUM AND CULTURAL CENTER TO ACCOMPANY THE EXHIBITION. GRANTS FROM THE NATIONAL ENDOWMENT FOR THE ARTS, A FEDERAL AGENCY; FIDELITY INVESTMENTS THROUGH THE FIDELITY FOUNDATION; THE GRACE SLACK McNEIL PROGRAM IN THE HISTORY OF AMERICAN ART; SKINNER, AUCTIONEERS AND APPRAISERS OF ANTIQUES & FINE ART, BOSTON; JACQUELINE LOEWE FOWLER; THE E. FRANKLIN ROBBINS CHARITABLE TRUST; THE MARGARET MULL ART MUSEUM FUND; AND THE WELLESLEY COLLEGE FRIENDS OF ART SUPPORTED THE EXHIBITION, CATALOGUE, AND ACCOMPANYING PROGRAMS.

Exhibition Dates
DAVIS MUSEUM AND CULTURAL CENTER
WELLESLEY COLLEGE
FEBRUARY 28 – JULY 14, 1997

THE RENWICK GALLERY OF THE
NATIONAL MUSEUM OF AMERICAN ART
SMITHSONIAN INSTITUTION
MARCH 6 – JULY 6, 1998

Project Director
JUDITH HOOS FOX

Consulting Curator
MARILEE BOYD MEYER

Catalogue and Exhibition Coordinator
MELISSA R. KATZ

Loan and Photography Coordinators
LISA McDERMOTT, SANDRA PETRIE HACHEY

Project Interns
SUSAN BROWNE AYLWARD, LAURA DeNORMANDIE, KATHERINE STEFKO

Content Editor
GERALD W.R. WARD

Copy Editing
MOVEABLE TYPE INC.

Indexers
NICHOLAS D. HUMEZ, PATRICIA PERRIER

Catalogue and Exhibition Design
DESIGN/WRITING/RESEARCH

JACKET FRONT: Wallace Nutting, *Wallace Nutting's Place, Framingham*, 1912, hand–colored platinum print; Society for the Presentation of New England Antiquities, Boston, Massachusetts (cat no. 121).
FRONTISPIECE: Jewelry workers in George J. Hunt's shop, ca. 1926; Vant Papers, collection of Stephen Vaughan.
JACKET BACK: Frank J. Marshall, Covered box with peacock medallion, ca. 1910, silver with enamel; collection of Alexander Yale Goriansky (cat no. 43).

LIBRARY OF CONGRESS CATALOGUE CARD NO. 96-86692
ISBN: 1-881894-08-8 (DAVIS MUSEUM) | 0-8109-6341-8 (ABRAMS)

COPYRIGHT © 1997 DAVIS MUSEUM AND CULTURAL CENTER
PUBLISHED IN 1997 BY THE DAVIS MUSEUM AND CULTURAL CENTER, WELLESLEY
DISTRIBUTED IN 1997 BY HARRY N. ABRAMS, INCORPORATED, NEW YORK
A TIMES MIRROR COMPANY

SECOND PRINTING

✸

Sandra Adams
Edith Alpers
The Baltimore Museum of Art
Rosalie Berberian
Richard Blacher
Thomas G. Boss Fine Books
Boston Public Library
W. Scott Braznell
Helen Vose Carr
David Cathers
Colby–Sawyer College Library
Cooper–Hewitt, National Design Museum,
    Smithsonian Institution
Cranbrook Art Museum,
    Bloomfield Hills, Michigan
Dedham Historical Society,
    Dedham, Massachusetts
Ellen Paul Denker and Bert Denker
The Detroit Institute of Arts
Drucker Antiques
R.A. Ellison
Fogg Art Museum,
    Harvard University Art Museums
Jacqueline Loewe Fowler
Barbara and Henry Fuldner
Johanna and Leslie Garfield
Arthur D. Gebelein
Ernest G. Gebelein
George Eastman House
Gilman Paper Company Collection
Alexander Yale Goriansky
Grace Episcopal Church,
    Manchester, New Hampshire
Gardiner G. Greene
Harvard College Library, Harvard University
The Manfred Heiting Collection, Amsterdam
Henry Ford Museum and Greenfield Village
Hingham Historical Society, Massachusetts
The Houghton Library, Harvard University
Betty and Robert A. Hut
Martin W. Hutner
Isabella Stewart Gardner Museum
Gilbert Jonas
John Heard House,
    Ipswich Historical Society, Massachusetts
James D. Kaufman
Jane D. Kaufmann
Lancaster Town Library, Massachusetts

Lee Gallery, Winchester, Massachusetts
James and Alice Lyons
The Yvonne Markowitz Collection
John Markus
The Family of Laurin Hovey Martin
Memorial Hall Museum,
    Pocumtuck Valley Memorial Association,
    Deerfield, Massachusetts
The Metropolitan Museum of Art
Marilee Boyd Meyer
Museum of Art, Rhode Island School of Design,
    Providence
Museum of Fine Arts, Boston
Museum of Modern Art, New York
National Museum of American Art,
    Smithsonian Institution
New Bedford Free Public Library
The New York Public Library, Rare Books and
    Manuscripts Division
Norwood Historical Society, F. Holland Day
    House, Norwood, Massachusetts
Tazio Nuvolari
The Oakes Family
Old York Historical Society, York, Maine
Judith Evans Parker
Mrs. Malcolm D. Perkins
William H. Perkins
Philadelphia Museum of Art
Pine Manor College,
    Chestnut Hill, Massachusetts
Pomfret School, Connecticut
Elizabeth Rose
John Rossetti
Sandwich Historical Society Glass Museum,
    Massachusetts
Society for the Preservation of New England
    Antiquities, Boston, Massachusetts
Tau Zeta Epsilon Art and Music Society,
    Wellesley College
Wellesley College, Wellesley, Massachusetts
Wellesley College Art Library
Wellesley College Library, Special Collections
Worcester Art Museum,
    Worcester, Massachusetts
Yale University Art Gallery,
    New Haven, Connecticut
Yale University Library
Private Collections

LIST OF COLOR PLATES

[sorted by catalogue number]

CONTENTS

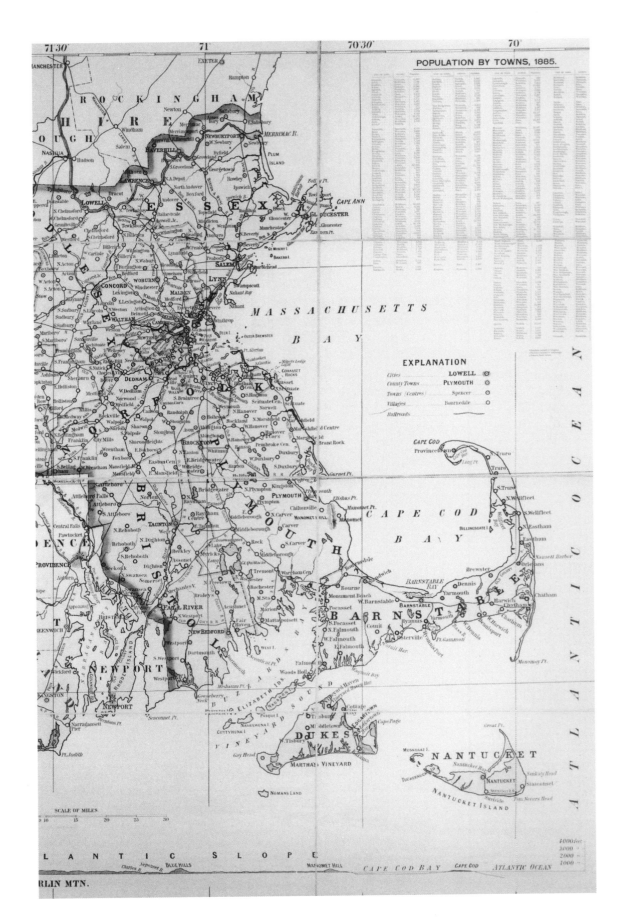

R.W. Smith & Co., map of Massachusetts, 1885, published in Philadelphia, Penn., 1888; Research Library, Boston Public Library.

TO MARK THE centenary of the founding of the Society of Arts and Crafts, Boston and the earliest American Arts and Crafts exhibition in 1897, the Davis Museum and Cultural Center has organized *Inspiring Reform: Boston's Arts and Crafts Movement.* The first comprehensive exhibition to examine Boston's contribution to the Arts and Crafts movement, it presents a rich selection of objects and artists, shown together for the first time in a century. The Davis exhibition has inspired research that adds significantly to our understanding of the ideas, ideals, and individuals that shaped Boston's unique response to this international movement. It also contributes to the growing study of American regional Arts and Crafts movements that, in recent years, has resulted in significant exhibitions of turn–of–the–century design in Chicago, Detroit, California, and upper New York state. ❡ This exhibition and accompanying catalogue explore the complex matrix of aesthetic ideals, historical circumstance, and social context that defined the Arts and Crafts movement in Boston and propelled it to national significance. Boston led the nation not only in the display of the new design ethos, but also in identifying the arts as a form of education, social welfare, and civic improvement. By relating Boston activity to the larger national movement, it is possible to identify what is uniquely regional about Boston designs. The proponents and practitioners of the Boston movement emphasized the American past through colonial revival, and the American future through the training and education of immigrants in schools and settlement houses, using the arts as a means to access American culture. ❡ The Davis Museum is a fitting institution to present this important exhibition, as both the town of Wellesley and Wellesley College had close, early associations with Boston's Arts and Crafts movement. C. Howard Walker, head of the Jury of the Society of Arts and Crafts, Boston until 1912 and design professor of the School of the Museum of Fine Arts, Boston, also taught a course in the History of Ornament at Wellesley College in 1897–98. Known to the Boston arts community as the "watch dog of taste," Walker was deeply committed to establishing rigorous standards for the movement and championing the expressive potential of the decorative arts. ⟨June Barrows Mussey, the son of a Wellesley College professor and an exhibiting member of the SACB, founded Merry Thought Press in Wellesley, publishing small books of poetry and color woodblock prints, while his mother ran an Arts and Crafts shop and tea room in the town. Carver Andrew Lees resided in Wellesley, printmaker Margaret Jordan Patterson taught at the Dana Hall school, and silversmiths George Christian Gebelein and Mary Knight (among others) worked in the Wellesley branch of the Handicraft Shop, a Boston metalsmiths co–operative. Their activities accurately reflect the diversity of direction taken by the movement in the early years of the twentieth century, a modestly scaled and community–based response to the Industrial Revolution. ⟨Like many of the outlying communities of Boston, the town of Wellesley offered upper– and middle–class patrons the possibility to realize the dream of domestic harmony through aesthetic unity that characterized Arts and Crafts ideals. While near to Boston, the towns of Wellesley, Winchester, Brookline, and Newton were also far enough removed to allow for the construction of homes and gardens that reflected essential principles of the Arts and Crafts movement. Isaac Sprague's *Belvedere* development in Wellesley Hills, begun around 1909, included a house designed by Gustav Stickley, completed ca. 1912. To this day, an Arts and Crafts–style sign on the corner of Abbott Road and Washington Street marks the entrance to this group of houses, visible expressions of this early twentieth–century ideal. ⟨Most significantly for Wellesley College is the *Tower Court* dormitory, which remains one of the most intact Arts and Crafts interiors in the Boston area. Designed by the firm of Coolidge and Carlson, *Tower Court* opened in September 1915. The program for *Tower's* Great Hall interior—influenced by the great architect of the American Gothic revival, Ralph Adams Cram, who served as architectural advisor to the Wellesley College Board of Trustees—includes hand–crafted furniture by William F. Ross & Co. and splendid ironwork by Krasser Iron Company. This remarkable ensemble of stained glass, furniture, lights, andirons, and cabinetry—capped by a hand–lettered Arts and Crafts inscription to the donor in the form of a manuscript page complete with historiated initial—provides an extraordinary record of the movement and its ambitions. ⟨We are particularly pleased to present an exhibition which so clearly demonstrates our commitment to the study, interpretation, and collection of these important examples of our material culture. The opportunity to present to our audience objects not yet widely featured in our permanent collection expands greatly the parameters of our own holdings. As both objects of beauty and documents of cultural development, the study and collection of the decorative arts complements Wellesley's multi-disciplinary approach to teaching and learning. ❬ The college museum is set apart from other institutions in the opportunities afforded by collaborations with faculty. They range from the occasional lecture and gallery talk to the most ambitious exhibition and publication. Over the years the museum has often joined with the Grace Slack McNeil Program in the History of American Art to present new research in American art. It is a pleasure to once again acknowledge the important role of program chair James F. O'Gorman in providing the initial stimulus for our investigations of the Arts and Crafts movement in Boston. This exhibition proposal, as is often the case, began in a conversation between Professor O'Gorman and Arts and Crafts expert Marilee Boyd Meyer, leading to the Wellesley College symposium of April 1993, *The Arts and Crafts in Boston and New England, 1897–1927*, sponsored by the Grace Slack McNeil program, which furthered the investigations of this material. We are indebted to Marilee Boyd Meyer for the tireless enthusiasm and commitment she has shown throughout the project in her role as consulting curator. ❬ In addition, I would like to thank our distinguished team of guest curators who shaped this exhibition, each focusing on a particular Arts and Crafts medium: David Acton, curator of prints and drawings, Worcester Art Museum; Edward S. Cooke, Jr., Charles F. Montgomery Associate Professor of American Decorative Arts, Yale University; Nancy Finlay, print specialist, New York Public Library; Marilee Boyd Meyer, independent consultant; Susan J. Montgomery, curator of Strawbery Banke Museum, Portsmouth, New Hampshire; and their three colleagues from the Museum of Fine Arts, Boston: Jeannine Falino, assistant curator of American decorative arts and sculpture; Anne E. Havinga, assistant curator of prints, drawings, and photographs; and Nicola J. Shilliam, assistant curator, textiles and costumes collection. Their contributions to the exhibition through the selection of objects, catalogue essays, and biographical research—completed in addition to the demands of their respective positions—exemplify the spirit of collaboration and enthusiasm that has distinguished this project. They were joined by catalogue essayist Beverly K. Brandt, associate professor of design, Arizona State University, and foremost scholar of the Society of Arts and Crafts, Boston. ❬ Every single member of the Davis Museum staff deserves special recognition for their commitment and vision for this, our most ambitious project to date. Each one has responded heroically to the challenge of mounting and presenting this exhibition to the public. Curator Judith Hoos Fox carefully and wisely guided the curatorial team and museum staff through the complex logistics of collaborative research and information sharing, loan and catalogue deadlines, and many other details great and small. Assistant curator Melissa R. Katz effected the herculean task of overseeing the checklist and loan requests, preparing the catalogue manuscript for publication, preparing the wall and label text, and coordinating the execution of the project. Their work with exhibition and catalogue designers, J. Abbott Miller and Paul Carlos of Design/Writing/Research, has resulted in this remarkable publication and the stunning transformation of the museum's galleries to create an historical and cultural context for the objects in the exhibition. The studio's work captures the integral roles of design, display, and function in the Arts and Crafts movement. Museum technicians John Rossetti and Santiago Hernandez brought to life the complex design and installation while ensuring the secure display of these rare and fragile objects. Associate director Kathleen Harleman played a central role in securing funding for the exhibition while, as always, her incisive questions kept the exhibition objectives focused on issues of content and quality. Registrar Lisa McDermott skillfully handled the multiple loan requests and complicated shipping arrangements for both the Davis Museum and Cultural Center and the National Museum of American Art. She was ably assisted by assistant registrar Sandra Hachey in the daunting task of securing photography rights and reproductions. Laura DeNormandie, curatorial assistant, provided administrative support with both competence and grace. Corinne Fryhle, curator of education, developed a program of lectures and events capturing the multifaceted nature of the movement, which has been diligently organized and overseen by education assistant Susan Browne Aylward. The exhibition's scope extends beyond the campus thanks to the self–guided tour of regional Arts and Crafts sites prepared by former education intern Katherine Stefko. Finally, the contributions of director of information and institutional relations Peter Walsh, including arranging distribution with our co–publisher, Harry N. Abrams, Inc., have ensured that this important exhibition and publication reach a truly national audience. ❡ We also wish to acknowledge the funding sources that have made the exhibition and catalogue possible. To the National Endowment for the Arts, we extend our gratitude—as we have so often in the past—for providing important support for this exhibition. For this and many other projects, funding from the Endowment has been the determining factor in the museum's decision to undertake the project. Its support has always been a catalyst in obtaining further necessary funding. The museum is particularly grateful for the support of Fidelity Investments through the Fidelity Foundation. We would also like to thank the Grace Slack McNeil Program in the History of American Art; Skinner, Auctioneers and Appraisers of Antiques & Fine Art, Boston; and Jacqueline Loewe Fowler for their support of the project, and acknowledge the moneys provided by the E. Franklin Robbins Charitable Trust and the Margaret Mull Art Museum Fund. The Wellesley College Friends of Art have also generously contributed to the exhibition. ❡ Ultimately, any exhibition depends on the generosity of its lenders. It is with gratitude that we acknowledge their significance to the exhibition at the Davis Museum and at the Renwick Gallery of the National Museum of American Art, Smithsonian Institution. Their willingness to part with their objects for an extended period at two venues has been critical to the success of this project. ❡ I would especially like to acknowledge our colleagues at the National Museum of American Art, Smithsonian Institution—Elizabeth Broun, director, and Charles Robertson, deputy director—and our colleagues at the Renwick Gallery of the National Museum of American Art, Smithsonian Institution—Kenneth R. Trapp, curator-in-charge, and Jeremy Adamson, curator—whose enthusiasm for the exhibition has enabled us to present *Inspiring Reform* in Washington, D.C., once again affirming the significant national contribution of Boston's Arts and Crafts movement.

SUSAN M. TAYLOR
DIRECTOR
DAVIS MUSEUM AND CULTURAL CENTER

The Davis Museum and Cultural Center, as a participant in the current national fascination with design reform at the turn of the century, has organized *Inspiring Reform: Boston's Arts and Crafts Movement*, the first exhibition to examine Boston's pivotal role in the American Arts and Crafts movement. This exhibition coincides with the one hundredth anniversary of the founding of the Society of Arts and Crafts, Boston—the first such organization incorporated in America, and the only such society still in existence. *Inspiring Reform* addresses the revival of interest in turn–of–the–century design and caps a decade of research that followed the landmark 1987 exhibition *"The Art that is Life": The Arts & Crafts Movement in America, 1875–1920*, organized by the Museum of Fine Arts, Boston. Since then, studies in California, upstate New York, and the Upper Midwest have revealed a pattern of New England connections within their regional adaptations, affirming Boston's role as a catalyst in the popularization of the Arts and Crafts movement in America. ⟨Originating in Britain in the nineteenth century, Arts and Crafts ideology called for aesthetic and social reform, in reaction to the decline in craftsmanship and the dehumanization of labor which accompanied the Industrial Revolution. John Ruskin and William Morris, among others, believed that quality hand–production would restore dignity to the maker and that objects of refined and elegant design would reestablish harmony and simplicity in the home. "Have nothing in your houses which you do not know to be useful or believe beautiful," stated Morris's credo, which elevated everyday objects into works of art. ⟨With its close ties to English culture, a heritage of cottage industries and crafts dating back to the seventeenth century, and its reverential support for art and education, Boston was well–placed to introduce Arts and Crafts ideals to an American audience. Boston's closely knit social leadership—wealthy, cultured patrons of the arts, philanthropic supporters, collectors, and members of the Church—believed in both aesthetic progress and traditional morality, a duality author William L. Vance coined "rebellious traditionalism" in *The Bostonians: Painters of an Elegant Age, 1870–1930*. The elite's Puritan lineage lay behind the Society of Arts and Crafts's emphasis on "sobriety and restraint" stated in its charter, and Boston's craftsmen responded to the call for more decorous, spiritually elevating design, but in a more conservative fashion than did their English, midwestern, or Californian counterparts. New England craftsmen and design reformers relied on historical models and practiced careful, meticulous workmanship. Indeed, the disciplined and brilliant execution of Boston's craftsmen would set a national standard. The tenets of the Arts and Crafts movement included a revival of medieval, Gothic, and Italian Renaissance precepts, along with pre–industrial design principles associated with the Japanese "craze" in the last quarter of the nineteenth century. Boston patrons were particularly responsive to the colonial revival, a style that embodied rationality, balance, and moderation, and also celebrated their historic past. One North End settlement house workshop, providing vocational training for young Italian and Jewish immigrant women, explicitly made the historical connection by naming itself "Paul Revere Pottery." ⟨ Boston's primary contribution to the Arts and Crafts movement was not style, however, but the transmission of ideas through its educational network. The Massachusetts public school system incorporated art education into its general curriculum in 1870. The state–sponsored Massachusetts Normal Art School and the Museum of Fine Arts's own School of Drawing and Painting soon followed. By the turn of the century, Boston–area colleges—including Harvard—offered public enrollment in summer arts classes. The study of art also gave teachers and artisans, including women, access to training in the basic design principles of their craft. ⟨ Boston's teachers and students of design carried these ideals to smaller communities outside the Boston metropolitan area, such as Worcester and Deerfield, and Providence, Rhode Island, where they set up workshops, studios, and schools. More importantly, Boston–educated craftsmen, architects, and teachers disseminated Arts and Crafts standards of good taste across the country. Arts and Crafts societies flourished from Portland, Maine to Portland, Oregon under Boston's intellectual leadership. ⟨ The Davis Museum and Cultural Center has assembled more than 150 objects to demonstrate Boston's complex response and contribution to Arts and Crafts reform. These works date from the 1890s through to the 1930s—from the inception through to the heyday of the Society of Arts and Crafts, Boston—and range from conventionalized designs to the dawn of the streamlined modernist aesthetic. *Inspiring Reform* also represents Boston's diversity through the number of artists discussed in both the essays and the biographies, especially those lesser–known figures often eclipsed by the famous few. Photography and book design, two specialties frequently ignored in Arts and Crafts studies, are included in this exhibition, since Boston artists played key roles in these fields. Other areas, which have received little study and are beyond the scope of this exhibition, include stained glass, exemplified by Connick Studios and by Sarah Wyman Whitman's windows in Harvard's Memorial Hall; the extensive basket–making of both the Deerfield and the Hingham societies; architecture; and landscape architecture, as influenced by Frederick Law Olmsted. ❨The essays and biographies present a significant body of new research, focusing on individuals and groups not previously identified or adequately studied. Each author has expressed a hope for scholarship continued beyond the limits of this exhibition to further examine the assumptions underpinning current historical interpretations. The scholarship supporting this exhibition, however, has laid the foundation for such research, and forms a comprehensive and pioneering study of Boston's unique and controversial role in the Arts and Crafts movement. ❨I would like to thank Beverly K. Brandt, a pioneer researcher of the Arts and Crafts movement in Boston, for her years of support on this project, and James O'Gorman, Grace Slack McNeil Professor of the History of American Art, Wellesley College, who proposed the venue for this exhibition.

MARILEE BOYD MEYER
CONSULTING CURATOR

A large debt of gratitude is due to Melissa R. Katz for the important role she played in organizing and shaping this introduction.

TALKING OR WORKING:
THE CONUNDRUM OF MORAL AESTHETICS IN BOSTON'S ARTS AND CRAFTS MOVEMENT

Edward S. Cooke, Jr.

THE EXPLORATION OF regional styles has been one of the cornerstones of studies in the decorative arts in the last thirty to forty years. Efforts to identify and interpret objects have been based upon analysis of the stylistic origins, form, decoration, materials, and construction of objects from particular regions. Such an approach has also guided scholarship on the Arts and Crafts movement and resulted in case studies on Chicago, California, and upper New York state.[1] Many of these regional studies of the Arts and Crafts movement have emphasized the aesthetics of the works of this period and relied upon a sense of the movement's monolithic origins. All cite John Ruskin, William Morris, and C.R. Ashbee as the inspirational leaders of regional efforts to unify the look of domestic space by reestablishing cooperation between different participants in the design process; to improve the quality of life by restoring aesthetic and structural integrity to everyday objects; and to preserve traditional methods of craftsmanship in a time of increased mechanization. Missing is an exploration of how different American centers responded to the various approaches or attitudes within the movement.[2] ❡ In an effort to analyze the diffusion of Arts and Crafts ideologies, this essay probes the whys and hows of artistic craft production in Boston in the late nineteenth and early twentieth centuries. Boston is considered a major center of the American Arts and Crafts movement because it supported the nation's first Arts and Crafts society (founded there in 1897), a number of important architects such as Ralph Adams Cram and Bertram Grosvenor Goodhue, and several critically acclaimed shops (for example, Grueby Pottery, the Handicraft Shop, and Merrymount Press). Yet to date there has been no thorough study of Boston's Arts and Crafts environment. Particularizing Boston's responses to the various strains of design reform provides a framework within which to examine the Society of Arts and Crafts, Boston, and the media in which Boston craftsmen and designers worked.

1. On regionalism as a decorative arts paradigm, see Philip Zimmerman, "Regionalism in American Furniture Studies," in Gerald W.R. Ward, ed., *Perspectives on American Furniture* (New York: W.W. Norton, 1988), pp. 11–38. Some of the specific studies include Sharon Darling's *Chicago Metalsmiths* (Chicago: Chicago Historical Society, 1977) and *Chicago Furniture: Art, Craft & Industry, 1833–1983* (New York: W.W. Norton, 1984); Kenneth Trapp, *The Arts and Crafts Movement in California: Living the Good Life* (New York: Abbeville, 1993); and Coy Ludwig, *The Arts and Crafts Movement in New York State, 1890s–1920s* (Hamilton, N.Y.: Gallery Association of New York State, 1983). See also Cheryl Robertson's bibliographic essay "The Arts and Crafts Movement in America," in Kenneth L. Ames and Gerald W.R. Ward, eds., *Decorative Arts and Household Furnishings in America, 1650–1920: An Annotated Bibliography* (Charlottesville: University Press of Virginia, 1989), pp. 343–57.

2. In "The Lamp of British Precedent: An Introduction to the Arts and Crafts Movement," Wendy Kaplan cautions about the varied convictions of Arts and Crafts reformers and the need to define participants broadly, but concentrates on regional aesthetics rather than regional dynamics: Wendy Kaplan, ed., *"The Art that is Life": The Arts & Crafts Movement in America, 1875–1920* (Boston: Museum of Fine Arts, 1987), pp. 52–60.

PRELUDE: THE 1870S

For the past fifty years, many cultural critics have lamented the decline of Boston during the last quarter of the nineteenth century. Whether considering the economic, political, or cultural vitality of the city, many writers have suggested that Boston had lost its leading role and was merely living smugly on its reputation. Making assumptions based upon the decline of certain types of manufacturing and entrepreneurial activity, the devastation of the 1872 fire, the rise of the Catholic Irish as a political force, and the exodus of writers such as William Dean Howells, the popular view portrays the former "Athens of America" imagining itself as a leader when in fact it was only experiencing a brief "Indian summer."[3] ❦ Such a pessimistic view of Boston has been based primarily on trends within popular literature— the rise to prominence of realistic, rather than Romantic prose, and the lure of New York as the center of commercial publishing—and the writings of such period pessimists and social critics as Henry James and George Santayana, who were voicing their own struggles. But is this a full or fair picture of Boston? As William Vance has recently demonstrated, shifting from a narrow consideration of literary production to a more inclusive evaluation of other activities helps revise our perceptions of late nineteenth–century Boston. Drawing insights from Justin Winsor's 1880 *Memorial History of Boston*, Vance sees vitality where other critics had seen only decline.[4] By linking together many different events, it is possible to view the 1870s as a pivotal decade in which Boston began to remake itself, shifting its attention from literary to visual culture: landscape design, architecture, painting, sculpture, and industrial arts. ❦ Several crucial events in that decade signaled a change in the city's orientation. In an 1870 Lowell Institute lecture, the landscape designer Frederick Law Olmsted argued the importance of different types of parks in urban areas, and later began to work with the city's Parks Commission on a plan for Boston's "emerald necklace" of parks connected by parkways. Continued development in the Back Bay, and in the downtown area devastated by the 1872 fire, prompted considerable discussion and activity among the city's newly organized architects, who were eager to prove their command of design. In the spring of 1874, the architect Henry Hobson Richardson, who had graduated from Harvard in 1859, returned to the Boston area and established a studio in Brookline. Richardson clearly valued the role of craftsmanship in architecture, and his circle of employees, which included Langford Warren, Waddy Longfellow, Robert Andrews, and Herbert Jacques, became some of the most active leaders in Boston's Arts and Crafts movement. The activities of the local architects prompted the expansion of the role of craftsmen within the building trades, benefiting numerous masons and small woodworking shops, and encouraging the immigration of such skilled carvers as John

3. Van Wyck Brooks, *New England: Indian Summer, 1865–1915* (New York: E.P. Dutton, 1940); Martin Green, *The Problem of Boston* (New York: W.W. Norton, 1966).

4. William Vance, "Redefining 'Bostonian'," in Trevor Fairbrother et al., *The Bostonians: Painters of an Elegant Age, 1870–1930* (Boston: Museum of Fine Arts, 1986), pp. 9–30.

Evans and Hugh Cairns. ❡ In painting, a number of patrons and a smaller number of painters reorganized the Boston Art Club to provide a forum for the discussion of techniques and aesthetics. At the center of the region's group of "spirited and progressive" painters, William Morris Hunt taught painting that emphasized impulsive imaginative compositions along with visible technique, and encouraged the collecting of French Barbizon and early Impressionist painting. At the same time Charles Callahan Perkins, the descendent of a China trader, recognized the importance of art education and a knowledge of drawing for America's citizenry and helped bring the Englishman Walter Smith to Boston in 1870 to set up compulsory drawing instruction for all school children and to establish the Massachusetts Normal Art School for the training of art teachers and workers skilled in the industrial arts. Perkins was also instrumental in establishing the Museum of Fine Arts in 1870 as a public repository to inspire artists, teach historical design, and instill good taste.[5] ❡ What prompted such a surge of interest in visual culture in the 1870s? Much of the interest accompanied the city leadership's transformation from an elite to a social class whose members had abdicated a political role, and parlayed the economic success of their ancestors into building non–profit organizations that defined appropriate taste and educated others who formed a community distinct from theirs, and who used their positions of authority to maintain their unassailable status. They were not manufacturing, railroad, or financial entrepreneurs but rather cultural capitalists, linked by common backgrounds, Harvard educations, intermarriage, and board memberships. They stressed their mastery and understanding of artistic genres and styles, the need for suitable leaders to lead and teach others, and the belief that the majority of citizens, although perhaps mechanically skilled, were incapable of creative, imaginative work. To counter what they viewed as popular vulgarities, these Boston Brahmins built institutions that defined visual culture and set the parameters of public discourse about such art. The value put on culture—and control of culture—and the social distinction between mind and muscle provided the defining framework for Boston's acceptance and adaptation of Arts and Crafts principles.[6]

THE LEGACY OF CHARLES ELIOT NORTON

At the heart of the transformation to visual culture was Charles Eliot Norton (1827–1908), who became the main spokesman in Boston on issues of design and craftsmanship. An 1846 graduate of Harvard, Norton initially earned great respect for his literary skills, pioneering the field of Dante scholarship, contributing often to the *Atlantic Monthly* and the *Nation*, and gaining a reputation as a valued editor. He held a deep interest in European history and culture, and in 1855 sought out John Ruskin. The two quickly

5. On the changes of this decade, see especially Cynthia Zaitzevsky, *Frederick Law Olmsted and the Boston Park System* (Cambridge: Harvard University Press, 1982); James O'Gorman, *H.H. Richardson and His Office: Selected Drawings* (Cambridge: Harvard College Library, 1974); Vance, "Redefining 'Bostonian'," and Fairbrother, "Painting in Boston, 1870–1930," in *The Bostonians*, esp. pp. 31–40; Bainbridge Bunting, *Houses of Boston's Back Bay: An Architectural History, 1840–1917* (Cambridge: Belknap Press of Harvard University Press, 1967); Douglass Shand–Tucci, *Built in Boston: City and Suburb, 1800–1950* (Amherst: University of Massachusetts Press, 1978); Walter Muir Whitehill, "Boston Artists and Craftsmen at the Opening of the Twentieth Century," *New England Quarterly* 50, no. 3 (September 1977), pp. 387–408; Diane Korzenik, *Drawn to Art: A Nineteenth–Century American Dream* (Hanover, N.H.: University Press of New England, 1985); and Elizabeth Herlihy, ed., *Fifty Years of Boston: A Memorial Volume Issued in Commemoration of the Tercentenary of 1930* (Boston: Subcommittee on Memorial History of the Boston Tercentenary Committee, 1930).

6. Paul Dimaggio, "Cultural Entrepreneurship in Nineteenth–Century Boston: The Creation of an Organizational Base for High Culture in America," *Media, Culture and Society* 4 (1982), pp. 33–50; Ronald Story, *The Forging of an Aristocracy: Harvard and the Boston Upper Class, 1800–1870* (Middletown, Conn.: Wesleyan University Press, 1980).

became friends who appreciated and respected each other's intellectual accomplishments. They shared a common belief in the moral power of art, the creative genius of the craftsman in a proper environment, and the aesthetics of craftsmanship. Norton, however, demonstrated a keener interest in the technical side of craftsmanship.[7] ❡ In 1873 President Charles Eliot of Harvard named Norton a Professor of Fine Arts, the first appointment in art history at an American university. Throughout his teaching career, Norton stressed the relationship of the arts to the study of history and literature, and the necessity of studying the underlying unity of expression in all the arts. Like Ruskin, Norton believed that close, firsthand study of historical artifacts would reveal the relationships of art and morals in past societies. He celebrated the Athenian Age, for he felt that the landscape and open–air lifestyle of ancient Greece checked materialism and hardness of heart, allowed every citizen to be an artist with an eye for balance, rhythm, proportion, and symmetry, and positively affected politics and writing as well as the visual arts. He also displayed a particular fondness for medieval Florence and Venice, where in his view a republican social structure and church–driven unity of spirit and morality led to great civic pride and craftsmanship. Norton found little of interest after 1600, believing that the Renaissance encouraged weak moral temper, permitted unchecked individuality, valued selfish luxury, cheapened taste, and undercut the artisan's devotion to craft.[8] ❡ Norton used the study of the morals and arts of societies past to refine the imaginative sensibilities of his Harvard students and to critique the cultural crises of America's Gilded Age. Distraught by the frenetic pace of life in the late nineteenth century that undercut poetic sensibility, the leisure of wealth that did not ensure the ability to differentiate between beauty and ugliness, and the lack of pride in workmanship that cheapened domestic objects, Norton looked to the past for guidance. As a description for his Fine Arts course in 1897 stated: "The object of this course is to show the relation of this study to the general studies of History and Literature, its importance for the understanding of the moral and intellectual life of mankind, its value in the cultivation of the powers of observation and discrimination of human experience, and its worth as one of the chief means for the culture of the imagination. The course begins with a discussion of the Fine Arts and their mutual relations, and of the modes in which they may be best studied in this country." In his examination questions, Norton always moved from an understanding of the past to a critique of the present beginning, for example, with a question on the place of art in twelfth–century Europe, following with one on regional variations in vaulting techniques, and ending with a question on the reasons for the decline of handicrafts in America or the merits of handicrafts in contrast to manufactured goods.[9] ❡ In his teaching and writing, Norton, like Ruskin,

7. On Norton's early years, see Kermit Vanderbilt, *Charles Eliot Norton: Apostle of Culture in a Democracy* (Cambridge: Belknap Press of Harvard University Press, 1959); and Leslie Workman, "'My First Real Tutor': John Ruskin and Charles Eliot Norton," in *New England Quarterly* 62, no. 4 (December 1989), pp. 572–86.

8. Vanderbilt, *Charles Eliot Norton*, esp. pp. 123–32; The Harvard University Catalogue for the years 1873 to 1910 (microfilm in the Harvard University Archives).

9. Vanderbilt, *Charles Eliot Norton*, esp. pp. 123–25 and 206–20; The Harvard University Catalogue for 1896–97; and Michael Brooks, "New England Gothic: Charles Eliot Norton, Charles H. Moore, and Henry Adams," in Elisabeth Blair MacDougall, ed., *The Architectural Historian in America: Studies in the History of Art* 35 (Washington, D.C.: National Gallery of Art, 1990), pp. 113–25.

espoused the moral foundations of art and argued that the most favorable artistic environment was that of an aristocracy in which there were mutual relations between the arts and between the intellectual leaders and skilled craftsmen. Repulsed by a democracy that "sweeps away natural distinctions of good breeding and superior culture" and permitted the bourgeois attitudes of the "illiterate" newly rich, Norton argued for an aristocracy in which a well–educated group of leaders would guide moral sentiment and taste. Norton did indeed have a profound influence on artistic reform and the Arts and Crafts movement while teaching the future leaders at Harvard. Among the students inspired by Norton and his associate Charles Herbert Moore, a Ruskinian who taught drawing, were the architects Waddy Longfellow, R. Clipston Sturgis, and Edmund Wheelwright; the scholars Ernest Fenollosa, Henry Chapman Mercer, Charles Fletcher Lummis, Denman Waldo Ross, and Bernard Berenson; cultural leaders J. Templeman Coolidge III and Arthur Astor Carey; the antiquarian Wallace Nutting; and even that champion of the vigorous life, Teddy Roosevelt.[10] ❰ Because of his friendship with Ruskin and his prominent role at Harvard, Norton became the filter through which the philosophy of the Arts and Crafts movement passed. His influence can be seen in the choice of past societies to be collected and studied, the way in which the existing social structure embraced design reform without revolution, and the central role of education in artistic regeneration. Norton influenced many scholars and collectors to focus upon Greek or Italian art, and provided the principles by which to study and appreciate art from other times and places. One of his earliest students was Ernest Fenollosa, whom Norton deterred from a career as a painter and for whom he arranged a teaching appointment in Japan. Fenollosa became fascinated with Japanese craftsmanship and the favorable conditions of artistic production there, and in turn influenced a number of collectors and scholars such as William Sturgis Bigelow and Arthur Wesley Dow. In the 1880s, Norton also began to value the associational meaning of American art and architecture before Jacksonian democracy. He wrote a passionate plea for the preservation of New England's historic houses and inspired early antiquarians such as William Sumner Appleton, the founder of the Society for the Preservation of New England Antiquities (SPNEA). Due to Norton's influence, Bostonians collected, appreciated, and studied classical, medieval, Japanese, and colonial American work as the foundation of a usable past. The Greek and Japanese collections at the Museum of Fine Arts, Boston and the Venetian and Florentine holdings of Isabella Gardner were held to be the best in America.[11] ❰ Norton's firm belief in an Arts and Crafts movement led by a cultured and educated aristocracy also served as a catalyst for the formation of several clubs or associations that encouraged high–minded talk about art and

10. In 1890 Norton described a redesigned Harvard campus consisting of buildings "with simple and beautiful design, in mutually helpful, harmonious, and effective relation to each other...," *Harper's New Monthly Magazine* 81 (September 1890). For Norton's critique of the newly rich and his influence as a teacher, see Vanderbilt, *Charles Eliot Norton*, pp. 219–20; T.J. Jackson Lears, *No Place of Grace: Antimodernism and the Transformation of American Culture, 1880–1920* (Chicago: University of Chicago Press, 1983), pp. 66 and 243–47; Sarah Giffen and Kevin Murphy, eds., "A Noble and Dignified Stream": The Piscataqua Region in the Colonial Revival, 1860–1930 (York, Maine: Old York Historical Society, 1992), esp. pp. 115–33; and Brooks, "New England Gothic," pp. 114–16.

11. Walter Muir Whitehill, *Museum of Fine Arts, Boston: A Centennial History* (Cambridge: Belknap Press of Harvard University Press, 1970); William Howe Downes, "Boston as an Art Center," *New England Magazine* 30, no. 2 (April 1904), esp. pp. 157–58; Charles Eliot Norton, "The Lack of Old Homes in America," *Scribner's Magazine* 5 (May 1888), pp. 638–40; and James Lindgren, "'A Constant Incentive to Patriotic Citizenship': Historic Preservation in Progressive–Era Massachusetts," *New England Quarterly* 64, no. 4 (December 1991), pp. 594–608.

design. Among the important associations in which Norton played a role were the Tavern Club, founded in 1884, and the Society of Arts and Crafts, founded in 1897. The former, of which Norton was vice–president from 1886–89 and president from 1890–98, was founded to promote "enlightened activity and enlightened leisure" in regard to all the arts, but played a particular role in the 1880s and early 1890s by bringing together various leaders in design. Members during this time included the architects and designers Robert D. Andrews, Francis Bacon, and Bertram Grosvenor Goodhue; the painters Frank Benson, John Singer Sargent, and Edmund Tarbell; the sculptors Daniel Chester French, Bela Pratt, and Augustus Saint–Gaudens; and museum professionals Martin Brimmer, Ernest Fenollosa, and Edward Morse.[12] The civilized gentility of the Tavern Club served as a wellspring from which ideas about civic morality and artistic progress bubbled up.[13] ⟨Seven members of the Tavern Club were also charter members of the Society of Arts and Crafts, Boston, which was organized shortly after an April 1897 exhibition of industrial arts, the first Arts and Crafts exhibition in America, held at Copley Hall. Harvard education or membership in one of the artistic clubs linked most of the founders. The only actual craftsmen involved were two book designers and printers— Henry Lewis Johnson and Daniel B. Updike, and three carvers—John Evans, John Kirchmayer, and Hugh Cairns. But such artisanal members were appropriate given the importance of book publishing to Boston's economy and continuing literary reputation and the prominence of carved architectural ornament. Carvers and book designers ranked at the top of the crafts hierarchy in Boston and frequently mingled with the leaders of the Arts and Crafts movement. The Society provided an important local forum for the discussion of design issues, lectures by prominent writers and designers, and exhibitions of high–quality handicraft. Beginning in 1900, the Society also maintained a salesroom in Boston. While intended to serve the Boston area, the Society quickly began to influence New England Arts and Crafts practitioners as far away as Providence, Worcester, and Portland, and soon had a national membership that included metalsmiths Robert Jarvie of Chicago, Mildred Watkins and Jane Carson of Cleveland, and Porter Blanchard and Douglas Donaldson of California; ceramists Henry Chapman Mercer of Pennsylvania, William Fulper of New Jersey, Adelaide Robineau of Syracuse, and Artus Van Briggle of Colorado; and glassblower Frederick Carder.[14] ⟨While some of the elite inspired by Norton and his circle themselves took up handicrafts in an attempt to test ideas or understand processes, most spent their time talking or writing about issues of design reform, and relied on others to realize their ideas. Following Norton's prescription of mutually helpful relations, the architects and learned elite were to supply to the artisans the informed, creative

12. Other prominent members of the Tavern Club included the architects and designers Herbert Jacques, Alexander Wadsworth Longfellow, Arthur Rotch, and C. Howard Walker; the painters Dwight Blaney, Dennis Miller Bunker, Frederic Crowninshield, Frank Duveneck, and Joseph Lindon Smith; and Arts and Crafts supporters Arthur Astor Carey and J. Templeman Coolidge III.

13. On the Tavern Club, see M.A. DeWolfe Howe, *Semi–Centennial History of the Tavern Club, 1884–1934* (Boston: The Tavern Club, 1934). On the Society of Arts and Crafts, Boston, see Beverly K. Brandt's "'All Workmen, Artists, and Lovers of Art': The Organizational Structure of the Society of Arts & Crafts, Boston, 1897–1917" in this volume, as well as her "The Essential Link: Boston Architects and The Society of Arts and Crafts, 1897–1917," in *Tiller* 2, no. 1 (September–October 1983), pp. 7–32. Other organizations that promoted discussion among the artistic elite included the Boston Art Club (whose dues structure favored the well–to–do connoisseur or gentleman painter), the Boston Architectural Club (a group of educators, designers, artists, and master craftsmen founded in 1889 that worked together with and supported the Boston Society of Architects, a professional group of practicing architects), and the St. Botolph Club (a group with a literary bent that also mounted art exhibitions). On the Boston Art Club and Boston Architectural Club, see Fairbrother, "Painting in Boston, 1870–1930," in *The Bostonians*, esp. p. 40; and Margaret Henderson Floyd, "Boston Architects: A Trained Profession 1889–1930," in Margaret Henderson Floyd, *Architectural Education and Boston* (Boston: Boston Architectural Club, 1989), esp. pp. 40–45. The role of pageantry and performance within all these clubs, as well as the activity of Bertram Grosvenor Goodhue, Joseph Lindon Smith, and others in designing sets and costumes, suggests that future research should explore this more ephemeral aspect of the movement.

14. The best source on the history of the SACB is Beverly Brandt's "'Mutually Helpful Relations': Architects, Craftsmen, and The Society of Arts and Crafts, Boston, 1897–1917" (Ph.D. diss., Boston University, 1985). The members of the Tavern Club who were charter members of the SACB included Waddy Longfellow, Robert D. Andrews, C. Howard Walker, Charles Eliot Norton, Morris Gray, Arthur Astor Carey, and J. Templeman Coolidge III. The importance of printing and carving is covered further in essays in this volume.

ideas arising from their study of historic artifacts and principles, which had bestowed upon them great powers of abstract reasoning. As the Harvard–educated psychologist/philosopher William James explained, the creative and productive thinking of an educated man was based upon the intellectual ability to associate and link things or events in both an analytical and aesthetic fashion, while the rote and reproductive actions of a technically skilled artisan was based upon an empirically derived response.[15] ❡ The difference between James's creative "man" and limited "brute" can be seen in the structure of handicraft production in Boston during the Arts and Crafts movement. The enthusiasts, who were well–educated gentlemen architects or artists, or educators, sought out skilled craftsmen—many of whom were immigrants—to execute their work. Non–Anglo–Saxon names were plentiful in the membership lists of the SACB, and most belonged to technically accomplished artisans, whom the elite patronizingly assumed were incapable of working by themselves. The leaders believed that, with appropriate designs supplied to them and with a shop tradition emphasizing flexible production of custom or small batch work, these "brutes" could execute high–quality, well–designed products. Such collaboration permitted the making of suitably artistic handicrafts, most of which only the well–to–do could afford, and offered further benefits to the cultural elite. Many of the leaders of the Arts and Crafts movement were anti–union and used the encouragement of skilled crafts to dampen labor unrest and uphold the existing social structure. Norton, C. Howard Walker, and Wallace Nutting all lamented that workers in mechanized factories had drifted toward mediocrity and artisanal indifference under the protection of unions. A craftsman working in a small shop carrying out the good designs of an educated man would discover the nobility and value of his work, accept his social role with pride, and act as a contented citizen who would not disrupt the social order. A similar impulse inspired philanthropists who used settlement house industries such as textile work in Denison House and pottery decoration in the Paul Revere Pottery to provide immigrants with craft skills that would give them a sense of civic pride and Americanize them, yet also provide appropriate objects to adorn the households of the wealthy.[16] ❡ Between the extremes of the leaders and technicians was a middle class that the cultural leaders recognized could be important contributors and consumers. Boston's prominent publishing industry, the dominant craft industry in the region, played a particularly strong role in improving the aesthetic literacy of this group, both through its book design, type styles, and graphic arts, and through its employment of a number of skilled workers in book production. Other members of this section of Boston society used their drawing skills or decorative design knowledge to gain employment as designers in

15. For James's argument, see his seminal *The Principles of Psychology* (1890; repr. New York: Dover, 1950), especially the chapter entitled "Reasoning." I am indebted to Paul Staiti for bringing this chapter to my attention. In his 1904 essay "The Future of American Architecture," Robert D. Andrews stressed the advantages of an American architect who, unhampered by the limits of local knowledge and traditional habits, could discerningly draw from the wealth of art history: *Boston Architectural Club Yearbook* (Boston: Boston Architectural Club, 1904), pp. 11–12. Denman Ross also distinguished between two classes, the thinker and the doer—the literati who have good taste, right judgment, and high ideals; and the craftsman who possesses knowledge of forces and resistances, can judge technical matters, and control their tools, materials, and methods: "The Arts and Crafts: A Diagnosis," *Handicraft* 1, no. 10 (January 1903), pp. 229–43.

16. On the dependence on skilled immigrant craftsmen, see "Handicraft in Massachusetts," *The Nation* 78, no. 2034 (June 23, 1904), pp. 489–90; Grant Hyde Code, "The Decorative Arts in Boston, 1880–1930," in Herlihy, *Fifty Years of Boston*, pp. 381–82; and H. Langford Warren, "Department of Woodworking," *Exhibition of the Society of Arts & Crafts: Copley Hall, Boston* (Boston: The Heintzemann Press, 1907), p. 86. On anti–unionism, see Vanderbilt, *Charles Eliot Norton*, pp. 197–99; C. Howard Walker, "The Museum and the School," *Handicraft* 2, no. 2 (May 1903), p. 35; and Wallace Nutting, *Wallace Nutting's Autobiography* (Framingham, Mass.: Old America Company, 1936), p. 245.

the making of wallpaper, textiles, or stained glass, or as interior designers. Still others, such as Hermann Dudley Murphy and Elizabeth Copeland, learned craft skills such as wood–carving or silversmithing through non–degree instruction or the formation of cooperative studios, and then marketed their work to the wealthy. The Society of Arts and Crafts, through its publications, meetings, and salesroom, provided an important sense of identity and common experience for these practitioners. Whether a young or single woman seeking economic livelihood or a male seeking career fulfillment, members of the middle class could control their status by improving themselves through craft work without threatening designers above or craftsmen below.[17]

17. On the activities of the native middle class, see the following essays in this volume as well as the Prospectus for the Department of Design (Boston: School of the Museum of Fine Arts, 1909), which lists employment of recent graduates.

THE EMPHASIS ON EDUCATION

Norton's leadership and the prominent role of Harvard–educated leaders distinguished the role of education in the creation of artistic handicrafts—and in the preservation of the class structures outlined above. Education was one of the premier "industries" in Boston, from the public school system up through the universities, and it is thus not surprising that education and educational status had a strong impact on the character of the city's Arts and Crafts movement. Above all else, Boston Arts and Crafts leaders emphasized education in the service of class structure at the expense of other concerns such as social reform and working conditions. Nevertheless, education meant different subjects for different classes: a broad–based liberal arts curriculum seemed appropriate for Norton's circle of gentlemen, while systematic artistic and manual training characterized that of the lower classes, and informal education and associational opportunities characterized that of the middle classes.[18] ❡ Although Norton retired in 1898, his approach was carried on and refined by two other Harvard professors, H. Langford Warren (1857–1917) and Denman Ross. Warren, an English–trained architect, worked from 1879 until 1884 in H.H. Richardson's office and then enrolled as a special student in Fine Arts at Harvard. After several years in private practice, in 1893 Warren became the first head of Harvard's new School of Architecture, then part of the university's Lawrence Scientific School but closely connected to the Department of Fine Arts headed by Norton. While he approved of the Beaux–Arts emphasis on rigorous education and detailed planning, Warren disagreed with its stylistic hegemony, under which Renaissance classicism was the only appropriate means of expression. Knowledgeable about classical, Gothic, Renaissance, and American colonial architecture, Warren stressed that the architect needed to be above all else a scholar with artistic impulses and artisanal knowledge. As he stated in his description of the program of study: "...architecture is essentially a Fine Art, the practice of which must

18. The emphasis on education came to a head in the early twentieth century and can be seen in two essays published in Handicraft in 1903: Denman Ross's "The Arts and Crafts: A Diagnosis," which emphasizes the importance of education, and Mary Ware Dennett's "The Arts and Crafts: An Outlook," which emphasizes the need to reform the social structure and to focus upon individual craftsmen: Handicraft 1, no. 10 (January 1903), pp. 229–43, and Handicraft 2, no. 1 (April 1903), pp. 3–27. Dennett, as well as Arthur Astor Carey and others interested in social reform, acceded to the dominant impulse and continued to interact with other Arts and Crafts leaders.

be based on a thorough knowledge of construction. Great stress has therefore been laid not only on continued practice in design and drawing, but on thorough instruction in the history and principles of the Fine Arts of Architecture and the arts allied with it...." A broad humanities education stressed the relationship of architecture to other arts and of the arts to their social and political context, so that the architect developed the scholarly acumen which would enable him to assess contemporary needs and materials and to apply the most appropriate principles of the past in the development of new or modified solutions. As a result, Warren's program produced a number of strong regionalists such as George Washington Smith in California and Harry Little in Concord, Massachusetts. Warren's history of architecture, which stressed construction and the history of culture rather than a linear progression of styles, and his keen interest in the craftsmanship of building made him a logical choice to head the SACB from 1903 until his death in 1917.[19] ❡ Warren's Harvard colleague Denman W. Ross (1853–1935) also preserved part of Norton's legacy. Ross, an 1875 Harvard graduate who had taken Norton's first Fine Arts course in 1873, initially pursued a Ph.D. in history. Nevertheless, the teachings of Norton inspired him to study painting in Europe and to travel throughout Europe, Egypt, China, and Japan, always looking for the connections between artistic production and its social and political context. After Norton's retirement in 1898, Ross became a special lecturer on design for the School of Architecture and offered a summer course on the Principles of Design from 1899 until 1914. Like Warren, Ross expressed displeasure with the narrowness of Beaux–Arts training—where "everybody does the same things in the same way for three, four or five years and going afterwards as teachers teaching the pupils to do it again in the same way"—but he did not emphasize the study of historical forms and craftsmanship as Warren did. He recognized that for many, the study of design became the study of historic ornament and resulted in weak, insipid reproductions. Instead, Ross sought to apply the methods of modern science to the study of past works in order to understand the universal principles of artistic design, those "fundamental principles of order which form the basis for design in all the arts." Rather than rely on the contextual approach of Norton, Ross sought to examine the object on its own to permit the appreciation of beauty, "no matter of what country, century, or type."[20] ❡ By developing mathematical models for criteria such as balance, harmony, and rhythm, or tone, shape, and area, Ross articulated his analysis of design in a way that established a middle ground between the rote abstractions of the South Kensington method and the free inspirations of Ruskin. Like his contemporary Oliver Wendell Holmes, Ross sought to straddle romantic historicism, derived from custom and tradition, and natural science, which sought to

19. The best source on Warren is the Quinquennial Files in the Harvard University Archives. The best statement of his educational philosophy, from which the quotation is taken, is "The Department of Architecture of Harvard University," *The Architectural Record* 22, no. 2 (August 1907), pp. 134–50. On the distinctiveness of his philosophy from Beaux–Arts training, see Anthony Alofsin, "Tempering the Ecole: Nathan Ricker at the University of Illinois, Langford Warren at Harvard, and Their Followers," in Gwendolyn Wright and Janet Parks, eds., *The History of History in American Schools of Architecture 1865–1975* (New York: Temple Hoyne Buell Center for the Study of American Architecture, 1990), pp. 73–88.

20. For information on Ross, see the Quinquennial Files in the Harvard University Archives; Mary Ann Stankiewicz, "Form, Truth and Emotion: Transatlantic Influences on Formalist Aesthetics," *Journal of Art & Design Education* 7, no. 1 (1988), pp. 81–95; and manuscripts pertaining to an autobiography in the Denman Waldo Ross Papers, Fogg Art Museum Archives, Harvard University. The quotations can be found in the Fogg manuscripts. For Ross's application of his theories and his rationale for them, see *A Theory of Pure Design* (New York: Peter Smith, 1907); and "The Arts and Crafts: A Diagnosis."

explain through the exercise of reason and logic. Throughout his courses and writings, and in his own collecting of art from a wide variety of cultures, including Peruvian textiles and Cambodian art, Ross attempted to explain the universal principles of beauty that a work of fine art embodied. He did not envision a democratization of artistic design, but rather was more interested in developing a discipline ensuring high standards of design that could be coordinated with high standards of technical craftsmanship in the production of artistic objects that would compare favorably with the best of the past. ❦ Distinct from Harvard's emphasis on informed creativity was the prescriptive, formulaic system that Walter Smith, trained in the South Kensington system in England, established at Massachusetts Normal Art School in 1870. In training workers in art industries or art instructors who might teach other workers, the state school used repetitive, rote methods of representation, thereby establishing a common but limited visual vocabulary to improve industrial production. The emphasis on mechanical drawing and drawing from memory was followed in 1883 by the introduction of manual arts, which gave elementary school children exposure to woodworking, metalworking, electrical work, and printing. These categories represented the four major industries in the Boston area. By 1898, manual training was compulsory in Massachusetts public schools. As in all Massachusetts public education, the curriculum was intended to shape a productive working class. Leaders justified the course of study in Ruskinian language, claiming it would increase efficiency, encourage the neatness and accuracy of the worker, provide some sense of engagement, and ensure standards of visual language and taste.[21] ❦ Between Harvard and the Massachusetts Normal Art School were the Lowell School of Practical Design, established in 1872; the School of the Museum of Fine Arts, opened in 1877; and the Cowles Art School, founded in 1882. While the first was intended primarily for the education of textile workers and designers, the latter two offered training in decorative design and encouraged individual exploration in the techniques of various media. Although the primary purpose of the Museum School was the teaching of drawing and painting, the charismatic Frederic Crowninshield, a stained–glass artist and muralist, began to teach principles of decorative design in 1879 and encouraged students to explore their impulses in a variety of media. The success of his instruction led to the establishment of the two–year class in decoration taught by C. Howard Walker, a Beaux–Arts trained architect who blended the geometric drawing exercises of the South Kensington methodology with an introduction to historical ornament and styles. In 1889, as the Decorative Design class swelled from seven to thirty–seven students, the school added a third year and offered instruction in the techniques of pottery, stained glass, textiles, and printing. By 1903

21. The best summaries of the impact of Smith are the essays in Donald Soucy and Mary Ann Stankiewicz, eds., Framing the Past: Essays on Art Education (Reston, Va.: National Art Education Association, 1990); and Korzenik, Drawn to Art. See also Jeremiah Burke and Louis Fish, "Education," in Herlihy, Fifty Years of Boston, pp. 449–89; Eileen Boris, Art and Labor: Ruskin, Morris, and the Craftsman Ideal in America (Philadelphia: Temple University Press, 1986), pp. 82–98; and Michael Katz, The Irony of Early School Reform: Educational Innovation in Mid–Nineteenth Century Massachusetts (Cambridge: Harvard University Press, 1968).

sixty–six students were formally enrolled, and many others simply attended a few classes. The studio emphasis on historic ornament, graphic design, and surface decoration was supplemented by lectures by Sarah Wyman Whitman, Denman Ross, Francis Bacon, Joseph Lindon Smith, Charles Eliot Norton, Ernest Fenollosa, Edward Morse, and Waddy Longfellow, thereby exposing the students to some of the main thinkers in Boston's Arts and Crafts community. ❡ The Museum School provided educational opportunities in artistic design for middle–class men and upper– and middle–class women who were unable to attend Harvard. Walker tended to be somewhat rigid in his approach to applied design and historic ornament, and his students most often found work as interior decorators or designers for wallpaper, textile, stained glass, jewelry, or publishing firms. Yet the overall looseness of the program in the late nineteenth century also permitted a variety of career choices: Lois Lilley Howe became an architect; Joseph Lindon Smith, Hermann Dudley Murphy, and Amy Sacker became artist/teachers. In the early twentieth century, the Museum School began to devote more attention to technical training in the decorative arts, hiring George Hunt to teach metalworking and silversmithing in 1906. In 1910 Walker sought to add instructors in wood–carving and enameling. Between 1907 and 1911, the Society of Arts and Crafts explored the possibility of expanding the artisanal training at the Museum School to create a School of Handicraft. The proposal never gained acceptance by the Museum Council, however, who wanted to maintain control of the school and were concerned about the number of design students already at the school, or by the SACB, who lacked sufficient finances to tempt the Museum with a new dedicated building.[22] ❡ The Cowles School of Art supported a more informal program that provided exposure to design as well as fabrication in metal, wood, fabric, and book arts. From the beginning it was a more process–oriented, less academic program. Among the teachers there in the 1890s were the architects Bertram Grosvenor Goodhue and Harold van Buren Magonigle, the metalworker Laurin Hovey Martin, and designer/craftsman Amy Sacker. The quality of work by such Cowles students as Sarah Choate Sears, a former Museum School student, and Elizabeth Copeland suggests that the program offered members of the middle class, particularly women, an important means of access to the shop floor.[23] ❡ Arthur Wesley Dow, a protégé of Ernest Fenollosa, offered another point of entry to the world of arts and crafts in his Ipswich Summer School. Like Ruskin and Norton, Dow believed in the poetic personality of the artist and sought the means to enter into the mystery of creativity. According to Dow, emotion was an important side of composition, but one needed principles to channel that emotion in certain ways: opposition, transition, subordination, repetition, symmetry. Unlike Ross, who emphasized the study of ob-

22. H. Winthrop Pierce, *The History of the School of the Museum of Fine Arts, Boston, 1877–1927* (Boston: Museum of Fine Arts, 1930); Roberta Sheehan, "Boston Museum School: A Centennial History, 1876–1976" (Ph.D. diss., Boston College, 1983); and Fairbrother, "Painting in Boston, 1870–1930," in *The Bostonians*, pp. 31–92. On the attempt to establish a School of Handicraft at the Museum, see Pierce, *The History of the School of the Museum of Fine Arts, Boston*, p. 100; *Handicraft* 3, no. 9 (December 1910), pp. 332–33; *Handicraft* 3, no. 10 (January 1911), pp. 363–64; and Beverly Brandt, "Mutually Helpful Relations," pp. 350–53.

23. There is no article or monograph on Cowles, but see Kaplan, "The Art that is Life," p. 268; and Nancy Finlay, *Artists of the Book in Boston, 1890–1910* (Cambridge: The Houghton Library, 1985), pp. 89–90, 96, and 103–04.

jects in order to derive principles, Dow emphasized the creation of objects in order to intuit principles. Dow met Fenollosa in February of 1891 and by that summer had opened his Ipswich Summer School. His school recognized no hierarchy of media, but rather encouraged students to cross media boundaries and create beautiful objects using a variety of materials. Among the offerings of the Ipswich Summer School were drawing, painting, woodcut printmaking, basket weaving, frame–carving, metalwork, and ceramic design. Dow ran his Summer School from 1891 to 1907, but also advised the curriculum at Byrdcliffe in Woodstock, New York, where a similar equality of all arts and emphasis on process prevailed. Although a product of the Norton circle and a friend of a number of Boston painters, Dow never had a strong local following but rather seemed to attract women from New York and Chicago. Most professionals were frustrated by the lack of medium–specific information and decorative emphasis. Amateurs and secondary school teachers who read his published works responded more favorably to his simplified procedures for ornament, pottery, embroidery, and furniture. In 1903 he accepted a position as the Director of the Department of Fine Arts at the Teachers' College of Columbia University and subsequently enjoyed a national platform for his ideas about art education.[24]

24. Frederick Moffatt, *Arthur Wesley Dow 1857–1922* (Washington, D.C.: Smithsonian Institution Press, 1977); Nancy Green, *Arthur Wesley Dow and His Influence* (Ithaca, N.Y.: Herbert F. Johnson Museum of Art, 1990); Foster Wyngant, "Art Structure: Fundamentals of Design Before the Bauhaus," in Brent Wilson and H. Hoffa, eds., *The History of Art Education: Proceedings from the Penn State Conference* (Washington, D.C.: National Art Education Association, 1985); and Arthur Wesley Dow, *Composition: A Series of Exercises Selected from a New System of Art Education* (Boston: Baker, 1899).

THE CHARACTER AND LEGACY OF THE
ARTS AND CRAFTS MOVEMENT IN BOSTON

In the late nineteenth and early twentieth centuries, the writings and patronage of Boston's cultural elite centered on the moral and aesthetic excellence of hand–crafted objects. Boston designers and makers did not demonstrate significant interest in Continental reform styles or in simple, honest forms. Boston objects of this period are characterized by a reliance on historical precedents, particularly American colonial styles, and British styles such as Gothic Revival and Celtic; an emphasis on traditional and expressive workmanship, especially joined solid wood furniture, raised or hammered silver objects, and thrown pottery; and a restrained celebration of labor–intensive and expensive ornament such as carving, modeling, or repoussé chasing. The colonial revival played a significant role, particularly in architecture, furniture, and metals, but also in the imagery for paintings and photography, evoking a simple, dignified past and providing optimism and confidence in the present. ⟨Given the influence of Norton, the Ruskinian qualities of associative meaning and expressive surfaces in Boston handicrafts are not really surprising. Yet equally important to the development of Arts and Crafts expression in Boston was W.R. Lethaby, a British architect and educator admired by leaders such as Bertram Grosvenor Goodhue and Langford Warren. Lethaby, who viewed architecture as a synthesis of common–sense construction, artistic craftsmanship, and a romantic summonsing of past traditions, delighted in materials and romantic associations. He therefore appealed greatly to those Boston architects and designers who rejected the unwavering rigidity of the Beaux–Arts tradition and favored the imperfections of visible workmanship. Thus the gouged marks on John Kirchmayer's carvings or Hermann Dudley Murphy's frames, the tooled modeling of Grueby pottery, and the hammered surfaces of Mary Knight's and Arthur Stone's silver all epitomize the Boston preference for expressive work by skilled artisans. What is striking in Boston is the lack of reference to William Morris, other than as a book arts practitioner, and to C.R. Ashbee, other than as a silver designer. The former's socialist leanings and the latter's emphasis on the happiness and welfare of the worker apparently did not play well in the social climate of Boston.[25] ❡ The emphasis on education in Boston led to numerous publications and students who spread ideas throughout the nation. The Society of Arts and Crafts, Boston, the first and most influential such organization, also played an important role in the dissemination of ideas about handicrafts. Boston thus became the main exporter of Arts and Crafts ideas rather than objects. Journals such as *American Architect and Building News*, *House Beautiful*, *Handicraft*, *Applied Arts*, and the short–lived *Knight Errant* were based in Boston. Norton, Warren, Ross, and Dow all wrote influential books or articles that inspired others to take up the cause of handicrafts. Arthur Wesley Dow drew inspiration from his association with Ernest Fenollosa at the Museum of Fine Arts, Boston and went on to become one of the most influential art educators through his publications and work at the Pratt School of Design, Byrdcliffe, and Columbia, all in New York. Ernest Batchelder studied at the Massachusetts Normal Art School and took a summer course with Denman Ross before going to Minneapolis, where he founded the Handicraft Guild, and to Pasadena, where he taught at the Throop Institute and established a tile manufactory. Batchelder also wrote *Design in Theory and Practice*, a publication that restated Ross's ideas about design. Many of the Newcomb Pottery designers also traveled to Boston to improve their design sensibilities—Marie Hoâ–LeBlanc, Gertrude Roberts Smith, and John Peter Pemberton studied with Ross, while Mary Sheerer studied with Dow. Ross and Dow probably taught most of those who in turn taught manual arts and industrial design in American schools in the 1910s. Several others who gained invaluable experience in Boston included the Pasadena architects Charles Sumner Greene, who worked for Langford Warren from 1891 until 1893, and his brother Henry Sumner Greene, who worked for Shepley, Rutan, and Coolidge, the firm that succeeded H.H. Richardson; Herbert S. Stone and Hannibal I. Kimball, 1894 graduates of Harvard, who established a printing business while undergraduates and then moved to Chicago in 1896, becoming that

25. On the importance of Lethaby, see Richard Oliver, *Bertram Grosvenor Goodhue* (New York: Architectural History Foundation, 1983), pp. 28–30. Lethaby's main publication was *Architecture, Mysticism, and Myth* (London: Percival & Co., 1892).

26. On Batchelder, see Trapp, *The Arts and Crafts Movement in California*; and Kaplan, "The Art that is Life," pp. 326–27. On Newcomb Pottery, see Jessie Poesch, *Newcomb Pottery: An Enterprise for Southern Women, 1895–1940* (Exton, Penn.: Schiffer Publishing, 1984); and Kaplan, "The Art that is Life," pp. 324–26; and Ross Class Lists in Harvard University Catalogue (Harvard University Archives). On the Greenes, see Jeff Wilkinson, "Greene & Greene Architects," *American Bungalow* 9 (1994), p. 6; and Barbara Ann Francis, "The Boston Roots of Greene & Greene" (M.A. thesis, Tufts University, 1937). Joseph Blumenthal identifies the importance of Stone & Kimball in *The Printed Book in America* (Hanover, N.H.: University Press of New England, 1989), pp. 43–46. On Wynne, see Kaplan, "The Art that is Life," pp. 264–65.

27. Ross, "The Arts and Crafts: A Diagnosis." On the Birmingham experience, see Alan Crawford, *By Hammer and Hand: The Arts and Crafts Movement in Birmingham* (Birmingham, U.K.: Birmingham Museums and Art Gallery, 1984).

city's premier Arts and Crafts publisher; and Madeline Yale Wynne, who studied painting at the Museum School and taught for several years in Boston, helped found the Society of Deerfield Industries, and was a founding member of the Chicago Arts and Crafts Society.[26] ❡ Boston's emphasis on moral aesthetics and education and its predilection for high–minded discussion—as Denman Ross himself stated, "It is more talk than work... we are playing at Arts and Crafts"—closely resembled the situation in Birmingham, England. In that center of British activity, the municipal elite created an atmosphere where the Arts and Crafts flourished: architects were among the primary leaders and the Municipal School of Art was an ideal center. It provided paying jobs for the leading craftsmen, served the artisanal needs for association and exhibition, and emphasized artistic laboratories in which students learned through making. Yet, as in Boston, the earlier experimental delight in expressive materials and ornament with romantic associations gave way to less personal work characterized by a more prosaic, formal approach to design. By 1915 Lethaby and his followers in Birmingham had accepted the inevitability of mechanized production and began to focus their attention on design rather than on the integration of design and craftsmanship.[27] ❡ In Boston, an emphasis upon education rather than sales or commercial viability restricted the vitality of the movement. A reliance on occasional grand exhibitions—in 1897, 1899, and 1907—and a single salesroom left most Arts and Crafts makers outside the growing culture of consumer capitalism developed by the proprietors of department stores during this period. One of the few real retail stores that carried the work of members of the SACB was Bigelow, Kennard & Co., a high–end jeweler that specialized in luxury goods. Thus the artisanal members of the Society did not benefit from the type of consumerism prevalent at the time and found it difficult to succeed financially. ❡ The attention devoted to education and the definition of terms also led to a form of academic fratricide. For example, in the early twentieth century, Denman Ross grew intolerant of the vocational leanings and pedagogical rigidity of C. Howard Walker at the Museum School and sought to develop a curriculum that integrated intellect and skilled technique. Ross believed that it was important for students not just to distinguish between historical styles but also to cultivate visual sensitivities and to discern quality in all types of objects. When the Museum School Council reviewed its curriculum in 1912, Ross recommended the appointment of Huger Elliot, formerly of the Rhode Island School of Design, as director. Elliot's philosophy of design was quite similar to Ross's and distinct from Walker's. Elliot believed that material and use determine form, structure determines design, ornament must emphasize structure, and natural ornament should be conventionalized. Elliot and his assistant in design, Henry Hunt Clark, a protégé of Ross's, thus moved the curriculum away from commercial and industrial design and towards theoretical and applied design. As a result, in the early twentieth century a new emphasis on formalism grew from the discussions about principles of design and composition. The writings of Dow and Ross became the foundation for a new reconciliation with the existing social order that emphasized mass–market consumerism. Thus the enthusiasm for a revival of artistic handicraft dispersed in Boston, although discussion continued in fragmented form and provided underpinnings for the preservation movement, the colonial revival, and modern design.[28]

I would like to acknowledge the help of many colleagues in the preparation of this essay, particularly Jonathan Fairbanks, Margaret Henderson Floyd, Marie Frank, Marilee Boyd Meyer, James F. O'Gorman, and Abby Smith. I would also like to thank James Cuno for allowing me access to the vast resources of the Harvard Libraries.

28. On the important changes in marketing and consumption, see William Leach, *Land of Desire: Merchants, Power, and the Rise of a New American Culture* (New York: Pantheon, 1993). For a discussion of the changes at the Museum School, see Sheehan, "Boston Museum School, A Centennial History: 1876–1976," pp. 69–81. There are some striking parallels between the Arts and Crafts leaders and the Mugwumps, a group of vigorous Harvard–educated wealthy idealists who sought to improve American politics through restoration of civic pride and the leadership of an intellectual elite in the period 1884 to 1893. However, this group was never effective as an organization nor did it create a style of politics. Their inability to agree upon the means to enact change, their blind spots, and the contradictions in their ideas undercut their effectiveness. Nevertheless, some of their ideas became part of the Progressive Party's platform: Geoffrey Blodgett, "The Mind of the Boston Mugwump," in Gerald McFarland, ed., *Moralists or Pragmatists? The Mugwumps, 1884–1900* (New York: Simon & Schuster, 1975), pp. 18–38.

"ALL WORKMEN, ARTISTS, AND LOVERS OF ART": THE ORGANIZATIONAL STRUCTURE OF THE SOCIETY OF ARTS AND CRAFTS, BOSTON

Beverly K. Brandt

THE DESIGN REFORM movement has attracted attention since its inception in the 1840s. One reason for its longevity as a topic for research, debate, exhibition, and acquisition may be its comprehensive nature. There were few aspects of turn–of–the–century culture not affected by the urge to improve the quality of the designed environment: the scholarship of design reform thus has been multi–disciplinary in scope, embracing everything from art to labor and industry, from politics to economics and marketing, and from philosophy to theory and creed. ❡ An implied but often overlooked aspect of design reform is its social dimension. Like most movements, design reform was significant for the people who defined and supported it, and expressed their belief in the power of the group to bring about change. We tend to identify the concept of design reform with strong individuals, such as John Ruskin and William Morris, Elbert Hubbard, and Gustav Stickley. Yet even these dominant personalities recognized design reform as too ambitious a quest for individuals working in isolation. Thus, all argued eloquently—in word, deed, and print—that improvement of the living and working environment required a concerted effort. ❡ Founded in the belief that design reformers could achieve more *en masse* than singly, the Society of Arts and Crafts, Boston (SACB) set out to attract a broad and growing constituency. Inviting the "help and cooperation of all Workmen, Artists, and Lovers of Art—of all men and women who are interested in improving the quality and raising the standards of Handicraft," it attracted professional craftspersons along with philanthropists, social reformers, educators, journalists, theorists, critics, and well–meaning amateurs. Its diversity and scale ensured its visibility and longevity, and it still exists today, a century after its birth. Paradoxically, its large and varied membership proved to be both a boon and a handicap and eventually compromised its ability to achieve many of the goals set forth in its early years.¹ ⟨The SACB was among the first American organizations patterned after earlier English models, reflecting its founders' desire to join the international pursuit of the restoration of usefulness and beauty to design while responding to the reforming impulse burgeoning within their city. Like its English predecessors—such as the Arts & Crafts Exhibition Society (founded in 1888)—it evolved from a display of handicrafts (fig. 1). Established shortly thereafter in the spring of 1897, it continued to hold "exhibitions of exemplary work...in every branch of industry in which Art and Craft are combined" (fig. 2). Providing "competent and sympathetic advice" for those members "desirous of instruction," it sought to change the appearance, function, and fabrication of everyday objects. Thus, as the essays in this catalogue reveal, it endeavored to display the best in American handicraft for a discriminating public, while inspiring production methods that were sound—ethically, ideologically, and economically.² ⟨Viewing itself as a leader in the reform effort, the SACB sought to distinguish itself from professional associations and trade unions. Expressing a self–importance matched only by its zeal, it regarded itself as *primus inter pares*. "This Society...is the first of its kind and has never been called the Boston Society of Arts and Crafts," explained one of its founders and presidents proudly, "but The Society of Arts and Crafts," an estimation reinforced by the uppercase "T" in its numerous publications.³ ⟨From its inception, it embarked upon a mission befitting the size, scope, and standing to which it aspired: "This Society was incorporated," its mission statement began, "for the purpose of promoting artistic work in all branches of handicraft. It hopes to bring Designers and Workmen into mutually helpful relations, and to encourage workmen to execute designs on their own. It endeavors to stimulate in workmen," it continued, "an appreciation of the dignity and value of good design and to counteract the popular impatience of Law and Form, and the desire for over–ornamentation and specious originality. It will insist," it concluded, "upon the necessity of sobriety and restraint, of ordered arrangement, of due regard for the relation between the form of an object and its use, and of harmony and fitness in the decoration put upon it." Underlying this statement of purpose are commitments to promote change through collaboration and to enforce a conservative aesthetic policy.⁴ ⟨To implement its goals, the SACB undertook a number of initiatives. It promoted education through lectures, workshops, and demonstrations, through its lending library and publications such as *Handicraft*, and through its (unsuccessful) attempt to found a School of Handicraft. It served the community by organizing events to attract the public, and by advising the legislature on industrial education. It provided frequent opportunities within Boston's artistic community for "social intercourse." It increased

1. Untitled prospectus pamphlet, *The Society of Arts and Crafts, Boston, Massachusetts, Incorporated A.D. MDCCCXCVII* The Thomas P. Smith Printing Company produced 250 pamphlets on December 9, 1897, for a cost of $2.50; Papers of the Society of Arts and Crafts, Boston, Archives of American Art, Smithsonian Institution, microfilm reel 316:frame 586 (hereafter cited as SACB archives, AAA/SI reel:frame). "For a Permanent Exhibition," [*Boston*] *Herald*, April 15, 1897; SACB archives, AAA/SI 322:222.

2. Untitled prospectus pamphlet. For a detailed institutional history, see Beverly K. Brandt, "'Mutually Helpful Relations': Architects, Craftsmen and The Society of Arts and Crafts, Boston, 1897–1917" (Ph.D. diss., Boston University, 1985).

3. Out of deference to Warren, I refer in my own research to the SACB—not the BSAC. F.W. Coburn, minutes of remarks made by Herbert Langford Warren at a dinner held on April 23, 1912 to honor Frederick Allen Whiting. SACB archives, AAA/SI 300:706–726.

4. Most likely this statement was drafted by Charles Eliot Norton (1827–1908) and Herbert Langford Warren (1857–1917), the organization's first and third presidents respectively. *Announcements for MDCCCXCIX, The Society of Arts and Crafts, Boston, Massachusetts*. The Thomas P. Smith Printing Company produced these in two batches on December 30, 1898 and April 2, 1899. *Scrapbook 1897–1904*, Archives of the Society of Arts and Crafts, Boston; Boston Public Library. For another version, drafted by Harold Broadfield Warren and titled *Announcements: The Society of Arts and Crafts, MDCCCXCVIII–IX*, see SACB archives, AAA/SI 316:484.

5. Elegant bulletins announcing the Society's upcoming meetings—such as that printed by Daniel Berkeley Updike on December 12, 1898—are in the *Scrapbook 1897–1904*; see item number 8. On the failed attempt to found a School of Handicraft, see the "Minutes of the Meeting of the Council," November 10, 1910, SACB archives, AAA/SI 316:102; "Minutes of the Meeting of the Council," January 10, 1912, SACB archives, AAA/SI 316:111; "Minutes of the Annual Meeting," February 14, 1912, SACB archives, AAA/SI 316:112. See various pamphlets drafted by Frederick Allen Whiting, ca. 1900–04, titled "Permanent Exhibition and Salesroom and the Bureau of Information;" SACB papers, Vertical Files, Fine Arts Library, Boston Public Library. Regarding industrial education, see: Whiting's minutes, SACB archives, AAA/SI 300:177.

6. "Permanent Society Formed With Many Members," [Boston] Herald, May 14, 1897; SACB archives, AAA/SI 322:201. This article indicates that Ralph Adams Cram approved of calling the new organization a "guild," a point challenged by Otto Fleishner, chief of the Fine Arts Department at the Boston Public Library, who condemned the term as "an English thing and a close corporation, with peculiar government and management." Early announcements regarding the proposed exhibitions and organization list some of the SACB's varied supporters in its early months. Later annual reports contain membership lists. For a three-decade survey of SACB members, see Karen Evans Ulehla, ed., *The Society of Arts and Crafts, Boston: Exhibition Record 1897–1927* (Boston: Boston Public Library, 1981). Bulletins, announcements, and annual reports define membership criteria in each category. Surveying annual reports along with the minutes of Council meetings illuminates these categories' evolution over time. Awarding medals to "members producing work of very rare quality" is first addressed on February 16, 1911; SACB archives, AAA/SI 316:106.

7. "For a Permanent Exhibition."

members' visibility by exhibiting, selling, and promoting their works within and beyond Boston. Most important, it functioned as an arbiter of taste in critical and theoretical matters. By imposing strict requirements upon candidates for membership and jurying every work they subsequently displayed or sold, it established an exacting standard that soon won national acceptance.[5] ❡ The Society's ideals and actions appealed to experienced practitioners, novices seeking professional guidance, and appreciative connoisseurs, who were distributed among three membership classifications—Masters, Craftsmen, and Patrons (later called Associates). Craftsmen comprised the largest group, Associates the smallest. Masters formed an intermediate group, a few eventually winning the title of "Medallist" by virtue of their superlative conceptual, aesthetic, and technical abilities (figs. 3 and 4). With its tripartite structure, the SACB resembled a medieval guild, in which master craftsmen trained apprentices and advised journeymen working in the service of patrons. It purposefully chose to call itself a "Society" rather than a "Guild," however, regarding the latter as exclusionary and socialistic. The former suggested a more comprehensive nature and a frankly apolitical agenda, dedicated to creating among members a nurturing, productive environment of "mutually helpful relations."[6] ❡ The Society's constituency was broader than its three official categories suggest. Augmenting its core of practitioners and patrons were non–members such as the local suppliers, manufacturers, and merchants who kept abreast of its activities and advertised in its catalogues, and the consumers who patronized its exhibitions, salesroom, and studios. The Society worked diligently to educate members and non–members alike, claiming that informed buyers who wanted both usefulness and beauty would inspire change in the marketplace by demanding high–quality goods from manufacturers and their workers. Thus it viewed its mission and its constituency as means to implement change throughout the production–and–consumption cycle. ❡ Neither size nor members' competencies determined the degree of influence exerted within the organization by Associates, Masters, or Craftsmen. Despite their numbers, Craftsmen had the least say in administering the SACB; instead, a select group of Associates and Masters established its policies and procedures and defined its mission and standards. Associates—"persons of culture and influence" who contributed social, political, and financial support—participated as founders, presidents, and silent partners who underwrote many of its activities. Masters—recognized as leaders in their respective fields for their expertise—also functioned as founders and presidents; members of both groups eventually held seats on the SACB's two official governing bodies, the Council and the Jury.[7] ❡ Yet election or appointment to either was less a reflection of expertise in the handicrafts than of professional credentials,

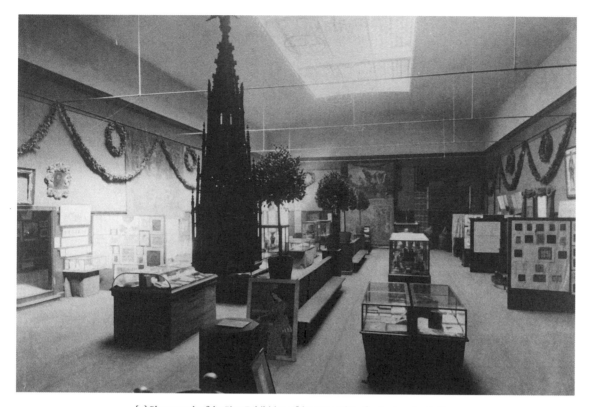

{1} Photograph of the First Exhibition of the Arts and Crafts, Boston, April 1897;
interior of Copley Hall showing display of contemporary handicrafts prior to the founding of the SACB;
Fine Arts Department, Boston Public Library.

and ironically those most involved in decision–making had least hands–on knowledge of the crafts. A small group of architects held fifty percent of the offices, thirty percent of the seats on the Council, eighteen percent of the positions on the Jury, and over twenty–five percent of the seats on four standing committees during the first two decades. Occupying a position as intermediaries between the connoisseurs who hired them and the craftsmen whom they employed, the architects' numbers were few but their influence pervasive.[8] ❴As this breakdown suggests, decision–makers comprised an elite group operating within the confines of the Council and Jury. The Council—the Society's chief administrative unit—controlled all decisions, policies, and actions in adherence with bylaws established in 1897 and left virtually untouched for the next several decades. The Jury—functioning as an aesthetic overseer led by architect and educator Charles Howard Walker (1857–1936)—was formed in 1900 in response to the salesroom's growth and members' increased participation in exhibitions. Charged with regulating the aesthetic and technical merits of all handicrafts produced and sold under the SACB's auspices, it reviewed all work submitted anonymously by members, accepting it—or more often rejecting it—and providing written or verbal critiques upon request. ❴During the SACB's first two decades, only five percent of the total membership of about 1,000 served as councilors. Two–thirds of these were Masters and

8. Connoisseurs and craftsmen far outnumbered the thirty–nine architects who ultimately ran the organization. At its founding, architects comprised only eleven percent of the total membership, shrinking to just three percent as the SACB grew. See Beverly K. Brandt, "The Essential Link: Boston Architects and The Society of Arts and Crafts," Tiller 2, no. 1 (September–October 1983), pp. 7–32; and Beverly K. Brandt, "'Sobriety and Restraint': The Search for an Arts and Crafts Style in Boston, 1897–1917," Tiller 2, no. 5 (Fall 1985), pp. 26–73.

one–quarter were architects. Others were connoisseurs, designers, educators, and varied craftspersons, including a concentration of six jewelers and metalworkers. Similarly, during its formative years, the Jury consisted almost exclusively of Masters, many of whom were multi–talented designer–craftspersons or educators. Some extended their influence—and control—by serving on both Council and Jury. Only seven women were elected or appointed to each, despite an overall participation by women in membership that approached fifty percent. Their lack of representation as decision–makers within the SACB has yet to be properly explained.[9] ¶ Nearly invisible as decision–makers, women nevertheless prevailed at SACB–sponsored displays and exhibitions. At its huge tenth anniversary show in 1907, they constituted two–thirds of the exhibitors, dominating displays of textiles, basketry, jewelry, and pottery. They were equally represented with their male colleagues in producing stained glass, metalwork, and printing, but were less evident in bookbinding and leather work. They seem to have appropriated the newly emerging field of photography as their own, but it is unclear whether they regarded it as a serious profession or merely a pleasurable pastime. Women were all but absent from glassblowing, woodworking, cabinetmaking, and ecclesiastical work, among the more physically demanding and lucrative fields; did women decline to pursue these, or were they simply discouraged from doing so by either convention or competition?[10] ¶ The SACB's tenth, twentieth, and thirtieth anniversaries were moments for celebration of past achievements and reflection upon future goals. In the year of its twentieth anniversary (1917), the Society conducted two surveys of its membership. One study revealed that over half its members lived in or around Boston, while another twenty–five percent resided in the state or region. Yet by that time, nearly twenty percent were from the Midwest, South, or far West. Altogether, members represented thirty states and seven foreign countries including England, Ireland, Canada, Norway, Denmark, Mexico, and the Philippines—a testimony to the organization's widespread reputation. What is more, members continued to be supportive over time as well as distance: twenty years after its founding, over half had been members for at least five years, one–third had been so for more than ten, and two–thirds of those who had served as founders still remained active.[11] ¶ The SACB benefited from international connections from its inception; such links were, in fact, partially responsible for its success. Many of its founders and members had first become aware of the design reform movement while traveling abroad, and their experiences ranged from studying architecture in France at the École des Beaux Arts, or in Italy courtesy of MIT's Rotch Traveling Scholarship, to working in the studios of such preeminent English artists and craftsmen as C.R. Ashbee (1863–1942), T.J. Cobden–Sanderson (1840–1922), Fred Partridge

9. Brandt, "Mutually Helpful Relations," Appendices A, C and D, pp. 433–438, pp. 428–438. Beverly K. Brandt, "'One Who Has Seen More and Knows More': The Design Critic and the Arts and Crafts," in Bert Denker, ed., The Substance of Style: Perspectives on the American Arts and Crafts Movement (Winterthur, Del.: Henry Francis duPont Winterthur Museum, 1996), pp. 117-42. The Council appointed Walker critic of the Jury on November 2, 1909; SACB archives, AAA/SI 316:92.

10. Brandt, "Mutually Helpful Relations," pp. 299–300. Exhibition of The Society of Arts and Crafts: Copley Hall, Boston, February 5–26, 1907 (Boston: Heintzemann Press, 1907); Mugar Library, Boston University.

11. A.W. Longfellow, Chair, "Report of the Membership Committee," The Annual Report of The Society of Arts and Crafts, Boston Massachusetts, for the Year 1916 (Boston: April 30, 1917), pp. 10–11. This misrepresents the number of founders, stating that there were twenty–six charter members; yet the charter bears only twenty–one signatures. Ralph Clipston Sturgis, Ralph Adams Cram, and Mary Crease Sears are erroneously included among the original group; SACB archives, AAA/SI 300:002. Warren, dinner remarks, April 23, 1912.

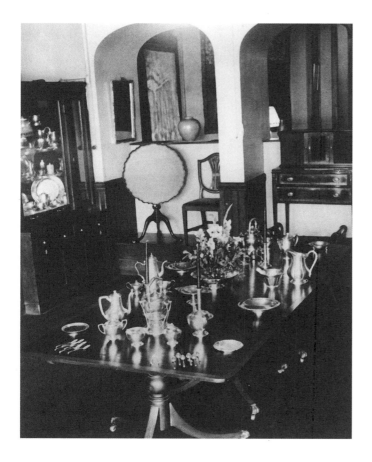

{2} Photograph of the interior of the SACB salesroom at 9 Park Street, Boston, post–1904; Fine Arts Department, Boston Public Library; showing furniture and metalwork in the colonial revival style. The Chippendale–style tilt–top tea table is attributed to F.W. Kulkmann.

(1877–1942), or Alexander Fisher (1864–1936). Charles Eliot Norton had forged an invaluable link with John Ruskin, Thomas Carlyle, and several of the Pre–Raphaelites while living abroad in the 1850s and 1860s. And many of the SACB's most prominent members were, in fact, British immigrants who settled in the Boston area, including Herbert Langford Warren (architect) and his brother Harold Broadfield Warren (painter), Arthur J. Stone (silversmith), and Hugh Cornwall Robertson and Charles Fergus Binns (potters). Additionally, Europeans, such as Karl F. Leinonen (a Finnish silversmith), John Kirchmayer (a German sculptor and carver), his countryman Carl H. Heintzemann (a printer), and others, played important roles within the organization. A curious feature of their acculturation is that many of these talented immigrants from countries with a well–established craft heritage eventually abandoned their native traditions in favor of a colonial revival style—which was, in essence, the "house" style of the SACB. Their interactions with local architects working in that style, coupled with their eagerness to satisfy the conservative strictures of the SACB Jury, may have influenced these immigrants' practices in New England.[12]

A second, more significant survey—categorizing members by profession or discipline—revealed that they practiced fifty–four different specialties ranging from architecture to wood engraving (see APPENDIX). Clustering these into twelve broadly defined divisions, the Council encouraged

12. Brandt, "Mutually Helpful Relations," pp. 23–25; and Brandt, "Sobriety and Restraint," p. 47.

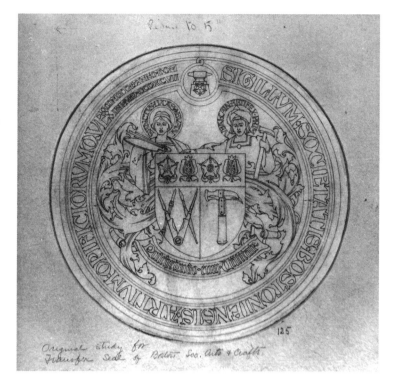
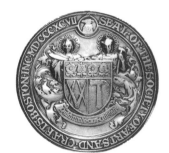
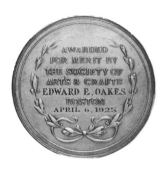

{3} Original study for the transfer seal of the Society of Arts and Crafts, Boston; drawing by Bertram Grosvenor Goodhue, 1909; MIT Museum. {4} Bronze medal of the Society of Arts and Crafts, Boston awarded to Edward Everett Oakes, 1923, incorporating the official seal of the SACB, designed by Goodhue in 1909; Oakes family collection.

members to wear color–coded costumes—in imitation of the "picturesque garb" worn by members of "old Florentine Guilds"—at all official meetings. These multi–hued smocks and gowns encouraged interaction among those with similar interests, while celebrating the SACB's ever–increasing scale and diversity.[13] ⟨ The survey indicates that members worked in a broader range of media and trades and with a greater range of techniques than current scholarship has acknowledged. It further suggests a need to ascertain how workers in each category viewed their professional distinctions and affiliations. What differentiated decorators from designers, interior decorators, porcelain decorators, and china decorators? What explained the segregation of metalworkers as silversmiths, chasers, ironworkers, brass workers, or pewter workers? What distinguished those working in cement from those working in concrete? And how did modelers, sculptors, and wood– or stone–carvers differ? Today's scholars and collectors must strive to comprehend the subtleties of these various crafts and trades, defining them as did their proponents—theorists, critics, educators, and practitioners—at the turn of the century. As this survey suggests, they must also broaden their definition of the arts and crafts beyond those categories defined by the traditional media of clay, wood, glass, fiber, and metal to embrace such areas as beadwork, photography, architectural model making, and ship modeling. ⟨ These seemingly arbitrary divisions

13. "Minutes of a Special Meeting of the Council," May 25, 1916; SACB archives, AAA/SI: 316:169. "Report of the Committee on Costumes, Preliminary Tally;" SACB archives, AAA/SI 316:159.

also suggest a hierarchy among craft categories and practitioners. The Jury acknowledged this in its annual reports: "The various classes of objects," it stated in 1913–14, "are different in intrinsic merit because of the materials and the skill required in the workmanship. It should be obvious," it continued, "that jewelry and enamels, wood carving and illuminating can be expressed in higher terms than the usual china painting and leather work and coarse basket making." Such an attitude—not exclusive to the SACB but commonly held among critics and theorists internationally—might have developed over time from divisions originally established and enforced by medieval guilds. Or it may have reflected distinctions based upon the value of the materials from which crafts were made, the degree of finesse required in their construction or finish, or their relative historical importance.[14] ❦ This implied hierarchy undermined the SACB's cohesiveness. Jewelers, enamelers, and metalworkers—practitioners of the so-called higher crafts—comprised fully one-third of the SACB's total membership, and their work generated over half of the salesroom's annual revenue. Holding more seats on the Council than any other group and one-quarter of those on the Jury, they influenced decision-making to a greater extent than did representatives of any other craft category—with the exception of architects.[15] ❦ Some of these individuals eventually formed special interest groups—called "guilds" despite reservations expressed by founders in the SACB's infancy—to augment their visibility and influence. Devoted to metalwork, woodworking, and ecclesiastical work, these guilds had varying effects: St. Dunstan's Guild, for example, supported its members' work by obtaining contracts for ecclesiastical commissions and then underwriting the high cost of materials. On the other hand, the highly political Guild of Metalworkers may have created more problems than it solved. Its members were particularly outspoken about the salesroom—whose success they deemed essential to their livelihood—provoking changes in its policies, procedures, and personnel. Thus it challenged one of the Council's formerly exclusive privileges.[16] ❦ Antipathies between the factions that inevitably arose during its first three decades ultimately jeopardized the SACB's ability to forge "mutually helpful relations" among groups whose interests often seemed mutually exclusive. Debates—some of which took place in the pages of *Handicraft*—ranged from the broadly philosophical to the petty and mundane. So divisive were these squabbles that some members resigned in protest. Others advised the SACB to split into two: one group for those interested in theory and ideas and another for those concerned with business matters and sales. As it stood, one member argued, Craftsmen were so excluded from the decision-making process that the SACB was united in name only.[17] ❦ A few disgruntled members argued that the SACB failed to achieve its mission, accusing it of merely "playing at Arts

14. C. Howard Walker, Critic for the Jury, "Report of the Jury," in The Report of The Society of Arts and Crafts, Boston Massachusetts, Incorporated MDCCXCVII, Nine Park Street, [April 12,] 1914, p. 10.

15. Brandt, "Mutually Helpful Relations," pp. 334–350. "Analysis of Sales for 1907," in Frederick Allen Whiting to Herbert Langford Warren, April 4, 1900; SACB archives, AAA/SI 300:500. "The Report of the Metalworkers Guild," in The Society of Arts and Crafts Twelfth Annual Report & List of Members: Boston 1909. "Analysis of Sales for the Year 1911 by Contributor," SACB archives, AAA/SI 317:752.

16. The 1906–07 annual report first mentions the Society's intention of forming "guilds" of those having "mutual interests" and desirous of "fellowship." The Guild of Metalworkers was subsequently formed ca. 1907–08. The Guild of Woodworkers is first mentioned in the annual report for 1907–08, and St. Dunstan's Guild in that for 1908–09. Those contributing to St. Dunstan's Guild fund included: Ralph Adams Cram, Frank Cleveland, Gustav Rogers, Guy Maginnis, Henry Hurt, John Kirchmayer, and Frank Fitzpatrick; SACB archives, AAA/SI 300:581.

17. Key components of the debate presented in Handicraft vols. 1 and 2 include essays by Arthur Astor Carey, Mary Ware Dennett, Denman Waldo Ross, and Charles Howard Walker. For a summary of the debate, ideas and contributors, see Brandt, "Mutually Helpful Relations," pp. 171–192.

and Crafts." But numbers suggest otherwise: few organizations of its type surpassed the SACB in terms of annual revenue and value of inventory in the salesroom, number of members, of exhibitions held, of attendees at those exhibitions, or of medals and honors awarded to its members. Few societies produced a magazine having the national distribution of *Handicraft*, or realized a degree of financial self–sufficiency.[18] ❲ Those same members would quickly point out that such facts and figures were less important than the overall quality of the Society's varied efforts. As early as 1897, they had advised that "the consideration [was] not how much but how good." Qualitative achievements included exhibitions that highlighted the close interaction of members working across disciplinary boundaries; catalogue entries that called attention to artistic collaboration by listing names of all who participated, whether designer, maker, manufacturer, or purveyor; the influence of its nationally accepted standards on displays of arts and crafts at international exhibitions; inclusion of members' works in the permanent collections of museums within and beyond the United States; and establishment of the Handicraft Shop—a metalsmiths' co–operative—that produced enough silver flatware, hollowware, and enamels to become financially independent. Even the Society's proposal to construct a new facility to house its headquarters and professional offices for those in allied fields—though never built—symbolized its commitment to banish disciplinary xenophobia.[19] ❲ Perhaps its chief accomplishment was its national stature, which prompted similar organizations hoping to further the cause of design reform to model themselves after the SACB: "the Society is looked to as the center of the movement," stated the *Annual Report* for 1906–07, "and as the one to which younger societies naturally turn for guidance and inspiration." The SACB inspired such emulation by encouraging the public to accept responsibility for the state of the applied arts and by molding perceptions regarding the role of handicrafts within American culture. The Society stimulated heated debates about design and social reform both within and beyond Boston while articulating a theory of good design as well as a standard by which to evaluate its implementation. It championed the contributions of the individual worker while promoting the additional benefits of artistic collaboration. And it argued that usefulness and beauty should be available to all. For reasons such as these, members chose to overlook occasional discrepancies between its stated intentions and its actual achievements, noting with obvious pride that "the Society is recognized as a leader in the Country."[20]

18. Ross, "The Arts and Crafts"; Brandt, "Mutually Helpful Relations," pp. 309–426.

19. *Prospectus: Exhibition of the Arts and Crafts. Copley Hall: Boston* [January 21, 1897]; SACB archives, AAA/SI 319:701. SACB exhibition catalogue (1907), passim. Carey developed plans to found a cooperative workshop in the fall of 1901. Illustrations of work produced at the Handicraft Shop appeared in *Handicraft* 1, no. 1 (April 1902). Regarding the SACB's participation at international expositions, see Beverly K. Brandt, "'Worthy and Carefully Selected': American Arts and Crafts at the Louisiana Purchase Exposition, 1904," *Journal of the Archives of American Art* 28, no. 1 (1988), pp. 2–16. The proposed new facility is discussed in Frederick Allen Whiting to Frederick Pickering Cabot, January 15, 1912; SACB archives, AAA/SI 300:682, and subsequently in reports of the so–called Building Committee to the Council in 1914; SACB archives, AAA/SI reels 300 and 316, passim.

20. "Report of the Council," in the *Annual Report* [for 1906–07] of *The Society of Arts and Crafts of Boston, Massachusetts, 9 Park Street*, MDCCCVII (May 1907). This report discusses formation of the National League of Handicraft Societies. Elizabeth Stone to Frederick P. Cabot, March 10, 1912; SACB archives, AAA/SI 300:691.

Survey of the SACB Membership conducted in 1916
by the Committee on Entertainment*

Architect................... 22	Lace Maker.................. 8
Basketry................... 21	Leaded Glass............... 2
Bead Worker............... 2	Leather 37
Book Plates 12	Metalworker.............. 96
Brass Worker 3	Modeler................... 22
Cabinet Worker........... 12	Needleworker.............. 7
Cement Worker............ 1	Painter 8
Ceramic Worker 1	Pewter..................... 2
Chaser 4	Photographer............. 23
China Decorator.......... 34	Porcelain Decorator........ 1
Color Printer............... 2	Potter 29
Colorist of Plaster Casts 1	Printer 5
Concrete Worker 2	Pyrographer 6
Crocheter 1	Sculptor................... 4
Decorator................. 29	Ship Modeler.............. 1
Designer................. 143	Silversmith 42
Draughtsman.............. 2	Stained Glass 5
Dyer....................... 4	Stenciler 7
Embroiderer.............. 33	Stone Cutter............... 1
Enameler 22	Tapestry Weaver 4
Frame Maker.............. 6	Tatting 1
Gem Carver 1	Textiles.................... 1
Illuminator 17	Toys...................... 12
Illustrator 1	Wood Block............... 2
Interior Decorator 2	Weaver................... 19
Iron Worker 3	Wood Carver 50
Jeweler.................. 129	Wood Engraver 2

* "Survey of the Membership, Conducted by the Committee on Entertainment of
the Society of Arts and Crafts, Boston, 1916;" SACB archives, AAA/SI 316:074

THE AESTHETICS OF CRAFTS-MANSHIP & THE PRESTIGE OF THE PAST: BOSTON FURNITURE-MAKING & WOOD-CARVING

EDWARD S. COOKE, JR.

S CHOLARS AND COLLECTORS of the American Arts and Crafts movement have paid little attention to the woodworkers of Boston. Such an oversight seems odd, given the region's extensive involvement in design reform, and prompts a fresh look at Boston's woodworking during that time. It is essential that we determine whether output in Boston was truly insignificant, or whether we have asked the wrong questions, proceeding from idealized aesthetics and rigid, formal definitions of what comprised "Arts and Crafts furniture."[1] ¶ A search through local shelter magazines and architectural journals indicates that Boston furniture–makers demonstrated moderate interest in a Mission or quaint style from about 1898 until around 1905. The *Boston Architectural Club Yearbook*, an annual of recent projects predominantly by Boston architects, illustrated a number of suburban or North Shore residences furnished in the craftsman style with oak paneling and Mission–style furniture. Local furnishing firms such as Paine Furniture Company or Cobb–Eastman Company (fig. 5) ordered large quantities of Gustav Stickley furniture during this period. They stressed the moderate cost of such furniture, the ability to acquire matching suites, and the appropriate fit with country houses, cottages, bungalows, or camps.[2] Yet many of the same firms also offered colonial revival forms. Mellish, Byfield & Co., a firm which provided Mission–style furniture for the Carnegie Library in Pittsburgh in 1897, also made Queen Anne, Chippendale, and Windsor oak chairs for the Boston Public Library. Paine continued to offer furniture in historic styles while retailing "bungalow furniture" in the Mission style from 1901 to 1905.[3] Beginning around 1905, Boston architects began to forsake Mission or craftsman interiors and concentrated instead upon colonial or post–medieval styles to evoke the simple life without sacrificing refinement or good taste. The *Boston Architectural Club Yearbook* illustrated new houses with furniture inspired by seventeenth–

1. Surveys such as Robert Clark, ed., *The Arts and Crafts Movement in America, 1876–1916* (Princeton, N.J.: Princeton University Press, 1972); *From Architecture to Object: Masterworks of the American Arts & Crafts Movement* (New York: Hirschl & Adler Galleries, 1989); and Leslie Bowman, *American Arts and Crafts: Virtue in Design* (Los Angeles: Los Angeles County Museum of Art, 1990) do not illustrate a single piece of Boston woodwork from this period. A local volume, Wendy Kaplan, ed., *"The Art that is Life": The Arts & Crafts Movement in America, 1875–1920* (Boston: Museum of Fine Arts, 1987), offers little more. It illustrates a Centennial turned chair and a chair designed by H.H. Richardson, both from the 1870s, a chest made in Deerfield in 1901, and a Windsor settee made by Wallace Nutting Period Furniture in 1927; but it does not include any consideration of the woodworking activities in Boston in spite of extensive discussion of Boston ceramics, silver, and stained glass. For a discussion of new ways of understanding furniture of this period, see Edward S. Cooke, Jr., "Arts and Crafts Furniture: Process or Product?" in Janet Kardon, ed., *The Ideal Home, 1900–1920: The History of Twentieth–Century American Craft* (New York: Abrams, 1993), pp. 64–76.

2. *Boston Architectural Club Yearbook* for the years 1902 through 1920; but see especially the 1904 volume which illustrates both craftsman and colonial revival interiors. For the advertisements of Cobb–Eastman and Paine, see *Boston Architectural Club Yearbook* 1902, p. 116; and *House Beautiful* 17, no. 6 (May 1905), p. 41. Susan J. Montgomery's research into the Stickley papers now at the Henry Francis du Pont Winterthur Museum Library revealed that Paine was Stickley's largest Boston account until about 1903, when Cobb–Eastman replaced it: letter from Susan Montgomery to the author, April 9, 1993.

3. On the work of Mellish, Byfield & Co., see *The Brochure Series of Architectural Illustration* 2, no. 12 (December 1896), pp. 197–98; *The Brochure Series of Architectural Illustration* 3, no. 11 (November 1897), p. xxiii; and Margaret Henderson Floyd, *Architecture After Richardson: Regionalism before Modernism—Longfellow, Alden, and Harlow in Boston and Pittsburgh* (Chicago: University Press of Chicago, 1994), pp. 207 and 347.

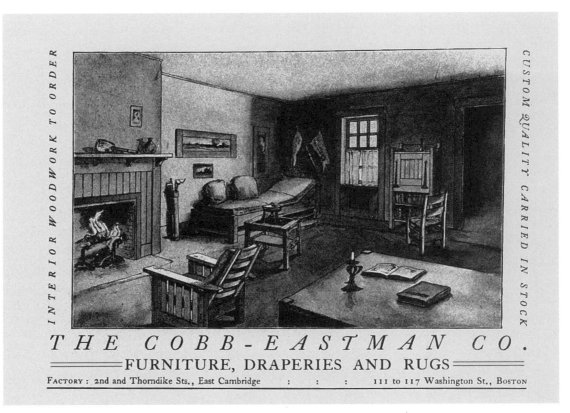

{5} Advertisement for Cobb–Eastman, *Boston Architectural Club Yearbook 1902*, p. 116.

century joined chests; William and Mary gate–leg tables; Queen Anne chairs, dining tables, lowboys or highboys; Chippendale chairs, tea tables, and chests of drawers; and Federal sideboards and urn–pedestal dining tables. Two different interior styles dominated the look of the first quarter of the century: the Georgian, most often seen in the paneled chimneybreasts flanked by fluted pilasters with Ionic capitals, fielded paneling, and staircases with twist turnings and scroll bracket designs derived from the demolished Thomas Hancock mansion on Beacon Hill (built 1736); and the Bulfinch neoclassical, distinguished by little or no paneling, light chair rails, carved or composition work with classical motifs, and light, curving staircases, all elements derived from the work of the Boston architect Charles Bulfinch (1763–1844). Yearbooks also featured historic Norman buildings, medieval churches, and English country houses and parish churches, as well as Samuel Chamberlain's photographs of North Shore colonial homes. The same sort of illustrations filled the pages of *The Brochure Series of Architectural Illustration* and suggest a commonly understood definition of historic style that linked American colonial work to medieval and post–medieval work in England and northern France.

Paine and Cobb–Eastman advertised colonial revival work exclusively, while other companies such as Irving & Casson, A.H. Davenport, and William F. Ross (cat. no. 16) offered interior woodwork and furniture in a range of historic styles from Gothic to Louis xv and xvi to colonial.4 ❡ The Mission style of furniture disappeared from the upper range of domestic work and became confined to the middle or lower–middle level of the market. Langford Warren stated that such furniture was superior to the "manifest ugliness and hopeless vulgarity" of other sorts of inexpensive furniture, especially that cursed by "tawdry and insipid" pressed or stamped ornament. To Warren and other architects and designers, absence of ornament was preferable to such debased workmanship. He praised works such as Mission furniture, which, "simple in outline and devoid of ornamentation, may properly be made by the machine and may be beautiful in its way."5 The last phrase indicates that class lines were being drawn: historic forms and decoration finished with skilled handwork for the upper classes; simple unornamented forms made by machines with no handwork for the middle and lower classes. Boston Consolidated Gas illustrated a model middle–class dining

4. On the general trends of the period, see Floyd, *Architecture After Richardson*, passim. For pertinent advertisements of Cobb–Eastman, Irving & Casson, A.H. Davenport, William Ross, and Paine, see *Boston Architectural Club Yearbook 1908*, p. 145; *Boston Architectural Club Yearbook 1911*, pp. 200–01; *Boston Architectural Club Yearbook 1912*, p. 218; and *Boston Architectural Club Yearbook 1914*, p. 172.

5. H. Langford Warren, "Department of Woodworking," *Exhibition of the Society of Arts and Crafts: Copley Hall, Boston* (Boston: Heintzemann Press, 1907), p. 86. For illustrations of the dining room and advertisements for Leavens, see *Boston Architectural Club Yearbook 1909*, p. 151; *House Beautiful 18*, no. 6 (November 1905), p. 50; and *House Beautiful 28*, no. 5 (October 1910), p. xiv.

room in the Mission style in 1909 (fig. 6), and the manufacturer William Leavens & Co. advertised Mission furniture for the same market until about 1915 (cat. no. 8). Yet Leavens also offered colonial revival furniture and employed advertising copy that stressed the colonial New England spirit of their simply designed straight–lined oak furniture (fig. 7). ⟨ Inextricably connected to the production of furniture in historic styles was the collecting of antiques. At the turn of the century, Boston had become the center of the antiques business, with numerous influential collectors and dealers. While many families in the area simply inherited colonial furniture, a number of gentleman collectors eagerly pursued early New England furniture, particularly that of the seventeenth and early eighteenth centuries. Such antiques not only possessed genealogical value and provided a sort of material jeremiad for New England's golden age, but also resonated with the Arts and Crafts principles of local materials (particularly the venerable oak), visible construction (pinned mortise–and–tenon joinery), honest craftsmanship (Puritan craftsmen being considered the noblest), and vernacular style (based firmly on the English styles). Gentleman artists such as Dwight Blaney (1865–1944) and J. Templeman Coolidge III (1856–1945), lawyers such

as H. Eugene Bolles (1838–1910) and Charles Hitchcock Tyler (1863–1931), and businessmen such as Francis Hill Bigelow (1859–1933) had all amassed significant collections of colonial furniture by the turn of the century. Bolles had assembled more than 600 pieces, which he valued for their "associations with customs, surroundings, and life of a provincial and colonial history." Three of the most prominent antiques shops, located along the same side of Charles Street, were Flayderman & Kaufman, Israel Sack, and Joseph Grossman. Boston also served as home for the magazine *Antiques* from its founding in 1922 until July 1929, when it relocated to New York City.[6] ⟨ The collecting of American antique furniture supported a number of craftsmen in the repair and reproduction trade. Olof Althin, a Swedish–trained cabinetmaker, worked extensively on the Tyler and Bolles collections, often improving the old furniture to its "original lines" during restoration. Althin also made his own furniture in the colonial style, drawing upon old techniques and using old wood to produce what he called "art furniture" (cat. no. 1).[7] The Harvard–educated minister Wallace Nutting, who suffered from neurasthenia, switched careers in 1904 to seek health and rejuvenation in the rural colonial world. Initially he sold hand–colored

6. On antiques collecting, see Elizabeth Stillinger, *The Antiquers* (New York: Knopf, 1980), esp. pp. 95–112; Harold Sack with Max Wilk, *American Treasure Hunt: The Legacy of Israel Sack* (Boston: Little, Brown and Company, 1986), esp. pp. 27–82; and *Antiques* 1, no. 1 (January 1922), p. 43.

7. For information on Althin, see his business papers in the library of the Winterthur Museum.

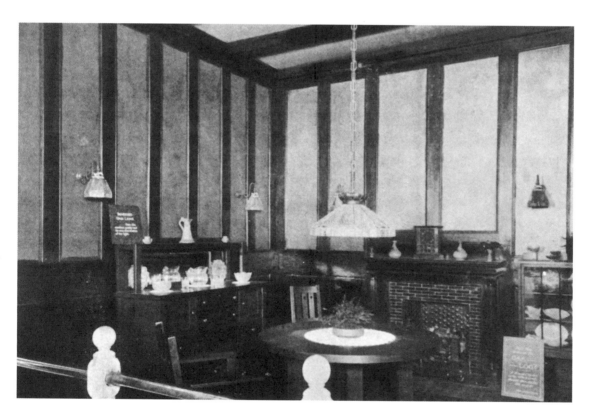

{6} Illustration of the Boston Gas Model Dining Room, *Boston Architectural Club Yearbook 1909*, p. 151.

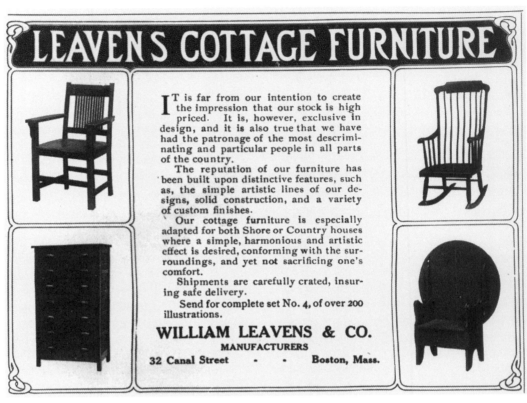

{7} Advertisement for Leavens Cottage Furniture, *House Beautiful* 28, no. 5 (October 1910), p. xiv.

photographs of rural landscapes and recreations of pre–Revolutionary interiors, but as he sought to recreate accurate settings, Nutting began to collect antiques and became a leading authority on American colonial furniture. In 1917 he published his first book about furniture, *A Windsor Handbook*, and opened a furniture shop. Nutting would often collect an authentic antique, study related examples, restore the prototype, and then have his craftsmen make reproductions (cat. no. 11). Among the "Ten Construction Commandments" that hung above the benches at his shop were "...2. If the old method is best, use it; 3. If the work can be done better by hand, do it that way; 4. Use long and large mortises, and large square white oak pins;...10. Let nothing leave your hands until you are proud of the work." Throughout his career, Nutting embodied the qualities common to the Arts and Crafts movement and the colonial revival.[8] ❡ Yet another manifestation of the interest in colonial furniture was the making of miniature antique furniture, a specialty of the Society of Arts and Crafts, Hingham. Around the turn of the century, a group of toy–makers from that town on the South Shore became known for their colonial revival furniture. Loring Cushing, Ezra Wilder, and William Luce

made works lauded for their simple charm and realistic imitation of the colonial period (cat. nos. 6 and 10). The use of colonial models for dollhouses—small domestic sets intended for young girls—was appropriate for the desired goals: it reinforced the notion of a simpler, controllable past, and it schooled young girls in "correct" taste.[9] ❡ The dominance of period styles, particularly American colonial, and the class associations of the new Mission style suggest the need to broaden our view of Arts and Crafts style. In articulating their response to the perceived ills of industrialization, urbanization, political corruption, and moral decay, Boston tastemakers looked to the past; in this, architects played a particular role. Warren observed that architects in Boston, well grounded in the history of architecture, had directly influenced the improvement of interiors and furniture in the late nineteenth and early twentieth centuries. Horace Dunham, a designer who taught furniture history at the School of the Museum of Fine Arts, found it natural to write an article on colonial chairs for an architectural journal in 1896. Citing the solid, logical construction and simple, functional lines of the Chippendale style, Dunham commented that American and English furniture from the last half

8. Among the best sources on Nutting are his autobiography, *Wallace Nutting's Biography* (Framingham, Mass.: Old America Company, 1936); Walter Dyer, "The New Mission of an Old Farmhouse," *Country Life in America* 20, no. 11 (October 1, 1911), pp. 35–38; William Dulaney, "Wallace Nutting: Collector and Entrepreneur," *Winterthur Portfolio* 13 (1979), pp. 47–60; Joyce Barendsen, "Wallace Nutting, an American Tastemaker: The Pictures and Beyond," *Winterthur Portfolio* 18, nos. 2/3 (Summer/Autumn 1983), pp. 187–212; and Marianne Woods, "Viewing Colonial America Through the Lens of Wallace Nutting," *American Art* 8, no. 2 (Spring 1994), pp. 67–86. On the relationship between neurasthenia and the vigorous life of the Arts and Crafts movement, see Tom Lutz, *American Nervousness, 1903* (Ithaca, N.Y.: Cornell University Press, 1991). The illustrated cupboard is a reproduction of Nutting's own Parmenter cupboard, his most cherished piece of case furniture: see Wallace Nutting, *Furniture of the Pilgrim Century, 1620–1720* (Boston: Marshall Jones, 1921), pp.124–25.

9. On the Society of Arts and Crafts, Hingham, see C. Chester Lane, "Hingham Arts and Crafts, Their Aims and Objects," *Craftsman* 3 (December 1903), pp. 276–81. For a general overview of the Hingham toy-makers, see Marshall and Inez McClintock, *Toys in America* (Washington, D.C.: Public Affairs Press, 1961), esp. pp. 83–84 and 98–101; and Ralph Bergengren, "Unusual American Toys," *House Beautiful* 39, no. 1 (December 1915), pp. 17–19 and xxv. Helpful in the interpretation of doll furniture as cultural artifact is Miriam Formanek–Brunell, *Made to Play House: Dolls and the Commercialization of American Girlhood, 1830–1930* (New Haven: Yale University Press, 1993). On Luce, see Karen Evans Ülehla, ed., *The Society of Arts and Crafts, Boston: Exhibition Record 1897–1927* (Boston: Boston Public Library, 1981), p. 140.

of the eighteenth century was "the best the world has yet produced" and far surpassed contemporary furniture "in point of style, appropriateness, and general usefulness." As a 1904 editorial in *House Beautiful* pointed out, all other styles were flawed: Art Nouveau and English quaint furniture were too showy and individualistic, Gothic either too crude or too ornate, French rococo too fanciful, and American Mission lacking a sufficient variety of motifs. Only the colonial revival style possessed "the prestige that age gives." Precedence and prestige rather than "new fashion" held forth, as cultivated Bostonians valued refined elegance based upon a reconfiguration of historical genres and details.[10] ¶ Another way to approach the study of Arts and Crafts furniture in Boston is to focus upon the makers themselves. Analysis of the SACB membership lists provides insights into who might have been active in the cause of handicraft and quality.[11] Several large firms noted for high–quality workmanship in historical styles—for example, A.H. Davenport and Lawrence Wilde & Co.—participated only in the earliest exhibitions of the Society. Some Society members were listed as furniture designers, but were often skilled in other media as well and, like architects, recognized the need to collaborate with skilled technicians: membership in the Society became a means to add moral value to their work. ¶ Only a few traditionally trained cabinetmakers maintained strong ties with the SACB. Samuel Hayward, who had worked as a carver and cabinetmaker in New York, consistently showed work in eighteenth–century styles and gained particular recognition for his painted decoration. Frederick W. Kulkmann, a German–trained "old style all–around cabinet maker" who worked with the carver Alfred Longuemere, seemed to be the Society's favored technician (cat. no. 5). He executed work for architects such as C. Howard Walker and Frank Cleveland and fabricated the basic furniture that others such as Estelle Nast, John Peabody, Mary Dawson, Martha Page, and Herbert Brown then carved and decorated.[12] ¶ The two largest groups of woodworkers active in the Society of Arts and Crafts were amateur woodworkers or cabinetmakers, and woodcarvers. Amateurs included Henry Hammond Taylor, a Bridgeport, Connecticut antique dealer and restorer; Charles Sladon, a music teacher in Newtonville, Massachusetts, who found creative satisfaction in woodworking; and J. Dwight Howard, a Newton clerk or salesman who used woodworking as a means of self–improvement, becoming a draftsman by 1919.[13] The

period's emphasis upon process, the establishment of woodworking as part of the manual arts training curriculum in all Boston public schools in 1891, and the appeal of crafts to the emerging white–collar managerial class all fueled the growth of this sector of the Society, but equally important were the economic realities that prevented individual self–sufficiency. The individual craftsman often found his values and approach out of step with the consumer's interest in matched sets and low prices, the manufacturer's lack of financial commitment to the value of design, and the Society salesroom's need for profit. Robert Brown, an SACB member from Pennsylvania, lamented in 1910: "Sales of pieces of furniture or woodwork at the Boston Society's rooms are few and far between and I venture to say that not one of the members engaged in woodworking, either as craftsmen or designers, makes an adequate livelihood."[14] ¶ Even more striking than the number of amateur woodworkers is the dominance of woodcarvers in the Society. In terms of numbers and length of membership, woodcarvers comprised the strongest set of woodworking members. Three of the twenty–one charter members of the SACB, most of whom were architects or artistically oriented members of Boston's upper class, were carvers: Hugh Cairns, John Evans, and John Kirchmayer. During this period, Bostonians expressed great interest in carving. Many felt that wood–carving was one of the craft skills least affected by the machine and that "any decoration must be carved by hand to make the slightest claim to artistic quality." Frederic Coburn, the art critic for the *Boston Herald*, remarked in 1910, "No other applied art, in fact—with the possible exception of printing and bookbinding—has advanced further in the United States in the past ten years" than wood–carving.[15] ¶ During the last quarter of the nineteenth century, wood–carving held a prominent position in the hierarchy of decorative arts and in discussions intended to improve both the taste of consumers and the style of manufacturers. In the old Museum of Fine Arts in Copley Square, where galleries were organized by medium rather than historical or regional classifications, the Lawrence Room was filled with a variety of carved work—English oak panels, Italian furniture, and Japanese panels and screens. The Women's Educational and Industrial Union (WEIU) demonstrated sufficient interest in carving to establish a School of Carving and Modeling at the museum, intended for women who needed to support themselves. They hired

10. T.J. Jackson Lears, *No Place of Grace: Antimodernism and the Transformation of American Culture, 1880–1920* (Chicago: University of Chicago Press, 1981); Warren, "Department of Woodworking," p. 86; Horace Dunham, "American Colonial Chairs," *The Brochure Series of Architectural Illustration 2,* no. 12 (December 1896), pp. 187–92; and *House Beautiful* 15, no. 4 (March 1904), pp. 232–33. See also Floyd, *Architecture After Richardson;* Trevor Fairbrother, *The Bostonians: Painters of an Elegant Age, 1870–1930* (Boston: Museum of Fine Arts, 1986); Beverly Brandt, "'Sobriety and Restraint': The Search for an Arts and Crafts Style in Boston, 1897–1917," *Tiller* 2, no. 5 (Fall 1985), pp. 26–73; and Brandt, "The Essential Link: Boston Architects and The Society of Arts and Crafts, 1897–1917," *Tiller* 2, no. 1 (September–October 1983), pp. 7–32.

11. The data compiled by Karen Ulehla provides a departure point for this discussion.

12. On Hayward, see *House Beautiful* 5, no. 5 (April 1899), pp. 208–13. For information on Kulkmann, see his entry in the biographical section.

13. Information on Sladon and Howard drawn from Newton directories. Taylor, the author of *Knowing, Collecting and Restoring Early American Furniture* (Philadelphia: J.B. Lippincott, 1930), also sold furniture to Francis P. Garvan: see David Barquist, *American Tables and Looking Glasses in the Mabel Brady Garvan and Other Collections at Yale University* (New Haven: Yale University Art Gallery, 1992), esp. pp. 389–92.

15. Brandt, "The Essential Link," p. 14; Warren, "Department of Woodworking," p. 86; F.W. Coburn, "Wood Carving and Architecture–Work by I. Kirchmayer and Others," *International Studio* (September 1910), p. lxi-ii. See also Warren's "The Qualities of Carving." *Handicraft* 1, no. 9 (December 1902), pp. 193–224.

14. *Handicraft* 3, no. 10 (January 1911), p. 384. Brown cited a personal example of the constraints faced by individual craftsmen. He had a mahogany piano stool on sale for $35, but a customer wanted a matched set for $60. Unable to produce the pair for that price, Brown sought an estimate from a commercial firm. The company could produce the set for $60, allowing $45 for the actual manufacture, $3 to Brown the designer, and $12 sales commission for the Society.

John Evans to oversee it, but they apparently overestimated the interest in the program, and the school was closed by 1880.[16] ❧ School training did not contribute significantly to the vitality of Boston carving. The WEIU's course lasted less than one year, and the Massachusetts Normal Art School did not offer woodworking or carving in its curriculum until 1911. Instead, carving remained the domain of trained immigrant men who followed the specifications of architects or designers in enhancing the beauty of an existing design. Bostonians favored a certain type of carving. An article in the Boston-based *American Architect and Building News* in 1877 criticized the work of Cincinnati's women carvers for their predilection to cover all plain surfaces with carved ornament, thereby emphasizing decoration to the disadvantage of form. Dismissing the enthusiasms of the amateur women, Boston designers insisted that architects should provide leadership and guidance in the encouragement of carving and that carvers should study historical models with the restrained use of carved ornament sensitive to form.[17] ❧ Langford Warren placed great emphasis upon the education of architects in the history of architecture, and a different sort of education for craftsmen. Through apprenticeship the latter not only learned their skills but also learned how to be patient and to observe the artistic hierarchy of designer and craftsman:

> The largest use of carved wood is...in the decoration of the interiors of buildings and in furniture, and this class of work has been directly controlled in most cases by educated architects. The growth and development of the profession of architecture in this country has therefore brought with it constant improvement and increased use of carved woodwork. ❧ In the first instance our carvers were immigrants, men trained in the workshops of Europe under the old apprentice system, which continues to produce excellent results there, and it is still the case that our best wood-carvers are such English, Scotch, Germans, Swedes, French, or Italians. Native Americans are now beginning to take up wood-carving, but it must be confessed that the entire absence of any proper apprenticeship system and lack of any adequate scheme of training which might conceivably take its place, still obliges us to depend on immigration from Europe to keep up our supply of skilled carvers.[18]

Among the foreign-trained carvers working for local architects were the Welsh-trained John Evans (b. 1850); the Scottish-trained Hugh Cairns (b. 1862) and Andrew Lees (b. 1844); the Swedish-trained Nils Kjellstrom (b. 1852) and Walfred Thulin (b. 1878) and the Spanish-born Domingo Mora (b. 1840), all of whom worked for Evans; the French-trained Alfred F.J. Longuemere (b. 1856); and the German-trained John Kirchmayer (b. 1860).[19] ❧ Kirchmayer, who enjoyed a long career as a carver for various manufacturers and architects, was considered by many the finest American carver of the period, famed for his technical ability, considerable volume of work, and commitment to expressive carving. The leading ecclesiastical architect of the period, Ralph Adams Cram, praised Kirchmayer as "the dean of American carvers," "a true creative artist...possessed of the whole Mediaeval tradition" yet "bent on working this out in vital contemporary forms" (cf. fig. 23).[20] ❧ Although he worked effectively in a variety of styles, including Renaissance, Romanesque, and Byzantine, Kirchmayer favored Gothic. He developed his own particular "American Gothic," not a simple reproduction, but rather an updated display of the same skill and spirit. For figural carving, he successfully blended a contemporary attention to the individuality of the face and hands of his subjects with a historical conventionalization of clothing and fabric. Looking at his work as simply traditional or "anti-modern" does not allow for the forwardness of his ideas and his abilities to execute them. While his embellishment of custom furniture for James Hill or George Booth and carved architectural elements for churches such as the reredos for All Saints' in Ashmont, Massachusetts or St. Paul's Cathedral in Detroit certainly showcase Kirchmayer's technical prowess and his rich and lively directness, it is his personal works, such as the tableau *Christmas in Heaven* (cat. no. 7), that truly reveal the strength and passion of his convictions, his architectural sense for composition, and his skill in giving life to wood. In such works, it is indeed easy to see how the carver believed that "every figure ought to be a poem by itself."[21] ❧ Andrew Lees was another immigrant carver who parlayed his craft skills into a broader artistic career. Earlier in his career, he carved architectural ornaments, fireplaces, custom-made furniture, and even figureheads for ships, but by the end of the century he was concentrating on special artistic work, carving the gun used as a model by Daniel Chester French for the *Minuteman* sculpture, and painting pastoral landscapes. In 1901 he joined the Society of Arts and Crafts, and gained particular renown for his mahogany bookends with carved acanthus leaf decoration (cat. no. 9).[22] ❧ While architects such as Warren and Cram praised the performance of

16. Walter Muir Whitehill, *Museum of Fine Arts, Boston: A Centennial History* (Cambridge: Belknap Press of Harvard University Press, 1970), pp. 36–51. For comparison, see Kenneth Trapp's discussion of Benn Pitman's wood-carving department at the University of Cincinnati's School of Design, established in 1873 and successful into the early twentieth century: "'To Beautify the Useful': Benn Pitman and the Women's Woodcarving Movement in Cincinnati in the Late Nineteenth Century," in Kenneth Ames, ed., *Victorian Furniture* (Philadelphia: The Victorian Society in America, 1983), pp. 174–92.

17. Whitehill, *Museum of Fine Arts*, p. 51; communication with Paul Dobbs, archivist at the Massachusetts College of Art, November 8, 1994; "Women as Wood-Carvers—The Movement in Cincinnati," *The American Architect and Building News* (March 31, 1877), pp. 100–01; Warren, "Department of Woodworking," p. 86; and Coburn, "Wood Carving and Architecture," pp. lxii–iv.

18. Warren, "Department of Woodworking," p. 36.

19. Evans and Cairns ran the two most respected architectural carving shops in Boston, Kjellstrom was the foreman of the Evans shop, Thulin's first American job was in the Evans shop, and Mora carved much of the woodwork for All Saints' Church in Ashmont: (Boston Directories); letter from Clarence Thulin to the author, January 14, 1995; Douglass Shand-Tucci, *All Saints' Ashmont: A Centennial History* (Boston: All Saints' Church, 1975). Biographical data on them was drawn from U.S. Census records: Evans 1910, vol. 133, E.D. 1647, sheet 7, line 20; Cairns 1900, vol. 70, E.D. 1304, sheet 9, line 69; Kjellstrom 1900, vol. 84, E.D. 1573, sheet 12, line 22; Mora 1900, vol. 71, E.D. 1321, sheet 16, line 22; Longuemere 1910, vol. 96, E.D. 1168, sheet 17, line 20.

20. Ralph Adams Cram, *My Life in Architecture* (Boston: Little, Brown and Company, 1936), pp. 187–88.

21. For sources on Kirchmayer, see his biographical entry.

22. Additional details about Lees's career can be found in his biographical entry.

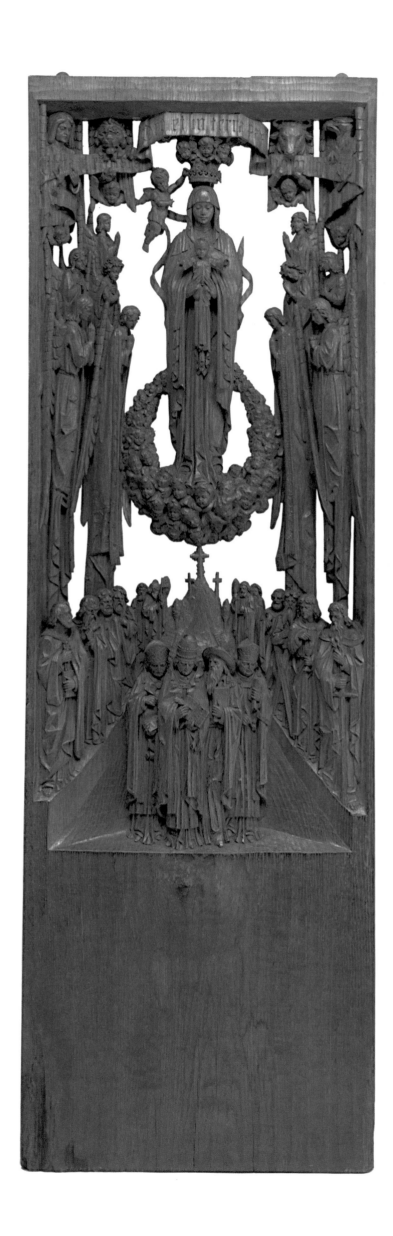

CAT. NO. 7
John Kirchmayer,
*A Christmas Festival
in Heaven*,
1918

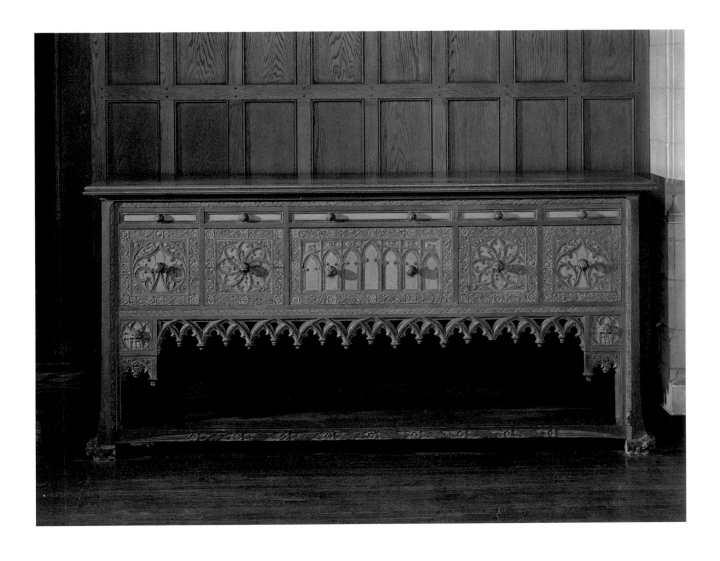

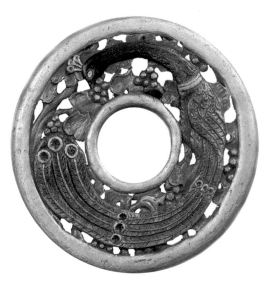

CAT. NO. 16 (*above*)
William F. Ross & Company,
Sideboard from *Tower Court*,
1916

CAT. NO. 13 (*right*)
Molly Coolidge Perkins,
Peacock medallion,
1899

CAT. NO. 11 (*opposite*)
Wallace Nutting,
Parmenter–Sudbury cupboard,
ca. 1920–30

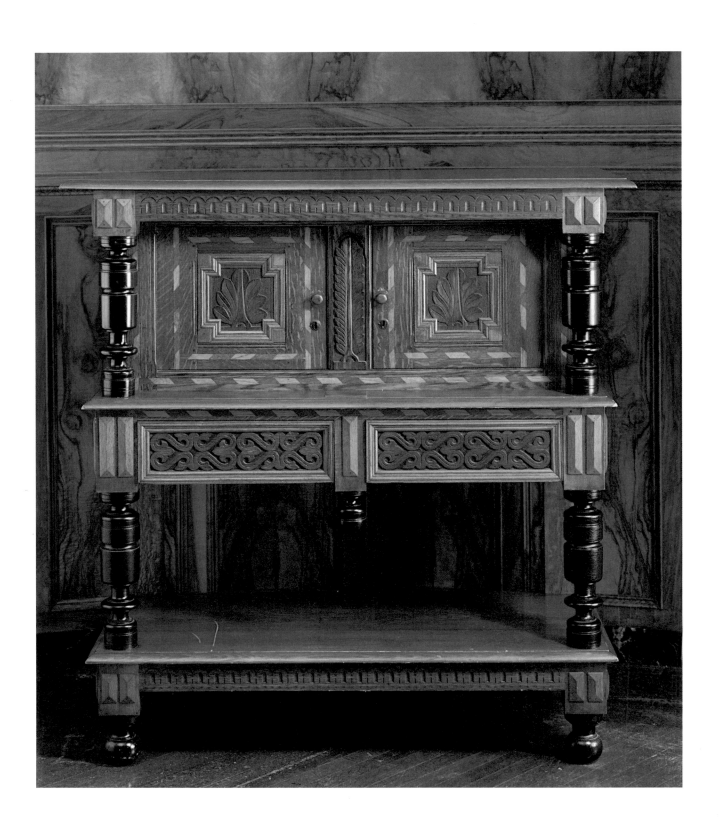

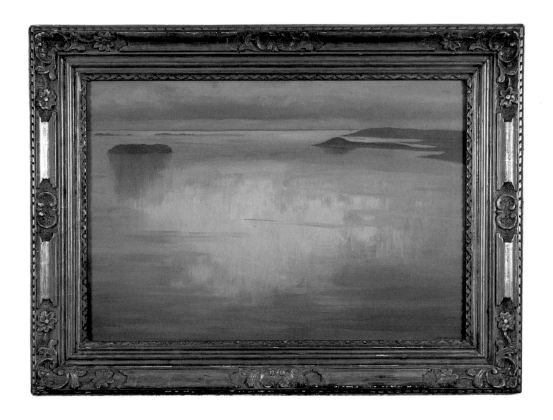

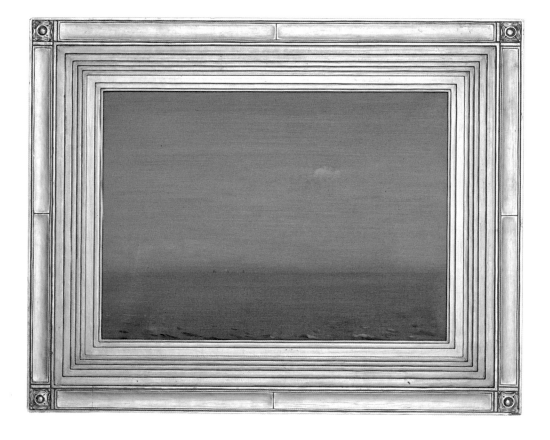

CAT. NO. 15 (top)   CAT. NO. 3 (bottom)
Arthur Wesley Dow,   Hermann Dudley Murphy,
painter;   painter;
Charles Prendergast,   Carrig–Rohane Shop,
frame–maker,   frame–makers,
The Mirror,   The Adriatic Sea,
1916   ca. 1908

skilled carvers, they were not the only tastemakers who recognized the value of carving to well–designed or artistic objects. At the turn of the century a distinct "Boston group" of artists also began to emphasize the importance of carving and took the lead in "frame reform." Deploring the dreadful frames of "ignorant and depraved frame–makers," these artists recognized the need for a sympathetic presentation of their work in custom frames, distinguished by links to Spanish or Italian examples, conscious use of the texture of carving, toning of the gilding to harmonize with the picture, and emphasis upon the lyrical qualities of framing rather than elaborate geometric and architectural layering. Turning away from overly elaborate examples with extensive cast ornament, dense carving, and complex combinations of moldings, the "Boston group" produced distinctive examples characterized by simplified, refined ornament and harmonious relationships of tones.[23] ❡ The Boston frame reformers couched their arguments within the language of craftsmanship, materials, and architectural context. First, they valued hand work: "If machine construction is necessarily involved, this must at least be made as unobjectionable as possible by elimination of all meretricious ornamentation. Wherever possible, however, the frame should be produced in strict accordance with handicraft methods." The reformers recognized the incongruity of presenting a freehand painting or watercolor within a machined frame in which ordinary moldings have merely been mitred and assembled. Such framing was suitable only for mechanical drawings or mechanically reproduced images. The "Boston group" emphasized the explicit textural surface of their carved areas and employed water gilding to achieve long–lasting variations in color and tone. They disliked precisely machined wood and pointed out the frailties and shortcomings of oil gilding or gold powders. The "Boston group" believed that good frames of proper craftsmanship, materials, and design "mediated effectively between frame and its surroundings," providing a desirable "decorative justification" that resulted in coherent beauty of the parts and the whole.[24] ❡ One of the early leaders in frame reform was Denman Ross, the Harvard historian–turned–painter who designed frames for the 1897 Society of Arts and Crafts exhibition. But Ross was more of an experimenter who brought critical attention to the frame but who neither undertook the carving himself nor established a frame–making shop.[25] The artists who immersed themselves in

frame–making were Charles Prendergast and Hermann Dudley Murphy. Prendergast, working in close collaboration with his brother, the painter Maurice Prendergast, drew inspiration from the carving and gilding of fifteenth– and sixteenth–century Italian examples, but tried to modify the designs to a more modern sensibility (cat. no. 15). Prendergast lamented the existing "mechanical results in wood–carving" and believed that the salvation of the great art of wood–carving lay with the recreational participation of "educated people" of taste like himself. They could study and draw ideas from old carvers and nature without slavishly copying them and would enjoy and highlight the beautiful irregularities of hand labor. When Prendergast moved to New York in 1914, his Boston experiences continued to influence his subsequent work. For his carved, painted, and gilded panels, screens, chests and boxes, and frames, he continued to draw ideas from a variety of historical precedents —Persian miniatures, Russian folk art, Coptic textiles, Byzantine mosaics, Etruscan murals, Egyptian carved panels, and colonial American needlework and japanned furniture—and to emphasize the energy and originality stemming from knowledge and appreciation of material and explicit use of craftsmanship. Throughout his career, Prendergast remained true to the artistic ideas of his Boston roots.[26] ❡ Hermann Dudley Murphy became interested in frames due to the influence of James McNeill Whistler and Denman Ross. From the former, Murphy developed an awareness of the importance of frames and realized that signing them with a personal cipher and the year implied that frames were art objects in their own right. From the latter, he learned the importance of historical study and of color harmony. With the help of Charles Prendergast, Murphy began making frames for his own paintings about 1898. Initially he worked in a "little crafts shop in a modest way," designing, carving, and gilding his own work, but also relying on other carvers and gilders.[27] ❡ By 1905 success apparently prompted Murphy to move his Carrig–Rohane frame shop (named after an Irish ancestral abode) from his home in Winchester into Boston. Contemporary reports noted that artists and collectors had responded so favorably to his frames that demand became "considerable and insistent," forcing Murphy to open his Boston shop where he "employed workmen whom he had trained to carry out designs which he sketched." While Murphy focused upon picture frames and mirrors (cat. nos. 3 and 4), his

23. The phrase "Boston group" was coined by Frederick Coburn, "Individual Treatment of the Picture Frame," *International Studio* 30, no. 117 (November 1906), pp. 12–16. The depiction of ignorant frame–makers is from *Academy Notes*, March 1907 (Hermann Dudley Murphy Papers, Archives of American Art, Smithsonian Institution, reel 4039, frame 282; hereafter AAA/SI reel:frame). Other good sources on the ideals of the frame reformers include Murphy's essay "Frames and Framing" (Hermann Dudley Murphy papers, AAA/SI reel 4039, frames 88–90) and Suzanne Smeaton, "American Picture Frames of the Arts and Crafts Period, 1870–1920," *Antiques* 136, no. 5 (November 1989), pp. 1124–37. Firms listed as makers of picture frames in *The Boston Directory* 1897 included Conant Bros. & Bragg Co.; F.H. Dennis; George A. Dew; and Robey, Horgan & Co.

24. The best summary of the Boston perspective is Coburn, "Individual Treatment of the Picture Frame," pp. xii–xvi, but see also clippings in the Hermann Dudley Murphy papers, AAA/SI reel 4039: frames 272–308.

25. *First Exhibition of the Arts & Crafts* (Boston: Thomas P. Smith Printing Co., 1897), p. 9; and Coburn, "Individual Treatment of the Picture Frame," p. 16.

26. For Charles's views on carving, see his essay "Revival of Wood–Carving," *House Beautiful* 26, no. 3 (August 1909), p. 70. See also the sources cited in his biographical entry.

27. On Murphy's early frame–making, see William Coles, *Hermann Dudley Murphy 1867–1945* (New York: Graham Gallery, 1982), and a review from April/May 1903 (Hermann Dudley Murphy papers, AAA/SI 4039:272). Murphy's accounts for the fall of 1904, which list the sources of his materials and the craftsmen working with him, are contained on pages 50 through 103 of his ledger for the years 1911–1944 (Hermann Dudley Murphy papers). It seems that Murphy designed detailing for frames or molding made elsewhere, then hired individual carvers, including Walfred Thulin, Frank L. Stimpson, and Giovanni Battista Troccoli, and gilders such as William Dixon, to work alongside him. A search of Boston directories for this period revealed that neither Thulin, Dixon, Troccoli, nor Stimpson were listed as working for Murphy or in Winchester and thus together comprised a cooperative shop. Among the suppliers of frames and frame stock were W.C. Stilphen of Lynn and Skinner & Matthews.

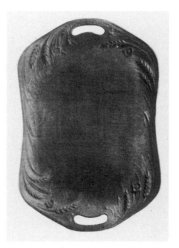
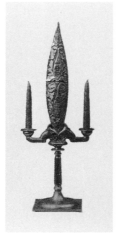
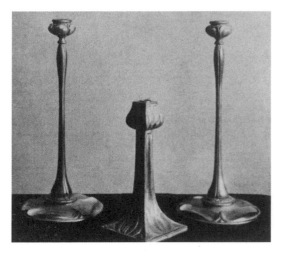
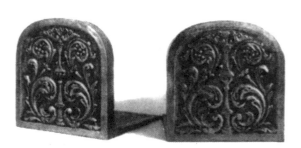

{8} Photograph of a carved wooden tray by Walfred Thulin, *House Beautiful* 37, no. 2 (January 1915), p. 18.
{9} Photograph of a carved wooden candlestick by Giovanni Battista Troccoli, *House Beautiful* 38, no. 1 (June 1915), p. 18.
{10} Photograph of carved wooden candlesticks by Martha Page, *International Studio* 41, no. 163 (September 1910), p. lxiv.
{11} Photograph of wooden bookends by Carrie and Mary Morse, *Bulletin of the Society of Arts and Crafts* 10, no. 7 (November 1926), p. 3.

shop also extended its "artistic principles into as many crafts as possible," turning out carved screens, candlesticks, panels, bookends, jewelry boxes (cat. no. 2), lamps, and even benches. For his leadership in the crafts field Murphy was elected president of the Guild of Woodworkers for the Society of Arts and Crafts, Boston in 1907 and his associate Martha Page was elected secretary.[28] ⁋ From 1906 to 1910 Murphy gained a reputation as the "commanding figure" in high–priced artistic frames. The reviews of his paintings during this period praise the frames and comment how the form, detail, and coloring of each frame perfectly suited its picture. Murphy actively promoted his work among the best circle of artists and collectors. Among his clients were Frank W. Benson, Edmund C. Tarbell, Childe Hassam, Charles Hopkinson, J. Alden Weir, Henry W. Ranger, and Frank Duveneck. Murphy also provided a monumental, architectonic frame for El Greco's *Assumption of the Virgin* in the collection of the Art Institute of Chicago. Murphy focused upon the high–priced market, specializing in frames for painters, collectors, and galleries, as well as mirrors sold to the Society of Arts and Crafts, Boston, the Detroit Society of Arts and Crafts, and Bigelow, Kennard & Co. Rather than

advertise, Murphy relied upon art journals, reviews, columns, and personal references to attract business.[29] ⁋ Foster Brothers, on the other hand, was a more commercial frame firm in Boston selling to middle–class households. It employed a traveling salesman to drum up business throughout the country, issued periodic catalogues, sent out announcements to remind customers to purchase wedding and Christmas presents, used trademarks and brass medallions affixed to the backs of their frames to establish marketing visibility, and held exclusive American rights to sell prints of the Medici Society. Foster Brothers relied upon stencil patterns to reproduce popular frames, with a set number of frame patterns and very accurate ways of establishing prices for each frame. The firm tried to enter the custom market in the first decade of the twentieth century, even copying the frames and candlesticks of Carrig–Rohane, but turned almost exclusively to colonial revival mirrors and frames for historic portraits and silhouettes in the 1910s.[30] ⁋ After 1910 Murphy devoted less attention to frame carving, but his former associates continued to carry out his ideals.[31] Walfred Thulin, a Swedish–trained joiner and carver who immigrated in 1900, worked with Murphy in

28. On the Guild of Woodworkers, see Beverly K. Brandt, "'Mutually Helpful Relations': Architects, Craftsmen and the Society of Arts and Crafts, Boston 1897–1917" (Ph.D. diss., Boston University, 1985), p. 335. For the growth of Murphy's frame shop to a full–time business, see clippings from 1907 and 1909 (Hermann Dudley Murphy papers, AAA/SI esp. 4039:82 and 308); James Spencer Dickerson, "Hermann Dudley Murphy—Painter—Craftsman," *The Sketch Book* 6, no. 6 (November 1907), pp. 303–06; "Making Carved Frames Choice Work," *Christian Science Monitor*, November 22, 1913, p. 4; and Coburn, "Individual Treatment of the Picture Frame," p. xvi On the organization of the shop, see the Carrig–Rohane Account Ledger 1908–1911 (Carrig–Rohane Shop Records, AAA/SI, box 6). Murphy solidified his personnel at this time, hiring William Dixon and Walfred Thulin as full–time employees, yet he continued to subcontract some of his work, paying Byron Moulton of Moulton & Webb (a custom woodworking firm) and Lindquist & Berggren for cabinetwork and Charles Emmel for carving from 1908 to 1910.

29. Murphy Biographical Questionnaire, Archives of the Society of Arts and Crafts, Boston; Boston Public Library (hereafter SACB papers, BPL); clippings of various shows (Hermann Dudley Murphy papers AAA/SI 4039:282–308); Coburn, "Individual Treatment of the Picture Frame," p. xvi.

30. Foster Brothers Records (AAA/SI).

31. Clippings of exhibitions after 1910 (Hermann Dudley Murphy papers AAA/SI 4039:308 ff.); Transcribed history notes of R.C. Vose (Carrig–Rohane Shop Records, box 7); *Worcester Telegram*, July 14, 1929, p. 10.

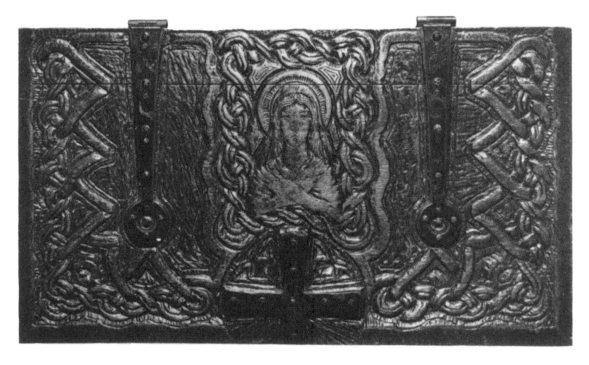

{12} Photograph of the cover of an oak dower chest by Madeline Yale Wynne, 1900; collection of Glenn C. Hjort.

Winchester and then Boston and became a shareholder in the shop before striking out on his own. Thulin made carved and gilded frames and candlesticks as well as carved furniture and trays until his death in 1949 (fig. 8). Giovanni Battista Troccoli, born in Italy and apprenticed as a carver to Hugh Cairns, studied with Ross and Murphy, and like Murphy was a multi–faceted artist. Better known today as a portrait painter, he was also a skilled carver of frames, chairs, and candlesticks (fig. 9). Troccoli taught at Ralph Radcliffe–Whitehead's Byrdcliffe Colony in Woodstock, New York in 1903 and 1904 and conducted classes on carving, gilding, and designing frames at his studio in Chestnut Hill. Martha Page and Estelle Nast, who collaborated with Thulin and F.W. Kulkmann, may also have studied with or worked for Murphy. Page gained a reputation as a maker of miniature frames and candlesticks which were "appropriately colored and gilded" (fig. 10). Nast, an artist and interior decorator who studied with Ross and Arthur Wesley Dow, painted decorative landscape scenes for folding screens, some of which were designed and carved by Page.[32] ❡ The accessibility of wood–carving—readily available materials, simple tools, opportunities to perfect techniques on one's own—and the physical and psychological benefits of manual work prompted a number of Bostonians, especially women, to take up carving. However, these women did not enroll in carving classes like the women in Cincinnati or New York.[33] Rather, Boston amateurs tended to learn through experiment, private tutorial, or books. Some of the non–professionals had studied painting or sculpture at art schools like the School of the Museum of Fine Arts and then proceeded to try wood–carving as an extension of sculpture. Murphy and Troccoli also offered private lessons. The SACB possessed a number of important reference books on carving, including George Jack's *Wood Carving: Design and Workmanship* (London: John Hogg, 1903), which a *Handicraft* review praised for its extended discussion on the principles of design derived from historical examples.[34] ❡ Many of the non–professionals used their carving skills to explore artistic processes, to make artistic household decoration for themselves, or to earn a living either as producers of small household objects or as art teachers. Molly Coolidge Perkins, daughter of J. Templeman Coolidge III, exhibited carved, gilded, and painted candlesticks at the 1897 Arts and Crafts exhibition and remained active as a

32. On Thulin, see Smeaton, "American Picture Frames of the Arts and Crafts Period," p. 1131; *Exhibition of the Society of Arts & Crafts* (Boston: Heintzemann Press, 1907), pp. 90–92; *House Beautiful* 37, no. 2 (January 1915), p. 44; letter from Clarence Thulin to Suzanne Smeaton, April 29, 1987; and letter from Clarence Thulin to the author, January 14, 1995. A carved chest of his was illustrated in *Handicraft* 5, no. 4 (July 1912), facing p. 49. On Troccoli, see his obituary in the *Boston Herald*, February 22, 1940; Troccoli Biographical Questionnaire (SACB papers, BPL); "The Studio of Giovanni Battista Troccoli at Chestnut Hill, Massachusetts," *House Beautiful* 43, no. 1 (December 1917), pp. 13–15; *The Byrdcliffe Arts and Crafts Colony: Life by Design* (Wilmington: Delaware Art Museum, 1984), pp. 8–10; Fairbrother, *The Bostonians*, esp. pp. 227–28; and *House Beautiful* 38, no. 1 (June 1915), p. 18. Page and Nast lived with each

33. On the accessibility of wood–carving and Karl von Rydingsvärd's role as a teacher, see Karl von Rydingsvärd, "Practical Points on the Art of Wood–Carving," *International Studio* 31 (1907), pp. lxxix–lxxxv; and *Hands That Built New Hampshire* (Brattleboro, Vt.: Stephen Daye Press, 1940), pp. 79–82. Von Rydingsvärd conducted his school in New York, but also taught at the Troy School of Arts and Crafts, the Institute of Arts and Science in Manchester, N.H., and the Swain School in New Bedford, Mass. Among his students were society women as well as young women intending to become art teachers, but he never found a following in Boston; perhaps he favored the Icelandic style of chip–carving that resulted in a dense overall manipulation of the wood, a bit of vulgarity not considered appropriate in Boston.

See also Boston City Directories; F.W. Coburn, "Wood Carving and Architecture" p. lxv; *Exhibition of the Society of Arts & Crafts* (Boston: Heintzemann Press, 1907), pp. 90–92; and Ulehla, *The Society of Arts and Crafts, Boston*, p. 166. Page and Nast are listed in Murphy's 1904 accounts for the purchase of gold leaf, and Page is debited for gilding small frames by Carrig–Rohane in 1908 (Carrig–Rohane Account Ledger 1908–1911, Carrig–Rohane Shop Records, Box 6, p. 13). Nast was listed as an "interior decorator" in Ross's class list for his 1907 "Theory of Pure Design" class: Harvard University Catalogue 1906–07, p. 210.

other at 398 Boylston Avenue in 1905–06 and on Highland Avenue in Winchester from 1906 to 1908. Frederic Allen Whiting described the charming cottage on Highland Avenue shared by Page and Nast: "While Miss Nast is busy with her painting in a studio on the first floor, Miss Page is occupied at her bench in an upper room designing, carving, gilding, coloring, and burnishing the charming miniature mirror and picture frames and the graceful candlesticks upon which her reputation as a successful craftswoman is based. It seems an ideal form of co–operation which brings these two busy young women together in so successful a combination of their various gifts:" Frederic Allen Whiting, "Modern Screens," (manuscript in the SACB papers, BPL).

34. For the review, see *Handicraft* 2, no. 10 (January 1904), pp. 219–22. Other titles in the library included Eleanor Rowe, *Hints on Chip–Carving: Class Teaching and Other Northern Styles* (London: R. Sutton & Co., 1892); Frank Jackson, *Wood–Carving as an Aid to the Study of Elementary Art* (London: Chapman & Hall, 1902); David Denning, *Wood–Carving for Amateurs* (London: L. Upcott Gill, 1898); and E.R. Plowder, *Progressive Studies and Other Designs for Wood–Carvers* (1894). Much of the library is presently housed in the Department of American Decorative Arts and Sculpture at the Museum of Fine Arts, Boston.

35. See Perkins's biographical entry for sources on her career.

36. On Nowell, see *Exhibition of the Society of Arts & Crafts*, Copley Hall, Boston (Boston: George H. Ellis, 1899); *Exhibition of the Society of Arts & Crafts* (Boston: Heintzemann Press, 1907); Boston City Directories; and Boston–New England Art Archives (Fine Arts Department, Boston Public Library).

37. Of the Morses, Carrie was the more accomplished carver, recognized for her "lovely" and "expensive" mirrors, frames, bookends, and trays. Mary, who seems to have executed some carving but mainly collaborated with her sister as a decorator (gilder or painter), was a teacher, employed at the Chestnut Hill School from 1905 to 1921 (where Troccoli also taught art in 1923) and at the Buckingham School in Cambridge from 1922 until the mid–1940s. See Newton Directories; Newton Births and Deaths (City Clerk's Office, Newton, Mass.); *Exhibition of the Society of Arts & Crafts* (Boston: Heintzemann Press, 1907), pp. 89–90; Juried Craftspeople of 1934 to 1938 (SACB papers, BPL); *House Beautiful* 38, no. 1 (June 1915), p. 18; and *Bulletin of the Society of Arts and Crafts* 10, no. 7 (November 1926), p. 3.

38. On Plummer, see his biographical entry. The interest of Bostonians in Japanese carving was stated and explained by J.T. Coolidge, Jr. in "A Few Considerations of Japanese Wood–Carving," *Handicraft* 2, no. 3 (June 1903), pp. 49–57.

39. For the Chicago story, see Sharon Darling, *Chicago Furniture: Art, Craft, & Industry, 1833–1933* (New York: W.W. Norton, 1984), esp. pp. 217–47.

40. Samuel McIntire was known more as a carver than as an architect at this time, as can be seen in the titles of two early monographs: Frank Cousins and Phil Riley, *The Wood–Carver of Salem: Samuel McIntire, His Life and Work* (Boston: Little, Brown and Co., 1916); and Fiske Kimball, *Mr. Samuel McIntire, Carver, The Architect of Salem* (Salem: Essex Institute, 1940).

carver through the 1920s (cat. nos. 12 and 13), but she also pursued photography and painting. She seemed to experiment with wood–carving as just one path in her creative pursuit.[35] Annie Nowell, a Winchester artist who maintained a Boston studio in the same building as Murphy, exhibited carved and decorated trays, stands, bookends, magazine holders, card boxes, and solitaire boards. In spite of her proximity to Murphy, she appears to have had no interaction with him.[36] Mary and Carrie Morse, sisters from Newton, studied with Troccoli, who boarded with them from 1909 to 1915, when he built his studio. Apparently Carrie was the more skilled carver and had a reputation for lovely but expensive work. A pair of bookends designed by Troccoli, carved by Carrie Morse, and decorated with Florentine water–sized gold leaf by Mary Morse reveals the cooperative ventures of these three (fig. 11).[37] As single women, the Morses found it socially acceptable and economically necessary to derive some part of their livelihood from carving, unlike Perkins who, once married, no longer actively showed her work and undertook work only for her family and friends. ❡ The only pupil of Karl von Rydingsvärd active in the Boston area was Leander Plummer, who turned from the Icelandic carving style of his teacher to develop his own genre—carved and stained panels of fish that he called "relief paintings" (cat. no. 14). Inspired by the expressive potential of depicting fish in swirling water, Plummer found his own artistic niche, constantly visiting the wharves of New Bedford to draw from nature, taking plaster casts of different species, and even building a pen to house fish so that he could study their movements and changing colors. His work also demonstrates an understanding of the Japanese carvings that received considerable attention in Boston during the first few years of the twentieth century. Many of Boston's cultural leaders, including Frank Benson and J. Templeman Coolidge III, noted the spiritual similarity between Plummer's work and Japanese panels, but praised the former for their naturalistic representation and decorative effect. Reviews of Plummer's work also noted the Japanese spirit of line and composition, but acknowledged that the realistic quality distinguished it from Japanese abstraction.[38] ❡ The importance of carving and historicism to Boston Arts and Crafts woodworking stands in striking contrast to other centers. In Chicago, for example, carving by Boston–educated Madeline Yale Wynne (fig. 12) and other women was carried on only from 1897 to about 1903, after which most Arts and Crafts woodwork consisted of Mission–style furniture made in manual arts programs or by shops and factories. Wynne and her peers turned to smaller, often less costly goods such as jewelry, needlework, and leatherwork.[39] ❡ In Boston, the hierarchical structure of producers—architects and artist–designers working with small–shop professionals and a vital, committed group of artistically inclined amateurs—retained its authority into the 1920s. The emphasis on historical sources and on the importance of process to an object's meaning or significance, and a fondness for the aesthetics of textured, handwrought work—which also led to the canonization of colonial craftsman Samuel McIntire, "the wood–carver of Salem"—was understood by many in the Boston area.[40] Conversant with John Ruskin's ideas about national vernacular traditions and the aesthetics of craftsmanship, and committed to the active cultivation of the colonial past, Boston's well–educated cultural elite provided important leadership in the production of distinctive woodwork. ◎

I would like to acknowledge the generous help of many friends and colleagues, especially Mark Coir (Archives, Cranbrook Educational Community); Paul Dodds (Massachusetts College of Art); Patty Dean and Craig Johnson (Minnesota Historical Society); Nancy Mowll Mathews (Williams College Museum of Art); William Hosley, Jr. (Wadsworth Atheneum); Suzanne Smeaton (Eli Wildner & Co.); Robert C. and Seth Morton Vose; Cindy Ott (Archives of American Art, Smithsonian Institution); Erica Hirschler and Andy Haines (Museum of Fine Arts, Boston); Sheila Perkins; and Shirley and Dean Prouty.

THE
POTTER'S
ART
IN
BOSTON:
INDIVIDUALITY
AND
EXPRESSION
SUSAN J. MONTGOMERY

CERAMICS PRODUCED IN the Boston area in the late nineteenth and early twentieth centuries established a standard of excellence for American art pottery. Within a fifteen–mile radius of the city, four major potteries made contributions to the field that earned national and international acclaim. Dedham, Grueby, Marblehead, and Paul Revere Pottery, each in its own way, responded to Arts and Crafts reform principles with spirit and tenacity. Other potters, less well known but equally committed, worked just outside the spotlight that shone on their more prominent colleagues. Russell Crook, William J. Walley, and Thomas Nickerson produced innovative, high–quality work. At the same time china painting moved out of the Victorian factory into the studios of professional decorators, teachers, and talented amateurs. As a major ceramic production center, the Boston area provides a unique opportunity to examine the complex practical and philosophical issues that define the American Arts and Crafts movement, including stylistic sources, craftsmanship, art education, and design reform.[1] ⁋Boston's rich ceramic tradition developed from the inexhaustible local claybeds that attracted and sustained redware potters in the seventeenth and eighteenth centuries. After the Revolution and well into the nineteenth century, utilitarian vessels were manufactured locally from stoneware clay imported from New York and New Jersey. In East Boston and Cambridge, nineteenth–century potteries grew into large–scale manufactories, producing direct imitations of English decorative ceramics; but imported fine earthenware and stoneware remained the norm. The constant influx of immigrant potters, particularly from England, transferred technical expertise and ensured that English ceramics remained the dominant model.[2] ⁋The Chelsea Keramic Art Works was established in 1872 by the Robertson family of English immigrant potters just outside of Boston.[3] Well aware of the work of their French and English contemporaries, James Robertson and

1. While Boston–area potters shared the efforts of local furniture–makers and silversmiths to revive craftsmanship, they did not succumb to the impulse to reproduce colonial designs. The colonial revival manifested itself in labor–intensive production—throwing on the wheel and hand–modeling or decorating. A generalized nostalgia for the past—common to the Arts and Crafts and the colonial revival reform movements—is apparent, however, in a variety of design sources employed by potters, including unblemished nature, pre–industrial Asian ceramics, and quaint illustrational styles. Amateur decorators and solitary potters seem to have expressed an urge for independence, respite, and self–sufficiency, in reaction to the increasing pressures of industrialized society.

3. Lloyd E. Hawes, *The Dedham Pottery and the Earlier Robertson's* [sic] *Chelsea Potteries* (Dedham, Mass.: Dedham Historical Society, 1986), is the best published source of information on Dedham and Chelsea pottery.

2. For the best overview of New England ceramics, see Lura Woodside Watkins, *Early New England Potters and their Wares* (Cambridge: Harvard University Press, 1950; repr. Hamden, Conn.: Archon, 1968).

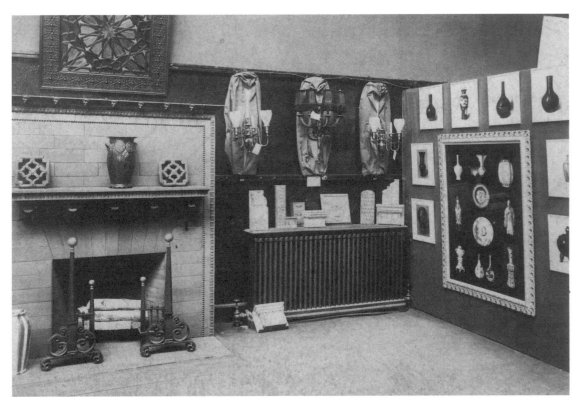

{13} Photograph of installation, First Exhibition of Arts and Crafts, Boston, Copley Hall, April 1897; Fine Arts Department, Boston Public Library; showing Grueby pierced tiles and vase on the mantel, and at right the Callowhill images for S.W. Bushell's *Oriental Ceramic Art*.

{14} Photograph of installation, Exhibition of the Society of Arts and Crafts, Boston (with a Loan Collection of Applied Art), 1907; Fine Arts Department, Boston Public Library; showing Grueby pottery on the center table, and pieces by Russell Crook— including his lion vase (CAT. NO. 19)—on the bottom tier of the table at right.

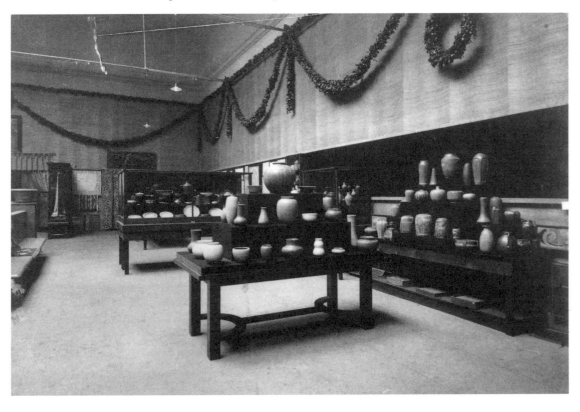

his sons developed their own versions of up–to–date decorative pottery. Hugh Cornwall Robertson devoted his energy and the company's resources to replicating the monochromatic Asian glazes he had seen at the 1876 Philadelphia Centennial Exposition. Robertson's success with his own *sang–de–boeuf* (oxblood) glazes introduced the Asian concept that glaze color over a simple ceramic form could achieve the status of fine art. He became a glaze expert, developing a dozen variations of pure color and texture that were admired as much for their rich beauty and rarity as for the extreme difficulty of producing them (cat. no. 21). ❰Robertson's single–minded pursuit of his elusive Chinese glazes, even at the cost of bankrupting his family's business, held great appeal for the artistic community in Boston. The Museum of Fine Arts, Boston amassed major collections of Japanese prints, paintings, ceramics, and other crafts in the 1880s and was recognized as a center for scholarship in the field. When the Chelsea Keramic Art Works closed in 1889, a group of prominent Boston artists, designers, and patrons who appreciated Robertson's talent financed another pottery for him, first in Chelsea and then in 1891 in Dedham, southwest of Boston. To guarantee their investment, the financiers insisted that Robertson develop a saleable line of dinnerware. Robertson selected the now famous Dedham crackle, based on another Asian prototype (cat. no. 20). This popular and resilient stoneware with a grey crackle "Corean" glaze, decorated in cobalt, supported the pottery and allowed Robertson to continue his experiments with exotic glaze effects. ❰When the First Exhibition of Arts and Crafts opened at Boston's Copley Hall in 1897, Hugh Robertson's "vases in 'dragon's blood' glaze" were featured. William H. Grueby, who was just beginning to realize his potential, exhibited reproductions of pierced Chinese tiles (fig. 13). Boston's fascination with Asian crafts was also nourished by images of Chinese and Japanese ceramics produced by Louis Prang, a prominent Boston printer.4 ❰In 1897 Grueby was about to introduce his major contribution to the field of glaze chemistry. As a direct beneficiary of Hugh Robertson's expertise, Grueby developed the matte green glazes that made the Grueby Faience Company famous.5 His velvety matte greens provided a perfect counterpart to the natural forms created by the company designer George Prentiss Kendrick. Kendrick was an experienced metalworker, book designer, and draftsman when he joined Grueby's company in 1894 (see cat. no. 41). In his designs of

leaves, stems, and flowers, Kendrick combined a metalworker's aesthetic of robust, sculptural mass with the ceramic technique of modeled clay to produce an original vision (cat. no. 22). ❰A founding member of the Society of Arts and Crafts, Boston in 1897, George Kendrick may have been responsible for the Grueby pottery's close correspondence with the Society's design guidelines printed in the catalogue for the 1899 exhibition. "The first thing to be recognized as essential to good work is that every form must be perfectly adapted to the use for which it is intended....Eccentricity of form is to be avoided as vulgar." Secondly, "...every form should be in harmony with the material in which it is executed." Finally, "...the decoration put upon any object must be in harmony with its form. The more intimate the relation between the form of the object and its decoration, the more beautiful it will be."6 The Society stressed the necessity of hand–craftsmanship to artistic quality. Grueby maintained high standards throughout his career, insisting on hand–modeled decoration on thrown forms rather than less expensive casting. The Society also called for "the necessity of sobriety and restraint, of ordered arrangement...,"7 clearly apparent in Kendrick's processions of dependable daffodils and stalwart broad leaves (cat. no. 22). ❰Introduced in 1898 and shown in the exhibition of the Society of Arts and Crafts in 1899, Grueby's matte glazed pottery won top honors at expositions in Paris (1900), Buffalo (1901), and St. Louis (1904), creating high demand for "good green ware."8 In the 1907 exhibition of the Society of Arts and Crafts, Grueby Faience Company was well–represented, with more than fifty individual pieces in a range of colors from apple to dark green, to blues, plum, and ivory crackle (fig. 14).9 ❰Although he exhibited only garden pottery in the 1907 show (fig. 15), Thomas Nickerson of the Merrimac Pottery in Newburyport, Massachusetts, about twenty miles north of Boston, had developed his own matte green (cat. no. 27). Unfairly criticized for imitating Grueby, Nickerson devised green glazes that were brighter in pitch than Grueby's rich, somber notes, and several other fine glaze effects, notably an iridescent metallic black (cat. no. 28).10 When modeled decoration appears on Merrimac pottery, leaves and blossoms tend to be much more sinuous than Kendrick's forthright flowers, suggesting the stylistic influence of Arthur Heygate Mackmurdo in England or French Art Nouveau designers. Yet form, decoration, and material are integrated and harmonious. ❰At the Marblehead

4. These were Louis Prang's colored lithographs for S.W. Bushell, *Oriental Ceramic Art*, 10 vols. (Boston: D. Appleton, 1896).

5. For a more detailed history of Grueby's accomplishments, see Susan J. Montgomery, *The Ceramics of William H. Grueby* (Lambertville, N.J.: Arts & Crafts Quarterly Press, 1993).

6. *Exhibition of the Society of Arts & Crafts* (Boston: George H. Ellis, 1899), p. 5.

7. SACB exhibition catalogue (1899), p. 7.

8. "Good Green Ware Gave Fame to Grueby Name," *Glass and Pottery World* (June 1908), p. 13.

9. *Exhibition of the Society of Arts & Crafts, Together with a Loan Collection of Applied Art* (Boston: Heintzemann Press, 1907), pp. 52–54.

10. Very little research has been published on the short–lived Merrimac Pottery. Paul Evans, in his landmark study of American art pottery, quotes a local newspaper report defending Merrimac's uniqueness: "Save in the color of certain green pieces, the resemblance is very little; and really the greens of Merrimac...are not at all comparable to the Grueby, with its soft, kid–glove–like surface and finish. The Merrimac has, however, so much to offer in scope and variety (and this cannot be said of the Grueby) that very interesting and charming products come up for consideration quite independent of the green specimens. Many of the Merrimac pieces show a cheerful, tender, bright, radiant character, which is wholly lacking in the Grueby. The soft color of the Merrimac is especially pleasing and the metallic glow on some of the articles is most effective, rich and brilliant. This metallic finish is the finer and more acceptable, as seen upon the low–tone pieces, such as on the soft dull violet, rose and similar colorings." Paul Evans, *Art Pottery of the United States: An Encyclopedia of Producers and their Marks*, 2nd ed. (New York: Feingold and Lewis, 1987), quoting Jane Layng, [Newburyport, Mass.] *Daily News* (January 24, 1903), p. 7.

Pottery the application of pure color glazes to simple forms found another individualized expression.[11] Although Robertson and Grueby glazes seemed more passionate in their rich variation of color and texture, Marblehead matte colors were dense and evenly applied in cool, flawless surfaces. It is certainly not coincidental that Robertson and Grueby were trained in traditional apprenticeship systems that relied on instinct, experience, and secrecy in glaze formulation, while Arthur Baggs, director of the Marblehead Pottery, had been trained in the scientific approach of glaze analysis at the newly opened New York School of Clayworking and Ceramics at Alfred University. There, under the guidance of Charles Fergus Binns, potters were trained in chemical analysis, precise formulae, and predictable results. ⟨At Marblehead decoration was painted on, not sculpted, ensuring a smooth, even surface. Flowers, animals, birds, and landscapes were reduced to linear, conventionalized patterns, another variation of the "sobriety and restraint, of ordered arrangement" mandated by the Society of Arts and Crafts design manifesto.[12] ⟨Flat pattern was part of the design credo of printmaker and teacher Arthur Wesley Dow. His seminal publication *Composition* (cat. no. 26B) analyzed Asian design principles, particularly those of Japanese prints, and dispensed them to a wide range of artists and craftsmen working in various media.[13] Dow's summer school in Ipswich undoubtedly had an effect on workers at Marblehead, just a few miles away. Designs such as the hollyhocks (cat. no. 26A) seem directly inspired by Dow's mandate to use simplified pattern to suggest beauty rather than depict reality. The mosaic bird frieze used on the cylindrical vase (cat. no. 25), probably adapted from a South American Indian source, has a similar abstract quality. ⟨Another potter whose work was exhibited in 1907 may epitomize the connections and collaborations nurtured by the Society of Arts and Crafts' philosophy of "mutually helpful relations" between architects and craftsmen. Russell Crook was a multi–talented individual who exhibited sculpture, plaster models for architectural woodwork, tiles modeled for Grueby, and his own pottery (cat. no. 19).[14] In 1900 he exhibited tiles based on Rudyard Kipling's *Jungle Book* in Paris. In 1902 he modeled the pumpkin tile mantel facing for Grueby Faience Company at the Scituate estate *Dreamwold*, a collaborative arrangement orchestrated by the mansion's architects (fig. 16). In the dining room, which featured a harvest theme, the Grueby/Crook pumpkin tiles

were complemented by Tiffany light fixtures, including a pumpkin chandelier and wall sconces. ⟨In 1907 Crook showed several pieces of unique salt–glazed stoneware pottery with cobalt decoration (fig. 14). Sometimes criticized by the conservative SACB jury for its crudeness, Crook's pottery was difficult to sell, and "too artistic to be practical." Crook was considered "well meaning and interested. Fitting example of craftsmen who will never be appreciated and who will never succeed."[15] ⟨Sustained financial success was a problem for all of these art potteries, large and small, at least in part because the profit motive was highly suspect. The Society advocated altruistic goals. "The motives of a true Craftsman are the love of good and beautiful work as applied to useful service, and the need of making an adequate livelihood. In no case can it be primarily the love of gain."[16] The irreconcilable conflict between art and money caused the Society—and its craftsmen—to struggle and ultimately collapse. As workers in the applied arts were elevated to the privileged status of painters and sculptors, they seemed to be required to become impractical, even incompetent, as business people. Hugh Robertson's obsession with oxblood glazes led to the bankruptcy of his pottery, yet he was rescued by more practical supporters. Other potters who had no patrons either survived on their own or went out of business. ⟨Some potteries were founded for reasons other than art or money. Marblehead Pottery began as a therapeutic enterprise at a clinic for patients suffering from neurasthenia, a debilitating depression identified by symptoms of overwhelming anxiety and fatigue. Dr. Herbert J. Hall theorized that neurasthenia was due to lack of meaningful activity and devised a program he called "the work cure." Intimately tied to his pioneering work in occupational therapy was the idea of the restorative power of nature and the psychological benefits of handicraft.[17] ⟨Marblehead Pottery rather quickly became a commercial venture, but the moral benefits of honest work, hand–crafted goods, and a small workshop remained closely associated with Arts and Crafts manufactories of all kinds. They shared the ideological position that handmade products were inherently better than machine–made goods, handicraft was more satisfying for employees than large–scale factory work, and better–designed objects improved the life of the consumer, who responded unconsciously to the creativity and joy with which his vase was produced. The Arts and Crafts interior offered a reprieve from twentieth–century hustle

11. Like Merrimac, Marblehead Pottery awaits an in–depth study of its history and production.

12. SACB exhibition catalogue (1899), p. 7.

13. Arthur Wesley Dow, *Composition*, 3rd ed. (New York: Baker and Taylor, 1900).

14. In the Society's 1899 show, work by Crook included a "Plaster sketch for fireplace front for Children's nursery," models for John Evans and Company woodwork, and a frieze or mantel facing entitled "Good Hunting"; SACB (1899), pp. 19–20. Very little is known about Russell Crook's background. Reportedly, he studied with Augustus Saint–Gaudens, worked at several potteries, including Grueby Faience Company, and attended the New York School of Clayworking and Ceramics at Alfred University; "Comments on Juried Craftsmen, 1936–1937," Archives of the Society of Arts and Crafts, Boston, Boston Public Library (hereafter SACB papers, BPL).

15. "Comments on Juried Craftsmen 1936–1937," SACB papers, BPL.

16. This was the first principle of handicraft, formally advocated by the Society in 1907. *Exhibition of the Society of Arts & Crafts, Together with a Loan Collection of Applied Art* (Boston: Heintzemann, 1907), p. viii.

17. Herbert J. Hall, "The Systematic Use of Work as a Remedy in Neurasthenia and Allied Conditions," *Boston Medical and Surgical Journal* (January 5, 1905), pp. 29–32. Herbert J. Hall, *The Work Cure* (Marblehead, nd).

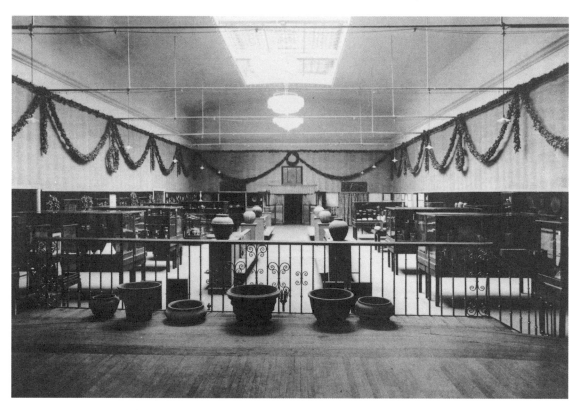

{15} Photograph of installation, Exhibition of the Society of Arts and Crafts, Boston (with a Loan Collection of Applied Art), 1907; Fine Arts Department, Boston Public Library.

{16} Photograph of the dining room mantel from *Dreamwold*, the Scituate estate designed by Coolidge & Carlson for Thomas W. Lawson, Esq.; *House Beautiful* (October 1902).

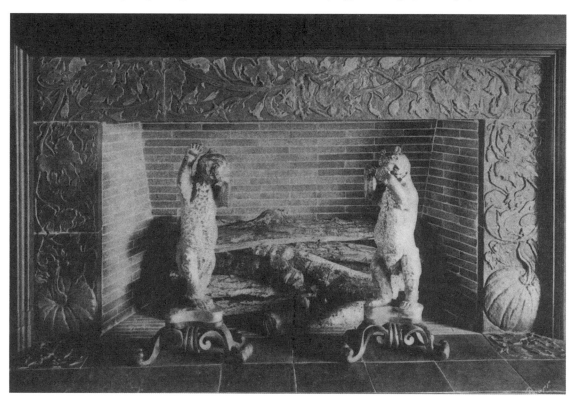

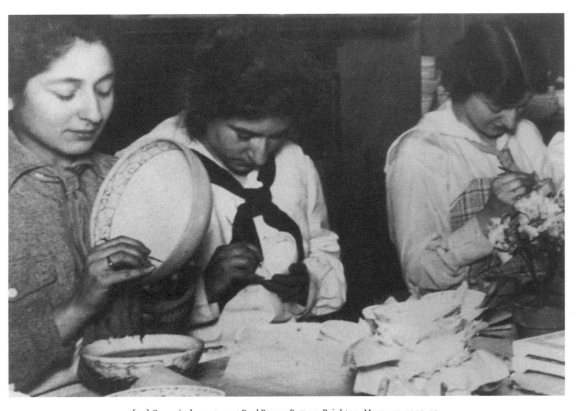

{17} Ceramic decorators at Paul Revere Pottery, Brighton, Mass., ca. 1909–10;
from left to right: Dena Harris, Lily Shapiro, Albina Mangini; collection of Mrs. Louise O'Neill, daughter of Albina Mangini.

and bustle, an antidote to modern life. ❡ For some potters, including Russell Crook and William J. Walley, Arts and Crafts philosophy also offered an opportunity for the individual to produce the work he believed in, independent of market demand. Walley's pottery in West Sterling, Massachusetts was entirely his own. Although trained in every detail of pottery manufacture at the Minton works in England, Walley ended up as a solitary redware potter with a strong personal Arts and Crafts attitude toward his work (cat. no. 32).[18] "I am just a potter trying to make art pottery as it should be made....Make one man's ideas, one man's work. Everything [is] made by hand. To me there is more true art in a brick made and burnt by one man than there is in the best piece of molded pottery ever made. What I feel we want is to be true to ourselves and let the art come out."[19] ❡ The psychological benefits of craftsmanship did not escape the notice of settlement houses and philanthropists. Paul Revere Pottery was founded by librarian Edith Guerrier with the support of Helen Osborne Storrow, a prominent Boston philanthropist, as a means of educating and training the young immigrant Jewish and Italian girls of Boston's North End.[20] Pleasant working conditions and liberal benefits,

including paid vacations, met the ideal standards of Arts and Crafts philosophy, but only with repeated infusions of cash from Storrow (fig. 17). Much of the work produced at Paul Revere Pottery was well–made dinnerware, charmingly decorated with simple animal motifs and homey mottoes. Several decorators became highly skilled, producing striking idealized landscapes that transcend any functional use (cat. no. 30). ❡ China painters tapped the same impulse for self–improvement among middle–class women as did the Paul Revere Pottery for young immigrants. Often conducted at home, china painting offered women an appropriate alternative to factory work, a more genteel and artistic means to increase one's income. Celia Thaxter, a prominent though impoverished New Hampshire poet, made a living from her china painting in the 1880s and 1890s. ❡ The popularity of china painting exploded after the turn of the century. Dozens of local china painters produced work for themselves and for sale, and taught classes as professionals and amateurs. Sidney Callowhill, one of a family of English immigrant decorators from the Royal Worcester factory, worked in the Trenton, New Jersey potteries before coming to Boston.[21] Probably the most prominent professional

18. Evans, *Art Pottery of the United States*, p. 316.

19. Autobiographical notes, 1906, SACB papers, BPL.

20. For the best source of information on Paul Revere Pottery as a settlement house, see Kate Clifford Larson, "The Saturday Evening Girls: A Social Experiment in Class Bridging and Cross Cultural Female Dominion Building in Turn of the Century Boston" (Master's thesis: Simmons College, 1995). Molly Matson, ed., *An Independent Woman: The Autobiography of Edith Guerrier* (Boston: University of Massachusetts, 1992) provides a more personal approach. The definitive history of the pottery remains to be written.

21. For more information on china painting in America, see Alice Cooney Frelinghuysen, *American Porcelain, 1770–1920* (New York: Metropolitan Museum of Art, 1989); and Ellen Paul Denker, *Lenox: A Century of Quality, 1889–1989* (Trenton: Lenox and New Jersey State Museum, 1989).

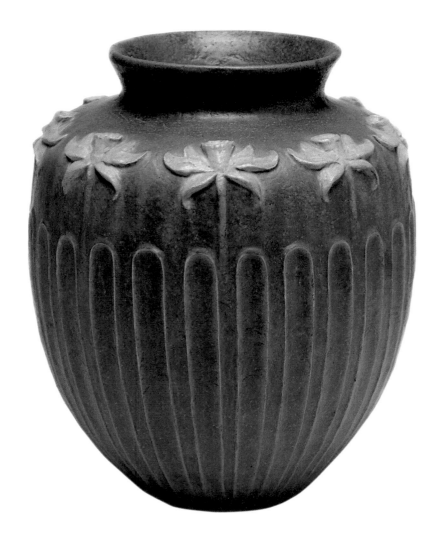

CAT. NO. 22
Grueby Pottery Company;
George P. Kendrick, designer;
Wilhelmina Post, modeler,
Urn–shaped matte green vase
with yellow daffodils, ca. 1901

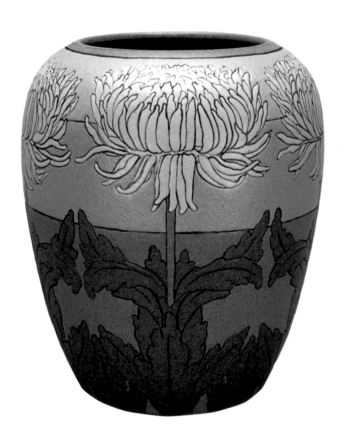

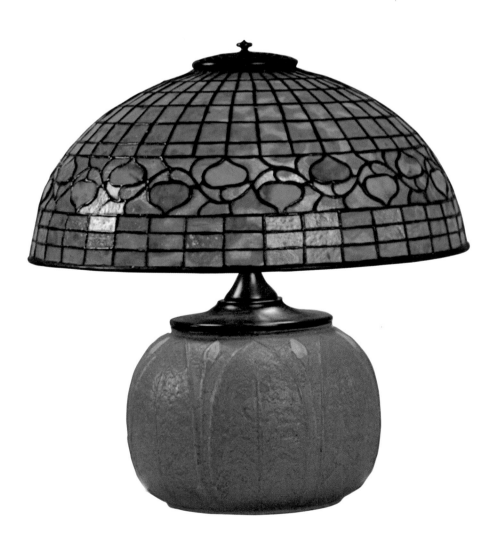

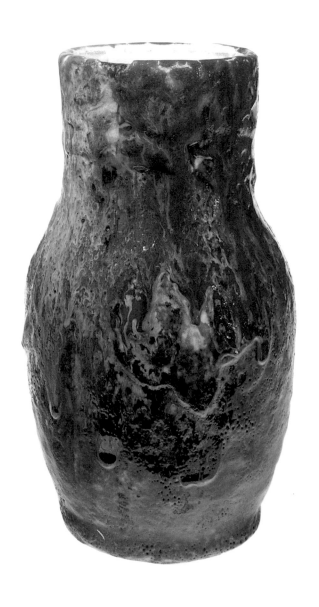

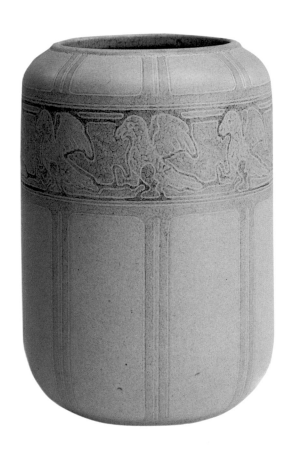

CAT. NO. 21 (*top*)
Dedham Pottery;
Hugh Cornwall
Robertson, maker,
Red–glazed vase,
ca. 1896–1908

CAT. NO. 25 (*bottom*)
Marblehead Pottery,
Cylindrical vase
with band of polychrome
mosaic birds, 1913

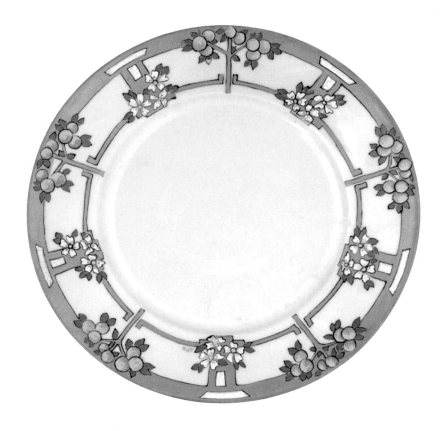

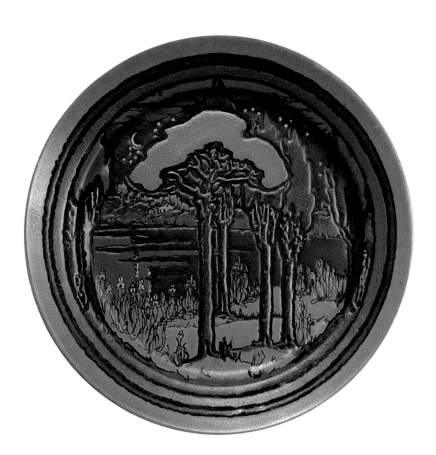

CAT. NO. 29 (*top*)
L.F. Nash, decorator,
Salad plate with
orange tree border, ca. 1910

CAT. NO. 30 (*bottom*)
Paul Revere Pottery;
Edith Brown, designer;
Sara Galner, decorator,
Matte–glazed charger
with nighttime landscape of
lake and cottage, 1915

decorator in the city, Callowhill exhibited frequently at the Society. Best known for his silver lustre work, he also experimented with Native American design (cat. no. 17). Sarah Ryel Comer, a middle–class woman from Newton, was a talented amateur (cat. no. 18).[22] At the other end of the spectrum were hundreds of anonymous artists. A plate signed by L.F. Nash found in Brookline represents those undiscovered talents awaiting the recognition they deserve (cat. no. 29).[23] Its restrained orange–tree border seems the perfect application of the Boston Arts and Crafts aesthetic to china painting. ⁋ By 1907 Boston–area Arts and Crafts ceramics had peaked. When the thirtieth anniversary show was mounted in 1927, Robertson, Grueby, and Walley were dead. Merrimac Pottery had burned in 1908 and had not reopened. Dedham Pottery, Marblehead, and Paul Revere Pottery remained open but seemed to produce more and more standardized ware, without the vitality of an earlier time. A cycle of creativity and excitement generated in part by the personalities involved, the economic atmosphere, and the opportunities available, was apparently over. In the 1920s and 1930s a transition toward studio pottery was already taking place, to a great extent initiated by the Arts and Crafts potters. The successes of Robertson, Grueby, Baggs, and others served as stepping stones for the next generation of potters who continued to use clay as an expressive medium in universities and studios across the country. ◯

Several colleagues assisted with this essay. Jim Messineo and Mike Witt of JMW Gallery offered several useful leads. David Rago, of David Rago Arts & Crafts, smoothed out some rough spots. Ruth Weidner, professor of art history, West Chester University, and Ellen Paul Denker, museum consultant, contributed generously to my understanding of the Callowhill family and their work. Marilee Boyd Meyer brought two published sources on Dr. Herbert J. Hall to my attention. I am grateful for these and innumerable other kindnesses.

22. Very little is known about Comer. She was married to fellow glass and china decorator Fred J. Comer. They lived in Newton Centre and frequently exhibited together at the SACB. See Karen Evans Ulehla, ed., *The Society of Arts and Crafts, Boston: Exhibition Record 1897–1927* (Boston: Boston Public Library, 1981), pp. 57, 279–283, 286.

23. L.F. Nash may be related to Mrs. William B. Nash of Brookline, who was a member of the Society from 1920 to 1926. Ulehla, *The Society of Arts and Crafts, Boston*, p. 159.

CIRCLES
OF
INFLUENCE:
METAL-
SMITHING
IN
NEW ENGLAND

JEANNINE FALINO

A REVIEW OF THE membership of the Society of Arts and Crafts, Boston in its first thirty years reveals that some 600 of a total of approximately 1,800 members claimed metalwork—including silver, gold, base metals, enamel, and jewelry—as their primary craft. This remarkable number represented approximately a third of the membership, exceeding that of any other craft represented in the Society from 1897 to 1927. Of the 600, 110 New England members attained Master craftsman status, the designation for accomplished practitioners. In addition, nearly half of the thirty–nine Society artists who were honored during this period with Medals of Excellence—the Society's highest distinction—were metalsmiths, ironworkers, or jewelers.[1] One can conclude from these figures that metalworking was one of the most popular crafts among the Society's membership, and that metalworkers, many of whom produced a combination of functional and ecclesiastical hollowware, flatware, and jewelry, were among its most accomplished artists. ⟨Society exhibition records also indicate that the use of base metals such as copper and wrought iron, and the long–dormant technique of enameling—evoking romantic images of pre–industrial culture in Europe and America—were revived to great effect by metalworkers during this period.[2] Due to its ease of handling, copper was the metal of choice for many beginning metalworkers, but its use by such proficient and highly skilled metalsmiths as Arthur Stone points to a blending of aesthetic, technical, and social reasons for its popularity. Stone used copper in combination with silver elements and patination to achieve color effects that would have been impossible in silver or gold. In 1904, Stone was awarded a silver medal at the Louisiana Purchase Exposition for metalwork that included a copper jardinière which he graced with a delicate wreath of oak leaves and silver acorns. Its democratic appeal as an inexpensive but sturdily useful metal may also account for Stone's fabrication

1. Karen Evans Ulehla, ed., *The Society of Arts and Crafts, Boston: Exhibition Record 1897–1927* (Boston: Boston Public Library, 1981), passim. Thanks to Jane Port for compiling information on Society membership and residences. For a fine survey of the national development in Arts and Crafts metalsmithing, see W. Scott Braznell, "Metalsmithing and Jewelrymaking, 1900–1920," in Janet Kardon, ed., *The Ideal Home 1900–1920: The History of Twentieth–Century American Craft* (New York: Abrams, 1994), pp. 53–63.

2. The tactile and reflective qualities of base metals have also been celebrated in two–dimensional art of this era; see two oil paintings in the Museum of Fine Arts, Boston: John Singer Sargent's *Miss Helen Sears (Mrs. J.D. Cameron Bradley)* of 1895, and John White Alexander's 1897 *Isabella and the Pot of Basil*, as well as the 1907 photograph by George H. Seeley, *Tribute*, reproduced in George Dimock and Joanne Hardy, *Intimations & Imaginings, The Photography of George H. Seeley* (Pittsfield: The Berkshire Museum, 1986), p. 6.

3. The jardinière and watering can by Arthur Stone are both in the collection of the Museum of Fine Arts, Boston.

4. Jane Port, "Elegant Iron: Turn–of–the–century Master Blacksmiths in Boston," *The Anvil's Ring* 23, no. 3 (Winter 1995–96), pp. 12–18.

of a copper watering can that he used at his home in Gardner, Massachusetts.[3] The survival of many utilitarian objects from this period suggests the twin economic and antimodernist attractions of the metal to those of modest means, as well as to those who wished to emulate the humble work of the medieval craftsman. Stylistically, much of the copperwork shares an affinity with the art of the Middle Ages as it was commonly perceived early in this century. Thus, there is an appealingly and consciously rough quality that is present in much copperwork produced during this era, which ranged in form from ornamental hardware to chafing dishes. As with much furniture produced at this time, the metalwork showed visible means of construction that included rivets, strapwork, and unplanished surfaces. ❡ Medieval influences are also evident in the many copper boxes made in New England with covers decorated with enamels. These boxes offered artists an opportunity to demonstrate their skill as both metalsmiths and painters who used copper, and occasionally gold–foil backing, as a warm–toned canvas upon which to spread their enameled colors. Mary Winlock, Frank Gardner Hale, and Rebecca Cauman were among a small group of recognized enamelists, yet there were many others whose names are lost to us who worked at this

craft. In general, the enamelwork produced during this period was floral in inspiration, and bilaterally symmetrical in execution, in a conscious or unconscious emulation of medieval decorative art. The most prolific metalsmith in silver who also worked in this style was Elizabeth Copeland, whose intentionally coarse cloisons and rich, if unrefined, enamels decorated boxes that cloaked the distant mist of the Middle Ages into a densely worked pattern of darkness, light, and brilliant color (cat. no. 35). ❡ The technical accomplishments and expressive style of the medieval craftsman were perhaps best understood by German–born and trained Frank Koralewsky, who strove to create works of art in wrought iron and cut steel that were the equal of any made in the pre–industrial world. To that end, he worked for seven years on *Schneewitchen* (Snow White), a twenty–square–inch lock embellished with imagery from the Grimm fairytale. Figures in the story were directly cold–carved in iron, ornamented with silver, bronze, and gold, and framed in richly patterned copper and brass Damascene work. Although such highly skilled work was financially impractical to maintain, as a *tour de force* it brought Koralewsky national recognition achieved by few in his field aside from Philadelphia ironworker Samuel Yellin.[4] ❡ The English

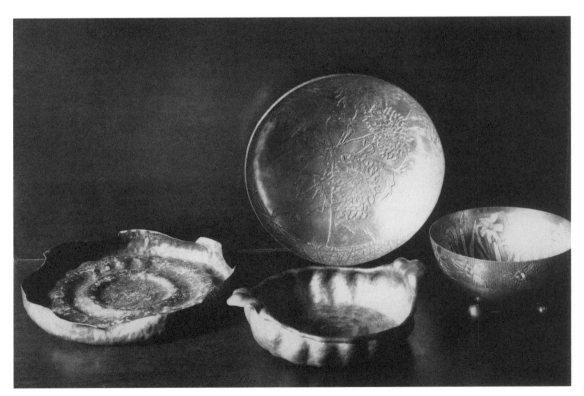

{18} Photograph of copper and silver bowls and trays by Madeline Yale Wynne, ca. 1900; Memorial Hall Museum, PVMA, Deerfield.

Arts and Crafts style—which blended design influences of medieval art with the lyrical lines of Art Nouveau—was popular among New England silversmiths only intermittently prior to 1914, and largely absent thereafter. The vogue may have been partly due to the importation of English–made silver to this area. According to W. Scott Braznell, a dish with two loop handles retailed by Shreve, Crump and Low of Boston between 1902 and 1914 was almost certainly produced by C.R. Ashbee's Guild of Handicraft.[5] The British origins of some Boston metalsmiths undoubtedly added to this aesthetic. Sheffield–born Arthur Stone produced a tea service in 1907 bearing crocus decoration in a conservative Art Nouveau design before settling into a comfortable colonial revival style with his trademark floral decoration. And on a return visit in 1904 to his native Liverpool, George Hunt fashioned a rather modern–looking teapot (cat. no. 40) that owed an equal debt to English Arts and Crafts and the influence of London botanist and designer Christopher Dresser.[6] These examples were in the minority, however, as they did not find a wide audience among their regional patrons. Rather, such works found their ways into the hands of urban museum curators and serious collectors such as George Booth (1864–1949) of Detroit who had a

keen appreciation for the history of metal-smithing.[7] The colonial revival style became the "house" style among New England patrons, who nestled new works comfortably among the colonial forms that were their cultural if not personal legacy. The overwhelming amount of silver that survives in this style seems to indicate that regional silversmiths worked to meet this preference. ¶ The prominence of metalsmiths and jewelers in the Society can be explained in several ways. By the late nineteenth century, New England had a well–established and thriving silver-smithing industry that was anchored by such giants in the business as Gorham, Reed and Barton, and others.[8] These firms required large numbers of trained workers, some of whom would have been expert silversmiths and designers. In order to enjoy independence and control over the process of metalsmithing, some of these individuals struck out on their own in private or cooperative workshops, including the Handicraft Shop of the Society of Arts and Crafts. Many joined the Society to gain a foothold in the crafts world, others to obtain an outlet to sell their works, which provided about a third of the Society's revenue. ¶ The burgeoning academic realm was another source of trained metalsmiths. In the last decade of the nineteenth century, crafts pro-

5. Alan Crawford, C.R. Ashbee: Architect, Designer, and Romantic Socialist (New Haven: Yale University Press, 1985), p. 209, fig. 200. W. Scott Braznell, "Influence of C.R. Ashbee," in Bert Denker, ed., The Substance of Style: Perspectives on the American Arts and Crafts Movement (Winterthur, Del: The Henry Francis du Pont Winterthur Museum, 1996), p. 44.

6. The Stone tea service and Hunt teapot are in the collection of the Museum of Fine Arts, Boston.

7. Some of the Boston metalwork listed in The Arts and Crafts Movement in Detroit, 1906–1976: The Movement, The Society, The School (Detroit: The Detroit Institute of Arts, 1976), cat. nos. 47, 51, 55, 56, and 59, was acquired by Booth either for himself, the Detroit Institute of Arts, or the Cranbrook Academy of Art, the latter founded by Booth in 1925.

8. See Charles L. Venable, Silver in America 1840–1940: A Century of Splendor (Dallas: Dallas Museum of Art, 1995) for a thorough discussion of this period.

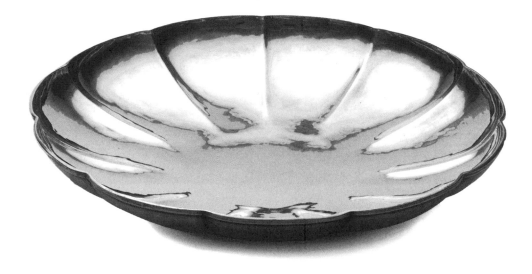

{19} L. Cora Brown, shallow silver bowl, ca. 1920; private collection.

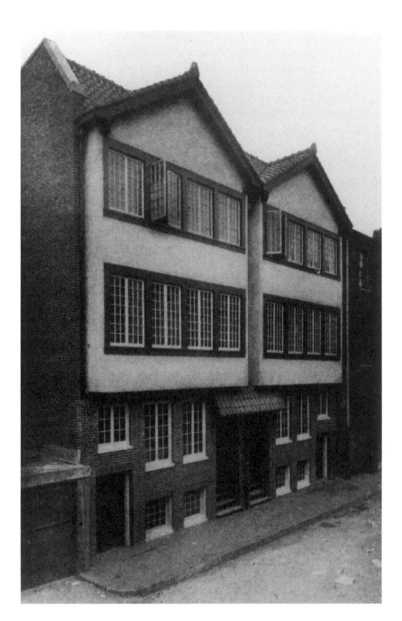

{20} Exterior view, Craftsmen Studios on Lime Street, Boston, *Craftsman* vol. XVI, no. 1 (April 1909), facing p. 92.
{21} Interior view, the Handicraft Shop, *The Providence Sunday Journal*, June 25, 1905, p. 30.

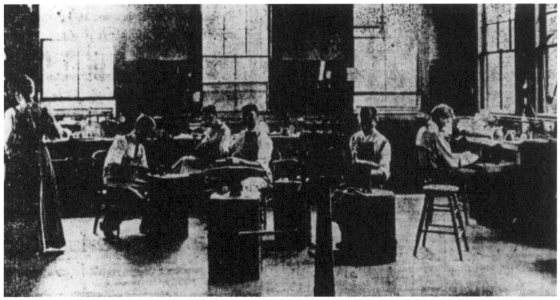

grams were established in the applied arts or decorative design departments of art schools in Boston and Providence, many of them founded in the 1870s to serve the region's educational and industrial design needs. These new departments attracted a female student population that was entirely new to the field and eager to make a living through the practice or teaching of a craft. ⟨ Talented silversmiths were among the wave of immigrants who arrived in Boston around the turn of the century. They quickly established themselves in the local manufactories, schools, and private workshops, where they often set a high standard for others to follow. These metalsmiths were men who had served traditional apprenticeships. They included Arthur Stone and George Hunt from England, George Germer and Frank Koralewsky from Germany, Frans J.R. Gyllenberg from Sweden, and Karl F. Leinonen from Finland. Those who received their training in an American and/or British academic setting, including Augustus Rose, Laurin Martin, and H. Stuart Michie, seemed content to remain within a school system rather than establish private workshops. A majority of their serious students were women; Elizabeth Copeland, Rebecca Cauman, Katharine Pratt, and Mary Winlock were four of the more prominent graduates who went on to independent careers.[9] ⟨ A smaller group experienced a less formal or more idiosyncratic education through chance contacts, family, or private lessons, and they tended to work outside the traditional framework of workshop or school. Among this latter group can be counted illuminator–turned–silversmith Janet Payne Bowles, and architect/designer George Prentiss Kendrick, who spent the more–celebrated part of his career working for Grueby Faience Company. Madeline Yale Wynne (fig. 18) drew upon the experience of her father, Linus Yale, Jr., the founder of Yale Lock, and her brother Julian, who was also a metalsmith, while amateur craftswoman L. Cora Brown (fig. 19) of suburban Concord worked in silver under the guidance of Karl Leinonen.[10] Artists in all three groups advanced their education through courses in design at Harvard University offered by Denman Ross.[11] Many also maintained membership in the Detroit Society of Arts and Crafts and participated in national exhibitions of arts and crafts in Providence, St. Louis, Detroit, and Chicago, extending Boston's range of influence far beyond New England.[12] These skilled foreigners, disaffected company metalsmiths, idealistic graduates, and several unconventionally trained but uniquely talented individuals contributed to a flowering of the craft that would enable New England to export both teachers and techniques to Arts and Crafts centers throughout the country. ⟨ Many of these artists worked independently yet in close proximity to one another. Workshops at 79 Chestnut Street, in two adjoining buildings at 26 and 28 Lime Street (fig. 20) and at successive locations of the Handicraft Shop served a number of silversmiths, some of whom probably shared bench space.[13] The familiarity engendered by these working arrangements encouraged the cooperative spirit that informs much of the work in silver produced during this period, as evidenced by the number of collaborative works that were produced (cf. fig. 23).[14] ⟨ Such a collegial attitude extended even to the more traditional and prolific workshop of Arthur Stone, whose journeymen were expected to follow the artistic lead of their master. The silversmiths there also benefited from Stone's profit–sharing on a semi–annual basis, in emulation of Ashbee's socialist ideals.[15] Moreover, those who had worked most closely with a particular object placed their own mark below that of the workshop; Stone's silversmiths produced a consistently high quality and quantity of silver for a national following among those of both modest and ample means.[16] ⟨ The Handicraft Shop (fig. 21), founded and financially supported by Society president Arthur Astor Carey, along with Frederick Allen Whiting and Mary Ware Dennett, was originally intended to support a variety of crafts. However, silversmithing quickly became the dominant craft. The primary shop members were supervisor Karl F. Leinonen, Frans J.R. Gyllenberg, George Gebelein, Seth Ek, Adolphe Kunkler, and C.G. Forssen, many of whom raised forms for decoration by designer, chaser and enameler Mary Knight, who studied at the Drexel Institute in Philadelphia under the guidance of Dennett and later worked as a designer for Gorham. It is likely that other silversmiths were affiliated with the shop over the years. Mary Winlock was with the group in 1903; Rebecca Cauman appears to have joined in 1924, and collaborated with both Gyllenberg and Leinonen on separate works submitted to the Society's 1927 exhibition.[17] ⟨ For some, the Handicraft Shop served as a means to an independent career. George Christian Gebelein had served an apprenticeship and worked with large firms before renting bench space with the Handicraft Shop in 1903. His early work in a modified Arts and Crafts style (cat. no. 36) soon evolved to include objects executed in the colonial revival style

9. For Cauman, see Ulehla, The Society of Arts and Crafts, Boston, p. 27; and the Archives, Massachusetts College of Art. Pratt Institute–educated Charles H. Barr chose to work independently in East Greenwich, Rhode Island, where he produced sconces, and table and desk accessories in an Art Nouveau style from around 1899 to 1901; "Metalwork and Amateurs with Illustrations from Photographs Designed and Executed by Charles H. Barr," House Beautiful (December 1899), pp. 16–24; obituary, New York Times, January 11, 1947, p. 19, col. 5. Death certificate for Frans J.R. Gyllenberg, Massachusetts Department of Vital Statistics.

10. Bowles studied in Boston sometime after 1896 with an unknown Russian artist working near the waterfront whose hammering produced "an orchestral tone which was the most beautiful thing [she] had ever heard." She left Boston in 1902 with her husband, the publisher Joseph Moore Bowles, who produced the Arts and Crafts periodical Modern Art and published works by Arthur Wesley Dow. Barry Shifman et al., The Arts and Crafts Metalwork of Janet Payne Bowles (Indianapolis: Indianapolis Museum of Art and Indiana University Press, 1993), p. 14. For Wynne, see Jessica H. Beels, "'I hate pretty work': Madeline Yale Wynne and the American Craft Revival" (Master's thesis, University of Delaware, 1995). For L. Cora Brown, see Ulehla, The Society of Arts and Crafts, Boston, p. 38.

11. Among Ross's summer school students were (as listed): Mary Peyton Winlock, designer, Cambridge (1899); L. Cora Brown, Concord (1902); Josephine Lillian Hartwell, teacher, William Penn Charter School, Philadelphia (1901–02); Augustus Rose (1903); Mary Catherine Knight, designer, Boston,

13. Silversmiths known to be working at 79 Chestnut Street, Boston: Arthur Williams (1906–15); George Hunt (1906–08); T. Christiansen (1907–13); James Woolley (1908); Adolphe C. Kunkler (1908); George Christian Gebelein (1909–15); Sybil Foster (1915); and Margaret Rogers (1910–15). Silversmiths known to be working at 26 Lime Street, Boston: Samuel R. Woolley (1909–12); Florence Richmond (1910–11); George Hunt (1911–15); Jessie Dunbar (1911–27); George Germer (1912–17); Adolphe C. Kunkler (1916–22); Margaret Rogers (1916–27); and Arthur Williams (1916–27). Silversmiths known to be working at 28 Lime Street, Boston: James Woolley (1909–27); Adolphe C. Kunkler (1909–15); George Hunt (1909); and Samuel R. Woolley (1913–17). Silversmiths known to be working at the Handicraft Shop, Wellesley: George Christian Gebelein (1906–07); Frans J.R. Gyllenberg (1906–07); Mary Knight (1907); Adolphe C. Kunkler (1906–07); C.G. Forssen (1906); and Seth Ek (1906). Silversmiths known to be working at the Handicraft Shop, 42 Stanhope Street, Boston: George Christian

Note 13 continued on next page

12. A sampling of exhibitions includes the Society of Arts and Crafts, Minneapolis, 1899, 1901; Art Institute of Chicago, 1897–1921; Louisiana Purchase International Exposition, St. Louis, Mo., 1904; Panama Pacific Exposition, San Francisco, 1915. Boston artists who also maintained membership in the Detroit Society of Arts and Crafts included Porter Blanchard, Elizabeth Copeland, George Gebelein, Frank Gardner Hale, the Handicraft Shop, Frank Koralewsky, Old Newbury Crafters, Mrs. Josephine Hartwell Shaw, Arthur Stone, Lester H. Vaughn, James T. Woolley, and S.R. Woolley. Eleventh Annual Report of the Society of Arts and Crafts, Detroit (1918).

Newton Centre (1903); William Edgar Brigham, student, North Attleboro (1905); Elizabeth Ethel Copeland, metalworker, Boston (1905); and Jessie Lane Burbank (1909, 1912). Students attending the afternoon and Saturday courses beginning in 1906–07 were: Arthur Irvin Hennessey, silversmith, Handicraft Shop, Marblehead; and George Joseph Hunt, silversmith and teacher of metalwork, School of the Museum of Fine Arts, Boston. Listed as attending Ross's 1905 class in Drawing and Painting was Mrs. Sarah S. Sears, probably Sarah Choate Sears, patron of Elizabeth Copeland.

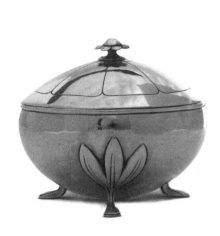

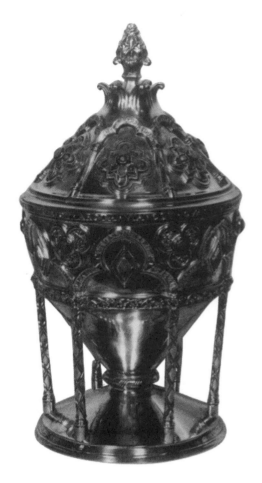

Note 13:
continued from page 75
Gebelein (1908);
Frans J.R. Gyllenberg
(1908–13); Mary Knight
(1908–13); C.G. Forssen
(1908–1910); and Karl F.
Leinonen (1909–13).
Silversmiths known to be
working at the
Handicraft Shop, 516
Atlantic Avenue, Boston:
Mary Knight (1914–18);
Frans J.R. Gyllenberg
(1914–27); K. [arl] Edwin
(son of Karl F.) Leinonen
(1923–27). Silversmiths
known to be working at
the Handicraft Shop, 514
Atlantic Avenue: Sybil
Foster (1916–18); Alfred
Swanson (1923–27), and
Rebecca Cauman,
(1924–27). Information
on the addresses of these
silversmiths was drawn
from Ulehla, *The Society of
Arts and Crafts, Boston*. See
also W. Scott Braznell,
contributor to Wendy
Kaplan, ed., "The Art that
is Life": The Arts & Crafts
Movement in America,
1875–1920 (Boston:
Museum of Fine Arts,
1987), p. 273, fn. 2.

14. For a sample of
collaborative work by
the Handicraft Shop
members, see St. Louis
exhibition catalogue
(1904), p. 81; SACB
exhibition catalogue
(1907), pp. 38, 40.

15. Crawford,
C.R. Ashbee, p. 34.

16. Elenita C. Chickering
with Sarah Morgan Ross,
*Arthur J. Stone 1847–1938,
Designer and Silversmith*
(Boston: The Boston
Athenaeum, 1994),
pp. 26–27.

17. For a review of the
Handicraft Shop, see
Braznell in Kaplan,
"The Art that is Life,"
pp. 272–75. cat. nos.
134–36. *The Townsman* 1,
no. 49 (March 8, 1907),
p. 8. Knight's work
experience at Gorham is
related in "Idealism at
'The Handicraft Shop',"
*The Providence Sunday
Journal*, June 25, 1905,
p. 30. *Tricennial Exhibition
of The Society of Arts &
Crafts* (Boston: Museum
of Fine Arts, 1927), p. 6,
nos. 72–73.

18. Little was a naval
architect and former
mayor of Salem. He
established a workshop
at his home on 27
Chestnut Street and also
maintained a bench at

{22} David Mason Little, silver powder box, ca. 1910; Peabody Essex Institute, Salem. {23} James T. Woolley, silversmith; Elizabeth Copeland, enamelist; John Kirchmayer, modeler; Frank E. Cleveland, designer; Cram, Goodhue, and Ferguson, architects; silver, parcel gilt, gold, and enamel baptismal font, 1920; private collection.

that was in great demand with his New England clients. With the success achieved through his affiliation with the Society, and the financial support of amateur silversmith David Mason Little (fig. 22),[18] Gebelein struck out on his own in 1909, opening his first shop at 79 Chestnut Street. In the early years he worked alone while accepting private students and apprentices, and after World War I, he employed several workmen to meet the growing demand for silver. Among Gebelein's apprentices were Museum School–graduates Katharine Pratt and Sybil Foster, who received a one–year scholarship from the Women's Educational and Industrial Union (WEIU) of Boston to study in his workshop.[19] Cleveland–educated Mildred G. Watkins studied privately with the silversmith before returning to the Cleveland School of Art (now the Cleveland Institute of Art), where she taught metalsmithing from 1919 to 1953.[20] Such educational support in what had hitherto been considered a man's field was consistent with the inroads made by women in many professions early in this century. ¶ After his apprenticeship with the Boston firm of Goodnow and Jenks, which traced its history to the workshop of Paul Revere, Gebelein considered himself the modern heir of the colonial silversmith. In his role as an

antique silver dealer, Gebelein also produced occasional reproductions of colonial objects. His most ambitious reproduction was of a John Coney sugar box made when the original came into his possession around 1935, and intended to prove that his skills were comparable to those of earlier silversmiths (cat. no. 37). However, just as eighteenth–century silversmiths cast certain elements to save time and money, Gebelein used such modern techniques as spinning and electroplating, and also jobbed out some work to commercial firms to keep costs down.[21] ¶ The nationwide flurry of church building and decorating in this period preoccupied many Boston architectural firms and offered prominent commissions for ambitious metalsmiths, particularly those who had arrived in this country with highly developed skills. Born and trained in Berlin, George Germer came to New England in 1891 and specialized in ecclesiastical metalwork. He designed and produced work for Catholic and Protestant churches from Boston to Washington and as far west as Denver, Colorado, always with richly repoussé and chased decoration. The 1907 exhibition of the Society of Arts and Crafts, Boston included a special section for ecclesiastical art that included metalwork as well as textiles, woodworking, and

Gebelein's shop. Little produced a variety of tablewares, a tea set, and a powder box. Martha Gandy Fales, *Silver at the Essex Institute* (Salem: Essex Institute, 1983), p. 60. Margaretha Gebelein Leighton in collaboration with Esther Gebelein Swain and J. Herbert Gebelein, *George Christian Gebelein, Boston Silversmith, 1878–1945* (Boston: Stinehour Press, 1976), pp. 61–63; 65–67.

19. For Foster, see "Woman is Training to be Silversmith," *Boston Post*, December 8, 1913. The WEIU also held an exhibition of Foster's work in 1915 (*Boston Post*, March 27, 1915), but Society records note that after moves to New Haven and New York City, she ceased producing metalwork around the time of the First World War.

20. For Watkins, see "Clevelander's Recognition by Chicago Art Institute," *Cleveland Town Topics*, November 10, 1913, p. 9; Grace V. Kelly, "Mildred Watkins Outstanding Artist in Making Jewelry and the Art of Silversmithing," *Cleveland Plain Dealer*, January 28, 1934, courtesy of the Library, Cleveland Museum of Art. See also Braznell in Kaplan, "The Art that is Life," p. 270, cat. no. 131. Before his appointment in 1935 as curator of the Yale University Art Gallery, John Marshall Phillips (1905–53) spent the summer of 1931 "investigating the hand manufacture of silver at the atelier of George C. Gebelein"; Leighton, *George Christian Gebelein*, pp. 62–63.

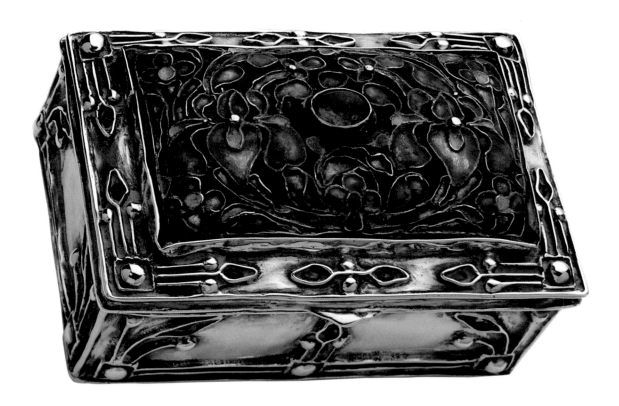

CAT. NO. 35
Elizabeth Copeland,
Covered box,
ca. 1915–37

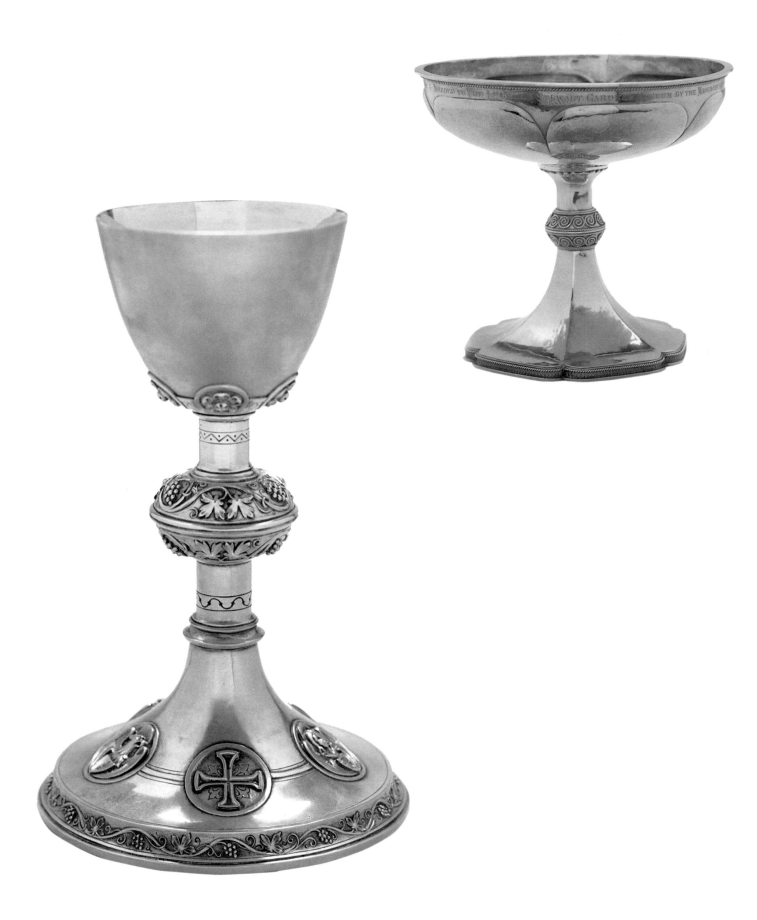

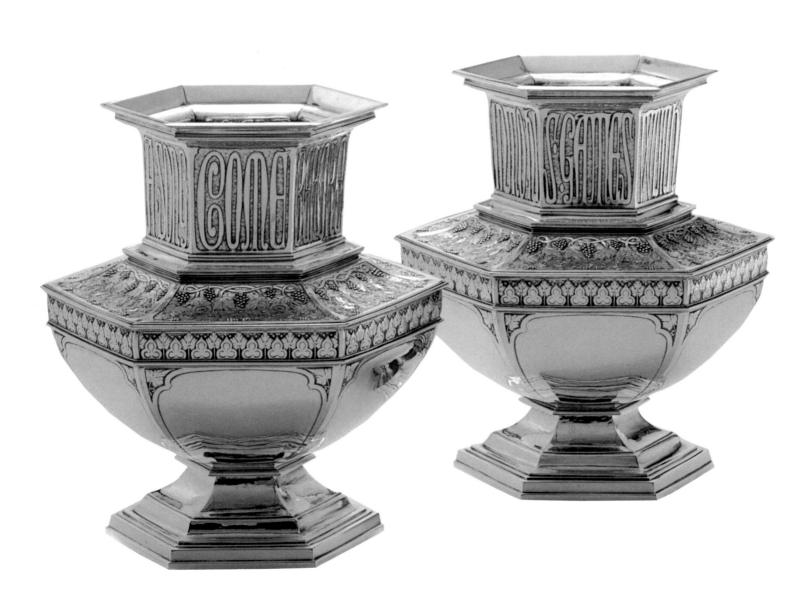

CAT. NO. 51
Arthur J. Stone and
Herbert Taylor,
Pair of altar vases, 1915

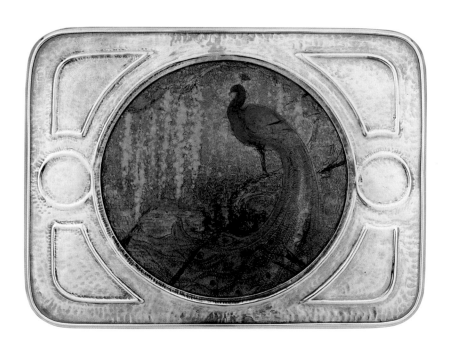

CAT. NO. 43
Frank J. Marshall,
Covered box with peacock
medallion, ca. 1910

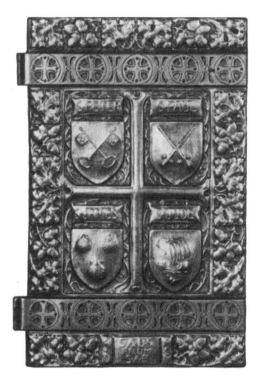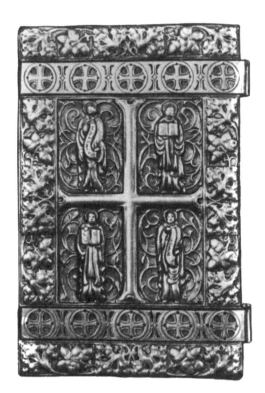

{24} Silver ecclesiastical binding by Laurin Hovey Martin, 1904, *International Studio* 24 (1904), pp. lxi–lxiv.

other crafts media.[22] Germer, Arthur Stone, and George Hunt were the regional silversmiths whose work was highlighted, and the exhibition may have led to Arthur Stone's most important collaborative commission, a gold pyx–monstrance–ciborium made in 1909 with the assistance of his journeyman, William Blair, with figures sculpted by woodworker John Kirchmayer and cast by Thomas Murray, for Boston's Church of the Advent. The renewed interest in medieval art also enabled Boston ironworker Frank Koralewsky to find church patrons for his elaborate cut steel candlesticks, strapwork, and lighting fixtures. Less well–known than Stone and Germer but equally adept was James Woolley, who with enameler Elizabeth Copeland was chosen by philanthropist George G. Booth (1864–1949) to fabricate a covered baptismal bowl (fig. 23) when Arthur Stone, Booth's first choice, was unavailable. Frank Cleveland of the architectural firm Cram, Goodhue, and Ferguson designed both the late Renaissance style pyx and the medieval form of the baptismal bowl.[23] ❦ The influence of academic training upon the craft was especially powerful in a state that in 1870 had instituted the first mandatory drawing classes in this country. Originally planned to benefit the state's manufacturing sector, the Massachusetts Normal School (now the Massachusetts College of Art) was established to train teachers of art and thereby to secure the technical and design future of the state's industries. The first professor of metalwork at the Massachusetts Normal Art School was Lowell–born Laurin Hovey Martin, whose formative artistic period was spent in England at the Birmingham School of Art from 1897 to 1899. Martin received several prizes during his time in England, and was singled out for special recognition by Sir William Blake Richmond, R.A., who stated that Martin's work was "not only extremely fine in design but almost as well worked out as could be." Martin left Birmingham for London to take private lessons from enameler Alexander Fisher. One of the most celebrated of his works was the repoussé and chased silver binding done in a medieval style for an ecclesiastical volume commissioned in 1904 by the Brown family of Rhode Island and printed at the Merrymount Press by Daniel Berkeley Updike (fig. 24).[24] ❦ Upon his return to the United States, Martin became a teacher at the Massachusetts Normal Art School, where he taught from 1901 until his death in 1939. The roster of Martin's students is impressive. Gertrude Twichell (cat.

21. Alexandra Deutsch "George Christian Gebelein: Craftsman and Businessman," Symposium, Emerging Scholars in American Art, Museum of Fine Arts, Boston, April 28, 1995. Gebelein was commissioned in 1928 and 1929 by collector Francis P. Garvan (1875–1937) to fabricate thirty copies of a Philip Syng, Jr. (1703–89) inkstand. Barbara M. Ward and Gerald W.R. Ward, eds., *Silver in American Life* (New York: American Federation of Arts, 1979), p. 101, cat. no. 76. Gebelein sold the Coney sugar box to the Currier Gallery of Art in 1955. William N. Hosley and Karen Blanchfield, contributors to Nancy B. Tieken et al., *American Art from the Currier Gallery of Art* (New York: American Federation of Arts, 1995), cat. no. 51.

22. Frank E. Cleveland, "The Arts and Crafts, An Account of a Recent Exhibition and the Relation of the Movement to Gothic Architecture," *Christian Art* 2, no. 1 (October 1907), pp. 72–80.

23. Chickering and Ross, *Arthur Stone*, p. 115, cat. no. 61. Individual correspondence between James Woolley, Arthur Stone, George Germer, Frederick Krasser, Frank Koralewsky, and patron George Booth, box 17:folder 4, 18:12, 22:6–10, Booth Papers, Cranbrook Archives.

24. Richmond's comments quoted by Martin in his SACB questionnaire. Archives of the Society of Arts and Crafts, Boston, Boston Public Library (hereafter SACB papers, BPL). Correspondence, Glennys Wild, Birmingham Museum and Art Gallery, England, to the author, October 31, 1995. Nathan Haskell Dole, "Some Sumptuous Book–Bindings Carried Out at the Merrymount Press, Boston," *International Studio* 24 (1904), pp. lxi–lxvi.

no. 52), Frank J. Marshall (cat. no. 43), and the prolific Elizabeth Copeland (cat. nos. 34 and 35), are known to have studied with Martin. Two other students of Martin who were responsible for the Cleveland Art Institute's early national reputation for enameling were Mildred G. Watkins and master enameler Kenneth Bates. Born in Scituate, Bates received his degree in 1926 before beginning his sixty–three–year teaching career at the Cleveland School of Art in 1927. Bates praised Martin as one of the greatest teachers and enamelers he had ever known.[25] ❡ Indeed, due to Martin's long career in Boston, a high percentage of enamelers in the Boston area studied with him or one of his students. No other enameler in the area (save jeweler Frank Gardner Hale, who preferred pictorial designs in a two–dimensional format) is known to have been recognized for leadership in this medium. The formal education of Chelsea–born Rebecca Cauman, Caroline Hay, and Eva M. Macomber remains uncertain (fig. 25). However, their preference for round copper boxes, stylized floral enamel designs, and gold foil backings—all features recalling works by Martin—suggest that they may have come into contact with him. Much more remains to be learned about the career of this important Boston artist.[26] ❡ The School of the Museum of Fine Arts, found-

ed in 1877, widened its initial focus on drawing and painting to include crafts around 1884, when C. Howard Walker was employed to head the Department of Applied Arts. In 1905, British–born George Hunt began to teach introductory metalwork. Among his students were Sybil Foster, class of 1913, and Katharine Pratt, who graduated in 1914. Hunt's hollowware ranged in style from British Arts and Crafts (cat. no. 40) and medieval (cat. no. 39) to colonial revival, the latter being in greater demand in his adopted city.[27] ❡ From the turn of this century, the Rhode Island School of Design (RISD) had a remarkable concentration of metalsmiths among its teaching staff. The multi–talented Theodore Hanford Pond, who had graduated from the Pratt Institute and worked for Louis Comfort Tiffany, lectured on decorative art at RISD in 1895; within a year he was teaching the first course on the subject at the school. Shortly thereafter, Pond was made head of the Department of Decorative Design. By 1901, with the support of school president Mrs. Gustav Radeke, Pond established a fully furnished metalwork studio headed by Laurin Martin. By the time he left to teach at the Mechanics Institute in Rochester in 1902, Pond had set RISD's decorative design department on a firm footing which was reinforced by the establishment of a Department of Jewelry,

25. Correspondence, Kenneth F. Bates to Massachusetts College of Art, March 30, 1993: "In several of my books I have given him credit as being my inspiration. One of his classroom techniques was to slowly unwrap from tissue one of his beautiful little trays or match box covers which was done in 'opalescent' enamel, a method which is little known today." Archives, Massachusetts College of Art.

26. Although Rebecca Cauman attended Massachusetts Normal School in 1898, it is not certain whether she came into contact with Martin; Archives of the Massachusetts Normal School; Archives, Massachusetts College of Art. Hay, who was listed as a Craftsman with the Society in 1905, was located at 256 Boylston Street. From 1906 to 1927, she worked at 74 Chestnut Street. Macomber may have begun working as a china painter, as a drawing signed by her appears in *Keramic Studio* (November 1900), p. 150. She lived in Hingham from 1905 to 1918, and moved to Montague in western Massachusetts in 1919. She was a Craftsman at the Society from 1905 to 1915; a Master from 1916 to 1927. Both Hay and Macomber participated in the Society's 1907 exhibition; see Ulehla, *The Society of Arts and Crafts, Boston*, pp. 104, 145.

27. Archives, School of the Museum of Fine Arts; SACB papers, BPL. "Jewelry and Silversmithing School at the Boston Museum of Fine Arts," *The Jeweler's Circular* (February 28, 1928); Ulehla, *The Society of Arts and Crafts, Boston*, p. 116. Hunt was the sole teacher of "metalry" at the Museum School until 1930.

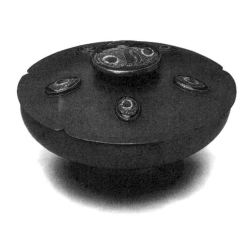

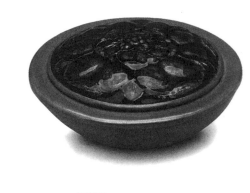

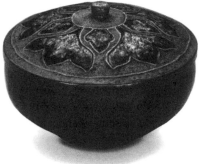

{25A} Rebecca Cauman, copper and enamel covered footed bowl, Boston, ca. 1920; Museum of Fine Arts, Boston; Gift of a Friend of the Department of American Decorative Arts and Sculpture. {25B} Caroline W. Hay, Hay Crafters, copper and enamel covered bowl, ca. 1907; Museum of Fine Arts, Boston; Gift of a Friend of the Department of American Decorative Arts and Sculpture. {25C} Eva M. Macomber, copper and enamel covered bowl, ca. 1910; Museum of Fine Arts, Boston; Gift of Lois and Stephen Kunian.

under the direction of Gorham jewelry foreman Charles E. Hansen, a graduate of the Cooper Institute and a veteran of Tiffany & Co.[28] ⊄ Augustus Foster Rose, who was to succeed Pond in his teaching position, was inspired to take up metalwork around 1901 while attending Martin's evening classes at RISD. The following year Rose traveled to England for further study, and upon his return embarked upon a long teaching career at RISD. Rose's lifelong concern for the importance of manual training was due in part to his friendship with artist, educator, and naturalist, Henry Turner Bailey (1865–1931), who worked for the promotion of industrial drawing from 1887 to 1903 as agent for the Massachusetts Board of Education. When Bailey became director at the Chautauqua School of Arts and Crafts in Lake Chautauqua, New York, he hired a number of New England metalsmiths to teach summer workshops, including George Hunt, Laurin Martin, and Augustus Rose.[29] Of the three teachers, however, Rose was most committed to encouraging crafts in public education. In 1925, he left RISD to become Director of Manual Arts in the Providence public school system. Rose's efforts to popularize metalsmithing led in 1927 to his establishment of a brochure series called *The Metal Crafts, Things In and About Metal*, for the met-

als educator and enthusiast; the series regularly featured student work from around the country, including in 1935 that of the young Harry Bertoia, who later joined the faculty of Cranbrook Academy. The longevity of the brochure, which endured until 1942, enabled the spirit of handcraftsmanship at the student level to be encouraged, until the 1950s brought both a new momentum and modernist aesthetic to metalsmithing.[30] ⊄ William E. Brigham (RISD class of 1906) became head of the Department of Decorative Design in 1914, where he developed a historically–based style of metalwork inspired by the works of art that he examined and painstakingly drew during his many trips to Europe and Asia (cat. nos. 54, 55, and 56). Brigham fabricated jewelry, hollowware, and sculptural compositions well into his retirement years using precious and semiprecious stones, enamels, silver, and gold, and often intermixed carved elements from exotic locales—a preference he shared with Josephine Hartwell Shaw and Marie Zimmermann. Although his passion for historical design was eventually displaced by a growing public interest in modernism, Brigham's essential message of craftsmanship did reach a new generation of metalsmiths in a short series of technical articles he wrote for the nascent *Craft Horizons*

28. Rebecca E. Lawton, Vassar College, unpublished manuscript; Rhode Island School of Design 1901 and 1903 school catalogues, courtesy of Thomas Michie, Museum of Art, RISD. Braznell in Kaplan, "The Art that is Life," p. 331, cat. no. 188.

29. Bailey's friendship with Rose was verbally recounted by the artist's family to the author between 1992 and 1994. Bailey also published *The Applied Arts Book* (1901–03), which was later published as *The School Arts Book* (1903–12) and *School Arts Magazine* (1912–35). Bailey was director at Chautauqua's school of Arts and Crafts from 1903 to 1917. Laurin Martin taught at Chautauqua in 1909 and 1913, George Hunt 1912, Rose 1914; Archives, Chautauqua Institute, Lake Chautauqua, N.Y. Rose was on the summer faculty in 1906 at the Bradley Polytechnic Institute in Peoria, Illinois. Wilfred E. Stone, "An Expression of Feeling in Terms of True Grace," *The Providence Journal*, December 30, 1934.

30. *The Metal Crafts, Things In and About Metal* 4, no. 1 (June 1935), p. 4.

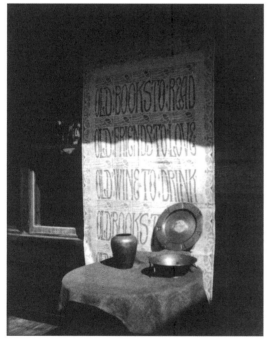

{26} Outdoor display, probably at the Byrdcliffe colony, N.Y., showing copper charger (CAT. NO. 46) and wall hanging (CAT. NO. 85) by H. Stuart Michie; private collection.

31. Correspondence, Museum of Art, RISD files, July 18, 1979; Garrett D. Byrnes, "Brigham Creates Individual Designs," The [Providence] Evening Bulletin, November 13, 1930. Brigham's wife, Clara Rust Brigham, became involved with Federal Hill Industries, in which textiles were produced by Italian immigrant women. She later established the Villa Handcrafts, a well-outfitted weaving workshop at their home on Rochambeau Avenue in Providence, where textiles, along with jewelry, metalwork, and woodwork, were made; Craft Horizons 3, no. 5 (May 1944), p. 17. Brigham edited a series of articles entitled "The Metalworker Suggests" between May 1944 and February 1947 for Craft Horizons.

32. Dow wrote a warm letter of introduction for Michie on July 24, 1903 (private collection), in which he stated: "His [Michie's] work was refined, well drawn and finished and strong in execution. With his education and equipment and his fine personal character, I should expect him to succeed anywhere."

33. See RISD Museum Notes 76, no. 1 (October 1989), p. 18, for a William Morris printed textile from Michie's teaching collection.

34. Both Martin and Michie signed the guest register at Byrdcliffe on July 1, 1907, and were housed in the "boy's shanty" cabin. It was the only trip that Michie is known to have made there; Martin also visited Byrdcliffe in 1904 and 1908. Joseph Downs Collection of Manuscripts and Printed Ephemera, Henry Francis du Pont Winterthur Museum.

35. H. Stuart Michie lecture notes, private collection. Augustus Rose files and lecture notes, private collection.

magazine, precursor of the present–day *American Craft*, a decade before his death in 1962.[31] Canadian–born Henry Stuart Michie, who became principal of the Worcester Art Museum School in 1909, enjoyed a varied Arts and Crafts education through schooling and travel (fig. 26). He studied at the Pratt Institute under his mentor and longtime colleague Arthur Wesley Dow, with whom he shared a love of Japanese art and design. From 1905 to 1906, Michie studied in England at the prominent Central and Camberwell Schools of Art in London, and met members of the Artificers Guild in London and Ashbee's Guild of Handicraft in Chipping Campden (cat. no. 45).[32] Once established in Worcester, Michie applied the Arts and Crafts aesthetic equally to his home and work life. His residence was graced with his handiwork and designs for a central staircase, copper downspouts, grillwork, and a wall fountain. He decorated his home with Japanese prints, stencils, and textiles he had assembled from around the world, which also served as his teaching collection.[33] The influence of Asian art upon Michie's own work can be discerned in the enameled carp, auguring good fortune, that appears in the center of his copper charger (cat. no. 46), which may have been made at the Byrdcliffe colony in Woodstock, New York in the summer of 1907, when Michie apparently traveled there with Laurin Martin.[34] With these small beginnings at schools in Boston, Providence, and Worcester, the pre–industrial tradition of teaching metalsmithing and its allied crafts was transferred from the workshop environment to that of academe. Surviving lecture notes by Michie and Rose reveal their hopes for the future of craft education in American schools. For Rose, it was to make the benefits of the manual training movement available to every school–age child and young adult. For his part, Michie lectured on the need for a national center of design for advanced art students. He advocated the establishment of schools, standards, and annual exhibitions in emulation of the National Art Training Schools begun in England in 1852 by Sir Henry Cole (1808–82), in order to place decorative arts in this country on a par with the fine arts.[35] The outbreak of the First World War and the Great Depression turned America's attention to other matters, and no such program was ever established. Still, the seeds sown by art educators in these early decades were reaped in the 1940s and 1950s, when crafts taught within the academic arena emerged with renewed vigor on the American cultural landscape. ◎

Special thanks are due to Jonathan Fairbanks for his long support of this project, to Gerald W.R. Ward and W. Scott Braznell for their thoughtful readings of the manuscript, and to the many colleagues who helped in its research and preparation, including: Aram and Rosalie Berberian; Elenita Chickering; Mark Coir and Karen Serotta (Cranbrook Educational Community); Ned Cooke; Patricia Cummings; Maureen Devine (Edsel and Eleanor Ford Museum); Paul Dobbs (Massachusetts College of Art); Virginia Fox; Marie Frank; Sam Hough; Deborah Martin Kao (Fogg Art Museum); Sylvia Kliman; Susmita Lavery, Jane Port, and Susan Reed (Museum of Fine Arts, Boston); Rebecca Lawton (Vassar College); Paul J. Weimerskirch (Providence Public Library); David Wood (Concord Museum); the descendants of the Brown, Michie, Rose, and Martin families; and my own family, David and Morgan Heath.

Life dates or working dates (as known) for artists whose works
are not included in this exhibition:

Kenneth Bates : 1904–94
Arrieto (Harry) Bertoia : 1915–78
William Blair : active 1904–09
Janet Payne Bowles : 1872/73–1948
Clara (Rust) Brigham : 1879–1954
Lucy Cora Brown : 1859–1937
Rebecca Cauman : b. 1872, active until 1927
Christopher Dresser : 1834–1904
Seth Ek : active 1906–12
Alexander Fisher : 1864–1936
C.G. Forssen : active 1903–10
Sybil Foster : active 1910–18
Goodnow and Jenks : 1893–1905
Gorham Manufacturing Company : 1865–1961
Frans J.R. Gyllenberg : 1883–1974
Caroline W. Hay : active 1905–27
Mary Knight : b. 1876, active until 1927
Adolphe C. Kunkler : active 1901–22
Karl F. Leinonen : 1866–1957
David Mason Little : 1860–1923
Eva M. Macomber : active 1900–27
Thomas Murray : 1869–1942
Theodore Hanford Pond : 1872–1933
Denman Ross : 1853–1935
Mildred G. Watkins : 1883–1968
James Woolley : active 1907–1926
Samuel Yellin : 1885–1940
Marie Zimmermann : 1878–1972

HISTORIC INTERPRETATIONS: BOSTON'S ARTS & CRAFTS JEWELRY

MARILEE BOYD MEYER

AMERICAN ARTS AND Crafts jewelry, which reinterpreted Victorian jewelry as a new art form, had its roots in the silversmithing community of Boston. As metalworkers who espoused design reform became more skilled with their hammering and cutting techniques, they turned their attention to the more meticulous art of jewelry–making. Jewelry required rich design sources and advanced technical skills. With its long–standing cultural wealth and flourishing economy, Boston offered both. There were many factors in the development of jewelry–making: dress reform from England, the new freedom of women, the setting of art criteria, and the dissemination of ideas. With its commercial silversmithing and jewelry industry, shaped in part by the taste of the elite, Boston produced outstanding practitioners and works. ❧Arts and Crafts jewelry of the 1890s differed from its Victorian antecedents. Beginning in England, the style eschewed the richly jeweled pieces that denoted the status, wealth, and power of the European nobility, and turned to seldom–used semiprecious stones and minerals of lesser cost. Both the color of stones and their size became important in harmonizing single large pieces of jewelry on the simple flowing gowns that were the expression of dress reform. Jewelry became a focal point on the dress, an artistic statement made by the wearer. Early forms were clasps and buckles of enameled silver and hammered copper that blended beauty with usefulness. Later, when metalworkers grew more proficient, brooches and pendants became lighter and more intricate in design. ❧The colors of turquoise, carnelian, tourmaline, peridot, and chrysoprase were often combined with the luminosity and texture of irregular blister pearls, opals, agates, abalone shells, or even pebbles for contrast. In addition, jewelry incorporated fragments from antiquity. Design became paramount. Motifs of peacocks, birds, flowers, and sailing ships from peasant art, and historical sources from India, China, and especially the

Italian Renaissance, were reintroduced by England's Charles Robert Ashbee, who is credited with returning jewelry–making to an art form. Enameling was resurrected for its inexpensive painterly color by Ashbee's contemporary, Alexander Fisher. Through American apprentices and publications such as *International Studio*, Ashbee and Fisher's ideas found their way into the Boston vernacular.[1] ❡ Through its Anglo–American ties, Boston readily embraced the Arts and Crafts movement. With their generations of accrued wealth and formal education, Bostonians had leisure time to travel to Europe and the Far East, educating themselves in the arts and culture of foreign museums while amassing private collections via the Grand Tour—collections which, on loan to museums, gave the public an awareness of the ancient arts. Included in these cultural studies were jewelry traditions. The thriving local diamond trade of the late nineteenth century soon expanded to include colored stones of lesser value but rising popularity. As a part of the larger Arts and Crafts movement, jewelry–making found its roots in the historical past. ❡ By the turn of the century, the Victorian role for women had been challenged. The invention of the typewriter and telephone introduced women to the possibility of economic independence outside the home. In ad-

dition, handicrafts provided women a vehicle for self–expression. In the late nineteenth century, many single women were employed in the flourishing manufacture of jewelry in North Attleboro and Providence. As this growing industry required an increasingly higher degree of skills, in 1870 Massachusetts mandated the teaching of drawing in the public schools, to encourage a potential workforce. Three years later, the Massachusetts Normal [Art] School was established—in part to meet the growing demand for art teachers under the new law—followed by the Rhode Island School of Design (RISD) and the School of the Museum of Fine Arts, Boston in 1877. Industrial arts training and fine arts training, usually separate disciplines, were joined in the new curricula. Women teachers were central to the plan, moving the creation of art into the domain of the working people and, in addition, providing women the opportunity to learn useful artistic skills. Women came into their own as a "mine of untapped resources." Courses in proportion, drawing, modeling, and sculpture would become basic training for art jewelers, the majority of whom in New England were women. Over the next thirty years, Massachusetts Normal gave out teaching certificates to 898 women but only 219 men.[2] ❡ Emerging from the Victorian era of gen-

1. Alan Crawford, *C.R. Ashbee: Architect, Designer and Romantic Socialist* (New Haven: Yale University Press, 1985), p. 363.

2. Walter Smith, *Art Education: Scholastic and Industrial Design* (Boston: James R. Osgood and Company, 1872), p.28; Alicia Faxon and Sylvia Moore, *Pilgrims and Pioneers: New England Women in the Arts* (New York: Midmarch Arts Press, 1987), p. 33; Anthea Gallen, *Women Artists of the Arts and Crafts Movement* (New York: Pantheon Books, 1979), p. 44. Walter Smith, the Massachusetts Normal Art School's first director and a strong advocate for working women, professed a need for identical training for women and men "without discrimination."

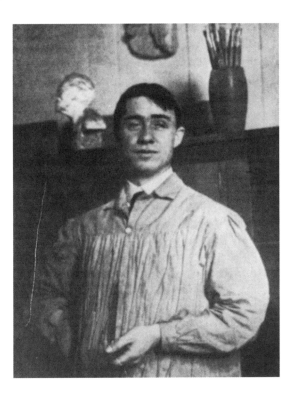

{27A} Photograph of Grueby designer, Addison Le Boutillier, ca. 1904, *Brickbuilder* (January 1905).

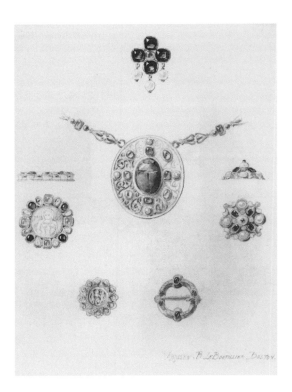

{27B} Drawings by Addison Le Boutillier, ca. 1899; Andover Historical Society, Andover, Mass.

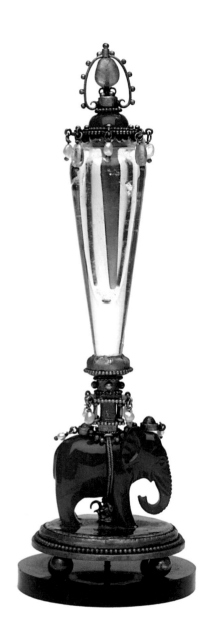

CAT. NO. 56
William E. Brigham,
Perfume bottle on an
elephant base, ca. 1920–25

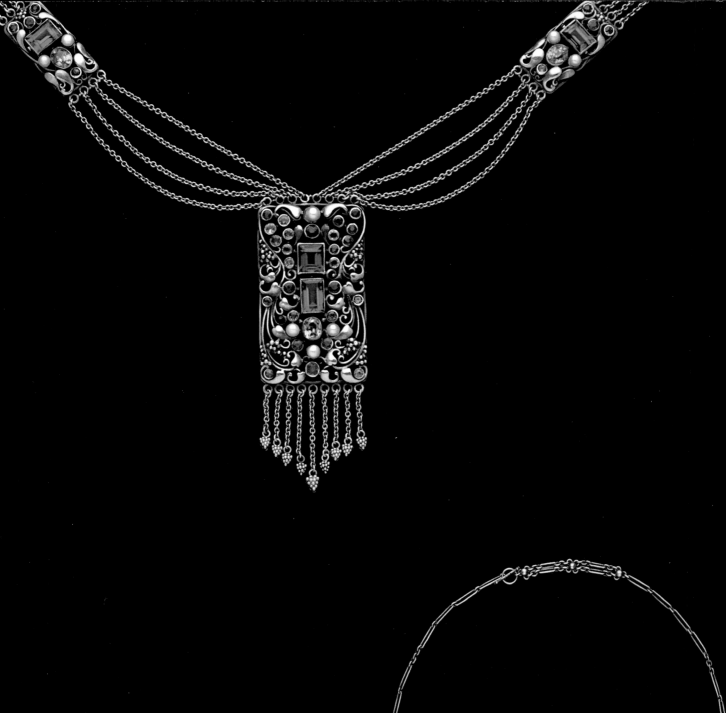

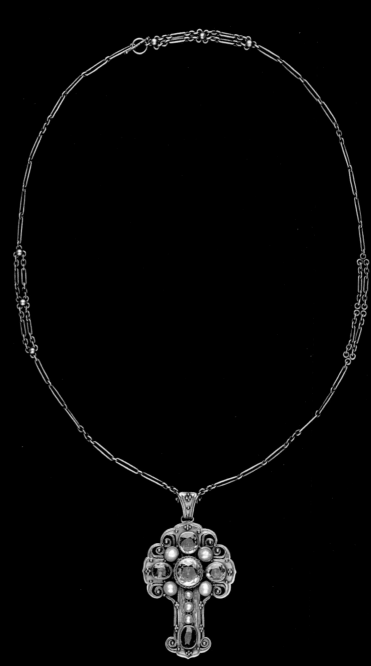

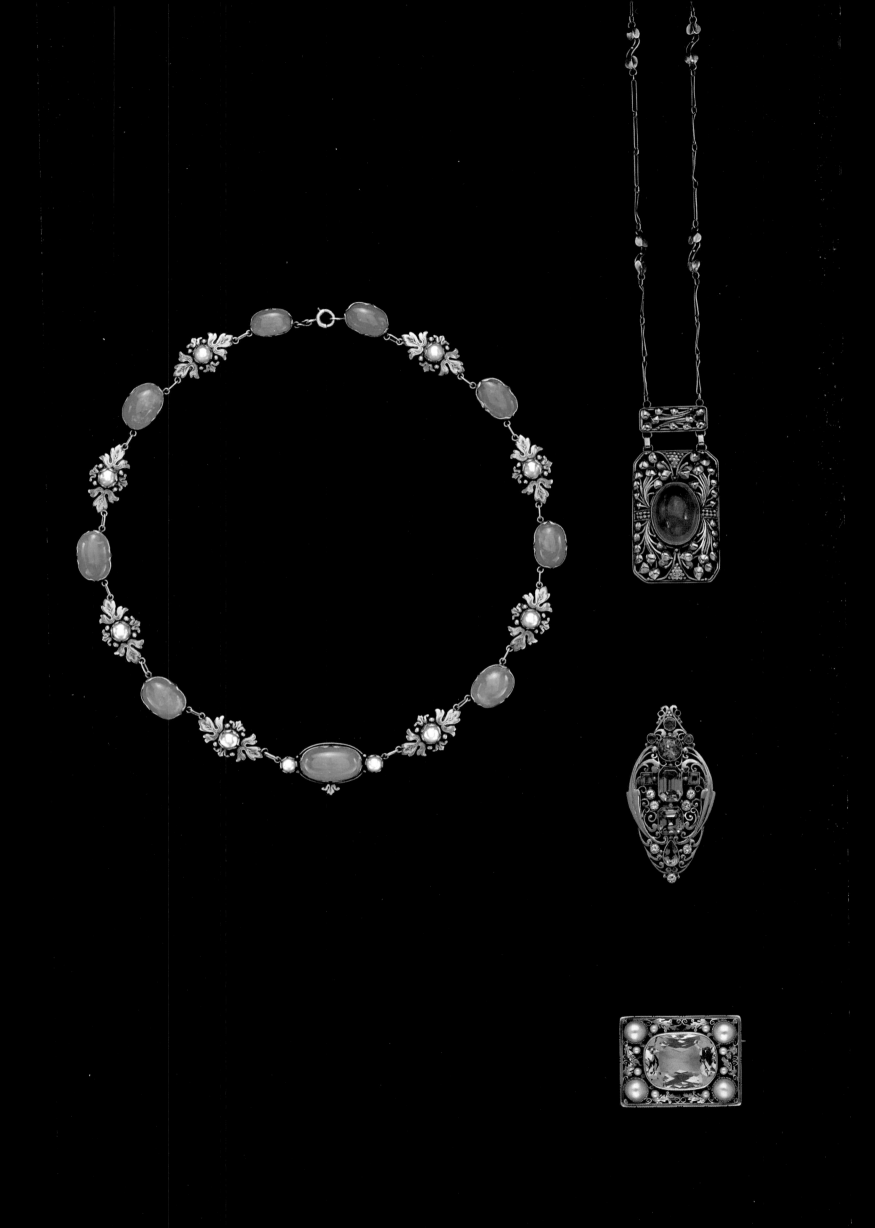

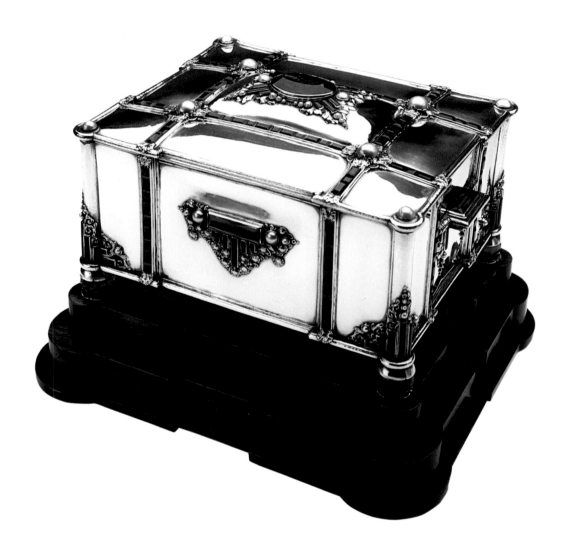

CAT. NO. 67
Edward Everett Oakes,
Jeweled casket,
ca. 1929

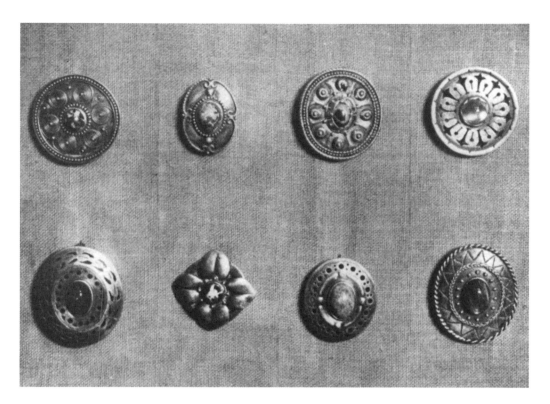

{28} Plate XVII from Augustus F. Rose and Antonio Cirino's book, *Jewelry Making and Design*, 1917.

teel philanthropy, women such as Madeline Yale Wynne of Deerfield and Jessie Luther (b. 1860) of Providence became pioneer practitioners of the handicraft movement. Wynne, a leading metalworker of the day, espoused a colonial revival approach in her silver shoe buckles (cat. no. 78) and medieval design elements in hammered copper pieces set with odd stones and enamel (cat. no. 77). Although considered primitive by later standards, at first they were reviewed as "original, gorgeous, barbaric."[3] Luther, as multi–talented as Wynne, also exhibited hammered enameled copper jewelry. Both women, however, spread the Arts and Crafts doctrine through their work in social service and occupational therapy—Wynne helping to establish both Deerfield's and Chicago's Arts and Crafts Societies and Luther working at Hull House in Chicago, the Handicraft Shop in Marblehead, and Sir Wilfred Grenfell's sanitarium in Labrador and Newfoundland.[4] ❧ In Boston, this idealism would be challenged by the first Jury of the Society of Arts and Crafts, Boston (SACB), founded in 1897. As part of the privileged class and with visual sophistication, the Jury was concerned with artistic design and the execution of the finished product, not its social implications. As Denman Ross wrote in *Handicraft* maga-

zine in 1903, "Consider the work of the Early and Middle Ages, of the Renaissance, the work of our own Colonial days, the work of the Far East, of China and Japan. We may have examples in our houses, in our museums, the masterpieces of earlier times. In comparison with these, the work which we are doing is most unsatisfactory."[5] ❧ Jewelry–making lagged behind metalwork and other media in development. In the Society's inaugural exhibition of 1897 and again in 1899, the New York firm of Marcus and Co. was the only jewelry contributor. Other than drawings of Etruscan–inspired jewelry by designer Addison Le Boutillier (1872–1951), entitled "Ancient Jewelry" and "Original Designs for Jewelry and work carved in gold" (fig. 27), works by individual art-jewelers did not appear.[6] From the beginning, jewelry–making was open to "almost anyone who possess[ed] a knowledge of design and a handiness with simple tools," and a small work space.[7] Those budding jewelers who could afford to, studied in Europe. Others applied metalworking skills learned in a factory setting or through art schools, but many apprenticed to a more knowledgeable craftsman. ❧ The establishment of the Society's showroom in 1900 under secretary–treasurer Frederic Allen Whiting brought

3. *House Beautiful* (June 1899), p. 6; (January 1901), p. 98; (July 1903), p. 71; and (January 1904), p. 106.

4. For biographical information on Jessie Luther, see the Papers of the Society of Arts and Crafts, Archives of American Art, Boston Public Library, microfilm reel 3468:frame 205 (hereafter SACB archives, AAA/BPL reel:frame).

5. Denman Ross, "Arts and Crafts: A Diagnosis," *Handicraft* I, no. 10 (January 1903), p. 229. This article was reprinted in the *Craftsman* magazine (December 1904), p. 335.

7. Henry W. Belknap, "Jewelry and Enamels," *Craftsman* (June 1903), p. 180.

6. Susan J. Montgomery, *The Ceramics of William H. Grueby* (Lambertville, N.J.: Arts & Crafts Quarterly Press, 1993), p. 56. Trained as an architect, Le Boutillier was hired by Bigelow, Kennard and Company to design jewelry, silver, clocks, and graphics for advertisements. He became director of design at Grueby Faience Company.

93

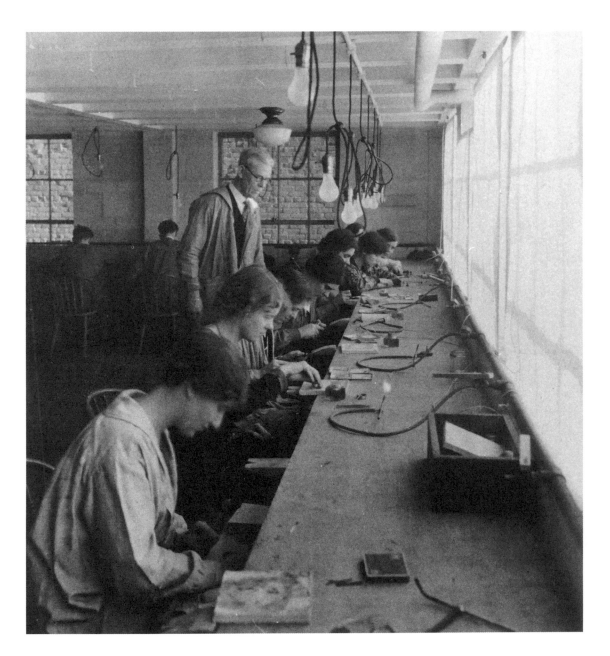

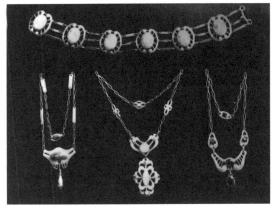

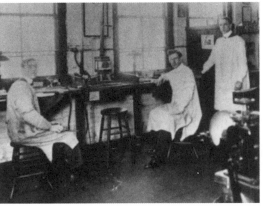

{29} Jewelry workers in George J. Hunt's shop, ca. 1926; Vant Papers, collection of Stephen Vaughan.
{30} Jewelry pieces designed by Mabel Luther, ca. 1905; Fine Arts Department, Boston Public Library.
{31} Apprentices Edward Everett Oakes and John Ballou with Frank Gardner Hale in Hale's shop, ca.1910;
collection of Susan Oakes Peabody.

together individual makers and patrons, thus creating a marketplace, while the Jury system ensured quality and growth.[8] To this end, craftsmen submitting objects for approval were assigned consignment numbers for more equitable judging. These factors contributed to Boston having the greatest concentration of individual art jewelers in the country by 1916.[9] The Jury, however, eventually became alarmed at the flood of inferior amateur products, calling to "strict account, the dabblers...[whose] work, if unchecked, would discredit the movement."[10] Decrying the lax methods of jewelry–making "in language which somehow suggests the vigorous English used by Mr. C. Howard Walker,"[11] the Jury "strongly suggested" drawing and proficiency in metalwork and enameling, and prescribed "simple line borders, repeats of units, the placing of foci before they attempt so–called rhythmical combinations of lines." Still seeing little improvement, the next year they added to their criteria filigraine of delicate wires, openness of space and repoussé leaf metals, subtle color and painted enamels.[12] Artists were expected to submit designs on paper and preferably in color (cat. no. 65). Art Nouveau style was specifically discouraged by the Jury as "untrained and undeveloped, of unstocked brain and faltering hand."[13] With its veto power, the Society controlled Boston's taste in jewelry by dismissing with "constructive criticism" anything not to their liking. There would not be another major exhibition in Boston until 1907 while the Jury directed its energies toward refining and dispersing its standards.[14] ❡ The years 1900 through 1915 became a formative time. Society members founded or taught in numerous summer schools: Arthur Wesley Dow taught in Ipswich, and Henry Hunt Clark at the Rhode Island School of Design summer school before going to teach in Cleveland, where Jury critic Frederic Allen Whiting and William Brigham also taught. Also at RISD was Augustus F. Rose, whose book *Jewelry Making and Design* (fig. 28, cat. no. 72B), written in 1917 with former student and assistant Antonio Cirino, was fundamental in teaching—as the subtitle states —"teachers, students of design, and crafts workers." Denman Ross taught at Harvard Summer School. Out of this ferment came important students: from silversmith and jeweler George J. Hunt (fig. 29) came Susan Leland Hill, Hazel Blake French, Margaret Vant (1905–89) and Gertrude Peet (b. 1880); from teacher Denman Ross, came students Josephine Hartwell (Shaw), William Brigham and Elizabeth Copeland with

her patron, Sarah Choate Sears. Laurin Martin, who studied under the English jeweler Arthur Gaskin, taught Mabel Luther (b. 1874) and Margaret Rogers. ❡ Society members also joined and strengthened other Arts and Crafts groups in the Boston area—Eva Macomber in Hingham, and Copeland and Rogers in Wayland.[15] Ideas were also dispersed through lectures, traveling exhibitions, and magazines such as *International Studio, Good Housekeeping, House Beautiful,* and Stickley's *Craftsman.* In 1896, the Gorham Manufacturing Company of Providence recognized the Arts and Crafts movement and attempted to compete by establishing a special department, headed by William Codman, where the most technically promising workers were encouraged to interpret and craft new designs by hand. Some pieces were marked "handwrought" (cat. no. 59). In 1903, in association with the Manufacturing Jewelers Association, of which Gorham was a member, RISD added a Department of Jewelry, under the guidance of Gorham Jewelry foreman Charles E. Hansen, with evening classes.[16] The year 1907 was a watershed in the development of New England Arts and Crafts because of three important events: the SACB's tenth anniversary show, which featured seasoned jewelry–makers; the formation of the Metalworkers' Guild, of which jewelers were a part; and the establishment of the National League of the Handicraft Societies, which helped spread standards through its magazine *Handicraft.*[17] ❡ The tenth anniversary exhibition of 1907 included the work of Mabel Luther (fig. 30), Margaret Rogers, and Josephine Hartwell Shaw, among many other known jewelry–makers who had previously exhibited in Chicago, Detroit, Minneapolis, New York, and Providence.[18] Elizabeth Copeland—with her interpretation of medieval designs (cat. no. 57)—was accepted, and William Denton of Wellesley received honorable mention for his butterfly pins under crystal. Newspaper reviews were extensive and favorable, noting the artists' work as being good, of original quality, and showing potential. The Jury, however, still considered the designs tentative and the execution somewhat crude. The significant fact, it would seem, was that thirty–four out of forty–six exhibitors were women, who were developing individual styles in jewelry–making "as no man with his knowledge of the intricacies of woman's mind and gowns could ever think to make."[19] ❡ One of Boston's most recognized jewelers, however, was not included in the 1907 show—Frank Gardner Hale, who was returning from an apprenticeship at Ashbee's

8. Beverly K. Brandt, "'Worthy and Carefully Selected': American Arts and Crafts at the Louisiana Purchase Exposition, 1904," *Journal of the Archives of American Art* 28, no. 1 (1988), pp. 2–14; SACB archives, AAA/BPL 300:306, 3468:113. Whiting, as director of Applied Arts and member of the International Jury of Award at the Louisiana Purchase Exhibition, was instrumental in bringing national attention to the SACB members who were awarded 27 out of a total of 43 medals. Whiting was chairman of the Jewelry Department in the Society's 1907 exhibition.

9. Emily E. Graves, "Handwrought Jewelry In America," *Magazine of American Art* (1916), p. 100. Other jewelry and silversmithing centers were Chicago, with its Scandinavian influence, and Cleveland, which looked to Boston for guidance from its teachers.

10. "Current Art Events," *International Studio* (September 1906), p. lxxxvii.

11. Typed unsigned manuscript (probably by Whiting) from the SACB to the *Boston Herald,* March 5, 1907, SACB archives, AAA/BPL 300:57.

12. The Report of the Jury, SACB Annual Report (1906 and 1907)—reviewed in "Current Art Events," *International Studio* (September 1906), p. lxxxvii—brought to public attention the Jury's comments on standards.

13. Report of the Jury (1906). C. Howard Walker mentions the "blessed absence of L'Art Nouveau" in his report to the Jury, *Bulletin of the Society of Arts and Crafts,* as late as 1920. According to Josephine C. Locke, "Nouveau is a revolt against the academic, the conventional, the formal of all kinds" (*Craftsman* [June 1902], p. 202). This was the antithesis of the Boston approach to decorative arts.

14. *Art Bulletin* (March 2, 1907); SACB archives, AAA/BPL 320.

18. *Exhibition of the Society of Arts and Crafts, Copley Hall* (Boston: Heintzemann Press, 1907), p. 21. Other jewelry exhibitors in 1907 included: Mary A. Bachelder, Jessie Burbank, Jane Carson (Barron), Jessie Luther, Martha Dyer, Toyoza Kobayashi, Grace Hazen, Florence Richmond, Gustave Rogers, Edmund B. Rolfe, Laurin Hovey Martin, Emily Peacock, Helen Keeling Mills, Horace Potter, Brainerd Thresher, Augustus F. Rose, Mildred Watkins, Mary Winlock, and James Winn.

17. Local societies that were members of the National League of Handicrafts Societies included: (in Massachusetts) Dorchester, Malden, Melrose, Brewster, Norwell, Greenfield, Springfield, Deerfield, and South Hampton; Providence, R.I.; Portland, Me.; and Hartford, Conn. SACB archives, AAA/BPL 300:225.

16. "Rhode Island School of Design—Department of Jewelry, 1901," folder, Archives, Rhode Island School of Design, Providence; W. Scott Braznell, "Metalsmithing and Jewelrymaking, 1900–1920," in Janet Kardon, ed., *The Ideal Home 1900–1920: the History of Twentieth–Century American Craft* (New York: Abrams, 1994), p. 55; Charlotte Gere and Geoffrey C. Munn, *Artists' Jewellery: Pre-Raphaelite to Arts and Crafts* (Woodbridge, Suffolk, U.K.: Antique Collectors' Club, 1989), pp. 182–86.

15. Although known primarily for her enameled copper boxes, Eva Macomber of Hingham showed necklaces in *Handicraft* (September 1911), p. 228. The Jury of Wayland's Society of Arts and Crafts, founded in 1906, accepted Elizabeth Copeland, Gertrude Twichell, and Margaret Rogers as members in 1907 (Wayland Society of Arts and Crafts papers, Wayland Historical Society).

19. SACB exhibition catalogue (1907), pp. 21–29; "A Craftsworker with Jewels: Rich Designs with American 'Stones'," Craftsman (January 1916), p. 422.

20. C. Howard Walker, "Queries," Handicraft (November 1910), p. 307.

21. For comments on clothing in relation to jewelry, see C. Howard Walker, "Queries," p. 307; and Carol Colbourne, "The New Art Jewelry," Good Housekeeping (November 1911), p. 587.

22. The Christian Science Monitor, March 6, 1913, gave accolades to the "Gain in Jewelcraft" (SACB archives, AAA/BPL 322:317). Participants in the Society's exhibition of jewelry at the Park Street showroom (where numerous small shows were held) included: Elizabeth Copeland, Eva M. Macomber, Frank Marshall, Mrs. M.I. Flagg, William D. Denton, Laurin Hovey Martin, Margaret Rogers, Josephine Hartwell Shaw, Frank Gardner Hale, Jessie Ames Dunbar, Mr. and Mrs. L.B. Dixon, Mrs. Lucretia M. Bush, Jessie L. Burbank, George J. Hunt, Carl H. Johonnot, George C. Gebelein, Mabel W. Luther, Susan Leland Hill, Martha Dyer, and Reginald F. Pierce. Exhibitors of small enamels included: Mabel W. Luther, Elizabeth Copeland, Arthur S. Williams, Mary P. Winlock, Caroline W. Hay, Frank J. Marshall, and Mr. and Mrs. L.B. Dixon. A contemporary reviewer noted, "The largest single exhibit is that of Frank Gardner Hall [sic] whose jewelry occupies an entire case." SACB archives, AAA/BPL 322:317.

23. Shaw, Rogers, Mabel Luther, and Elizabeth Copeland were featured in Claire M. Coburn, "Specimens of Craftsman Jewelry," Good Housekeeping (November 1906), p. 507. Shaw was also the focus of Ralph Bergengren, "Some Jewels and a Landscape," House Beautiful (April 1915), p. 147.

Guild of Handicraft and the study of enamel with Fred Partridge in London. Hale became one of the most influential Boston jewelers. As early as 1901, Hale had drawings included in the Design Department of the Minneapolis Arts and Crafts Exhibition and had designed covers for music books. His skill in jewelry and enamels was quickly recognized and he later took on several apprentices, including eighteen-year-old Edward Everett Oakes (fig. 31) before Oakes studied with Josephine Hartwell Shaw. Much of the progress made by other craftsmen was due to Hale's example. It would not be until twelve years later, however, under Hale's guidance, that art jewelers reached maturity with the creation of their own guild. ❦ The burgeoning of the many local Arts and Crafts societies permitted much experimentation and fed into the 1907 show, the outgrowth of which led to the establishment of the National League of Handicraft Societies. Uniting the smaller groups into a cohesive force, the League provided lectures and technical handbooks, and mounted professional shows, thus advancing standards. Accomplished members disseminated ideas beyond the classroom through Handicraft magazine, re–issued in 1910. Gustave Rogers, who taught in Worcester and Marblehead, wrote articles on design in jewelry, while Laurin Martin included instructional illustrations in his article, "Jewelry Making." In addition, the magazine provided a forum for answering questions from the public. Regarding the worth of the new "inexpensive jewelry," critic C. Howard Walker replied that the value was in the timelessness of design and the perfection of workmanship: "The tone, color, material, design arrangement is of permanent value."[20] ❦ During the first decades of the new century crafts, in general, gained in sophistication. Changing fashions encouraged a corresponding adaptation in jewelry. Although craftsmen's jewelry was appreciated, it was considered too casual and thus inappropriate for the "grand dames." The use of satin, velvet, and lace in evening wear required jewelry of delicacy, openness, and richness.[21] In addition to the earlier cabochons, faceted stones were used. Josephine Hartwell Shaw created intricate pieces wrought in gold and costly platinum. Margaret Rogers redesigned necklaces to fit the new styles. Hale made longer necklaces with filigree and colored stones. By 1913, the quality of Arts and Crafts objects merited the establishment of the Medal of Excellence by the SACB; jewelers and metalsmiths were predominant among the winners.[22] ❦ The jewelers' own Guild around 1919 carried on the

old ideas, but allowed jewelers new freedom to combine historical sources with fresh ideas. The Guild's dean, Frank Gardner Hale, and members such as William Brigham of Providence lectured regularly. Historical influences appeared in the naturalism of William Morris's twisted tendrils; the symmetrical, repeating designs inspired by Arthur Wesley Dow and the Orient; the medieval elements of hand–hammered metals and cabochons; and the granulation, small round pearls, and colored stones of the Italian Renaissance, a period when goldsmiths were at their artistic pinnacle as creators of personal adornment. The more imaginative jewelers incorporated fragments from antiquity into their jewelry: ancient jade from Boston's China trade (cat. no. 63), old glass, Wedgwood, and other antique objects. Workmanship in silver, gold, and platinum required both more refined modeling and techniques of chasing, overlapping, and piercing, with both sides formally finished. Commissions for special pieces were growing, especially the resetting of family jewels into modern "timeless" designs. ❦ Following the earlier historical imitation, individual styles emerged. As early as 1906, Shaw's jewelry showed her discipline and talent as a designer.[23] The irregular organic pearl of

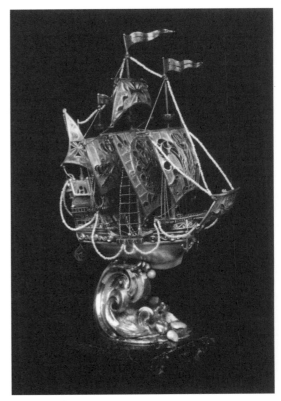

{32} The Argosy, ca. 1927, jeweled ship by William Brigham, present whereabouts unknown; RISD owns a similar jeweled ship by Brigham.

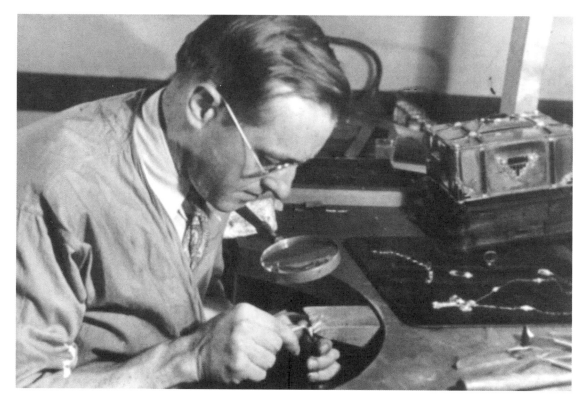

{33} Edward Everett Oakes at his jewelry bench with silver jeweled casket (CAT. NO. 67) in background, ca. 1930; collection of Susan Oakes Peabody.

her gold necklace dictates the shape of the piece, which is surrounded with wirework and beads (cat. no. 74). The gold pendant with Mexican fire opal cabochon (cat. no. 75) made use of Dow's concept of ordered nature, while the Greco–Roman overtones of her cross pendant with amethysts, pearls and granulation (cat. no. 73) paid tribute to the Ecclesiastical movement so popular in Boston. It was given by Shaw to the Museum of Fine Arts, Boston in memory of her silversmith husband, Frederick, in 1914, the same year Shaw received the Society's Medal of Excellence. Margaret Rogers, a colleague of Shaw's, combined Renaissance and medieval elements with the simplicity of Dow's aesthetic in her works by using a basic pattern of colored stones alternating with pearls and gold leaves (cat. no. 71); her smaller pieces used smooth stones and repeating leaf–and–bead motifs (cat. no. 70). ⁌Frank Gardner Hale translated the scrolls of his earlier music book covers into three–dimensional jewelry. His early circular pin used classical motifs of grapes and leaves with a stone focal point (cat. no. 61), while his later work, still using scrolls, balls and semiprecious stones, became almost abstract in form—a symmetrical, highly developed structure. This densi-

ty can be seen in his large, predominantly tourmaline and sapphire brooch (cat. no. 60) and long jeweled pendant (cat. no. 64). Equally skilled in the art of enameling, Hale used foil backing in his Limoges–type plaques to highlight the colors of his subjects, which ranged from religious themes to fish (cat. no. 62). Another prolific enameler, though less well known, was jeweler Mabel Luther (b. 1874) who did miniature landscapes. ⁌By 1910, the second generation of art jewelers did not have to go to Europe for apprenticeship as had the earlier pivotal figures, Martin, Rose, and Hale. Hazel Blake French, for example, studied with C. Howard Walker at the Museum of Fine Arts, Boston in 1913 and continued with George J. Hunt. A lone studio craftswoman, she nurtured the pure ideals of the craft, making special use of Sandwich glass from the nearby factory on Cape Cod in her "interpretive jewelry" (cat. no. 58), giving each piece a name such as *Blue Ship* and *Red Currant*.[24] ⁌Edward Everett Oakes avidly studied historical ornament in museums, gleaning ideas for his jewelry from older sources. From his apprenticeship with Hale he inherited his use of wirework and from Shaw the use of pearls and stones. He was awarded the Medal of Excellence in 1923

24. For biographical information on Hazel Blake French, see SACB archives, AAA/BPL, 3468:247.

(cat. no. 76), the same year the Metropolitan Museum of Art purchased his ball pendant on cord, a piece evoking both Renaissance and Indian Moghul styles (cat. no. 66). Typical of Oakes's work was the use of foliate wirework, beading, and his trademark oak leaves contained in a notched frame (cat. no. 68). His consummate skill as a goldsmith is shown in his filigree bracelet, which is both delicate in detail and bold in design (cat. no. 69). ❡ Having combined the art of design and the techniques of craft in an ultimate execution of wearable jewelry, the craftsmen extended their imagination to *objets d'art*. William Brigham, a student of Denman Ross and Henry Hunt Clark, was a brilliant and unorthodox designer and jeweler. In European travels, he made watercolor studies of works by Benvenuto Cellini in the Uffizi, and Indian and African art in London museums (cat. no. 55).[25] It was only after his retirement from teaching that he put his seasoned study of "Old World" objects into practice. Fanciful objects became his forte, such as *The Argosy*, a sailing ship in jeweled form which drew much acclaim (fig. 32). Incorporating an antique crystal vial, his perfume bottle displays the effects of intricate jewelry techniques, with the beading and jewel styles of the Italian Renaissance combined with an elephant form from Indian art (cat. no. 56). It was no longer wearable art, but embraced that most personal body adornment, perfume.[26] The bottle's style contrasts with the simplicity of the cylindrical cigarette jar with cabochons (cat. no. 54), and points to objects created for personal use in the 1920s and 1930s. ❡ This edging toward the simple planes of modernism is clearly exemplified in Edward Everett Oakes's jeweled silver box (cat. no. 67). The casket is architectural in design, with contained, symmetrical key panels. The pearl and amethyst devices, which are every bit as rich as his jewelry, are integral parts of the structure. The cover is embedded with translucent amethysts and, when opened, the light coming through suggests the religious overtones of stained glass windows. An original thrust toward a new age, this casket fulfills an Arts and Crafts ideal for beautiful objects, in which the artist—with no thought for time, cost, or gain—creates art for art's sake (fig. 33). Immediately highly praised, Oakes's casket was displayed in both Boston and Detroit as "one of the finest pieces of art craftsmanship produced in contemporary America."[27] ❡ Boston's vision in jewelry continued. Oakes, Rogers, and many others worked well into the 1940s, while the larger aspects of the Arts and Crafts movement were assimilated into American life.[28] The guidance of the Jury system instilled the rudiments of design, discipline, and workmanship, leaving a legacy upon which other movements built. But with the passing of the old guard of Jury critics and the growth of individual guilds, artists had the confidence to go beyond the fading Arts and Crafts movement to the studio experimentation and clean lines of modernism. ◉

I would like to thank the generous help of many friends and colleagues, especially Gloria Lieberman (Skinner, Inc.); Judy Anderson (Marblehead Historical Society); Aram Berberian (Ark Antiques); Evelyn Lannon and Janice Chadbourne (Boston Public Library); Robert Brown (Archives of American Art); Shannon Kozak; Jane Port; Suzanne Flynt (Memorial Hall Museum, PVMA); Laurie K. Whitehill (RISD Library); Thomas Michie and Jane Stokes (RISD); Paul Dobbs (Massachusetts College of Art); Rosalie Berberian; Stephen Vaughan; and my editor, Mary Louise Meyer.

25. Grace Slocum, *Who's Who in Rhode Island Art* vol. I (Providence: RISD Library, 1945).

26. *The Argosy* and this perfume bottle were shown together at the Society's thirtieth anniversary exhibition in 1927, and the bottle was featured on the cover of the Society's *Bulletin* that same year. According to commentary in the *Bulletin*, the *Argosy's* creation was "suggested by the boat-shaped piece of amethyst." The ship appears in a period photograph with the penciled identification as the *Argosy*. Its present whereabouts are unknown, but it is often confused with a similar ship in the RISD collection with a hull of amber. Both pieces appear to have rigging and sails made of seed pearls, enamels, and semiprecious stones.

27. Albert Franz Cochrane, "Edward E. Oakes at Arts and Crafts–Museum School Guild's First Display," *Boston Evening Transcript*, May 17, 1929. See also the review in the *Boston Evening Transcript*, October 16, 1929, which called the jewel casket "itself a jewel," and the Edward Everett Oakes papers, AAA/BPL 2805.

28. Many known craftsmen with roots in the Arts and Crafts movement continued their particular style late into the decade, while others evolved clean designs in their later works, which were considered modern. See Jewel Stern, "Striking the Modern Note in Metal," in Janet Kardon, ed., *Craft in the Machine Age, 1920–1945* (New York: Abrams, 1995) p. 122. Jewelers exhibiting at the Worcester Art Museum on April 23, 1943 included William Brigham, Jessie Dunbar, Frank Gardner Hale, Mabel Luther, Edward Everett Oakes, Reginald Pierce, Gertrude Peet, Gertrude Rosendahl, Florence Whitehead, and Hazel Blake French; silversmiths included George Gebelein, James Woolley, Katharine Pratt. SACB archives, AAA/BPL 320:19.

BOSTON

AND THE

SOCIETY

OF

ARTS &
CRAFTS:
TEXTILES

NICOLA J. SHILLIAM

O
F ALL THE products of the American Arts and Crafts movement, textiles—though key features of the adornment of interiors and their inhabitants —remain the least studied, partly because so few of them survive, by reason of their inherent fragility, and partly because the names of their designers and makers were seldom recorded.[1] Given the limitations of current research, any definition of regional characteristics in Arts and Crafts textiles is even more elusive. Nonetheless, factors that may have contributed to the evolution of textile design in Boston include the following: a marked taste for the products of the English Arts and Crafts movement, nurtured by the social elite's ties of heritage, trade, and travel; a nostalgia for the colonial era embodied in treasured ancestral textiles; and an appreciation for the art of the past and of other cultures that was expressed in the great museum and private collections of Boston. The high value that Bostonians placed on art and education also played a significant role in the encouragement of the decorative arts and their application to industry: Boston was the center of a network of thriving educational institutions and great art collections, and of a powerful textile manufacturing industry that drew its designers and craftspeople largely from the local populace. Finally, the prominence of Boston women in reform movements and philanthropy also influenced aspects of the production of textiles. ⟪All of these factors similarly shaped the Society of Arts and Crafts, Boston (SACB) and its influence on textile design and production when the Society was at its zenith (ca. 1897–1927). Textiles produced during this period encompass such a wide variety of techniques that it is not possible to give each sufficient attention here. The rise or fall in popularity of some of these techniques is, to a certain extent, reflected in the membership, exhibitions, and sales records of the SACB. During the last quarter of the nineteenth century, America, as well as Europe, experienced a widespread

1. For recent essays devoted to textiles alone, see Gillian Moss, "Textiles of the American Arts and Crafts Movement," in Linda Parry, William Morris and the Arts and Crafts Movement: A Source Book (New York: Portland House, 1989), pp. 16–22; Christa C. Mayer–Thurman, "Textiles: As Documented by The Craftsman," in Janet Kardon, ed., The Ideal Home, 1900–1920: The History of Twentieth–Century American Craft (New York: Abrams, 1993), pp. 100–10; Nicola J. Shilliam, "Emerging Identity: American Textile Artists from Arts and Crafts to Art Deco," in Marianne Carlano and Nicola J. Shilliam, Early Modern Textiles: From Arts and Crafts to Art Deco (Boston: Museum of Fine Arts, 1993), pp. 28–44.

renewal of interest in handmade textiles, especially needlework. The exhibition of English embroidery at the Philadelphia Centennial Exposition in 1876 inspired Americans to revive traditional needle skills, which had declined by mid–century, overshadowed by such fruits of the industrial revolution as garish aniline dyes and a taste for printed kit embroidery, known as Berlin woolwork.[2] Regional decorative arts and needlework societies established during this period and modeled after English examples facilitated the teaching of skills, the search for sources of good design, and exhibitions of finished works, and in some cases acted as social organizations, offering support for those who desired to make a living by their expertise. ❡ One of the first of these self–help organizations was Boston's Women's Educational and Industrial Union (WEIU), founded in 1877 by Dr. Harriet Clisby, one of America's first female physicians, with the support of prominent Boston women. Created in response to the social problems of a city undergoing rapid industrialization and with a growing immigrant population, the Union was a nonprofit organization formed "to increase fellowship among women with the purpose of promoting the best practical methods for securing their education, industrial, and social advancement," an aim shared by sister organizations such as the New York Society of Decorative Art, also founded in 1877.[3] The Union shop helped women support themselves and their families by the sale of crafts, especially needlework, and classes were offered to prepare women for careers in textile production, retailing, and interior decoration. ❡ Needlework was prominent among the textile crafts represented in the SACB.[4] In its early exhibitions, English Arts and Crafts embroidery was seen as a powerful influence. As Candace Wheeler wrote: "Even in Boston, where, owing to the decided cultivation of art and the early introduction of drawing in the public schools, one would have looked for a rather characteristic development, English designs and English methods have been somewhat closely followed."[5] But others sought inspiration in America's own needlework traditions. Possibly the best known and most studied local group that contributed to the colonial revival style in embroidery was the Society of Blue and White Needlework, Deerfield, founded in 1896 by artists Margaret Whiting (1869–1946) and Ellen Miller (1854–1929).[6] Conceived out of the friends' concern to preserve and record eighteenth–century embroideries in the local museum in Deerfield, the Society grew into a modestly lucrative co–op-

erative enterprise based on Ruskinian principles that numbered thirty–one workers by 1901 (fig. 34).[7] The SACB catalogue commented that their work, displayed at the 1899 exhibition, "while in one sense a revival, may also be considered a survival of the embroidery practised [sic] by the women of Colonial times, when the handicrafts were still part of the natural way of living."[8] Over time, some of the Blue and White Society's work, though still loosely derived from examples of embroidery discovered in institutional and private collections in the Connecticut River Valley, evolved into original work in a more modern style (cat. no. 89). Perennially popular, however, were the doilies and table covers decorated with floral and bird motifs inspired by patterns in the eighteenth–century originals (cat. no. 88). ❡ The work of other groups and individuals—such as the WEIU, with its own notable embroiderers (many of whom also belonged to the SACB), including Mrs. Edward Warren, Mrs. Fred S. Moseley, Mrs. John L. Hall, and Mrs. Harold P. Mosher; and Mrs. Samuel Cabot, an Associate Member of the SACB and a notable scholar of textile history—testified to the continued popularity of colonial revival and English Jacobean needlework patterns in the Boston area well into the 1930s.[9] Although largely inspired by antique textiles, work exhibited by the Guild of Thread and Needleworkers (particularly that of Mildred Mowll, who was active in both the SACB and WEIU) at the SACB's 1926 exhibition in Boston and New York was commended for its suitability to "modern home decoration."[10] Embroideries of this type were also a major component of the needlework shown at the SACB's 1927 exhibition. ❡ A constant concern of the SACB was the improvement of the work of the present through appreciation of the great art of the past. Members were continually urged to study the objects in local institutions and private collections: "We have examples of Greek, Gothic, Renaissance, Chinese, Persian, Japanese, and Moorish craftsmen all around us, in our museums and collections, our homes, in books and photographs, to inspire and guide the worker."[11] The Museum of Fine Arts, Boston in particular provided textile artists with a rich resource of great cultural diversity, thanks to early collectors and educators such as Denman Waldo Ross, Edward Sylvester Morse, and William Sturgis Bigelow. The Textile Study Room was established in 1898 to assist students and members of the local textile manufacturing industry to seek inspiration in the museum's holdings.[12] The School of the Museum of Fine

2. Anthea Callen, *Women Artists of the Arts and Crafts Movement, 1870–1914* (New York: Pantheon Books, 1979), pp. 100–02.

3. Act of Incorporation, April 23, 1880; Archive of the Women's Educational and Industrial Union, 1877–1974, the Schlesinger Library, Radcliffe College, Cambridge, Mass. On the New York Society of Decorative Art, see Candace Wheeler, *The Development of Embroidery in America* (New York and London: Harper, 1921), pp. 112–18.

4. Karen Evans Ulehla, ed., *The Society of Arts and Crafts, Boston: Exhibition Record 1897–1927* (Boston: Boston Public Library, 1981). About 240 individuals or groups are listed in the SACB's craftsman/exhibitor index under the category of "needlework." This figure includes those listed as "designers" if they stated a specialization in embroidery designs.

5. Wheeler, *The Development of Embroidery in America*, p. 118. Included in the SACB's first exhibition was a group of carpets and embroideries designed by William Morris but executed by SACB members.

6. See Georgiana Brown Harbeson, *American Needlework* (New York: Bonanza Books, 1938), pp. 152–55; Margery Burnham Howe, *Deerfield Embroidery* (New York: Scribner, 1976); Wendy Kaplan, ed., "The Art that is Life": The Arts & Crafts Movement in America, 1875–1920 (Boston: Museum of Fine Arts, 1987), pp. 174–75.

7. Margery Burnham Howe, "Deerfield Blue and White Needlework," *Bulletin of the Needle and Bobbin Club* 47, nos. 1 and 2 (1963), p. 50. Receipts for this date totaled $2,126.76 and the workers shared in the profits proportionally to their labor.

8. *Exhibition of the Society of Arts & Crafts, Together with a Loan Collection of Applied Art: Copley and Allston Halls, Boston, 4–15 April 1899* (Boston: Heintzemann Press, 1899), p. 38.

9. Surviving records from the 1930s at the WEIU contain many orders for such patterns. Examples of work in the colonial revival style by some of these women are illustrated in Harbeson, *American Needlework*, between pp. 188 and 191. Mrs. Samuel Cabot (Nancy Graves Cabot) organized several important exhibitions of eighteenth–century American needlework during this period.

10. For an illustration of a wall hanging by Mildred Mowll in the Jacobean style in this exhibition, see "Fine Needlework in Modern Times," *Bulletin of the Society of Arts & Crafts* 10, no. 3 (April 1926), p. 1.

11. *Annual Report of the Society of Arts and Crafts, Boston* (1910), p. 16.

Arts provided classes in design, color, art history, and interior decoration for countless students, some of whom, such as Elwyn G. Gowen (later a teacher at the Museum School) did not specialize in textiles, but worked successfully in various media. Gowen's eclectic block–printed textiles (cat. nos. 82 and 83) suggest his study of the diverse sources available at the museum. Other SACB members studied in different institutions, such as Massachusetts Normal Art School, the School of the Worcester Art Museum, and the Rhode Island School of Design, or in summer schools such as that at Ipswich. Some members, among them H. Stuart Michie, spent substantial periods in England where they absorbed even more of the English Arts and Crafts influence (cat. no. 85). In 1920, American Arts and Crafts objects were compared favorably to a visiting exhibition of English Arts and Crafts—a style still preferred in Boston for its "blessed absence of L'Art Nouveau as expressed by loops and goops."[13] ❡ Ecclesiastical textiles, listed under ecclesiastical art rather than with other textiles, received prominent attention in the Society, especially during the first decade of exhibitions. The participation of Boston's elite in the Anglo–Catholic Episcopalian Church movement was accompanied by a flowering of ecclesiastical art of

English inspiration, including textiles. The architect Ralph Adams Cram and his partner Bertram Grosvenor Goodhue, both members of the SACB, contributed designs for such work, some of which are known to have been executed by the Sisters of the Society of St. Margaret.[14] Established in Boston in 1873 as a branch of an English order based in East Grinsted, Sussex, the Sisters of the Society of St. Margaret achieved a reputation for needlework of high quality, which they exhibited in the 1897 SACB exhibition.[15] Apart from exquisitely embroidered vestments created for their own use, including a cope with embroidered hood (cat. no. 86) whose stylized Tudor rose and pomegranate design bears a striking resemblance to Goodhue's cover for the 1897 SACB exhibition catalogue (fig. 35), the work of the Sisters was commissioned by major Boston churches, including All Saints', Ashmont; St. John the Evangelist, Bowdoin Street; the Church of the Advent, Brimmer Street; and, further afield, the Church of St. James the Less in Philadelphia.[16] ❡ Others who exhibited noteworthy ecclesiastical textiles at the Society included R. Clipston Sturgis, a member of the advisory board of the Society (exhibiting in 1897, 1899), Julia DeWolf Addison (1897, 1899, 1907, 1927), Emma Trevor Bush and the Massachusetts Altar

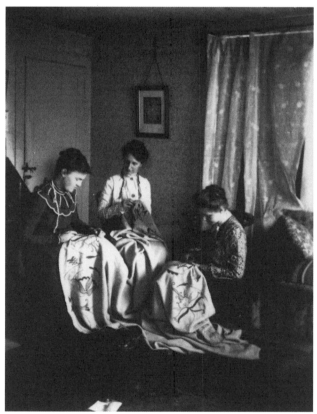

{34} Frances and Mary Allen, *Members of the Deerfield Society of Blue and White Needlework Embroidering a Bed Cover*, ca. 1900, platinum print; Memorial Hall Museum, PVMA, Deerfield.

12. Larry Salmon et al., *From Fiber to Fine Art* (Boston: Museum of Fine Arts, 1980), pp. 3–4. The extent to which local textile manufacturing was directly affected by the Arts and Crafts movement in general and work shown at the SACB in particular remains to be explored. American textile manufacturers had a reputation for copying foreign designs and undervaluing their own designers. Unfortunately, the resources of the Museum of American Textile History, North Andover, Mass., which are particularly relevant to this topic, were unavailable throughout the preparation of the exhibition, owing to the Museum's relocation to new premises.

13. *Annual Report of the Society of Arts and Crafts, Boston* (1920), p. 8. As early as 1906 a dislike of Art Nouveau—"the work of the untrained, underdeveloped, unstocked brain and the faltering hand"—was expressed in the Society's publication, the *Annual Report of the Society of Arts and Crafts, Boston* (1906), p. 7.

14. See Douglass Shand–Tucci, *Boston Bohemia, 1881–1900: Volume One of Ralph Adams Cram: Life and Architecture* (Amherst: University of Massachusetts Press, 1994), pp. 297–99, 422.

15. *First Exhibition of the Society of Arts & Crafts, Copley Hall, Boston, 5–16 April 1897* (Boston: Heintzemann Press, 1897), pp. 6–7.

16. On the embroidery of the Sisters of the Society of St. Margaret, see Sister Catherine Louise, S.S.M., *The House of My Pilgrimage: History of the American House of the Society of St. Margaret, 1873–1973* (Boston: publ. by the Sisters of the Society of St. Margaret, ca. 1973), pp. 26–27; Sister Mary Elisabeth, S.S.M., "St. Margaret's School of Embroidery," *The Church Militant* (May 1955), pp. 9–10. On All Saints', Ashmont, see Robert Brown, "All Saints' Church," *Architectural Review* 7 (August 1900); Ralph Adams Cram, "All Saints' Church, Dorchester (Boston), Mass.," *The Churchman* 79 (April 15, 1899), pp. 560–63. For an illustration of the altar cloth at All Saints', see Douglass Shand–Tucci, *All Saints', Ashmont, Dorchester, Boston: A Centennial History of the Parish* (Boston: All Saints' Church, 1975), front cover illustration.

Society (1917, 1927), and Mrs. Marion Sousa and Saint Catherine's Guild (1927). Beyond Boston, fine ecclesiastical work was made by groups such as the Newport–based Aquidneck Cottage Industries, an example of whose work was a cutwork and embroidered linen altar cloth designed by Louisa Sturtevant for St. George's School, Newport, Rhode Island.[17] In 1906, the SACB Jury explicitly encouraged the submission of more ecclesiastical art, perhaps in response to a decline in the quantity or quality of such work.[18] By the 1927 exhibition, listings of ecclesiastical art, particularly textiles, had dwindled significantly. ⟨Lace–making was one of the traditional immigrant crafts that was well represented in the SACB, and this subject offers insight into the sometimes conflicting viewpoints of SACB members. During the second half of the nineteenth century, the revival of lace–making in Europe was often sponsored by upper–class women who regarded the patronage of peasant women exercising "traditional" skills as their philanthropic duty.[19] This notion of philanthropy found fertile ground in the United States in the early twentieth century, in urban centers such as the Scuola d'Industrie Italiane, New York, and at Denison House and South End House, social settlement houses in Boston. There recent immigrants were encour-

aged to revive traditional lace–making, thus achieving several Arts and Crafts ideals: hand labor, fulfillment through work, and the creation of beautiful, useful objects.[20] Concerning the 1899 SACB exhibition, the *Boston Daily Advertiser* reported: "To the women one of the most interesting collections at the Arts and Crafts is the Italian lace, which is very beautiful. It is certainly pleasing to know that a great part of it was made by Italian women right here in Boston."[21] The daily demonstrations of lace–making on a lace pillow by a young Italian woman were particularly popular (cat. no. 92). ⟨In 1902, the Circolo Italo–Americano was established at Denison House to foster good community relations between Americans and Italian immigrants in the Boston area. As Eileen Boris has noted, "Denison House emphasized 'immigrant gifts' when cultural pluralism was a radical idea."[22] One of the driving forces of the Circolo was its president, Vida Scudder, a Wellesley professor and social activist. "Few people realize the rising importance of the Italians in Boston as a political factor," Scudder argued forcefully. "They now number over 60,000 and they are beginning to waken to their political power....Let us all—we Americans who are trying to look ahead, to guard against the 'melting–pot' melting out the best and leaving

17. Illustrated by Georgiana Harbeson, *American Needlework*, opp. p. 168.

18. *Annual Report of the Society of Arts and Crafts*, Boston (1906), p. 7.

19. On the revival of lace–making in Europe in this period, see Santina Levey, *Lace: A History* (London: Victoria & Albert Museum; Leeds: W.S. Maney, 1983), pp. 111–15.

20. On lace–making in Boston and New York, see Kaplan, "The Art that is Life," p. 311; Eileen Boris, *Art and Labor: Ruskin, Morris, and the Craftsman Ideal in America* (Philadelphia: Temple University Press, 1986), pp. 134–38; Eva Lovett, "An Italian Lace School in New York," *International Studio* 29 (July 1906), p. xii.

21. *Boston Daily Advertiser*, April 8, 1899, p. 8.

22. Boris, *Art and Labor*, p. 133.

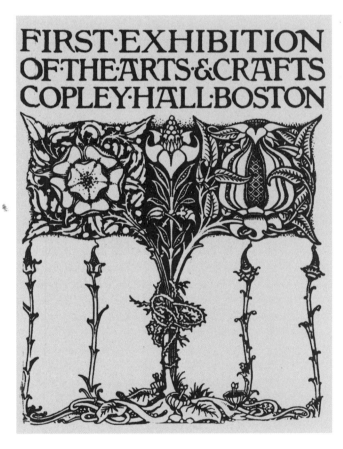

FIRST·EXHIBITION OF·THE·ARTS·&·CRAFTS COPLEY·HALL·BOSTON

{35} SACB exhibition catalogue cover, 1897, designed by Bertram Grosvenor Goodhue; Fine Arts Department, Boston Public Library.

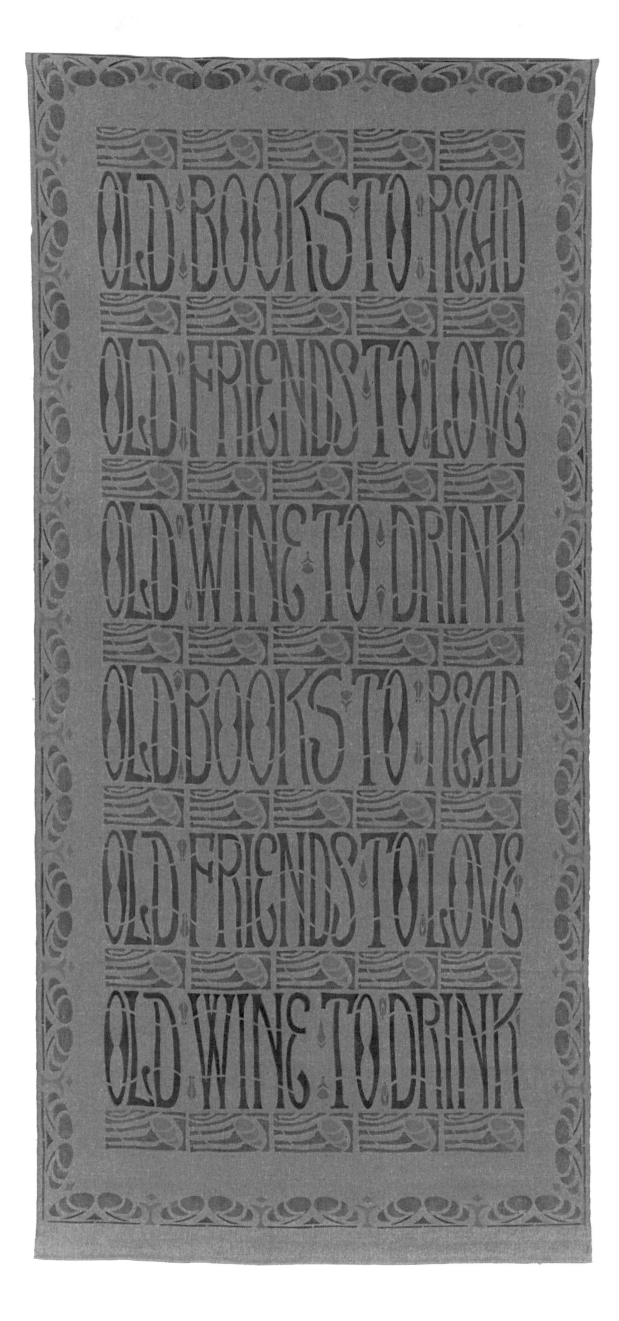

CAT. NO. 85
H. Stuart Michie,
Old Books to Read,
ca. 1905

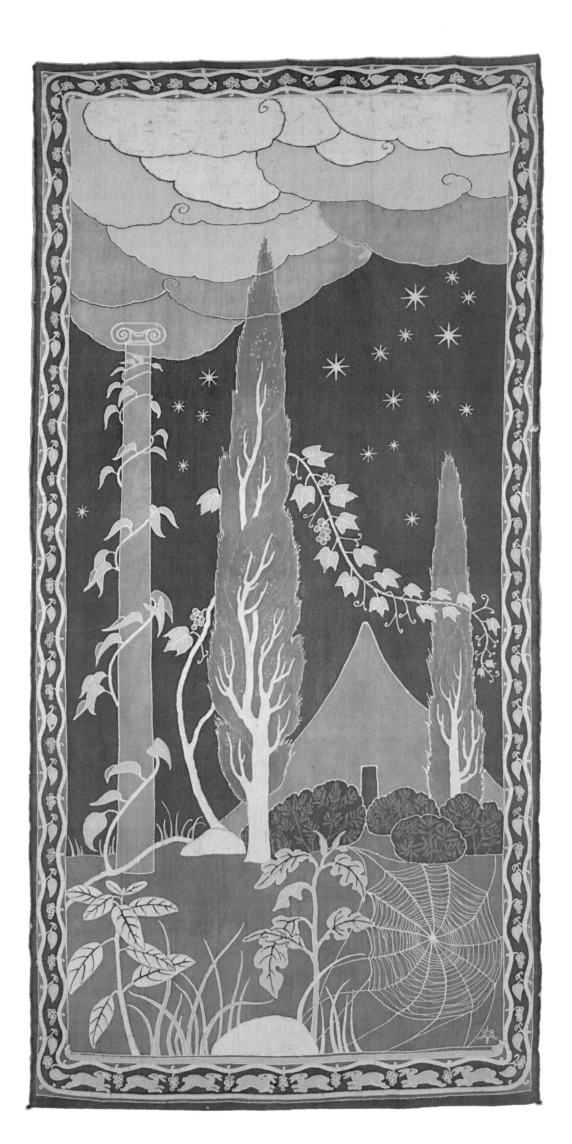

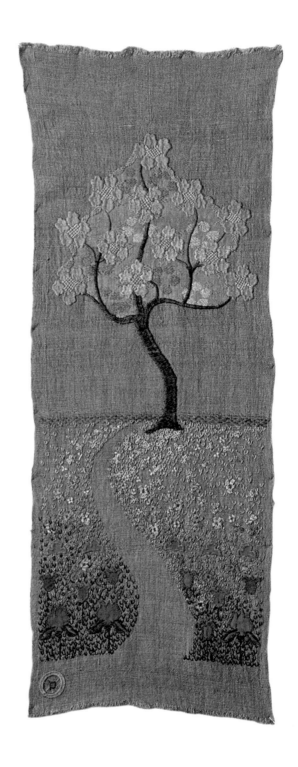

CAT. NO. 89
Society of Blue and
White Needlework,
Deerfield, makers,
Rose Tree,
ca. 1896–1926

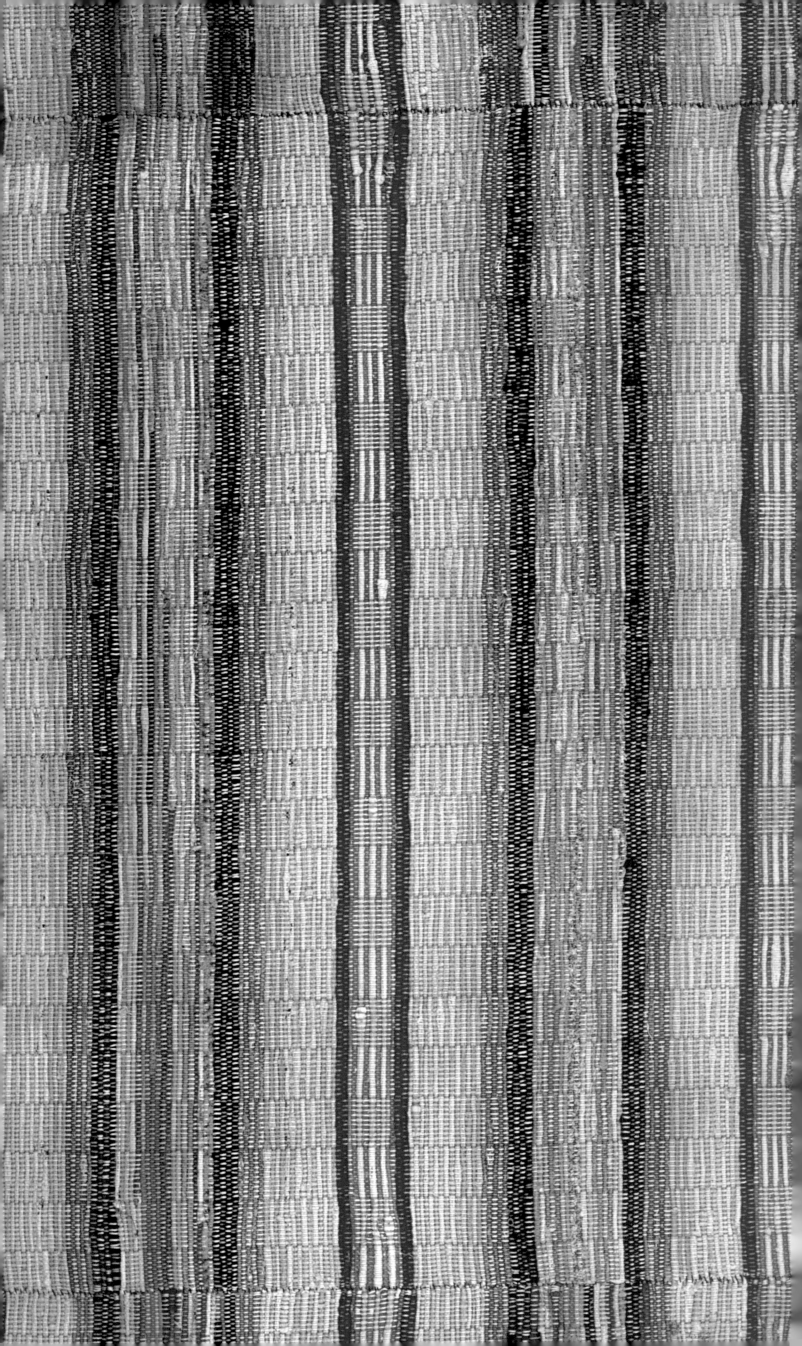

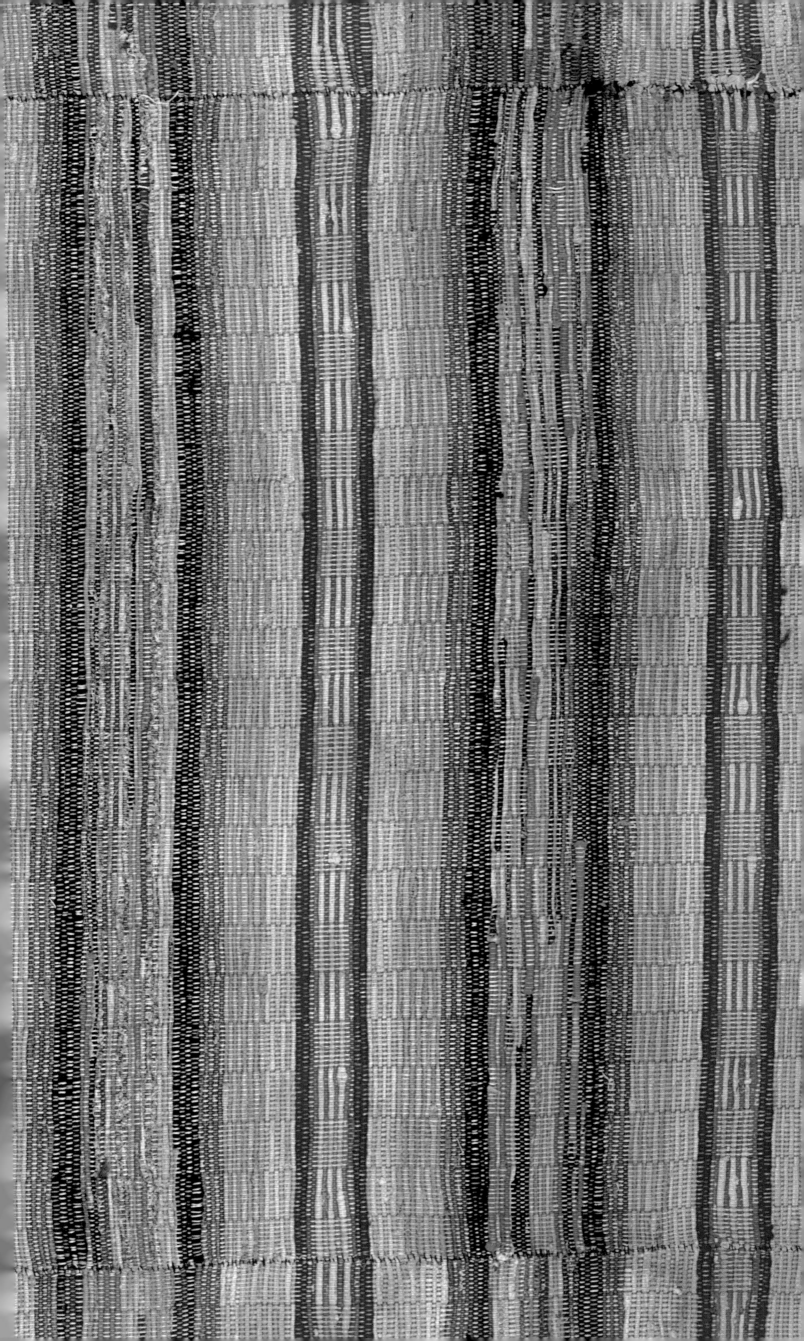

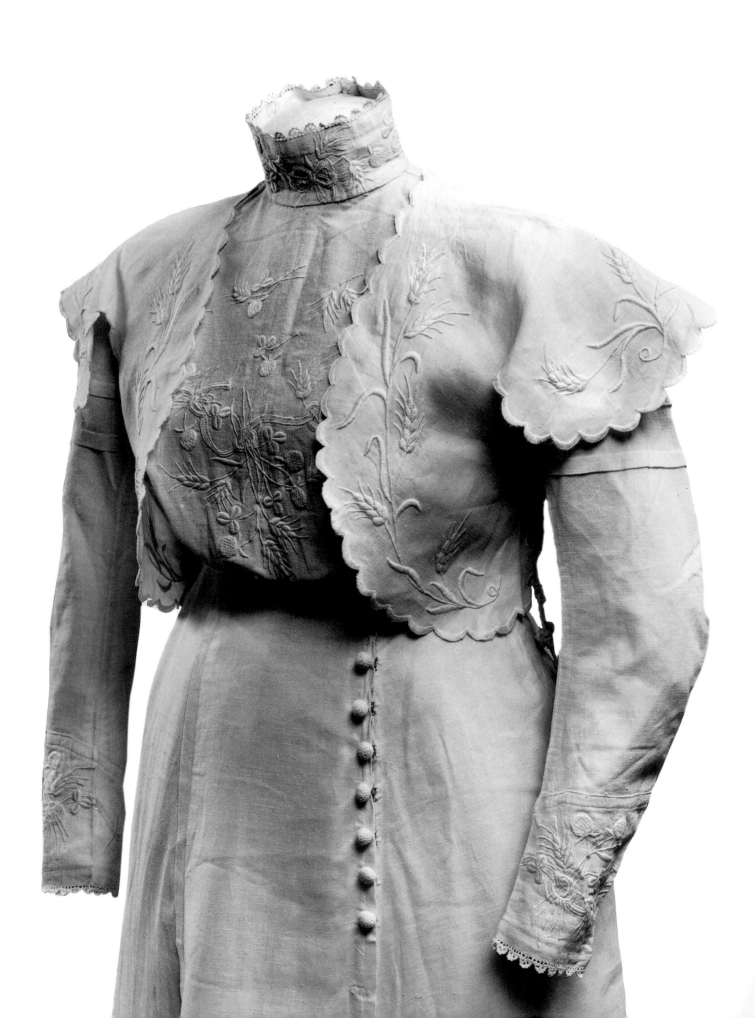

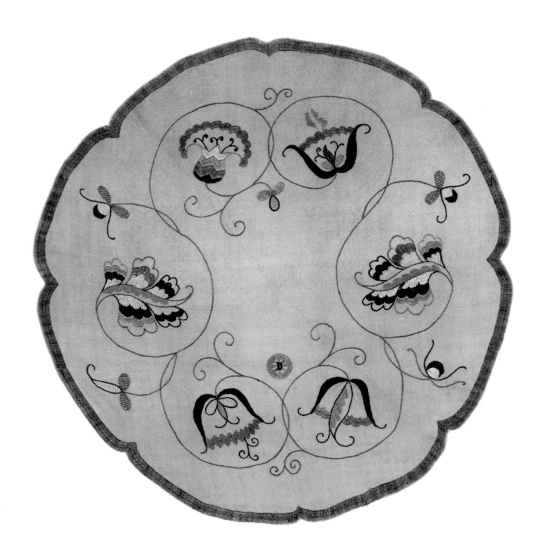

CAT. NO. 88A
Society of Blue and White
Needlework, Deerfield,
makers; Margaret Whiting,
probable designer,
Circular cover with floral
design, ca. 1896–1926

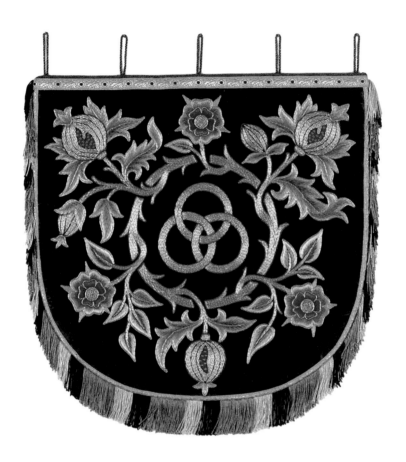

CAT. NO. 86
St. Margaret's School
of Embroidery, makers;
Bertram Grosvenor Goodhue,
possible designer,
Embroidered hood (from a
cope) with Tudor rose and
pomegranate design, ca. 1900

the dross to be fused into our national character —let us help to save as much as possible of this quality by actively interesting ourselves in this Arts and Crafts movement."[23] From 1908, the activities of the Women's Club at Denison House included a lace–making class, originally comprised of four young girls (fig. 36), under the instruction of Mabel Foster, listed as a Craftsman in the SACB between 1906 and 1909.[24] In addition, Denison House acted as a clearinghouse for Italian–American and, later, other immigrant groups' crafts, including lace–making (cat. no. 80). A notable Italian–American lace–maker associated with the Circolo Italo–Americano was Teresa Pellegrini, who was elected a Master in the SACB in 1912.[25] ❲ Sylvester Baxter, however, in his article in *Handicraft* on lace–making in Boston, took a more patrician attitude by emphasizing the role of Mrs. E.J. Weber as a pioneer of the lace–making revival in the city. Florence Weber, a Master in the SACB and a student of the Museum School, had access to the lace collection in the Museum of Fine Arts, and studied related literature at the Boston Public Library. Baxter contrasted this scholarly study of lace with "the making of pillow lace in its coarser forms [that] had long been carried on in Boston by women of the large colony that occupies the 'Little Italy'

quarter of the city."[26] He suggested that three lessons in lace–making given by one of "these Italian women" to Mrs. Weber were a symbolic link: "the lace–workers afforded the connecting link that joined the higher developments of the art on this side of the water with the industry in its manifold historic aspects." According to Baxter, when Weber introduced her work to the SACB, the Society "saw in it the suggestion for a new local industry that perhaps might to a considerable degree advance the realization of its ideals for work that would interest and delight the workers in making things of beauty, and would correspondingly benefit the world."[27] Weber implemented these ideals at South End House, where she instructed girls in making higher–priced "refined" laces rather than coarser "peasant" laces, with the result that "from shop–girls they find themselves transformed to artist–artisans" who are "happy in their work."[28] ❲ Textiles for interior decoration formed quite a large proportion of the textiles exhibited by the Society (fig. 37). Specialty shops like that of George Fenety, who supplied kits and custom–made textiles such as curtains and covers (cat. no. 81) to local customers for several decades, used the Society's early exhibitions as occasions for self–promotion by showing high–quality,

23. "La Nostra Piccola Esposizione," *Bollettino del Circolo Italo–Americano* 3, no. 2 (December 1910), p. 1.

24. Ulehla, *The Society of Arts and Crafts, Boston*, p. 85.

25. There is a discrepancy between the dates given for Teresa Pellegrini as a Craftsman and a Master in the original biographical sheets on consignors in the Papers of the Society of Arts and Crafts, Boston, Archives of American Art/Boston Public Library, and in the published exhibition record (Ulehla, *The Society of Arts and Crafts, Boston*, p. 170, where Pellegrini and listed as a Craftsman 1907–12 and Master 1913–27).

26. Sylvester Baxter, "Lace–making in Boston," *Handicraft* 1 (1902), p. 64.

27. Baxter, "Lace–making in Boston," p. 66.

28. Baxter, "Lace–making in Boston," pp. 71–72.

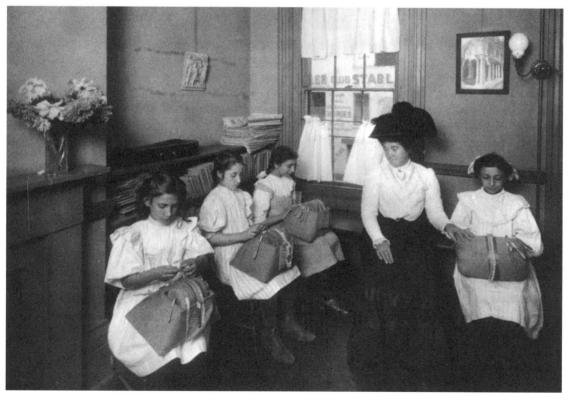

{36} Photograph of lace–making class at Denison House, ca. 1908; the Schlesinger Library, Radcliffe College.

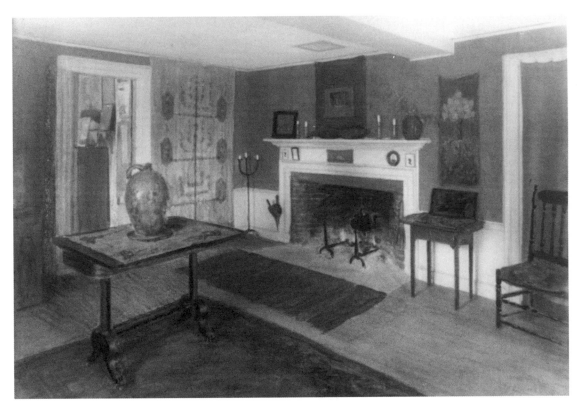

{37} Hand–colored photograph of the north parlor of the Nims House, Society of Blue and White Needlework, Deerfield, showing the *Rose Tree* wall hanging (CAT. NO. 89); Memorial Hall Museum, PVMA, Deerfield.

hand–decorated textiles. On the other hand, although textiles for personal adornment appear to have been less numerous in the SACB exhibitions, hand–decorated clothing was certainly popular during the period (cat. no. 84) and dress was, undoubtedly, a concern of Boston women, who had been in the forefront of the dress reform movement in America.[29] ⟪ A particular form of textiles for interior decoration that appears to have attracted the criticism of the SACB was rug–making.[30] Wealthy Bostonians had typically favored expensive, imported Oriental rugs or English Arts and Crafts carpets. Yet homemade rugs, with their colonial revival connotations of traditional "craft," and inexpensive, easily cleaned rugs and disposable summer carpeting that could be changed with the season, were popularized by magazines such as *House Beautiful*. This renewed interest in rug–making encouraged the production of simple hooked or woven rag rugs by many local individuals and Arts and Crafts societies.[31] More than thirty individuals and societies are listed as "rug–makers" in the SACB list. Enthusiastic rug–makers, such as Madeline Yale Wynne, waxed lyrical on the topic of the humble rag rug: "Rag rug, indeed! It is the summer, the hillside, and the sweet Adirondack fragrance coming to

one in short lengths."[32] Candace Wheeler subtitled her *How to Make Rugs* (1903), significantly, "How to Make Happiness and to Awaken Social Consciousness." Rugs that achieved wider acclaim were those with labels, such as the hooked Abnákee rugs with Native American motifs, from Pequaket, New Hampshire (shown by Helen Albee at the SACB's 1899 exhibition), and Sabatos and Cranberry Isles rugs, both from Maine. Perhaps less well known are Subbekashe rugs, again with Native American–inspired designs, first made in 1902 by Lucy D. Thomson in Belchertown, Massachusetts; the rag rugs produced by the Society of Arts and Crafts, Hingham (cat. no. 87); the Deerfield Rug Makers; and "Pilgrim" rugs from Pittsfield.[33] By 1915, even the SACB Jury noted that "woven rag mats have improved in their combination of color."[34] Basketry, which also underwent a revival in such centers as Hingham and Deerfield during this period, but which is not represented in this exhibition, also drew some rather elitist criticism from the Jury.[35] ⟪ One textile technique featured in exhibitions of the Society of Arts and Crafts, Boston in the 1910s and 1920s was not a revival but an innovation. Batik, a wax–resist dyeing technique used primarily for the decoration of textiles, was virtually

29. On dress reform in Boston see Sally Buchanan Kinsey, "A More Reasonable Way to Dress," in Kaplan, "The Art that is Life," pp. 358–69; Marianne Carlano, "Anti–Fashion in Boston: Rational, Hygienic and Artistic Dress during the Second Half of the Nineteenth Century," *Textile and Text* 13, no. 3 (1991), pp. 23–42.

30. "On the Making of Hooked Rugs," *Handicraft* 3 (1910–11), pp. 284–91.

31. An exhibition of "Furnishings for a Summer Home" at the SACB Gallery in 1914 "was something of a novelty and proved interesting and successful. There was a showing of furniture, suggestions for interior decoration, hangings, embroideries, pottery, baskets and hand–woven rugs suitable for summer cottages"; see *Annual Report of the Society of Arts and Crafts, Boston* (1914), p. 13.

32. Madeline Yale Wynne, "How to Make Rugs," *House Beautiful* 13 (August 1903), p. 162.

33. On rug–making see Boris, *Art and Labor*, pp. 127–29 and bibliography; Max West, "The Revival of Handicraft in America," U.S. Bureau of Labor, *Bulletin* 55 (November 1904), pp. 1573–97; Allen H. Eaton, *Handicrafts of New England* (New York: Bonanza Books, 1949), pp. 118–131. On Hingham, see Susan Willard, "The Hingham Society of Arts and Crafts" in *Hingham* (Hingham, Mass.: Old Colony Chapter, Daughters of the American Revolution, 1911), pp. 120–21.

34. *Annual Report of the Society of Arts and Crafts, Boston* (1915), p. 10.

35. "The Jury wishes to call attention to the classes of least developed work present. First, basketry: It is disappointing that Philippines, Indian, or Mexican basketry should be so much finer than others, and that coarse, loose weavings should be so persistently offered for acceptance."; *Annual Report of the Society* (1914), p. 10.

unknown in America before the early twentieth century. Inspired by Javanese batik textiles from the Dutch East Indies first displayed at the Paris International Exposition in 1900, avant–garde artists, first in Europe and then in America, began to experiment with the technique. Young American artists, including Marguerite Thompson Zorach (wife of printmaker William Zorach), Hazel Burnham Slaughter, Martha Ryther (born in Boston), and Lydia Bush–Brown began to make batik textiles in the 1910s. Batiks took major prizes in an important series of competitions, sponsored by the Art Alliance of America and *Women's Wear* between 1916 and 1920, intended to encourage innovation in American textile design through the study of primitive and non–Western art in American museum collections. From an early date, local artists were able to study authentic Javanese batiks in the Museum of Fine Arts, Boston. The museum, through Denman Ross, had acquired five batiks from the Javanese Village at the 1893 World's Columbian Exposition, and Ross added sixty–six more in 1911.[36] Batik–decorated clothing—originally considered rather bohemian, since it was often worn by the artists who made it—was sold in "artistic" boutiques and later by the more avant–garde department stores, and became quite fashionable in the 1910s and 1920s.[37] ❰ Although New York artists pioneered the use of batik, the new technique soon spread to other American art centers, including Boston. Articles in popular journals and do–it–yourself manuals encouraged amateurs to try the new technique, which shared something of the appeal of stenciling, although it was technically more demanding.[38] As more batiks were submitted to the SACB, the Critic of the Jury remarked: "Batik has steadily improved, the dyes are excellent, and there is more pattern in the designs. Too violent color transitions are less frequent."[39] In 1919, a curious comparison was made between the relative merits of batik and embroidery: "Batik is becoming better in design but is unfortunately superseding embroidery."[40]

Some of the better known batik artists, such as Hazel Burnham Slaughter and Lydia Bush–Brown (cat. no. 79), exhibited several times at the SACB. Local artists who showed batiks at the SACB included Francisca Machado Warren, hailed as "the first to exhibit her original work in this line at the rooms of the Society of Arts and Crafts"; Laura Lee; Richard Wight Sprigings; and Roy P. Williams.[41] As the Society declined during the 1920s, batik, which appears to have been considered more modern and original than much of the embroidery submitted, also sold better than embroideries. ❰ The conflict between the refined taste of the elite of the SACB, shaped by the art of Europe's great museums, and the philanthropic impulses of that same elite, engaged by the textile skills of immigrants and the revival of the "simple" crafts of colonial ancestors, was reflected in the struggles between the different factions within the SACB—and in the often paternalistic pronouncements of the SACB juries, to which textiles were frequently subjected.[42] Ultimately, elitism and tradition may have prevented the evolution of the Society toward modernism in the decorative arts during the second quarter of the twentieth century. ◎

Of the many people who helped to make this project possible, I would like to give special thanks to Sister Adele Marie and Sister Esther (Sisters of the Society of St. Margaret); Oliver D. Avens; Anne M. Donaghy and Richard Nylander (SPNEA); Suzanne L. Flynt (Memorial Hall Museum, PVMA); Marie–Hélène Gold, Bert Hartry, and Eva Moseley (the Arthur and Elizabeth Schlesinger Library on the History of Women in America, Radcliffe College); Kristin Hardin (Prairie Avenue House Museums, Chicago); Shannon Kozak; Deborah E. Kraak (Henry Francis du Pont Winterthur Museum); Marilee Boyd Meyer; Gillian Moss (Cooper–Hewitt National Design Museum); Pamela B. Parmal (Museum of Art, RISD); Brother Eldridge Pendleton; Anne B. Poulet (Museum of Fine Arts, Boston); Janet Schallenberger (WEIU); Nancy B. Tiffin (Hingham Historical Society); Susan Ward; and the staff of the Fine Arts Library, Boston Public Library.

36. Susan MacMillan Arensberg, *Javanese Batiks* (Boston: Museum of Fine Arts, ca. 1978), introduction.

37. See Nicola J. Shilliam, "From Bohemian to Bourgeois: American Batik in the Early Twentieth Century," in *Contact, Crossover, Continuity: Proceedings of the Fourth Biennial Symposium of The Textile Society of America* (Los Angeles: Fowler Museum of Cultural History, UCLA, 1994), pp. 253–63.

38. Particularly influential were Amy Mali Hicks, "Batik, Its Making and Its Use," *House & Garden* (November 1913), pp. 289–90, 318–19; Frances Gifford, "How Batiks Are Made," *American Silk Journal* 37 (May 1918), pp. 67–71; and Pieter Mijer, *Batiks and How to Make Them* (New York: Dodd, Mead and Company, 1919).

39. *Annual Report of the Society* (1920), p. 9.

40. *Annual Report of the Society* (1919), p. 7.

41. See "Batiks by Miss Warren," *Boston Evening Transcript*, May 3, 1920, p. 14.

42. For example, on the conflict between SACB members Mary Ware Dennett and H. Langford Warren, which contributed to Dennett's decision to resign from the council in 1905, see Boris, *Art and Labor*, pp. 37–45.

A MILLENNIUM IN BOOK-MAKING: THE BOOK ARTS IN BOSTON

NANCY FINLAY

IN 1922, WHEN the Boston printer Daniel Berkeley Updike published his treatise, *Printing Types: Their History, Forms and Use*, he claimed that the Kelmscott editions of William Morris "opened the millennium in book–making."[1] "Millennium" here is meant in the Biblical sense, as the age that was to begin with the Second Coming of Christ, when there would be a new heaven and a new earth, after the old heaven and the old earth had passed away. So radical and far–reaching were the changes in printing practices ushered in by the Arts and Crafts movement that Updike's statement hardly seems an exaggeration. Although by 1922 Updike and his contemporaries had rejected the heavy types and elaborate ornaments typical of Morris's work, they continued to seek a unity of effect and a typographic style appropriate to the content of their books. The idea that the overall design of a book should be in the control of a single individual was virtually unheard of prior to the 1890s; by the 1920s, book design was a highly esteemed profession. ❡ No one in Boston in the early 1890s was more impressed by the work of William Morris than Daniel Berkeley Updike. Updike came to Boston from Providence in 1880 and went to work for Houghton Mifflin and Company to learn the printing trade. Boston in the 1890s was still unrivaled as a center of printing and publishing, with large commercial houses such as Little, Brown and Company and Ginn and Company; small literary publishers such as Copeland & Day and Small, Maynard and Company; and a host of allied industries. Although Boston's day as the literary capital of the nation was over, the quality of Boston book–making was widely admired and many New York publishers still had their books printed or bound there. At Houghton Mifflin, Sarah Wyman Whitman had been campaigning since the early 1880s to improve the appearance of the firm's trade bindings, introducing light colors and simple designs (cat. no. 109). Whitman was a society matron who designed stained glass as well as book covers,

1. Daniel Berkeley Updike, *Printing Types: Their History, Forms and Use: A Study in Survivals*, 2nd ed. (Cambridge: Harvard University Press, 1937), p. 204.

and was personally acquainted with many of the authors for whose books she provided cover designs. ❡ Updike designed one book reflecting Morris's influence before leaving Houghton Mifflin to establish his own Merrymount Press. *A Day at LaGuerre's* by F. Hopkinson Smith (fig. 38), published in 1892, has been described as the first American book to reflect the influence of Kelmscott.[2] Although there is nothing radical about the layout of the text, the cover and title-page incorporate a black and white vine border by Harold van Buren Magonigle and a printer's mark designed for Houghton Mifflin and Company by the British designer Walter Crane during a visit to Boston in 1891–92.[3] Updike's contribution was the arrangement of the page, the juxtaposition of type and ornaments, the use of red for the title, and the choice of the Arts and Crafts style. Other Boston publishers also were quick to imitate Morris's decorations. From Copeland & Day came editions of Dante Gabriel Rossetti's *House of Life* (1894) and Wilfred Scawen Blunt's *Esther: A Young Man's Tragedy* (1895), both with elaborate decorations by Bertram Grosvenor Goodhue.[4] In 1896, Houghton Mifflin published Thomas Bailey Aldrich's *Friar Jerome's Beautiful Book*, with decorations by William Snelling Hadaway, and Updike produced *The Altar Book*, perhaps the

finest of all American Arts and Crafts books, a large folio with lavish borders, initials, and type by Goodhue, as well as full-page illustrations by the British artist Robert Anning Bell (cat. no. 97). ❡ Morris's was not the only style to influence Boston bookmaking, however. Sarah Wyman Whitman looked to the book covers of Dante Gabriel Rossetti for inspiration for her cover designs. Walter Crane's visual influence was apparent in posters and poster-style book cover designs and decorations by Ethel Reed and Amy Sacker. The decadent images of Aubrey Beardsley were another important influence on Reed, as well as on Will Bradley, who moved from Chicago in 1894 to set up his Wayside Press in Springfield, Massachusetts. Bradley was also aware of the work of contemporary French poster artists Eugène Grasset and Henri de Toulouse-Lautrec. An enthusiasm for French Impressionist and post-Impressionist art was shared by Thomas Buford Meteyard—who produced book designs for Copeland & Day and Lamson, Wolfe & Co.—and Arthur Wesley Dow, who is best known for his color woodblock prints, but who also designed a few book covers and at least one poster. An interest in Japanese art was common to many artists and is especially apparent in the work of Whitman and Dow. ❡ Throughout the nineties,

2. Susan Otis Thompson, "The Arts and Crafts Book," in *The Arts and Crafts Movement in America, 1876–1911* (Princeton, N.J.: Princeton University Press, 1972), p. 97.

3. See Nancy Finlay, *Artists of the Book in Boston, 1890–1910* (Cambridge: Houghton Library, 1985), p. 4. On Crane's experiences in Boston, see Walter Crane, *An Artist's Reminiscences* (London: Methuen, 1907), pp. 360–409.

4. For a bibliography of the work of Copeland & Day, see Joe Walker Kraus, *Messrs. Copeland & Day, 69 Cornhill, Boston, 1893–1899* (Philadelphia: G.S. MacManus Co., 1979).

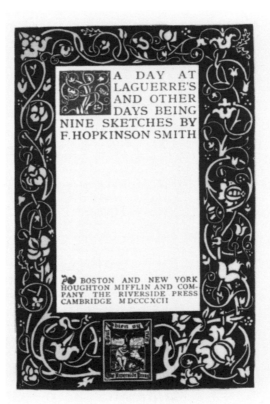

{38} Title-page of F.H. Smith's *A Day at LaGuerre's and Other Days*, designed by Daniel Berkeley Updike; border by Harold van Buren Magonigle; printer's mark by Walter Crane; Houghton Library, Harvard University.

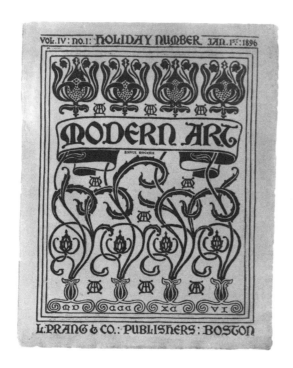

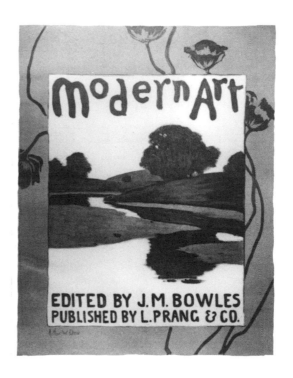

{39A} Bruce Rogers's cover design for L. Prang and Company's *Modern Art* 4, r.o. 1 (January 1, 1896); Houghton Library, Harvard University.

{39B} Poster by Arthur Wesley Dow for L. Prang and Company's *Modern Art*, 1895; Fine Arts Department, Boston Public Library.

Boston book artists drew freely on these widely differing styles, producing designs of great richness and lavishness; their unfettered exuberance remains extraordinarily appealing, perhaps at least in part because it is so clearly a reflection of youthful enthusiasm and high spirits. This enthusiasm also found an outlet in various associations between artists and writers, among them the Pewter Mugs and the Visionists.5 A forum for self–expression was provided by an array of periodicals, ranging from such informal and personal efforts as the *Courrier Innocent*—printed by Thomas Buford Meteyard and a changing cast of companions with linoleum blocks and a rolling pin—through ambitious manifestos such as the *Knight Errant* and *Modern Art*. The *Knight Errant*, established in 1892 by Bertram Grosvenor Goodhue, his architectural partner Ralph Adams Cram, and the printer Francis Watts Lee, survived only a few short months, but its influence lasted much longer. Bruce Rogers accompanied *Modern Art* to Boston when it moved east from Indianapolis in 1895. His design for its cover (fig. 39A) shows how thoroughly he had absorbed the lessons of Crane and Morris. In contrast, Dow's poster for *Modern Art* (fig. 39B, cat. no. 133) is purely French, echoing Monet's

Mornings on the Seine, with which it is roughly contemporary. ❨ The first Exhibition of the Arts and Crafts in Copley Hall in 1897 provided an effective showcase for what was by then widely perceived as a "new movement" in the book arts (fig. 40). Notices of Whitman's book covers for Houghton Mifflin and Company (cat. no. 111), Rogers's designs for *Modern Art*, and a grouping of book covers, bookplates, and illustrations by Amy Sacker and her students at the Cowles School were generally favorable. The *Altar Book* was among the stars of the show, and a specimen page for Updike's *Tacitus* (cat. no. 98), which would not be published until 1904, was widely admired.6 Other reviewers were attracted by the flamboyant Art Nouveau decorations of Will Bradley and E.B. Bird.7 ❨ In every mention of the exhibition, the book arts figured prominently, often more than any other branch of the Arts and Crafts. Some criticism was directed at the exhibition for its commercialism, however, and for its supposed lack of understanding of the true principles behind the Arts and Crafts movement. Although this criticism was not directed specifically at the book arts, it might well have been, for much of the work on view had been executed for commercial publishers, and in

5. The Pewter Mugs was a drinking and dining society; the Visionists appear to have been more mystical and philosophical in their interests, though high spirits and good fellowship were still much in evidence. The membership of the two groups overlapped to a large extent. Ralph Adams Cram, *My Life in Architecture* (Boston: Little, Brown and Company, 1936) is still the best account of this period. More recent interpretations are found in Estelle Jussim, *Slave to Beauty: The Eccentric Life and Controversial Career of F. Holland Day, Photographer, Publisher, Aesthete* (Boston: D.R. Godine, 1981) and Douglass Shand-Tucci, *Boston Bohemia, 1881–1900: Volume One of Ralph Adams Cram: Life and Architecture* (Amherst: University of Massachusetts Press, 1994).

7. *Boston Daily Globe*, April 14, 1897; *Springfield Republican*, April 17, 1897.

6. Sarah Wyman Whitman, on viewing the *Tacitus* specimen at this exhibition, is said to have exclaimed, "Phoebus, what a page!": Ray Nash, *Printing as an Art* (Cambridge: publ. for the Society of Printers by Harvard University Press, 1955), p. 33. When *Tacitus* was finally published in 1904, lettering by Whitman adorned the cover.

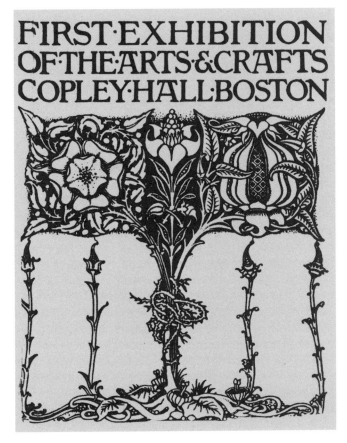

virtually all of it the artist's role had been limited to that of designer. "Decorative design" was on the point of becoming "commercial art," and many of the artists who started out designing posters and gold–stamped trade bindings would wind up producing advertisements. Aside from the craft of printing, there were very few examples of handicraft among the book arts. A great many of the best book artists did not produce the things they designed. That was left to someone else, and often it was done mechanically, taking advantage of the latest technology (fig. 41). ⅭAmong the printers who played a prominent role in the founding of the Society of Arts and Crafts, Boston (SACB) were Carl H. Heintzemann, Henry Lewis Johnson, and Daniel Berkeley Updike. Johnson had learned the craft of printing from Heintzemann and was one of the chief instigators of the 1897 exhibition. Although Updike's involvement with the Society of Arts and Crafts has often been minimized, he was extremely active during the Society's early years, serving on numerous committees with Heintzemann and Johnson. Sarah Wyman Whitman (cat. nos. 109–111) and later Julia DeWolf Addison (cat. no. 93), Amy Sacker (cat. nos. 106 and 107), and Mary Crease Sears (cat. no. 108) were also tireless

committee members, devoting much time and energy to the Society's activities. Perhaps one reason printers took a special interest in the Society is that, like architects, they were frequently obliged to orchestrate the talents of craftsmen in many different fields. Just as an architect might call upon stone–carvers, wood–carvers, and workers in metal, stained glass, and textiles to carry out and amplify his or her designs, a publishing project such as *The Altar Book* could enlist the talents of illustrator, decorator, designer, and binder, in addition to the compositors and pressmen who actually printed the book. Other projects might employ calligraphers and illuminators in an attempt to rival early manuscripts. The Society of Arts and Crafts provided a forum where practitioners of these crafts could meet, examine one another's work, and make useful contacts. ⅭThe founding of the Society of Arts and Crafts occurred at a propitious moment for the book arts, a moment when many talented men and women had been drawn to Boston by the prospect of a career in book design or book decoration in the city's printing and publishing industries. Most of these artists were young and much of their work was deliberately experimental. The purpose of the SACB, as stated by its first

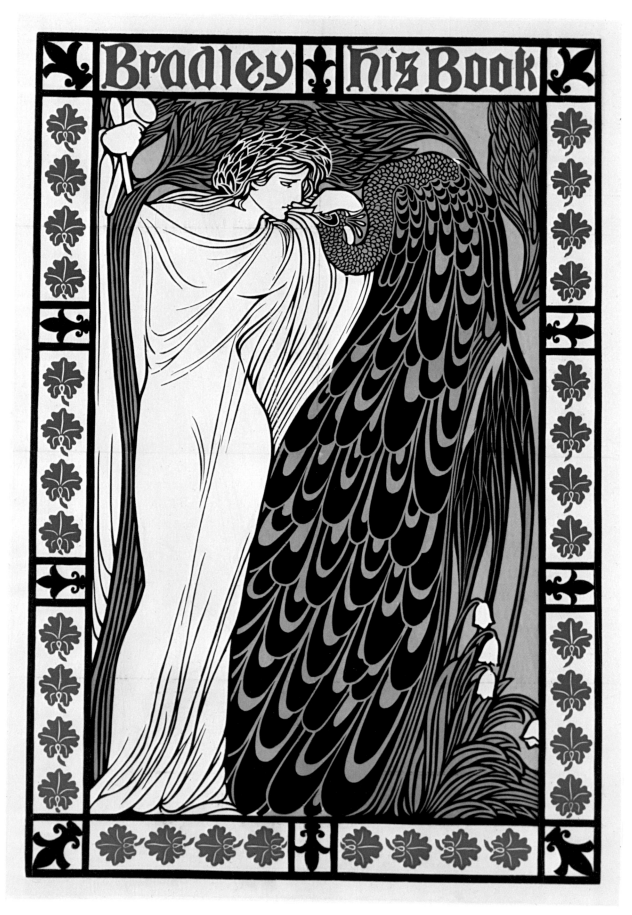

CAT. NO. 95
Will Bradley,
poster designer;
Bradley: His Book, No. 30
[*The Kiss*], 1896

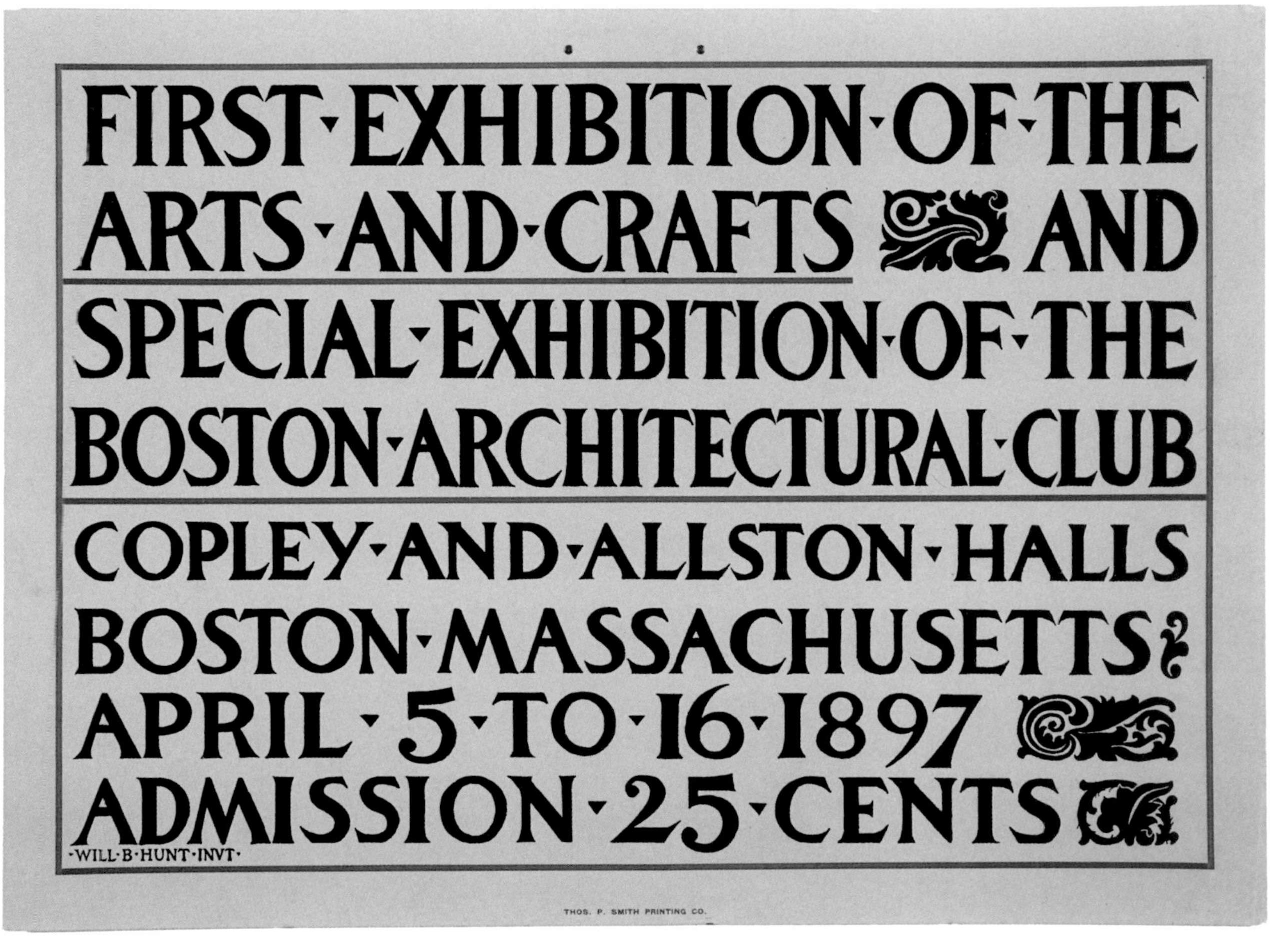

FIRST·EXHIBITION·OF·THE
ARTS·AND·CRAFTS 🍃 AND
SPECIAL·EXHIBITION·OF·THE
BOSTON·ARCHITECTURAL·CLUB
COPLEY·AND·ALLSTON·HALLS
BOSTON·MASSACHUSETTS
APRIL·5·TO·16·1897
ADMISSION·25·CENTS

·WILL·B·HUNT·INVT·

THOS. P. SMITH PRINTING CO.

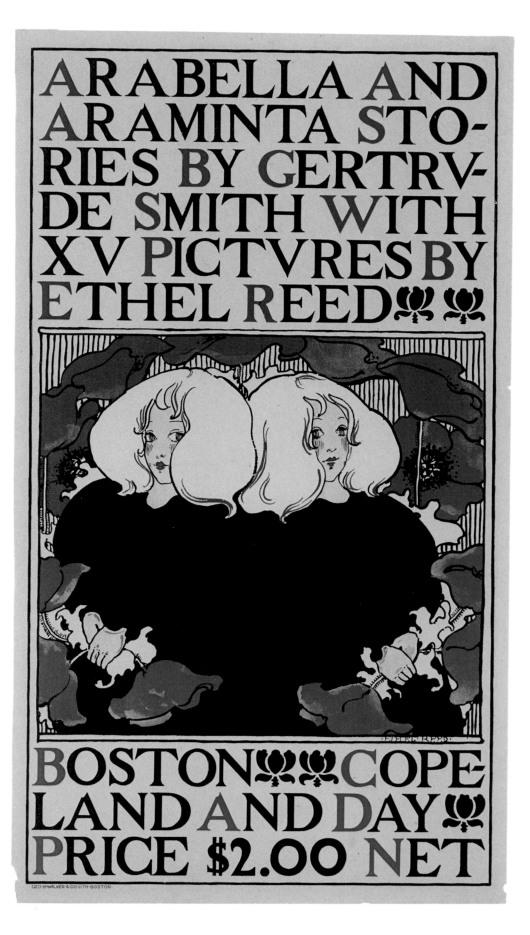

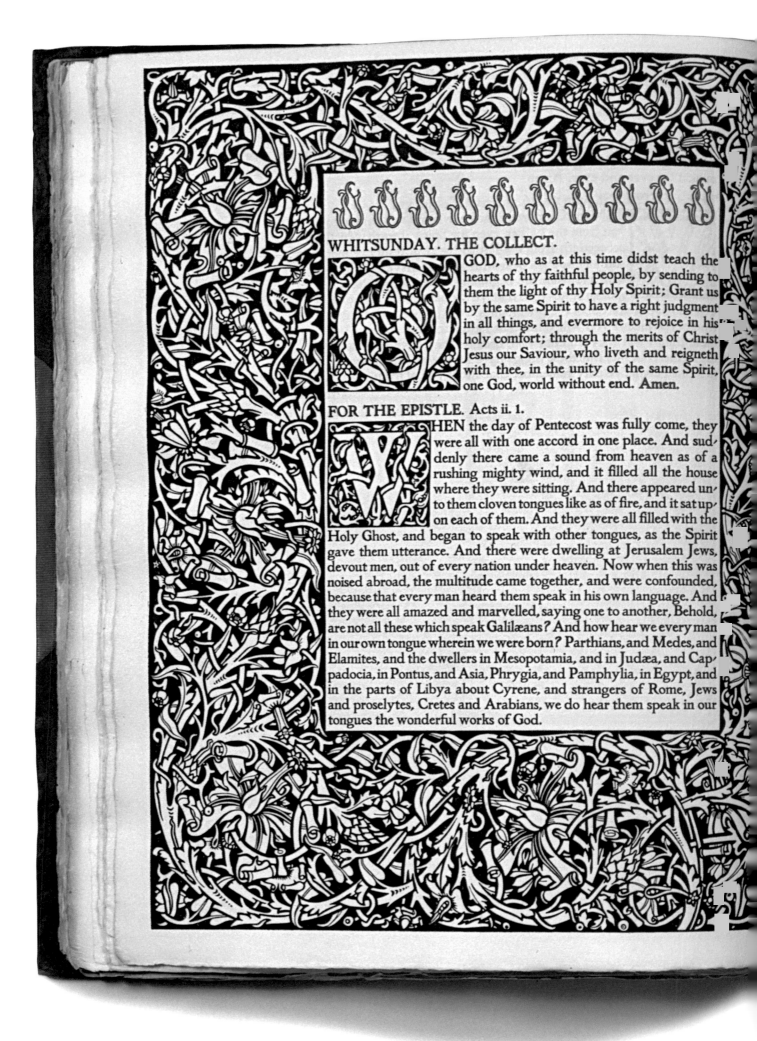

WHITSUNDAY. THE COLLECT.

O GOD, who as at this time didst teach the hearts of thy faithful people, by sending to them the light of thy Holy Spirit; Grant us by the same Spirit to have a right judgment in all things, and evermore to rejoice in his holy comfort; through the merits of Christ Jesus our Saviour, who liveth and reigneth with thee, in the unity of the same Spirit, one God, world without end. Amen.

FOR THE EPISTLE. Acts ii. 1.

WHEN the day of Pentecost was fully come, they were all with one accord in one place. And suddenly there came a sound from heaven as of a rushing mighty wind, and it filled all the house where they were sitting. And there appeared unto them cloven tongues like as of fire, and it sat upon each of them. And they were all filled with the Holy Ghost, and began to speak with other tongues, as the Spirit gave them utterance. And there were dwelling at Jerusalem Jews, devout men, out of every nation under heaven. Now when this was noised abroad, the multitude came together, and were confounded, because that every man heard them speak in his own language. And they were all amazed and marvelled, saying one to another, Behold, are not all these which speak Galilæans? And how hear we every man in our own tongue wherein we were born? Parthians, and Medes, and Elamites, and the dwellers in Mesopotamia, and in Judæa, and Cappadocia, in Pontus, and Asia, Phrygia, and Pamphylia, in Egypt, and in the parts of Libya about Cyrene, and strangers of Rome, Jews and proselytes, Cretes and Arabians, we do hear them speak in our tongues the wonderful works of God.

CAT. NO. 97 Bertram Grosvenor Goodhue, type designer and dece

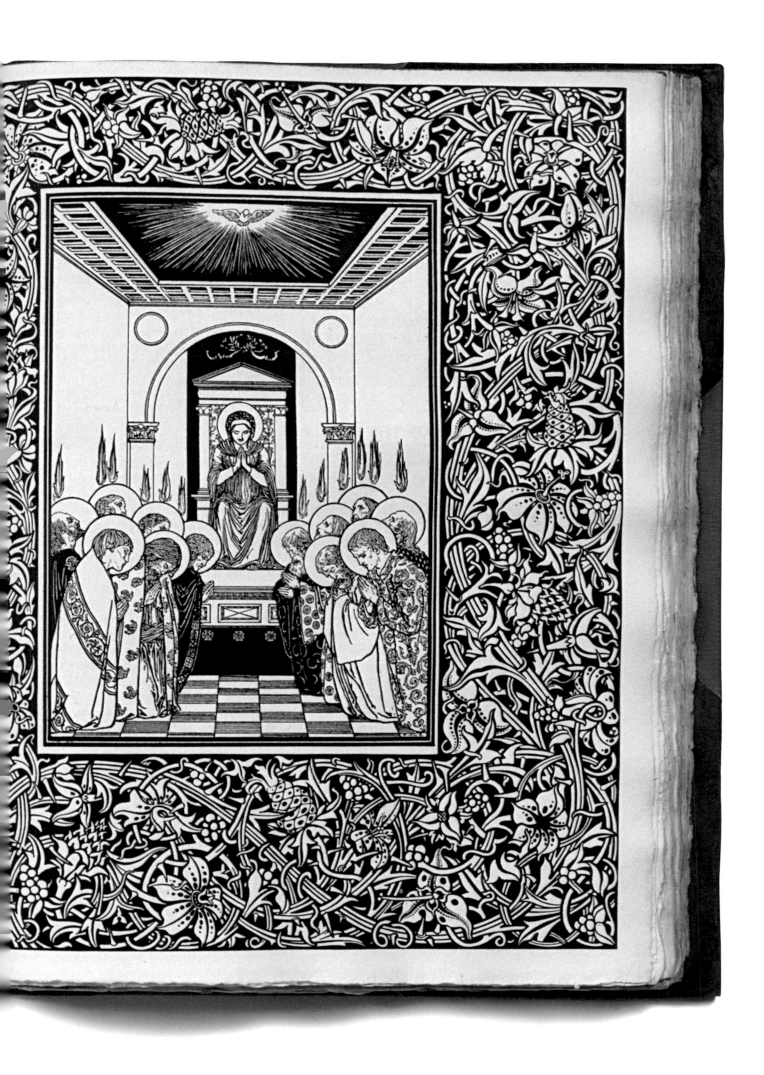

Berkeley Updike, printer; Robert Anning Bell, illustrator, *The Altar Book*, 1896.

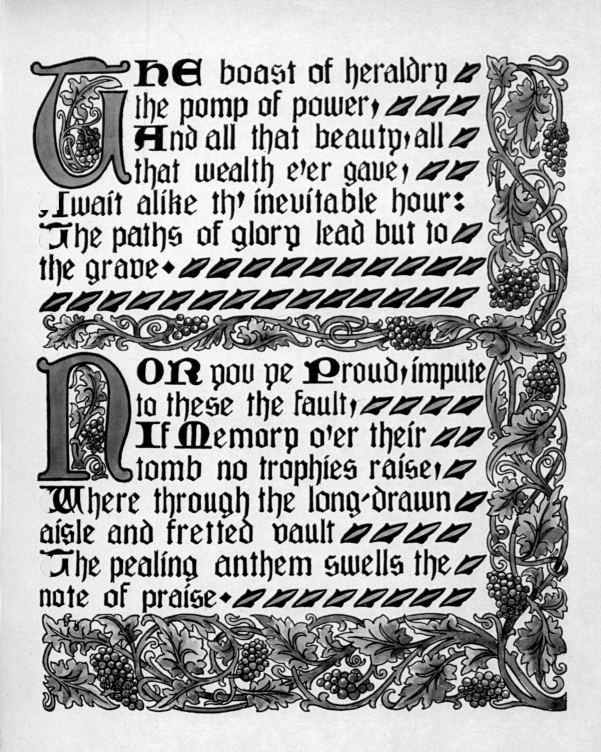

The boast of heraldry,
the pomp of power,
And all that beauty, all
that wealth e'er gave,
Await alike th' inevitable hour:
The paths of glory lead but to
the grave.

Nor you ye Proud, impute
to these the fault,
If Memory o'er their
tomb no trophies raise,
Where through the long-drawn
aisle and fretted vault
The pealing anthem swells the
note of praise.

CAT. NO. 99
Herbert Gregson,
calligrapher;
Anna Lessman,
illuminator;
Carl H. Heintzemann,
printer;
Thomas Gray, *Elegy Written
in a Country Churchyard*,
1901

THE CENTAUR. WRITTEN BY MAURICE DE GUÉRIN AND NOW TRANSLATED FROM THE FRENCH BY GEORGE B. IVES.

I Was born in a cavern of these mountains. Like the river in yonder valley, whose first drops flow from some cliff that weeps in a deep grotto, the first moments of my life sped amidst the shadows of a secluded re' treat, nor vexed its silence. As our mothers draw near their term, they retire to the cav' erns, and in the innermost recesses of the wildest of them all, where the darkness is most dense, they bring forth, uncomplaining, offspring as silent as themselves. Their strength'giving milk enables us to endure with' out weakness or dubious struggles the first difficulties of life; yet we leave our caverns later than you your cradles. The reason is that there is a tradition amongst us that the early days of life must be secluded and guarded, as days engrossed by the gods.

My growth ran almost its entire course in the darkness where I was born. The innermost depths of my home were so far within the bowels of the mountain, that I should not have known in which direction the opening lay, had it not been that the winds at times blew in and caused a sudden coolness and confusion. Some' times, too, my mother returned, bringing with her the perfume of the valleys, or dripping wet from the streams to which she resorted. Now, these her home'comings, although they told me naught of the valleys or the streams, yet, being attended by emanations there' from, disturbed my thoughts, and I wandered about, all agitated, amidst my darkness. 'What,' I would say to myself, 'are these places to which my mother goes and what power reigns there which sum' mons her so frequently? To what influences is one there exposed,

CAT. NO. 105
Bruce Rogers,
type designer and typesetter;
Carl Purington Rollins,
printer;
Maurice de Guérin,
The Centaur, 1915

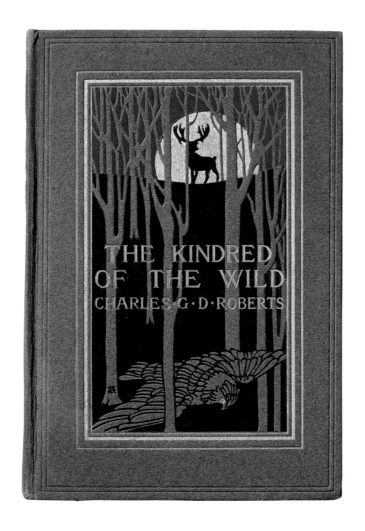

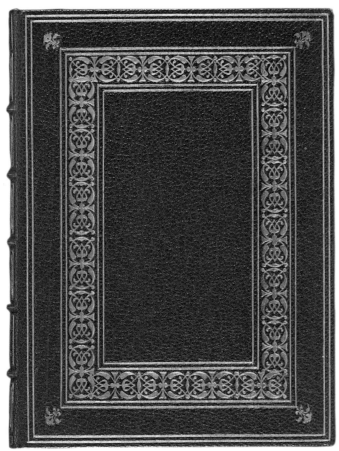

CAT. NO. 107
Amy Sacker,
cover designer;
Charles G.D. Roberts,
The Kindred of the Wild, 1902

CAT. NO. 108
Mary Crease Sears,
cover designer;
Agnes Saint John,
binder;
Dante Gabriel Rossetti,
Hand and Soul, 1899

president, professor Charles Eliot Norton, must have sounded like a direct challenge to much that they believed in:

> The Society of Arts and Crafts...endeavors to stimulate in workmen an appreciation of the dignity and value of good design; to counteract the popular impatience of Law and Form, and desire for over–ornamentation and specious originality. It will insist upon the necessity of sobriety and restraint, of ordered arrangement, of due regard for the relation between the form of an object and its use and of harmony and fitness in the decoration put upon it.[8]

In the book arts, this entailed the rejection of Morris's style and the adoption of simpler models. ❡ Norton's influence on the book arts may have been especially pronounced, both because of his friendship with printers and publishers, and because he judged several of the competitions in printing and binding during the early years of the Society.[9] A glimpse of this change is provided by Janet Ashbee, the wife of C.R. Ashbee, whose Essex House Press was carrying on the Morris tradition in England. During a visit to Boston in November 1900, the Ashbees dined with Norton and "quite a little knot of typographists," including Updike, Goodhue, and Rogers. Knowing that the Ashbees continued to admire Morris's work, Norton condemned it strongly, finding "type, paper, drawing and style all ugly." Decoration was to be eschewed in favor of pure typography—the simple, austere work of T. J. Cobden–Sanderson's Doves Press being recommended as a model.[10] ❡ Of course, not all of the Boston book artists adopted this chastened style. Bradley, Goodhue, Heintzemann, and Henry Lewis Johnson remained proponents of the use of borders, decorations, and ornaments to give color to the printed page. As late as 1923, Johnson published Historic Design in Printing, a compendium of decorative material for use by his students in Business Printing at Boston University.[11] Lavish decoration was deemed acceptable as long as it was securely based on historical precedents. This attitude led to the flowering of revival styles in printing at the beginning of the twentieth century. The term "allusive typography," which is often used for printing of this kind, simply refers to design in a period style, reflecting the historical origins and literary content of a book. The idea may be derived from the Arts and Crafts notion that the purpose of an object should be reflected in its decoration. ❡ The most popular revival styles in bookmaking, as in architecture, were the colonial and the Renaissance. Will Bradley was responsible for the rediscovery of early American printing.[12] As early

8. Papers of the Society of Arts and Crafts, Boston, 1897–1924, Archives of American Art, Smithsonian Institution (hereafter SACB archives, AAA/SI), quoted in Karen Evans Ulehla, ed., The Society of Arts and Crafts, Boston: Exhibition Record 1897–1927 (Boston: Boston Public Library, 1981), p. 5.

9. For example, in February 1897 and January 1900. SACB archives, AAA/SI.

10. Alan Crawford, C.R. Ashbee, Architect, Designer and Romantic Socialist (New Haven: Yale University Press, 1985), p. 95. The quotes from Janet Ashbee are from "The Ashbee Journals," King's College Library, Cambridge, England.

11. Henry Lewis Johnson, Historic Design in Printing: Reproductions of Book Covers, Borders, Initials, Decorations, Printer's Marks and Devices, Composing Reference Material for the Designer, Printer, Advertiser and Publisher (Boston: The Graphic Arts Company, 1923). A second volume, Printing Type Specimens: Standard and Modern Types with Notations on their Characteristics and Uses: A Printing Guide for Printers, Advertisers and Students of Printing, was published by The Graphic Arts Company in 1924.

12. Will Bradley, Picture of a Period, or Memoirs of the Gay Nineties and the Turn of the Century, also a Few of the Years that Followed (San Marino, Calif.: Rounce & Coffin Club, 1950), n.p.

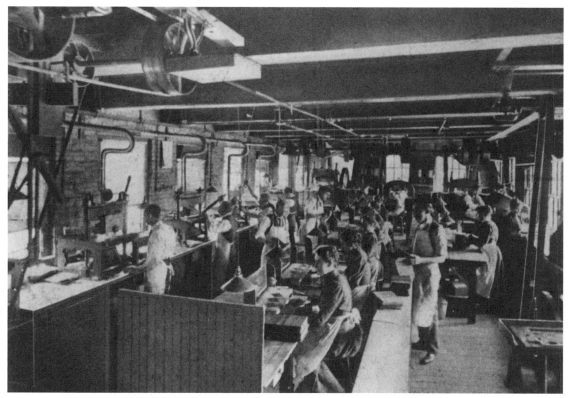

{41} Cover–stamping room at The Riverside Press, ca. 1910; New York Public Library.

as January 1897, the influence of the colonial imprints he discovered at the Boston Public Library is evident in the layout of Bradley: His Book (fig. 42). An exaggerated adaptation of this style—involving a liberal use of rules, type ornaments, and over–sized baskets of fruit and flowers—was sometimes called "Bradleyism." Similar devices appeared almost simultaneously in the work of other designers and printers, including Theodore Brown Hapgood, Jr. (cat. no. 100) and Carl Heintzemann. The style was used for works of fiction set in colonial times, for advertisements, and for numerous facsimiles and reprints of early American books (cat. no. 102). ❲Although he never hesitated to evoke early American printing or to use other period styles where appropriate, Updike's real love was the Italian Renaissance. According to Charles Eliot Norton, "it was the printers in Italy who, during the first fifty years after [the] discovery [of printing], took chief advantage of it, and carried the art to an excellence which was not attained in other countries."[13] Although the fifteenth–century Venetian types of Nicolas Jenson had been the models for William Morris's Golden type and Goodhue's Merrymount, both Morris and Goodhue were more interested in the arts of Northern Europe than in

those of Italy, and created types to match the bold black and white ornaments they both favored. Montallegro, the type that Updike commissioned from the British type designer Herbert Horne, was likewise based on fifteenth–century models, but was infinitely more refined. Updike used it for the Humanist's Library, his attempt at limited edition publishing. In these self–effacing, eminently readable little books, Updike deliberately sought "to print in a form akin to the great traditions of the printer's art in its earliest days."[14] The title–pages by T.M. Cleland and W.A. Dwiggins (cat. no. 96), printed in red–orange and black, allude to, but do not precisely imitate, Renaissance models. None of them could be mistaken for anything but a twentieth–century book, and they were soon recognized as a significant landmark of twentieth–century printing.[15] ❲Bruce Rogers too, though he experimented in every conceivable style, was strongly drawn to the printing of the Renaissance. His Montaigne and Centaur types were both based on Jenson's. Although Rogers would later decide that Centaur was "too definitely an Italian Renaissance letter,"[16] it proved popular with small private presses. Rogers himself first used it in a privately published edition of The Centaur, by Maurice de

13. Charles Eliot Norton, "The New Humanistic Type," The Printing Art 6, no. 5 (January 1906), p. 273.

14. Prospectus for the Humanist's Library (Boston: The Merrymount Press, 1907).

15. George Parker Winship, The Merrymount Press of Boston: An Account of The Work of Daniel Berkeley Updike (Vienna, Austria: printed for Herbert Reichner, 1929), p. 16.

16. Quoted in Joseph Blumenthal, Bruce Rogers: A Life in Letters (Austin, Tex.: W. Thomas Taylor, 1989), p.33.

Guérin (cat. no. 105), for which his wife set the type while he printed it on a handpress in the Dyke Mill printing office of Carl Purington Rollins in rural Montague, Massachusetts. Although in appearance it is not a typical American Arts and Crafts book, *The Centaur* is decidedly a work of handicraft, and stylistically compares favorably with the later productions of the British Arts and Crafts movement. ❡ Calligraphy and hand–bookbinding were not crafts for which Boston was noted prior to 1897, but both flourished following the founding of the Society of Arts and Crafts. Many calligraphers and bookbinders were members of the Society from its earliest years, but few examples of their work survive. Some calligraphers, like Julia DeWolf Addison, were talented amateurs who produced carefully lettered and illuminated manuscripts on vellum (cat. no. 93). Others specialized in Christmas cards which were sold through the SACB shop. William Addison Dwiggins, Herbert Gregson, and Theodore Brown Hapgood were among the most skillful of the professionals. Their lettering appears in a handful of small books in which the text was photomechanically reproduced from calligraphic originals. Examples include a 1900 edition of Thomas Gray's *Elegy Written in a Country Churchyard*, with lettering by Gregson (cat. no.

99), and *Two Lyrics*, by John Bannister Tabb, lettered by Hapgood. Both were published by the short–lived Craftsman's Guild in small limited editions with hand–colored decorations.[17] An edition of the *92nd Psalm*, with text reproduced from his own calligraphy, was among the first books issued by Dwiggins from his press in Hingham.[18] ❡ The craft of bookbinding necessarily caters to an elite clientele, but a city of bibliophiles like Boston provided opportunities for a few talented binders. Perhaps the most influential was Mary Crease Sears, who for many years operated a small bindery and school of bookbinding (fig. 43). Sears's work ranges from an elaborate mosaic binding with a repeating pattern of irises through a binding in the style of the sixteenth century, blind–tooled with heavy metal bosses, executed as a gift for Isabella Stewart Gardner.[19] In 1916, she designed a special binding for a copy of *The Altar Book*, decorated with silver bosses and a silver crucifix with gold inlay executed by Arthur J. Stone, following detailed models by John Kirchmayer, both fellow members of the Society of Arts and Crafts.[20] One of Sears's students Rosamond Loring, specialized in making the decorated papers used by bookbinders.[21] Her paste papers were used by Sears and her students as covers on several Merrymount Press books,

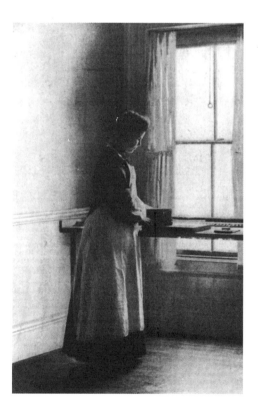

{43} Mary Crease Sears at the bench in the finishing–room in her bindery (79 Newbury Street, Boston), ca. 1908; *The Outlook* 90 (1908), p. 438.

17. See "The Craftsman's Guild," *Publisher's Weekly* no. 1493 (September 8, 1900), p. 486; and no. 1500 (October 27, 1900), p. 1176. This interesting venture remains inadequately documented.

18. See Dwight Agner, *The Books of WAD: a Bibliography of the Books Designed by W.A. Dwiggins* (Baton Rouge, La.: Press of the Night Owl, 1974).

19. Joseph Newman of the Northeast Document Conservation Center in Andover, Mass. has uncovered most of the information that is available about this binder. For a good early discussion of Sears's work, see Claire Coburn Swift, "The Fine Art of Bookbinding," *The Outlook* 90 (October 24, 1908), pp. 433–40.

20. This binding is reproduced in Elenita C. Chickering and Sarah Morgan Ross, *Arthur J. Stone, 1847–1938: Designer and Silversmith* (Boston: The Boston Athenaeum, 1994), cat. no. 116, p. 64.

21. Loring also collected historical specimens of decorated papers; her collection is now in the Houghton Library. See Rosamond B. Loring, *Marbled Papers* (Boston: Club of Odd Volumes, 1933) and *Decorated Book Papers: Being an Account of their Designs and Fashions* (Cambridge: Department of Printing and Graphic Arts, Harvard College Library, 1942).

TRICENNIAL
EXHIBITION
OF
THE SOCIETY OF
ARTS & CRAFTS
BOSTON
1897-1927

MARCH 1 TO 20, 1927
MUSEUM OF FINE ARTS

{44} SACB exhibition catalogue cover, 1927, designed by Daniel Berkeley Updike; Fine Arts Department, Boston Public Library.

and on the cover of the 1930 Riverside Press edition of Sophocles's *Antigone* (cat. no. 103). ❡The book arts were well represented in the Tricennial Exhibition of the Society of Arts and Crafts in 1927 (fig. 44), with illuminated manuscripts by Julia DeWolf Addison and Theodore Brown Hapgood, bookplates by Amy Sacker, and bookbindings by Mary Crease Sears and her students. A large section devoted to printing—including a selection of Merrymount Press books, books designed by Carl Rollins at Yale University Press, and a copy of Henry Lewis Johnson's *Historic Design in Printing*—demonstrated the Society's success in promoting good design. ❡Today, the legacy of the Arts and Crafts movement is evident not only in the small private presses that maintain the traditions of type set by hand and original prints as illustrations, but also in the efforts of contemporary designers to adapt the new digital technology to the requirements of good book design. The 1990s are a period of transition, not unlike the 1890s. Another new age of book–making is beginning, in which the traditional role of books as the primary purveyors of information is being challenged, while public awareness of the book as a physical object—as an art object—is being enhanced. Early twentieth–century designers sought to make the best and most beautiful books they could with the most advanced technology available; it remains to be seen what designers will do with the infinitely more challenging technology of the late twentieth century. ○

The following individuals were especially helpful in my research: Sue Allen; Stanley Cushing (Boston Athenaeum); Priscilla Juvelis; Joseph Newman (Northeast Document Conservation Center); Danny D. Smith; Jean–François Villain; and Philip Weimerskirch (Providence Public Library). Sandra Adams, Thomas G. Boss, and Sinclair Hitchings all went far beyond the call of duty, providing moral support as well as useful information.

PICTO-RIALISM

AND

NATURALISM

IN

NEW ENGLAND

PHOTO-GRAPHY

ANNE E. HAVINGA

LONG VIEWED AS being outside mainstream aesthetic styles, photography has had to fight to find its place among the arts, a struggle that has persisted since the earliest photographers discovered that they could create not merely objective translations of reality, but also artistically expressive images. As with all the fine and applied arts, current aesthetic trends have influenced photography's interpretation of the world. At the turn of the century, the major impetus in photography was to gain recognition as an art form. Seeking to achieve this, in part through a response to the principles of the Arts and Crafts vision and in rejection of the mediocre quality of industrialized society's increasingly mass–produced images, leaders in photography advocated fine craftsmanship combined with back–to–nature simplicity and harmonious design.[1] ❦ Photography had undergone tremendous technological advances by the time of its fiftieth birthday in 1889, advances that signaled major changes for the field: the development of the gelatin dry plate process, the availability of commercially–prepared paper and pre–mixed chemicals, and the introduction of small, relatively inexpensive hand–held cameras. Taking pictures had become simplified, and virtually anyone could master its technique. For many, photography became a pastime, and by the end of the 1880s the majority of its practitioners were amateurs. This new generation of photographers came from a broad range of society—urban and rural, well–to–do and not so well–to–do, male and female—who took pictures primarily for pleasure. Photography as a hobby was commended by critics as a way to enrich the soul, and was especially encouraged for women. "Amateur photography is of special interest and importance to women. It has provided for them a peculiarly interesting field. It is ever an incentive to good health. Many a ruddy cheek there is whose hue has been won on long camera tramps, many an elastic step which would have been slow and halting, many a spirit dull and languid,

1. Much research on Arts and Crafts photography has been carried out by Christian A. Peterson. See his "The Photograph Beautiful 1895–1915," *History of Photography* 16, no. 3 (Autumn 1992), pp. 189–232.

2. W.S. Harwood, "Amateur Photography of To–day," in *The Cosmopolitan: An Illustrated Monthly Magazine* 20, no. 3 (January 1896), p. 253.

3. As quoted from the society's constitution by Benjamin Kimball in "Boston Camera Club," *New England Magazine* 8, no. 2 (April 1893), p. 188. The Boston Camera Club is still in operation and is the longest surviving organization of its type.

4. *Exhibition of the Society of Arts & Crafts, Copley Hall, Boston, April 4–15, 1899* (Boston: George H. Ellis, 1899), pp. 15–17.

5. Denman W. Ross, "How Design comes into Photography," *Photo–Era* 4, no. 1 (January 1900), p. 2 (notes from Dec. 13, 1899 lecture at the Harvard Camera Club).

6. William F. Robinson, *A Certain Slant of Light: The First Hundred Years of New England Photography* (Boston: New York Graphic Society, 1980), pp. 146–47.

but for the leading of the lens," noted a writer in *Cosmopolitan* magazine.[2] ❡ Camera clubs, where men and women photographers came for instruction and to exhibit their work, opened in every large and mid–size city across the country, and in some small towns as well. Among the New England cities that established clubs were Boston, Providence, Hartford, Manchester, Portland, Worcester, Cambridge, Lowell, Brockton, and Melrose; even Harvard and Yale Universities had clubs. One of the earliest photographic associations in the country was the Boston Society of Amateur Photographers, founded in 1881 by a handful of aficionados including Wilfred A. French, a particularly active member best known for his photographs of colonial homesteads. Renamed the Boston Camera Club in 1886, this organization became the first official camera club in the country, set up for "the advancement among its members of the knowledge of photography in its various branches by the aid of discussions, lectures, experiments and such other methods as may be deemed best."[3] The club, located at 50 Bromfield Street, provided not only technical advice and exhibition space, but also darkrooms and a library. ❡ The first exhibition of the Boston Society of Amateur Photographers, with more than seven hundred prints, was held at the Massachusetts Institute of Technology in November 1883; this and subsequent annual exhibitions helped set the standard for photography shows across the country. In 1885 the Society of Amateur Photographers of New York and the Pacific Coast Amateur Photographic Association in San Francisco held their first annual exhibitions, and in 1886 the Photographic Society of Philadelphia collaborated with the Pennsylvania Academy of the Fine Arts to present an ambitious exhibition of 1,871 prints by prominent English and American photographers. In 1887 the country's three leading photographic societies—Boston, New York, and Philadelphia—embarked on the most significant series of photographic exhibitions of the time, the Joint Annual Exhibitions, which rotated from club to club from 1887 to 1894 (except in 1890). In 1892, when the Boston Society hosted the Exhibition, it chose a jury of well–known painters to emphasize the aesthetic value of photography—although, since the jury knew little about the medium, the results were less than satisfactory. ❡ The association of photography with other arts continued in Boston when the medium was well–represented in the 1897 and 1899 exhibitions of the Society of Arts and Crafts. In the April 1899 exhibition, pho-

tography was grouped with books, bookbindings, illustrations, and engraving. The influential Norwood, Massachusetts photographer F. Holland Day—who was intimately involved with the organization of this exhibition and its inclusion of photography—contributed a total of eleven platinum prints and was instrumental in obtaining representative works by Mary Devens, Gertrude Käsebier, Joseph T. Keiley, Sarah Choate Sears, Alfred Stieglitz, and Clarence H. White, among others.[4] Photography was increasingly accepted among the arts in the Boston cultural community: Denman W. Ross, the influential Lecturer on the Theory of Design at Harvard University, pronounced in a talk presented to the Harvard Camera Club in December 1899 that he had accepted photography as a fine art, as long as "the artist conceives his subject in a design; and this design must be beautiful in itself, apart from what it suggests or signifies." His lecture was published a month later in *Photo–Era* magazine. He continued, "it is not the beauty of the subject which makes it a work of fine art, but the beauty of the form which the imagination of the artist gives to the subject."[5] ❡ Amateur photographers looked largely to camera clubs and to magazines for guidance. Articles on photography appeared in popular publications such as *Cosmopolitan* and *Harper's Weekly*, as well as in the *Craftsman*. Several magazines, started in the late 1880s and 1890s and devoted solely to photography, were based in New England: *American Annual of Photography* (begun in 1887, published in New York and Boston); *American Amateur Photographer* (begun in 1889 in Brunswick, Maine), which merged in 1907 with Chicago's *Photo–Beacon* to become *American Photography* (published in Boston) under the editorship of Frank Roy Fraprie, who was also a photographer of note; *Photo–Era* (begun in 1898 in Boston), which was one of the most widely read, as it affiliated itself almost immediately with the Boston Camera Club; and *The Photographic Monthly* (published in Providence) which lasted only one year, 1901–02.[6] The most influential journals devoted to photography at this time were Alfred Stieglitz's *Camera Notes* (1897–1902), the vehicle of the Camera Club of New York; followed by *Camera Work* (1903–17), the voice of the elite Pictorialist group, the Photo–Secessionists—both journals were known for their high–quality photogravures. Stieglitz, who had returned to the United States from Germany in 1890, settling in New York City, became the most respected figure in photography and strongly advocated the medium's recognition as an art form. ❡ The dominant

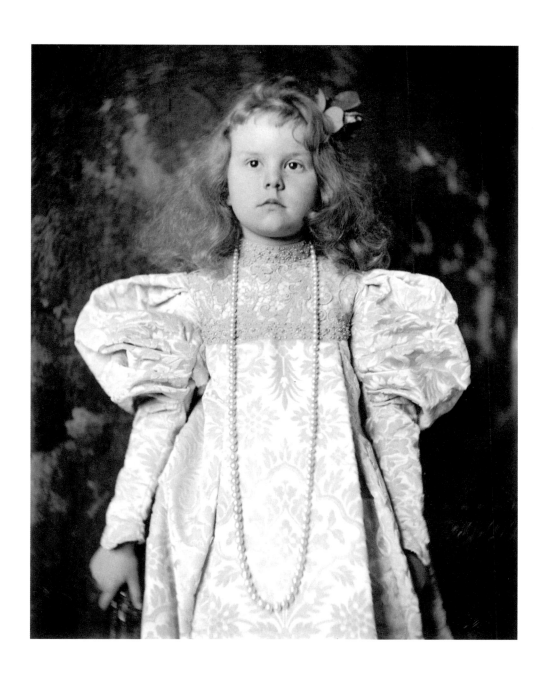

CAT. NO. 123A
Sarah Choate Sears,
Helen Sears,
ca. 1897

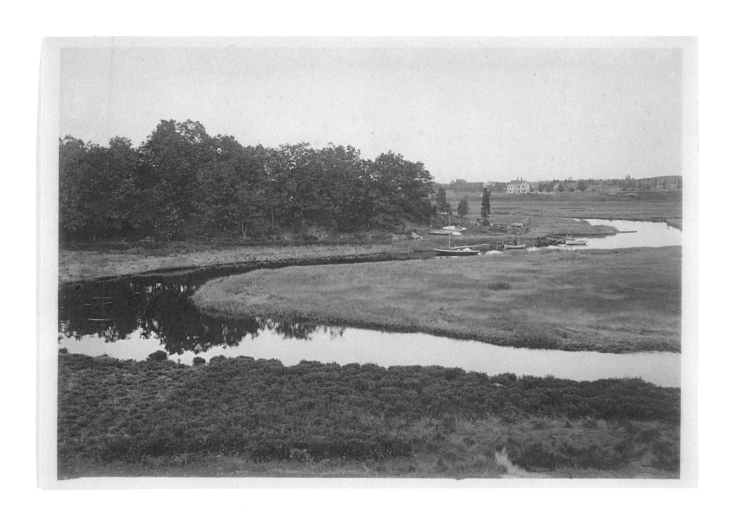

CAT. NO. 118
Arthur Wesley Dow,
Salt Marsh, Ipswich River,
ca. 1904

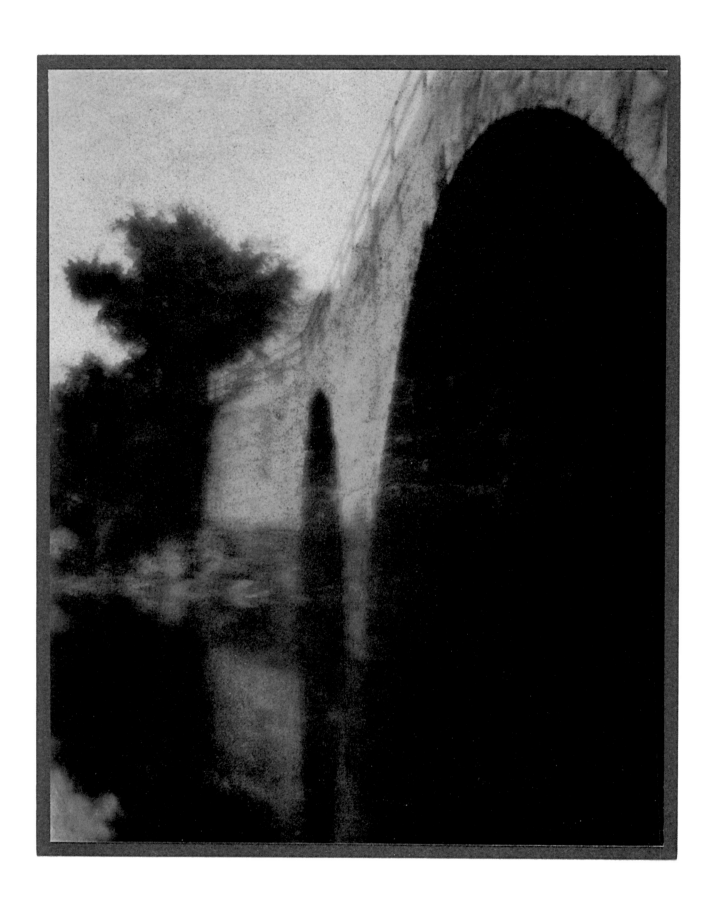

CAT. NO. 113
Alvin Langdon Coburn,
The Bridge, Ipswich, 1903

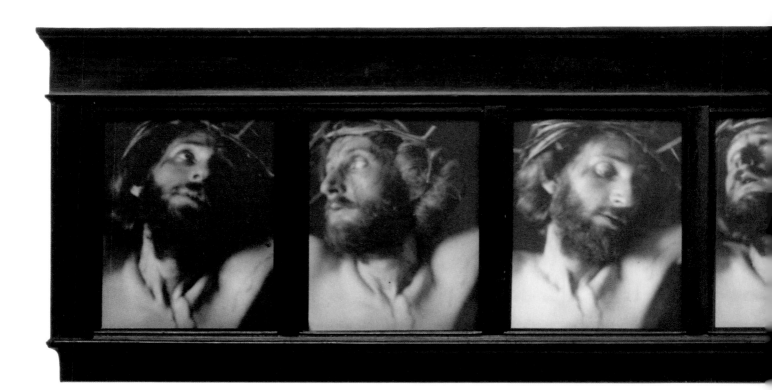

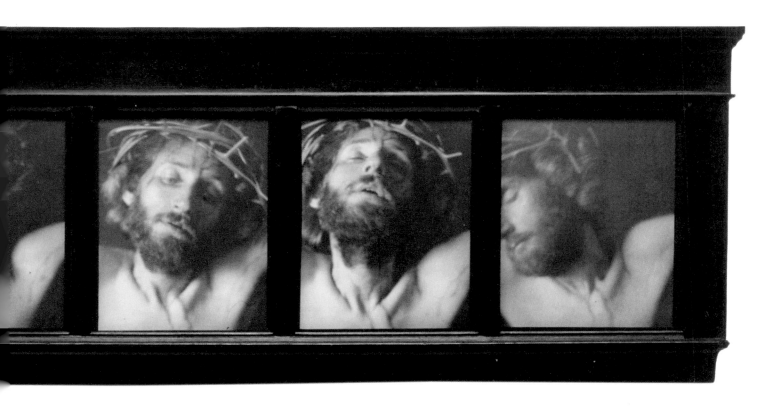

CAT. NO. 116
F. Holland Day,
*The Seven Last Words
of Christ*, 1898

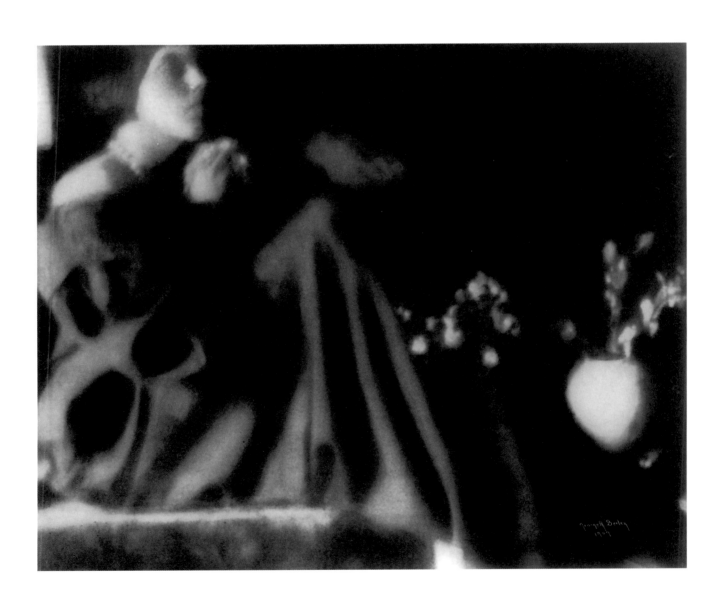

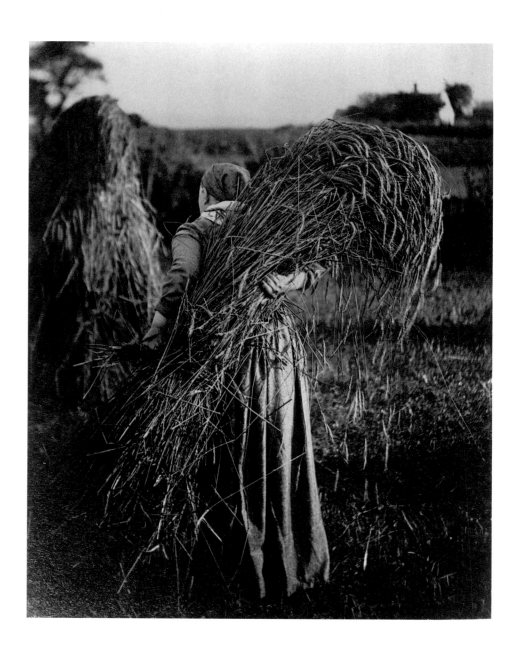

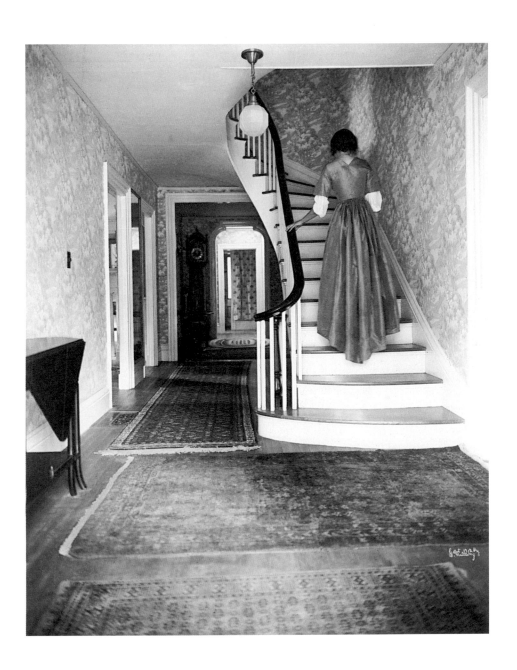

CAT. NO. 121
Wallace Nutting,
Wallace Nutting's Place,
Framingham, 1912

trends in photography at the turn of the century were Pictorialism and Naturalism, each of which stressed its own Arts and Crafts approach to nature, simplicity of design, and refinement of technique. Pictorialism and Naturalism had their roots in the rival ideas of two influential British photographers: Henry Peach Robinson, whose *Pictorial Effect in Photography* appeared in 1869, and Peter Henry Emerson (a distant relative of Ralph Waldo Emerson), whose *Naturalistic Photography for Students of the Art* was published in 1889. Emerging as a reaction to the smothering effects of industrialization, urbanization, and the increasing volume of mass–produced images and poor–quality amateur photographs that were considered to be trivializing the medium, these two approaches were intended to provide guidelines for expression in a medium that still had few organizing principles. The term "Pictorial" was chosen to indicate "artistic" photography, and both Pictorialist and Naturalist photographers frequently addressed themes, subjects, and styles found in paintings, prints, and drawings in an effort to justify the artistic merit of their medium. In particular, Naturalist photographers derived much from the Barbizon school of painting of the middle decades of the century, and the Pictorialists were influenced by a range of end–of–the–century movements including Impressionism, Symbolism, Tonalism, and Art Nouveau. ❡ In America, Naturalism overlapped with Pictorialism and is generally seen as an offshoot of it; Stieglitz included Naturalist as well as Pictorialist photographs in *Camera Notes* and *Camera Work*. Many of the Pictorialists emphasized a decorative and romanticized portrayal of the world, using soft–focus lenses and manipulated printing. The purest Naturalist photographers, whose subjects usually related to the outdoors, strove for a plain but artistic description of reality and expressions of earnest sentiment through unretouched, artistically arranged images. In New England, Naturalist and Pictorialist photographers operated side by side, employing the platinum and gum bichromate printing processes to produce a broad variety of coloristic and tonal effects, and create images intended to resemble etching, charcoal drawing, or even watercolor. ❡ Working in Boston, southern Maine, and western Massachusetts, Emma Lewis Coleman was an early artistic photographer who in the 1870s began to make unmanipulated platinum prints of pastoral life. Inspired by the Barbizon paintings (and presumably photographs) that she came in contact with while studying in Paris in the 1860s,

Coleman made naturalistic images related in spirit to those of Peter Henry Emerson frequently reproduced in American photographic magazines in the 1880s. Between 1883 and 1886, Coleman made a series of staged photographs, in which her friends posed in traditional costume making colonial New England crafts and performing rural tasks in York, Maine (cat. no. 115). These images illustrated Sarah Orne Jewett's popular preservationist novel, *Deephaven*, published in 1893. ❡ Pictorialism flourished as a celebration of individual artistic presentation, and a number of photographers working in New England produced photographs that were innovative in their style, technique, and subject. Many Pictorialist photographers found that by using soft focus, printing in gum bichromate or platinum (sometimes in combination), and manipulating the negative or print, they were able to modulate tonalities, introduce highlights, and subdue certain details to achieve especially poetic effects. Stieglitz, shortly after returning to the United States, expressed it thus: "Simplicity, I might say, is the key to all art—a conviction that anybody who has studied the masters must arrive at. Originality, hand–in–hand with simplicity, are the first two qualities which we Americans need in order to produce artistic pictures....Atmosphere is the medium through which we see all things... what *atmosphere* is to Nature, *tone* is to a picture."[7] ❡ One of the more extraordinary New England influences on "artistic photography" was that of Arthur Wesley Dow, who derived from Japanese design concepts a system emphasizing purity of form, flat tonal harmonies, and an absence of deep spatial perspective.[8] Dow's principles of design, when put into practice, imparted a distinctly decorative aspect to many Pictorialist images. Most of the small number of photographs he began making in the 1890s are cyanotypes, although he also produced silver prints of landscape and documentary subjects.[9] He occasionally submitted his photographs to camera club exhibitions. Dow's use of blue cyanotype (cat. no. 118) parallels his experimentation with color in woodcut (see "The Flourish of Color Relief Printmaking in New England" in this volume) and underscores his interest in the rhythm of form and color values, albeit with a narrower coloristic range. The application of Dow's precepts to photography was promoted not only in his own teachings and writings, but also specifically through the influence of successful students such as Alvin Langdon Coburn, who wrote: "Dow had the vision...to recognize the possibili-

7. Alfred Stieglitz, "A Plea for Art Photography in America," in *Photographic Mosaics* 28 (1892), pp. 136–37.

8. Dow's fascination with oriental art and design was stimulated in large part by his association with the collection of Japanese art at the Museum of Fine Arts, Boston, where he was a curator in the 1890s.

9. See Nancy E. Green, *Arthur Wesley Dow and His Influence* (Ithaca, N.Y.: Herbert F. Johnson Museum of Art, 1990), pp. 12–13.

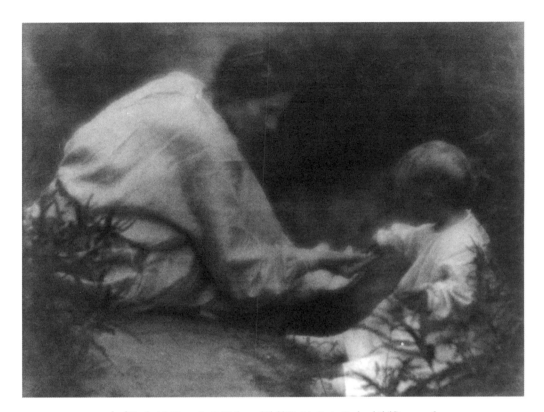

{45} Frederick Haven Pratt, *Mother and Child (Beatrice Baxter Ruyl and Child)*, ca. 1906, platinum print; Lee Gallery, Winchester, Mass.

10. Helmut and Alison Gernsheim, eds., *Alvin Langdon Coburn, Photographer: an Autobiography* (New York: Dover Publications, 1978), p. 22. See also Peterson, "The Photograph Beautiful 1895–1915," p. 204.

11. Article by Sadakichi Hartmann, reprinted in Harry W. Lawton and George Knox, eds., *The Valiant Knights of Daguerre: Selected Critical Essays on Photography and Profiles of Photographic Pioneers by Sadakichi Hartmann* (Berkeley: University of California Press, 1978), p. 91.

ties of photography as a medium of personal expression. I learned many things at [his] school, not least an appreciation of what the Orient has to offer us in terms of simplicity and directness of composition....I think that all my work has been influenced to a large extent and beneficially by this oriental background, and I am deeply grateful to Arthur Wesley Dow for his early introduction to its mysteries."[10] ❡ Coburn studied with Dow at Ipswich in the summers of 1902 and 1903, and a decade later traveled to the Southwest with him. Having got his start in photography through his distant cousin F. Holland Day in his native Boston, Coburn was particularly active as a photographer in New York and London, where he eventually settled. Many of his photographs taken on the North Shore around Ipswich are prime examples of his ability to make boldly harmonious compositions, and to create combination platinum and gum prints, a technique in which he was an early innovator and especially adept in producing rich tonal effects (cat. nos. 113 and 114). Coburn later completely removed the subject in photography when in 1917 he made his so–called "vortographs," pictures of prisms reflected in mirrors—the first intentionally non–representational photographs. ❡ The Pictorial-

ists, and to a lesser extent the Naturalists, took great care in the presentation of their images, attaching them to mounts of earthy shades of green or brown and framing them in simple, often specially–crafted frames, sometimes in Mission–style oak. The noted critic Sadakichi Hartmann recorded that "some photographers apparently mistook their packing paper mounts for sample–books of paper warehouses" which they then tried to order for mats or mounts. He also wrote, in a 1907 essay entitled "The Influence of Artistic Photography on Interior Decoration," that "artistic photographers...argue that a picture is only finished when it is properly trimmed, mounted, and framed, and that the whole effect of prints, mount or mat, signature, and frame, should be an artistic one, and the picture be judged accordingly."[11] ❡ Fred Holland Day was particularly concerned with the presentation of his photographs, often mounting them on several layers of colored paper, and designing individual frames for them. An early admirer of Symbolist art and literature, Day, who had first started a publishing business, became the most influential early American Pictorial photographer after Stieglitz. He had avid followers nationally and internationally, especially in England. In the Boston area, he was frequently asked to speak and to judge camera club exhibitions. He also wrote a number of articles on artistic photography. ❡ Day was the first photographer to show combination gum bichromate and platinum prints, although Cambridge photographer Mary Devens was the earliest practitioner of the combination technique in New England. He was very involved with the Boston Camera Club and with the Society of Arts and Crafts, Boston. He contributed to the first Exhibition of the Arts and Crafts held in Copley Hall in April 1897, and to the second exhibition in April 1899, and served as well on the organizing committee with Sarah Choate Sears. He lobbied with Sears for an international exhibition of photography to be held in 1900 at the Museum of Fine Arts, Boston—almost successfully, had it not been for the rivalry that had developed with Stieglitz, who was holding out for such a show in New York.[12] Photographers came from near and far to see him; Clarence White and Gertrude Käsebier were frequent visitors to his Norwood and Maine homes, and the Worcester Pictorialist Frederick Haven Pratt made a series of figure and landscape compositions in 1906 while at Day's estate in Maine (fig. 45). ❡ In a number of photographs, Day posed nude boys and men in hazy atmospheric landscapes, often on the rocks by the Sheepscot

River at his summer home in Five Islands, near Georgetown, Maine, sometimes including props suggestive of the Antique (cat. no. 117). Day's most audacious photographic work was his series of "sacred" images, *The Seven Last Words*; the most important of these is *The Seven Last Words of Christ* (cat. no. 116), made in the summer of 1898, in which Day himself posed as the dying Christ.[13] He exhibited the series in its entirety at the Philadelphia Photographic Salon in 1898 and at the Royal Photographic Society exhibition in London in 1900. Day showed two variants of one of the images, *Father forgive them*, at the second exhibition of Arts and Crafts held at Copley Hall in 1899 to contrast unmanipulated and manipulated prints made from the same negative. A number of critics found Day's combination of photography and religion difficult to accept; wrote Charles Caffin, "the limit of mistake is reached by one [series of photographs] of seven heads crowned with thorns, purporting to represent the 'Seven Last Words' from the Cross, and the other, a dead Christ with the Magdalen bathing his feet with her tears."[14] ❡ Longtime friend of F. Holland Day and a member of the prominent Sears family, Sarah Choate Sears was extremely generous in her philanthropic efforts on behalf of the arts in Boston. Sears not only spoke out for

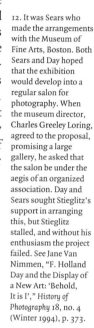

12. It was Sears who made the arrangements with the Museum of Fine Arts, Boston. Both Sears and Day hoped that the exhibition would develop into a regular salon for photography. When the museum director, Charles Greeley Loring, agreed to the proposal, promising a large gallery, he asked that the salon be under the aegis of an organized association. Day and Sears sought Stieglitz's support in arranging this, but Stieglitz stalled, and without his enthusiasm the project failed. See Jane Van Nimmen, "F. Holland Day and the Display of a New Art: 'Behold, It is I'," *History of Photography* 18, no. 4 (Winter 1994), p. 373.

13. Day wrote about this work in "Sacred Art and the Camera," *Photo–Era* 6 (February 1899), pp. 545–49.

14. Charles Caffin, "Philadelphia Photographic Salon," *Harper's Weekly* (November 5, 1898), p. 1087.

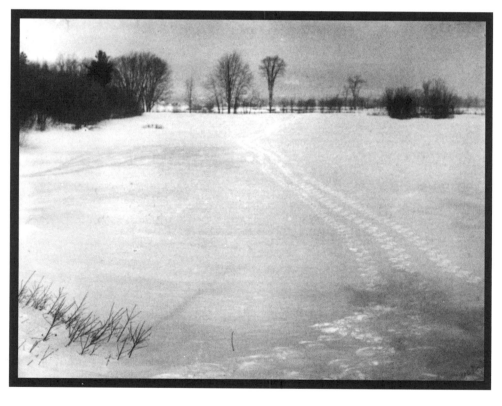

{46} William B. Post, *Intervale, Winter*, 1898, platinum print; Hallmark Photographic Collection.

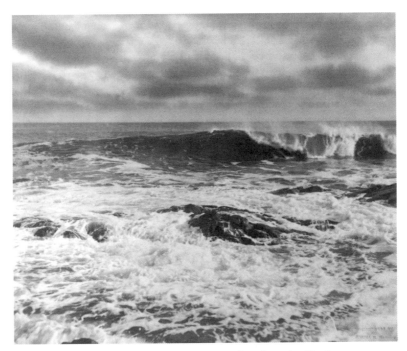

{47} Martha Hale Harvey, *After the Storm*, 1897, silver print; Fine Arts Department, Boston Public Library.

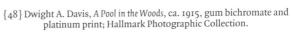

{48} Dwight A. Davis, *A Pool in the Woods*, ca. 1915, gum bichromate and platinum print; Hallmark Photographic Collection.

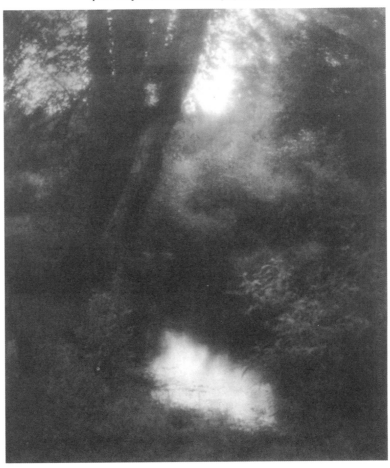

artistic photography but was herself a photographer. Encouraged by Day, in the 1890s and around 1900 she made pictures of her family and friends that on occasion were startlingly direct; some of her portraits of her daughter Helen are sweetly pretty while others convey a penetrating intensity (cat. no. 123). She also made a series of photographs of softly lit flowers that are especially romantic (cat. no. 124). Sears was a founding member of the SACB and a member of the first jury. ❡ Day also encouraged Clarence H. White, originally from Newark, Ohio, whom he had met at the Philadelphia Photographic Salon in 1898, and was so impressed by his photographs that he arranged a one–man show for White at the Boston Camera Club the next year. In 1906, White and his family moved to New York, and from there visited Day in both Norwood and Maine. An influential teacher at Columbia University Teachers College in New York and at "Seguinland," a summer photography school he started in 1910 in an old hotel near Day's home in Maine, White taught his students to be especially sensitive to the subtleties of "almost infinite variations of surface quality, depth, luminosity and color suggestion" available in photography.[15] White's refined studies of the female figure, shown in an enchanted landscape, can be interpreted as symbols of femininity and motherhood (cat. no. 128). In 1907-08 he collaborated with Stieglitz to photograph the female nude, and in the same decade he made several portraits of Day with a black man cloaked in shadow, in which it seems likely that both photographers had a hand (cat. no. 127).[16] ❡ From New York City, where he was a successful financier, photography collector, and friend of Alfred Stieglitz, William B. Post was an active amateur photographer who summered and eventually retired to Fryeburg, Maine. With careful framing Post made poetic, naturalistic views of the Maine rural landscape that include his scenes of peaceful winter snow (fig. 46), summer water lilies, and fields of grain (cat. no. 122). The "elegance and grace" and "astonishing" simplicity of Post's style were praised by Sadakichi Hartmann in a 1901 review for Camera Notes.[17] Other lesser-known photographers in New England working in a direct, naturalistic approach were Herbert W. Gleason, Bertram H. Wentworth, and Martha Hale Harvey (fig. 47). ❡ Many women photographers of the era followed the convention that they should specialize in the documentation of family life and domestic customs, conventional subjects that related to women's traditional roles in soci-

ety. Sarah Choate Sears, Chansonetta Emmons, and the Allen sisters of Deerfield all addressed domestic themes in their photographic works. Chansonetta Emmons captured in her platinum prints charming, picturesque groups of children at play that are sometimes reminiscent of the paintings and watercolors of Winslow Homer (cat. no. 119A), as well as farming scenes meant to convey the beauty of honest work (cat. no. 119B). Frances and Mary Allen made large numbers of photographs, also primarily in platinum, of children playing in the fields and streams around Deerfield and of local folk, primarily women, making traditional crafts (cf. fig. 34), and acting out, in costume, daily moments of colonial life (cat. no. 112). ❡ A large number of the photographs of American furniture historian Wallace Nutting, like those of Frances and Mary Allen, were concerned with providing information about American colonial life (cat. no. 121). Nutting was especially important for seeking to engender a reverence for the purity and elegance of the customs of an earlier time. He reportedly sold nearly ten million hand–colored prints of nostalgic views of colonial interiors and bucolic landscapes between 1900 and 1936, while also producing a series of books with tipped–in photographs—including five on New England states: Vermont Beautiful (1922), Massachusetts Beautiful (1923), New Hampshire Beautiful (1923), Connecticut Beautiful (1923), and Maine Beautiful (1924). The photographs were hand–colored by women in his Old America Company publishing house in Framingham, Massachusetts. ❡ Working initially in the Boston area, Edwin Hale Lincoln made platinum prints of sailing ships before moving in 1893 to western Massachusetts, where he photographed trees, orchids, and the palatial summer residences in and around Lenox. Lincoln's deep affection for natural science enabled him to make an extended series of 400 platinum prints of New England plants which he titled Wildflowers of New England (1914). These botanical images, which he began making in the early 1890s, were acclaimed by Gustav Stickley in the Craftsman: "The Craftsman has had the good fortune to secure from Mr. Lincoln a series of pictures of flowers which bloom from April, May and June throughout our Northeast country. These will appear in our magazine in the months in which they appear in the New England wild gardens and we feel secure that they will meet with the response that such simple beauty must always win from Nature's true lovers."[18] ❡ One of the most daring composers of the Pictorialist photographic im-

15. Clarence H. White, "The Educational Value of Photography as an Art," in Art and Industry in Education: A Book Illustrative of the Principles and Problems in the Courses in Fine and Industrial Arts at Teachers College (New York: Teachers College, Columbia University, Arts and Crafts Club, 1912), p. 87.

16. Barbara L. Michaels clarified the authorship and approximate dating of these portraits of Day with a black man in "New Light on F. Holland Day's Photographs of African Americans," History of Photography 18, no. 4 (Winter 1994), p. 339 and fns. 45 and 46.

17. Sadakichi Hartmann, "Exhibition of Prints by William B. Post," Camera Notes 4, no. 4 (April 1901), p. 27, as reported in Keith F. Davis, An American Century of Photography, from Dry–plate to Digital: The Hallmark Photographic Collection (Kansas City, Mo.: Hallmark Cards, Inc., 1995), p. 37.

18. Unknown (Gustav Stickley?), "A New England Flower Lover," Craftsman 28, no. 6 (March 1915), p. 689. See also William B. Becker, "'Permanent Authentic Record': The Arts and Crafts Photographs of Edwin Hale Lincoln," History of Photography 13, no. 1 (January–March 1989), p. 23.

19. Sadakichi Hartmann, "Boston Art Gossip," *Art News* 1, no. 4 (June 1897), p. 6, reprinted in Jane Calhoun Weaver, ed., *Sadakichi Hartmann, Critical Modernist: Collected Writings* (Berkeley: University of California Press, 1991), p. 79.

age was, like Lincoln, also active in western Massachusetts, Stockbridge photographer George Seeley. After picking up the camera in 1902—later than many of his Pictorialist peers—Seeley exhibited for the first time in 1904 at the First American Photographic Salon in New York, where his work was widely acclaimed. This exhibition, which occurred despite the lack of sanction by Stieglitz, included work by a number of worthy New Englanders such as the editor and writer on photography, Frank Roy Fraprie, and the Worcester photographer Dwight A. Davis (fig. 48). Seeley's success prompted Stieglitz to invite him to join the newly organized Photo–Secession and to feature his photographs in subsequent issues of *Camera Work*. Seeley's compositions employ flat, decorative tonalities on a bolder scale than many of his contemporaries to make increasingly abstract interpretations of the Stockbridge landscape (cat. no. 126). His photographs were well received, partly because of their sense of timelessness and their monumentality. Occasionally Seeley made images of rural life that in contrast have an engaging immediacy and directness, such as his close–up of two pigs (fig. 49). Animals as subjects were more common in the domain of Naturalist photographers such as William Lyman Underwood, who explored taking pictures of wild and domesticated animals,

including a pet bear. ⟪ Sadakichi Hartmann wrote in 1897 that "Boston seems to be a kind of preparatory school for New York and other cities."[19] Many aesthetic styles, techniques, and practices in photography originated in New England. Precedents for the establishment of camera clubs and for photography exhibitions were first set in Boston, and advocates of the artistic value of the medium looked to Day, Coburn, and later Seeley, among others, for inspiration. These Pictorialists and the Naturalists affirmed the role of the beautiful, the utilitarian, and the natural in photography early in the Arts and Crafts movement through their compositional styles, their innovative techniques, and their advocacy for the medium. Just as Southworth and Hawes had set the standard for the art of the daguerreotype in the middle of the century, New England Pictorialist and Naturalist photographers established important precepts for Arts and Crafts photography at the century's end. ◎

The author would like to thank in particular Clifford S. Ackley of the Museum of Fine Arts, Boston; Verna Posever Curtis of the Library of Congress; Karen Haas; Mack Lee of Lee Gallery, Winchester, Mass.; Christian A. Peterson of The Minneapolis Institute of Arts; and George R. Rinhart for their assistance and support.

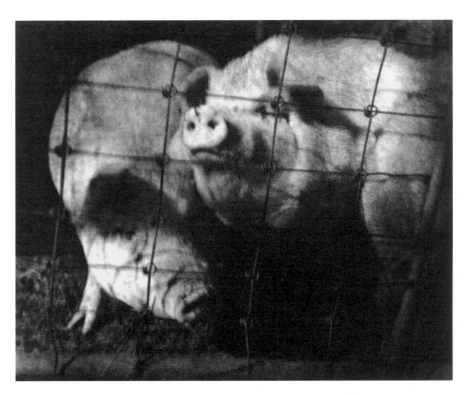

{49} George H. Seeley, *Untitled (Pigs)*, ca. 1920s, toned silver print; Museum of Fine Arts, Boston.

THE
FLOURISH
OF
COLOR
RELIEF
PRINT-
MAKING
IN
NEW ENGLAND

DAVID ACTON

AT THE TURN of the twentieth century an unprece-dented surge in the production and popularity of original prints accompanied changing values con-cerning their status as works of fine art. The Boston area became the country's most important region for color relief printmaking at that time, rivaled only by California for its concentration of artists, their stylistic breadth, and the scale of their production. The cosmopolitan character that made Boston a capital of American publishing (see "A Millennium in Book–Making: the Book Arts in Boston" in this volume) also helped to nurture New England as a center for printmaking. Artists were drawn from afar to historic New England villages and picturesque towns on the Atlantic shore, where artists' colonies thrived. The region's vast academic community provided teaching opportunities that helped keep many artists in the area. A fad in the 1890s for making and collecting color art posters flourished in Boston, where many designers were inspired and influenced by transatlantic antecedents: the Arts and Crafts movement from England, Art Nouveau from France and Belgium, Jugendstil from Munich, Sezessionstil from Vienna, and especial-ly color woodcuts from Japan.[1] ❦ Printmaking possessed an un-usual status, for despite the time and manual dexterity required by its complex techniques, their two–dimensionality and reliance on drawing allied prints more closely to painting than to the dec-orative arts. Many galleries that concentrated on painting also presented exhibitions of prints during this period, and they sold well. Most of these works of art were purchased by middle–class consumers, one at a time. They were conceived as and destined to be wall decoration. In 1918 the reviewer of a New York exhibition of color woodcuts observed: "Many of the prints would grace my lady's boudoir or add cheer to a morning room, because, al-though not costing much, they are real art and fulfill their mis-sion to be decorative and bring happiness. Many others would

1. David Kiehl, *American Art Posters of the 1890s in the Metropolitan Museum of Art* (New York: Abrams, 1987).

2. Peyton Boswell, "The New American School of Wood Block Printers in Color," Arts and Decoration 9 (1918), p. 168.

3. Prints were sold, for example, from Arthur Wesley Dow's exhibition at the Museum of Fine Arts in 1895, and from Gustave Baumann's show at the Worcester Art Museum in 1930.

4. For a list of the print-makers who exhibited at the P.P.I.E., see Raymond L. Wilson, Index of American Print Exhibitions, 1882–1940 (Metuchen, N.J.: Scarecrow Press, 1988), pp. 522–49.

5. For an historical survey of woodcut in Europe, see Arthur Mayger Hind, An Introduction to the History of Woodcut, 2 vols. (London: Constable and Company, Ltd., 1935); for an outstanding technical manual of the period, see Julius J. Lankes, A Woodcut Manual (New York: H. Holt and Company, 1932).

6. On the techniques of Japanese color woodcut, see Margaret Miller Kanada, Color Woodblock Printmaking: The Traditional Method, Ukiyo-e (Tokyo: Sfunotomo, 1992); for a period technical manual in English, see Frank Morley Fletcher, Wood-block Printing: A Description of the Craft of Woodcutting & Colourprinting Based on the Japanese Practice (London: J. Hogg, 1916).

add just the artistic touch needed to the walls of a bungalow or the especially appointed rooms of a country home."[2] This was the period when many American museums started to collect prints, and it was not unusual for prints to be offered for public sale at museum exhibitions.[3] Printmakers sold their work singly from their studios, often by mail order. ❡ Printmaking societies, large and small, sprang up around the country, and annual exhibitions were a common feature of their activities. These shows often traveled to small museums and libraries, and prints were sold at each venue. Printmakers often joined distant clubs and sent their work to distant shows, thus establishing geographically extensive markets for themselves. Competitive printmaking exhibitions were featured in the Panama–Pacific International Exposition in San Francisco in 1915, for example, and many of the awards went to color woodcut artists with ties to Massachusetts.[4] Occasionally color woodcuts were exhibited by the Society of Arts and Crafts, Boston; however, never were they a consistent or significant feature of the shows. Those printmakers whose works were presented there seem to have produced few woodcuts, for generally little is known of them today. ❡ Woodcut became almost as common as etching in this era of hand–craft, because of its simplicity, econ-

omy, and the universal availability of required materials and tools. Basically this technique begins with a design drawn on the smooth side of a wooden plank; the unmarked areas are then carved away. Ink is applied to the remaining surface and transferred to paper under pressure. This rudimentary procedure was shared by two independent traditions that developed over centuries in Western Europe and in Japan. Both were professional endeavors, in which teams of craftsmen produced large numbers of prints. ❡ European artisans used thick, oil–based carbon inks, applied to the blocks with leather pads or rollers.[5] They printed on papers that were mold–made from cotton or linen, usually in sheets thick and opaque enough to be printed on both sides. Mechanical presses that employed screw, lever, or roller mechanisms were used to apply strong, even pressure vertically against the woodblock. For color prints a different printing matrix was used for each hue, and registration—the proper overlapping alignment of component images— was achieved by securing blocks and paper in fixed positions on the press. ❡ Color woodcut developed independently in Japan as a means of manufacturing popular printed ephemera.[6] Known as ukiyo–e, or "pictures of the floating world," these prints represented stylish actors

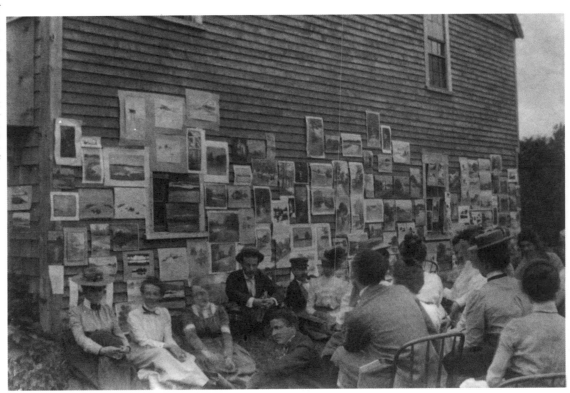

{50} Undated photograph of students at Arthur Wesley Dow's Ipswich (Mass.) Summer School; Ipswich Historical Society.

and fashionable courtesans—from the realm of worldly pleasures to be found in the pleasure quarter of the city of Edo (Tokyo)—or landscape views of famous places. Japanese printers brushed their water–based inks onto the blocks, with a medium of rice paste to blend colors and modulate tones. They printed on traditional papers handmade from the long, delicate fibers of the inner bark of mulberry trees. With the paper face down on the inked block, these artisans printed by rubbing the back of the sheet with the *baren*, a disklike pad covered with a palm leaf. For multiblock color prints, Japanese craftsmen registered their overprinted images by carefully placing the paper in guide marks, or *kento*, carved at the same positions in the corners of each woodblock. ❡ The Japanese method was a great inspiration to Arthur Wesley Dow, the central figure in New England color woodcut.7 He grew up in the small coastal town of Ipswich, north of Boston. After studying with a succession of local artists, Dow went to Paris in 1884, where he attended the Académie Julian, and then spent several months painting at Pont Aven in Brittany. Though he had been exposed to a wide range of styles and ideas, his work remained fairly conventional when he set himself up in Boston in 1889 as a painter and teacher. Then, early in 1891 Dow discovered the

work of the great *ukiyo–e* master Katsushika Hokusai, and was enchanted. He studied the prints at the Museum of Fine Arts and came to know Ernest F. Fenollosa, the curator of Oriental art, who enabled him to confront Japanese art and culture firsthand on its own terms.8 Dow began to explore Japanese design in his own work, and he experimented with color woodcut. He worked on a small scale, cutting his blocks from pine and printing in watercolor by hand–rubbing on Japanese papers. His works still represented landscape views of the shore, hay fields and salt marshes of Ipswich, but he abandoned the imitation of nature and Western systems of perspectival composition and illusionistic modeling (cat. no. 132). ❡ Dow and Fenollosa became close friends, and together they sought to combine Asian and European aesthetic principles in a new style. The artist consciously reduced his design vocabulary to line, color, and *notan*, a Japanese concept for the balance of dark and light. In 1893 he related some of his discoveries and evolving theories in "A Note on Japanese Art and What the American Artists May Learn Therefrom," in the Boston art magazine *The Knight Errant*.9 Dow's notions of the artist's self–reliance remained distinctly western. He believed that spiritual benefits came from the creative and physical process of

7. On Dow, see Frederick C. Moffatt, *Arthur Wesley Dow 1857–1922* (Washington, D.C.: Smithsonian Institution Press, 1977); Nancy E. Green, *Arthur Wesley Dow and His Influence* (Ithaca, N.Y.: Herbert F. Johnson Museum of Art, 1990); Julia Meech–Pekarik and Gabriel P. Weisberg, *Japonisme Comes to America: The Japanese Impact on the Graphic Arts, 1876–1925* (New York: Abrams, 1990), pp. 163–79.

8. Dow also met the museum's curator of graphic arts, Sylvester Rosa Koehler, who taught the artist how the prints were made. Note the article that Koehler edited on Japanese woodcut printing technique: T. Tokuno, "Japanese Wood–cutting and Wood–cut Printing," *Report of the United States National Museum of 1892* (Washington, D.C.: Government Printing Office, 1894), pp. 221–24.

9. Arthur Wesley Dow, "A Note on Japanese Art and What the American Artists May Learn Therefrom," *The Knight Errant*, vol. 1 (January 1893), pp.114-16.

{51} Vojtěch Preissig, *Arts and Crafts of the Homeland*, 1919, color linocut; Worcester Art Museum, Sarah C. Garver Fund.

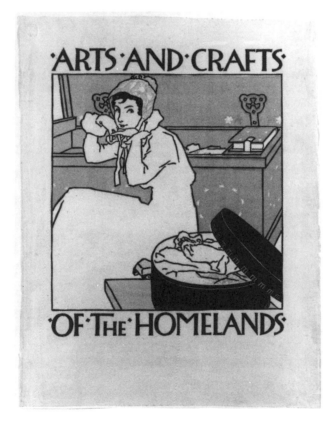

CAT. NO. 132A
Arthur Wesley Dow,
View in Ipswich, 1895

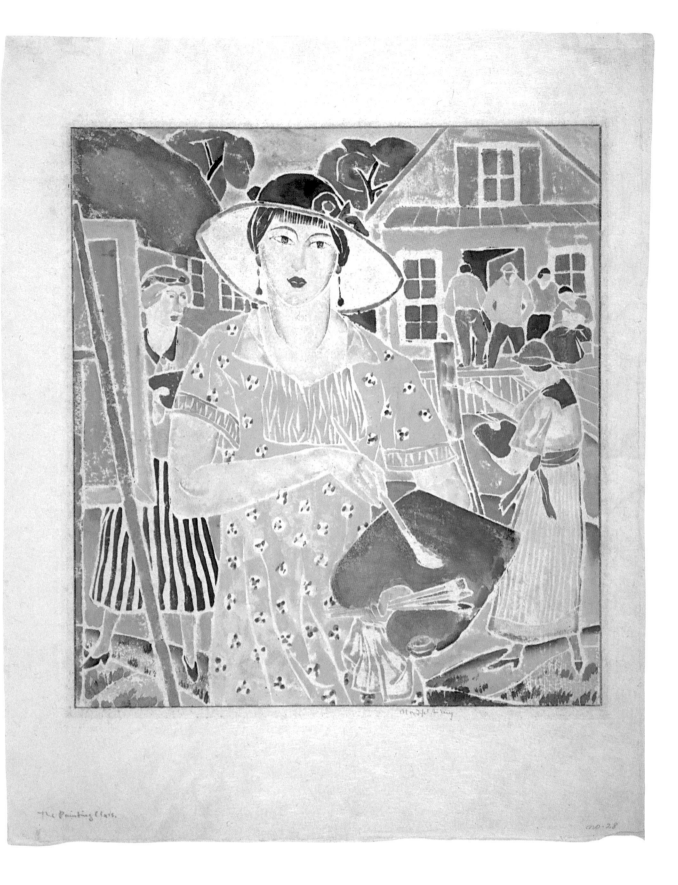

The Painting Class.

Nordfeldt imp

cno-28

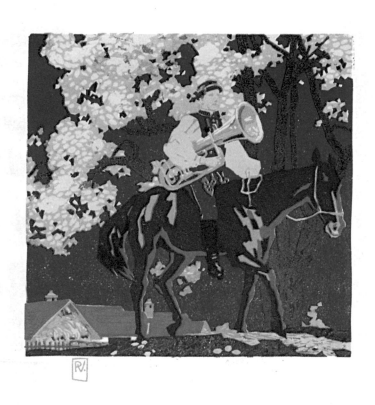

Vojtěch Preissig: Bohemian Musician
Linoleum Cut

CAT. NO. 142
Vojtěch Preissig,
The Bohemian Musician, 1916

1914.[17] This master printmaker had been the proprietor of his own workshop in his native Czechoslovakia.[18] Like the Wiener Werkstätte, his Prague studio produced both practical and decorative materials, but Preissig could not generate sufficient demand for these products and the business failed. In 1910 he joined his brother in New York, and worked as a commercial artist and illustrator specializing in the medium of linocut, or linoleum block printing.[19] During World War I the artist made linocut propaganda posters for distribution in Czechoslovakia, and he taught the technique in his courses at the Art Students League in New York. Preissig seems to have been the first to employ linocut as an artists' medium in the United States and to teach students its use. Dow recognized that this durable, soft material—easier to work than wood—had great educational potential. ❡ Preissig moved to Boston in 1916 to teach at the Wentworth Institute of Technology, and he headed its graphic arts department through the mid-1920s. His own prints often depicted Czech subjects in a direct, decorative manner redolent of the perfume of Art Nouveau. This is apparent in the linocut poster for the exhibition *Arts and Crafts of the Homeland*, printed at the Wentworth Institute in 1919 (fig. 51).[20] While the furniture, bookbinding, costumes, and textiles in the exhibition display English and colonial revival influences, the use of a languorous young woman is reminiscent of the designs of Alphonse Mucha, for whom Preissig worked as an assistant in Paris from 1898 to 1903. ❡ In 1914 Edna Boies Hopkins first visited the artists' colony at Provincetown, on the tip of Cape Cod.[21] The activity of this artist, teacher, and intermediary was pivotal for relief printmaking in Massachusetts. A decade earlier, after studying with Dow in Brooklyn, she traveled to Japan to acquire a deeper knowledge of an *ukiyo–e* printmaking. Afterwards, in Paris, the artist combined the Japanese manner with influences from French wood engraving. Borrowing equally from *ukiyo–e* and Post–Impressionism, she made popular woodcuts of flowers and foliage, arranged as artfully as *ikebana* and cropped as eccentrically as a *ukiyo–e* print (cat. no. 134). Hopkins taught her color woodcut technique in Paris, and among her pupils were two old friends from Cincinnati, Ethel Mars and Maud Hunt Squire (cat. no. 144). After moving to France in 1906, the lifetime companions Mars and Squire were drawn to bohemian art circles in Paris.[22] Both were watercolorists in whose work *japonisme* was combined with the influence of the Nabis. Mars's vivid woodcuts of Parisian café life were well received at the Salon d'Automne, where they were shown from 1907 to 1913. She taught the color woodcut technique to Ada Gilmore and Mildred McMillen, two young artists from Chicago (cat. nos. 130 and 137). ❡ In the spring of 1915—shortly after the outbreak of the First World War, when many American artists returned from Europe—Mars, Squire, Gilmore, and McMillen all arrived in Provincetown.[23] They may have been recommended to the place by Hopkins, or attracted by the Continental atmosphere of this picturesque seaside village with its Portuguese fishing community and its summertime influx of artists, writers, actors, and musicians. B.J.O. Nordfeldt and Juliette Nichols came to Provincetown that summer, making up a group of six printmakers who stayed after Hopkins and the other artists left town in the autumn. Their mutual enthusiasm for color woodcut drew them together, and they worked steadily through the winter, sharing ideas, and planning for a group exhibition the following season. Some produced still lifes, while others made genre, landscape, and seascape prints. ❡ It was Nordfeldt who originated the method and look that came to distinguish Provincetown printmaking. He had been using the Japanese technique to create color woodcuts closely inspired by *ukiyo–e* prints since 1900.[24] Also a skillful intaglio printmaker, Nordfeldt was familiar with the technique of applying several colors to a single etched plate and printing in one pass through the press; in Provincetown he adapted this principle to the hand–printed woodcut. After penciling his design in simple outlines on a pine block, the artist cut them away in unadorned grooves. He tacked the paper to one edge of the block, so the sheet was folded over the printing surface and back, thus assuring proper registration. When the artist applied watercolors to the block with a brush, the grooves dividing the colored cells kept them from mixing and embossed the unprinted white lines. He then moistened the paper, folded it over, and rubbed on the back to print. Nordfeldt completed one impression at a time of these large and intensely colored prints, which represented genre images of the lives of the fishermen and artists of Provincetown (cat. no. 140). ❡ That winter, several Provincetown artists made woodcuts by this new technique, and were featured in a May exhibition at the Berlin Photographic Company in New York. Later in the summer, another show was mounted at Ambrose Webster's oceanside studio in Provincetown. Many others

17. In 1914 Dow and Preissig shared an exhibition at the Montclair Art Museum in New Jersey; see *Oil Paintings and Block Prints by Arthur Wesley Dow, Graphic Works by Vojtěch Preissig* (Montclair, N.J.: Montclair Art Museum, 1914–15).

18. Tomáš Vlček and Jiri Zantofsky, *Vojtěch Preissig, 1873–1944* (Prague: Narodni Galleri, 1968); and Irena Goldscheider, *Czechoslovak Prints from 1900 to 1970* (London: British Museum Publications, 1986), pp. 21–22.

19. Developed in England in the 1860s principally for use as a floor covering, linoleum seems to have been first used for printmaking around 1900 in Germany and Eastern Europe. It was made from powdered cork or wood bound together with oxidized linseed oil, calendared in sheets and applied to a burlap backing. The softness of the material and its absence of grain made it easier to cut than wood, and ideal for printing by hand or press.

20. Preissig's influence in Boston continued through his successor, the Czech–American Louis K. Novak, who taught at the Wentworth Institute and continued to produce his own Arts and Crafts–influenced color relief prints through the 1930s. A selection of Novak's prints and related technical materials were given to the Museum of Fine Arts, Boston after the artist's death in 1981.

21. Mary Ryan Gallery, *Edna Boies Hopkins: Color Woodcuts, 1900–1923* (New York: The Gallery, 1986); David Acton, *A Spectrum of Innovation: Color in American Printmaking, 1890–1960* (New York: W.W. Norton, 1990), pp. 64–65, 268; and Meech–Pekarik and Weisberg, *Japonisme Comes to America*, pp. 180–89.

22. The descriptions of what provocative figures Mars and Squire were in Paris include those of the American artist Anne Goldthwaite (see Adelyn D. Breeskin, *Anne Goldthwaite: A Catalogue Raisonné of the Graphic Work* [Montgomery, Ala.: Montgomery Museum of Fine Arts, 1982], p. 25), and of Gertrude Stein, who mentioned them in *The Autobiography of Alice B. Toklas*, and used the two women as the models for her short story, "Miss Furr and Miss Skeene."

24. On Nordfeldt, see Meech–Pekarik and Weisberg, *Japonisme Comes to America*, pp. 200–13; and Fiona Donovan, *The Woodblock Prints of B.J.O. Nordfeldt, A Catalogue Raisonné* (Minneapolis: University Art Museum, University of Minnesota, 1991).

23. According to the account of Ada Gilmore—who later married the artist Oliver Newberry Chaffee—published in *The Provincetown Advocate* in 1933, and reprinted there in 1952; see Ada Gilmore Chaffee, "Cape End Early Cradled Gifted Group of Print Makers Who Added to Art," *The Provincetown Advocate*, October 30, 1952, p. 5. On the Provincetown Printers group, see Janet Flint, *Provincetown Printers: A Woodcut Tradition* (Washington, D.C.: Smithsonian Institution Press, 1983); William Evaul, "The Provincetown Printers: Genesis of a Unique Color–Woodcut Process," *Print Review* 18 (1983), pp. 57–66; and Matthew Marks, "Provincetown Prints (review of the National Museum of American Art exhibition)," *Print Collector's Newsletter* 15 (September–October 1984), pp. 131–33.

anxiously took up the new technique, which was easy and encouraged personal adaptation. Provincetown became a mecca for relief printmaking, and artists who employed an array of techniques were drawn there. Some, like Blanche Lazzell and Maud Ainslie, settled there; some, like Gustave Baumann and Tod Lindenmuth, came only as summer visitors; and others, like Eliza Draper Gardiner and Margaret Jordan Patterson (fig. 52), simply sent their prints to group shows there. ❮ Color woodcut in Provincetown seems to have reached its apogee in the summer of 1918, when a large print show was presented at the Town Hall, and the Provincetown Printers, the first printmaking society in America devoted solely to woodcut, was founded. Nordfeldt had lost interest by this time, but the white line woodcut technique was fully exploited by Blanche Lazzell (cat. no. 135).[25] She made her first print at Provincetown in 1916, taught the technique in her wharf studio through the 1940s, and executed her last color woodcut in Morgantown, West Virginia

in about 1954. Lazzell went to Paris in 1923 to study with Fernand Léger, Albert Gleizes, and André Lhote. After she returned to Cape Cod, many of her prints reflected the influence of Cubism. Lazzell shared these ideas in the still–vital Provincetown artistic community, and artists such as Agnes Weinrich and Karl Knaths, whose color woodcuts of the 1910s have the unmistakable decorative rhythm of Arts and Crafts style, used the medium for new explorations of modernism. ❮ By 1927 the fashion for relief printmaking in the Arts and Crafts style was on the wane. However, its enormous influence on the proliferation and appreciation of American printmaking was apparent five years later when these prints predominated in the landmark exhibition at the Brooklyn Museum.[26] This trend had helped to transform printmaking from a method of reproduction into an original creative medium for both serious artists and hobbyists. Color relief prints had been accepted in the thousands into American museums and homes. ◎

25. On Lazzell, see John Clarkson. *Blanche Lazzell* (Morgantown, W.Va.: Creative Arts Center Galleries, West Virginia University, 1979); Flint, *Provincetown Printers*, pp. 34–35; Acton, *A Spectrum of Innovation*, pp. 82–83, 270–71.

26. *American Color Prints* (Brooklyn, N.Y.: Brooklyn Museum, 1933).

NO. 1
Olof Althin
Chest with drawer,
1900–15
Oak
36 1/2 inches H x
60 1/2 inches W x
23 1/2 inches D
Private Collection

NO. 2
Carrig–Rohane Shop;
Adrian Eckberg,
head carver
Jewelry box, 1915
Yellow–poplar with sgraffito
decoration and inset stones
2 3/4 inches H x 8 3/4 inches W x
5 3/4 inches D
Collection of Helen Vose Carr

NO. 5
Frank Cleveland, designer;
Frederick W. Kulkmann, maker;
Alfred Longuemere, carver
Credence table, 1907
Oak
39 1/4 inches H x 30 inches W x
18 inches D
Rector, Wardens, and Vestry of
Grace Episcopal Church,
Manchester, New Hampshire

NO. 3
Hermann Dudley Murphy, painter;
Carrig–Rohane Shop, frame–makers
The Adriatic Sea, ca. 1908
Oil on canvas, with gold leaf on
carved yellow–poplar frame
30 3/4 inches H x 37 7/8 inches W x
2 3/8 inches D (framed); 20 inches H x
27 1/8 inches W (unframed)
Frame marked, with insignia:
"19 ["M" in circle] 08/Carrig Rohane/593"
Museum of Fine Arts, Boston;
Gift of Miss Mary Thacher, 45.777

NO. 4
Edmund Tarbell, painter;
Carrig–Rohane Shop, frame–makers
New England Interior, ca. 1906 (painting),
1908 (frame)
Oil on canvas, with gold leaf
on carved yellow–poplar frame
42 inches H x 37 1/8 inches W x
2 1/4 inches D (framed);
30 1/8 inches H x 25 1/8 inches W (unframed)
Frame marked, with insignia:
"19 ["M" in circle] 08/Carrig Rohane/607"
Museum of Fine Arts, Boston;
Gift of Mrs. Eugene C. Eppinger, 1985.66
(DMCC venue only)

NO. 6C
Advertisement for
Loring Cushing,
ca. 1912
12 1/2 inches H x
6 1/2 inches W (sheet)
Hingham Historical Society,
Hingham, Massachusetts

NO. 6A
Loring Cushing
Miniature slat-back chair
ca. 1910
Yellow–poplar
9 inches H x 3 1/2 inches W x
3 1/8 inches D
Hingham Historical Society,
Hingham, Massachusetts

NO. 6B
Loring Cushing
Miniature desk
ca. 1910
Yellow–poplar
9 1/2 inches H x 7 7/8 inches W x
4 1/2 inches D
Hingham Historical Society,
Hingham, Massachusetts

NO. 7
John Kirchmayer
A Christmas Festival in Heaven,
1918
Oak tableau
66 inches H x 24 inches W x
4 inches D
The Detroit Institute of Arts;
Gift of George G. Booth,
19.67

NO. 8
William Leavens and Company
Sideboard
ca. 1910
Oak, white pine, and copper
45 1/4 inches H x 48 inches W x
21 inches D
Labeled on backboard:
"WILLIAM LEAVENS & CO. /
[chair–table image] /
MANUFACTURERS/BOSTON, MASS."
Tau Zeta Epsilon Art and Music Society,
Wellesley College

NO. 9
Andrew Lees
Pair of bookends,
1910–30
Mahogany
5 3/8 inches H x 4 1/4 inches W x
4 5/8 inches D
Private Collection

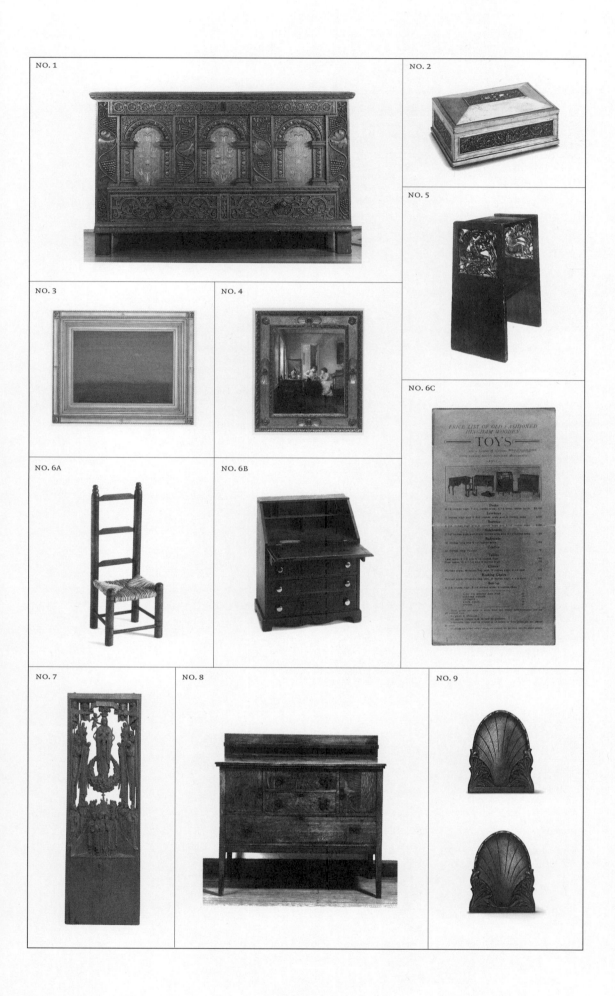

NO. 1

NO. 2

NO. 3

NO. 4

NO. 5

NO. 6C

NO. 6A

NO. 6B

NO. 7

NO. 8

NO. 9

167

NO. 10A
W.B. Luce
Miniature looking glass,
ca. 1910
Yellow–poplar
7 1/2 inches H x 3 7/8 inches W
Ink–stamped
on backing:
"W.B. LUCE/HINGHAM CEN. MASS."
Hingham Historical Society,
Hingham, Massachusetts

NO. 10B
W.B. Luce
Miniature chest of drawers,
ca. 1910
Maple and yellow–poplar
4 1/2 inches H x 3 1/2 inches W x
1 3/4 inches D
Ink–stamped on drawer bottom:
"W.B. LUCE/HINGHAM CEN. MASS.";
labeled on bottom:
"APPROVED/HINGHAM–SOCIETY/
[bucket image]/ARTS–AND–CRAFTS"
Private Collection

NO. 11
Wallace Nutting
Parmenter–Sudbury cupboard
ca. 1920–30
Oak and white pine
55 1/2 inches H x 54 inches W x
23 1/4 inches D
Branded on drawer bottom:
"WALLACE NUTTING"
Pine Manor College,
Chestnut Hill, Massachusetts;
Gift of Mr. and Mrs. George Olmsted, Jr.
in memory of their daughter Virginia

NO. 12
Molly Coolidge Perkins
Hanging bear cabinet, 1926
White pine and glass
32 3/4 inches H x 27 1/2 inches W x
10 1/2 inches D
Initialed and dated, bottom center:
"M.D.P./1926"
Collection of William H. Perkins

NO. 13
Molly Coolidge Perkins
Peacock medallion,
1899
Carved, painted, and gilded white pine
9 inches diameter x 1 inch D
Labeled on reverse:
"Miss Mary Coolidge/
114 Beacon Street, Boston"
Collection of Mrs. Malcolm D. Perkins

NO. 14
Leander Plummer
A School of Bluefish and Tern Over Sand Smelt,
1911
White pine with stain
26 inches H x 67 1/2 inches W x 6 inches D
Signed and dated, lower right:
"L.A. Plummer/1911"
Board of Trustees of the New Bedford
Free Public Library

NO. 15
Arthur Wesley Dow, painter;
Charles Prendergast, frame–maker
The Mirror, 1916
Oil on canvas, with gold leaf on carved
and gessoed yellow–poplar frame
35 1/2 inches H x 45 3/4 inches W
(framed)
John Heard House,
Ipswich Historical Society

NO. 16
William F. Ross & Company
Sideboard from
Tower Court, 1915
Oak with polychrome decoration
47 3/4 inches H x 96 inches W x
29 inches D
Wellesley College, Wellesley,
Massachusetts

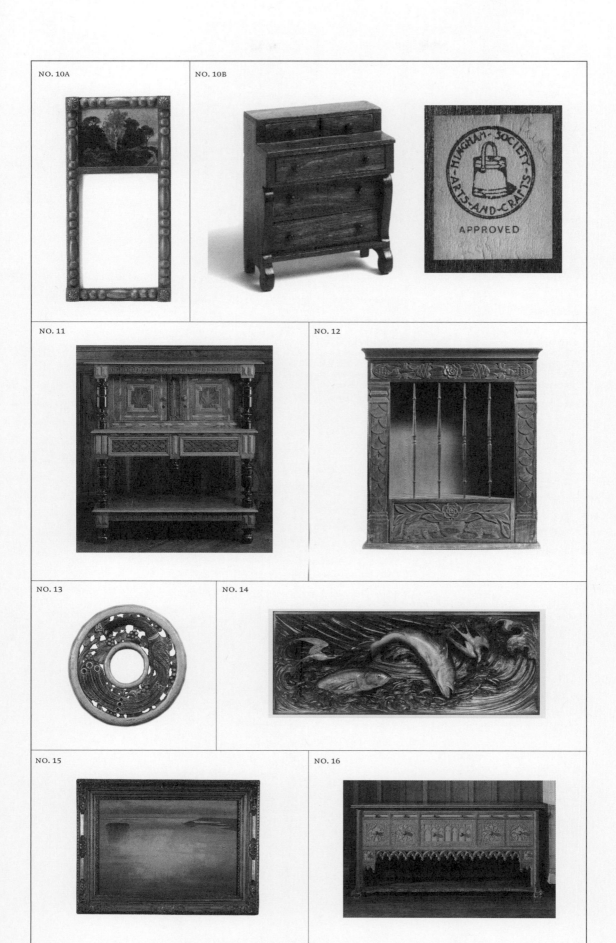

NO. 10A

NO. 10B

NO. 11

NO. 12

NO. 13

NO. 14

NO. 15

NO. 16

NO. 17
Sidney T. Callowhill,
decorator
Salad plate with South
American Indian design,
ca. 1920–30
China painted German
porcelain blank
7 5/8 inches diameter
Signed: "Sidney T. Callowhill"
Private Collection

NO. 18
Sarah Ryel Comer,
decorator
Charger with Persian border,
1913–27
China painted French
porcelain blank
11 3/4 inches diameter
Signed: "Sarah Ryel Comer"
Collection of
Rosalie Berberian

NO. 19
Russell S. Crook
Vase with lion
decoration,
ca. 1907
Salt–glazed stoneware
9 1/2 inches H x
7 inches diameter
Monogrammed in ligature: "RSC"
Society for the Preservation of
New England Antiquities,
Boston, Massachusetts;
Gift of Edward Buckingham Sears

NO. 20
Dedham Pottery;
Maude Davenport, decorator
Plate with grey crackle glaze and
cobalt horse–chestnut border,
ca. 1904–28
Stoneware
8 9/16 inches diameter
Marked: Maude Davenport circle,
blue company stamp
Collection of James D. Kaufman

NO. 21
Dedham Pottery;
Hugh Cornwall Robertson,
maker
Red–glazed vase,
ca. 1896–1908
Stoneware with "volcanic" glaze
11 5/8 inches H x
5 1/4 inches diameter
Marked: "Dedham/Pottery/HCR"
Yale University Art Gallery;
Mabel Brady Garvan Collection,
by exchange

NO. 22
Grueby Pottery Company;
George P. Kendrick, designer;
Wilhelmina Post, modeler
Urn–shaped matte green vase
with yellow daffodils,
ca. 1901
Stoneware
10 inches H x 8 inches diameter
Impressed circular mark:
"GRUEBY POTTERY/BOSTON USA";
monogrammed in ligature: "WP"
Private Collection

NO. 23
Grueby Faience Company
Oxen cart mantel
from *Dreamwold*, Scituate, Mass.,
1902
Stoneware tiles
Three tiles, across mantel top:
each 12 inches H x 2 inches D;
left tile 16 3/4 inches W,
center tile 25 5/8 inches W,
right tile 17 5/8 inches W
(60 inches W overall)
Private Collection

NO. 24
Grueby Faience Company;
Ruth Erickson, modeler;
Tiffany Studios
Spherical matte ochre lamp base
with white buds;
leaded glass brickwork shade
with vine pattern border,
ca. 1900–05
Stoneware and glass
19 inches H x
16 inches diameter (shade)
Base monogrammed:
"RE"; circular paper label:
"GRUEBY POTTERY/
BOSTON USA"; shade stamped:
"TIFFANY STUDIOS/
NEW YORK", "1435"
Collection of David Cathers

NO. 25
Marblehead Pottery
Cylindrical vase with band of
polychrome mosaic birds,
1913
Earthenware
9 inches H x
4 1/2 inches diameter
Impressed on base:
Marblehead mark with
sailing ship
Collection of Betty and
Robert A. Hut

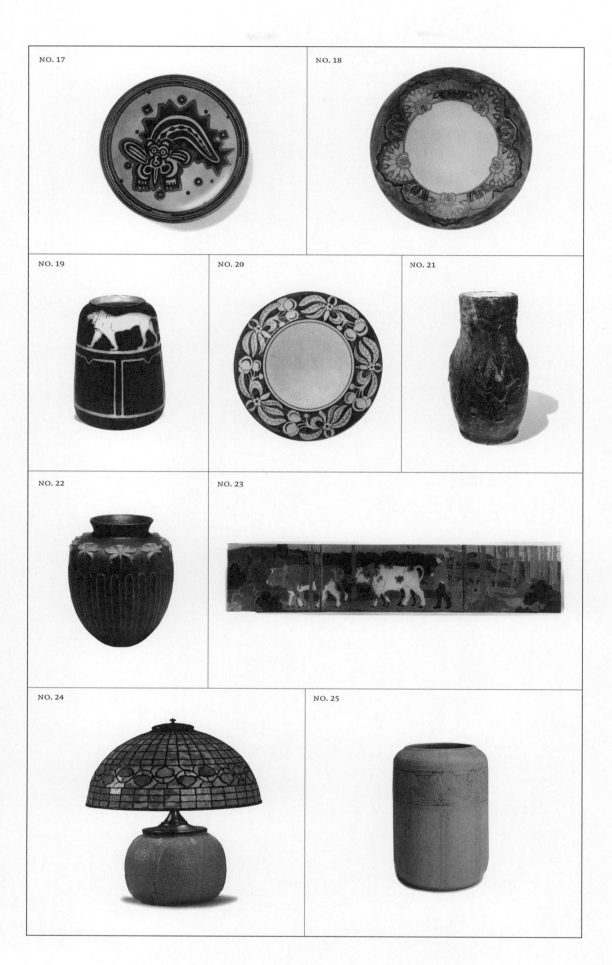

NO. 17

NO. 18

NO. 19

NO. 20

NO. 21

NO. 22

NO. 23

NO. 24

NO. 25

171

NO. 26A
Marblehead Pottery
Vase with hollyhocks,
1904–08
Earthenware
9 3/4 inches H x
3 1/8 inches diameter
Marked: M over T
with stylized seagull
through M
Collection of Betty and
Robert A. Hut

NO. 26B
Arthur Wesley Dow
Composition: a Series of Exercises
in Art Structure... (6th ed.)
(New York: Baker and
Taylor, 1905)
Printed book, detail of page 63
11 1/4 inches H x 9 inches W
Wellesley College Library

NO. 27
Merrimac Pottery;
Thomas Nickerson
Matte green vase with
four–petal flowers at rim,
1900–01
Earthenware
7 1/4 inches H x
4 1/4 inches diameter
Marked on bottom:
large paper label with sturgeon
Collection of Barbara and
Henry Fuldner

NO. 28
Merrimac Pottery;
Thomas Nickerson
Spherical vase with black
metallic glaze and four
loop handles, 1903–08
Earthenware
9 3/4 inches H x
11 5/8 inches W
Collection of R.A. Ellison

NO. 29
L.F. Nash, decorator
Salad plate with orange
tree border, ca. 1910
China painted German
porcelain blank
7 5/8 inches diameter
Initialed: "LFN"
Collection of Ellen Paul
Denker and Bert Denker

NO. 30
Paul Revere Pottery;
Edith Brown, designer;
Sara Galner, decorator
Matte–glazed charger with
nighttime landscape of lake
and cottage, 1915
Earthenware
12 inches diameter
Initialed: "SG"
Collection of John Markus

NO. 31
Paul Revere Pottery;
Ida Goldstein, decorator
Matte green and yellow vase
with large chrysanthemum
blossoms, ca. 1908
Earthenware
8 3/4 inches H x
7 1/2 inches diameter
Initialed: "IG"
Collection of R.A. Ellison

NO. 32
William Walley
Narrow–necked vase
with four handles,
1898–1919
Red earthenware
11 9/16 inches H x
5 inches diameter
Initialed, on base: "WJW"
Private Collection

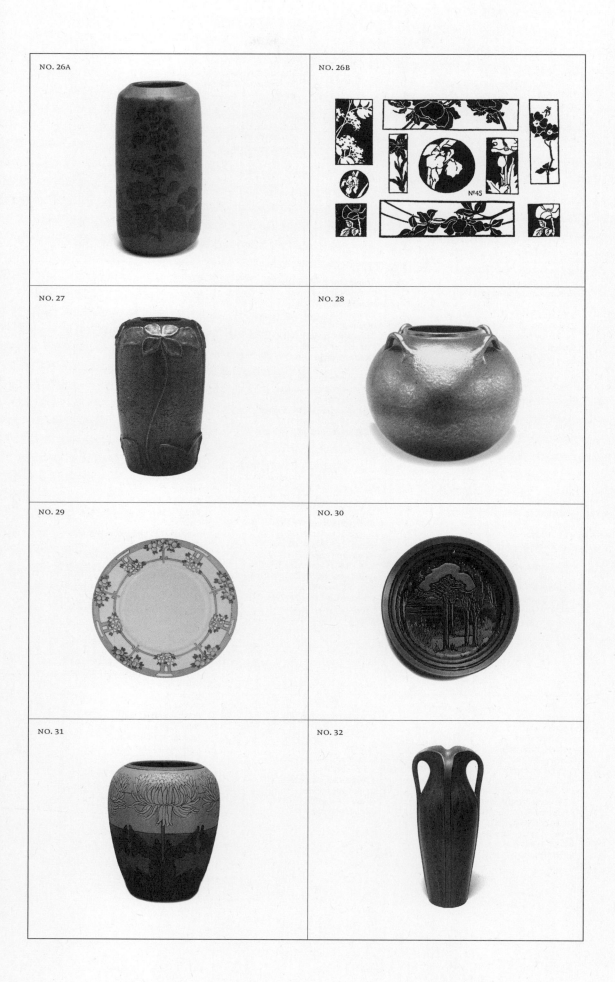

NO. 26A

NO. 26B

Nº45

NO. 27

NO. 28

NO. 29

NO. 30

NO. 31

NO. 32

NO. 33
Mary Batchelder
Table lamp with pierced
shade and fringe, ca. 1907
Metal, possibly copper
13 inches H (without
chimney) x 14 inches
diameter (shade)
Incised on bottom, with
monogram: "MB"
Private Collection

NO. 34
Elizabeth Copeland
Footed bowl, ca. 1904–05
Silver
3 3/4 inches H x 9 7/8
inches diameter (7 3/8
inches at opening)
Scratched on base: "EC"
Private Collection

NO. 35
Elizabeth Copeland
Covered box, ca. 1915–37
Silver with enamel
3 3/4 inches H x 6 1/4 inches W x
4 inches D
Marked on bottom in raised,
applied letters: "EC"
Collection of Jacqueline Loewe
Fowler

NO. 36
George Christian Gebelein
Coffeepot and creamer,
ca. 1903–06
Silver with ebony handle
and finial
Coffeepot: 6 1/2 inches H x
7 1/2 inches W x 4 inches D
Creamer: 3 inches H x
5 inches W x 3 inches D
Each stamped on underside,
incuse, within cut-cornered
rectangle: "GEBELEIN"; hallmark within rectangle, in raised
letters: "H [anvil image] S"
Collection of Arthur D. Gebelein

NO. 37
George Christian Gebelein
Sugar box, ca. 1935
Silver
5 1/4 inches H x 9 inches W x
7 1/2 inches D
Stamped inside on bottom, in
raised letters within shaped
cartouche: "GEBELEIN"
Collection of Arthur D. Gebelein,
Ernest G. Gebelein, and
Gardiner G. Greene

NO. 38
George E. Germer
Chalice, 1924
Silver with gilt bowl
9 inches H x 4 inches W
(cup, 5 3/4 inches W at base)
Stamped on base:
"G.E. GERMER/BOSTON,
MA./STERLING"
Isabella Stewart Gardner
Museum; Gift of the Trustees,
Christmas 1924 in memory
of Isabella Stewart Gardner

NO. 39
George J. Hunt
Award in form of a chalice, 1934
Gold
6 inches H x 7 3/16 inches W x
4 7/8 inches D
Inscribed around rim: "•ALBERT
CAMERON BURRAGE VASE•AWARDED
TO THE ISABELLA STEWART GARDNER
MUSEUM BY THE MASSACHUSETTS
HORTICULTURAL SOCIETY FOR THE
MOST OUTSTANDING EXHIBIT OF
THE YEAR 1934"
Marked on base: "18K/ENTIRELY/
HAND–WROUGHT/G.J. HUNT"
Isabella Stewart Gardner Museum;
Horticulture Society Award to Isabella
Stewart Gardner Museum for Flower
Show, 1934

NO. 40
George J. Hunt
Teapot, 1904
Silver with ivory
insulators and finial
6 inches H x 9 inches W x
5 1/2 inches diameter
Marked on body: "GJH" in
triangle; lion passant;
Chester (England) hallmark, "C"
(1904 datemark); marked
inside lid: lion passant, "C"
Museum of Fine Arts, Boston;
Gift of Joseph B. and
Edith Alpers

NO. 41
George Prentiss Kendrick,
designer
Tobacco jar (or tea caddy),
ca. 1897
Copper with silvered interior
4 1/2 inches H x
4 11/16 inches diameter
Stamped on bottom,
incuse: "G.P.K."
Private Collection

NO. 42
Frank L. Koralewsky
Hinges, lock, and key, 1932
Steel inlaid with brass
Hinges: 9 1/2 inches H x
6 1/2 inches W
Lock: 13 1/2 inches H x
14 1/4 inches W
Key: 6 3/8 inches L
Inscribed over keyhole:
"When you do/do/it"
Cranbrook Art Museum;
Gift of George and Ellen Booth
through the Cranbrook
Foundation, 1932.3

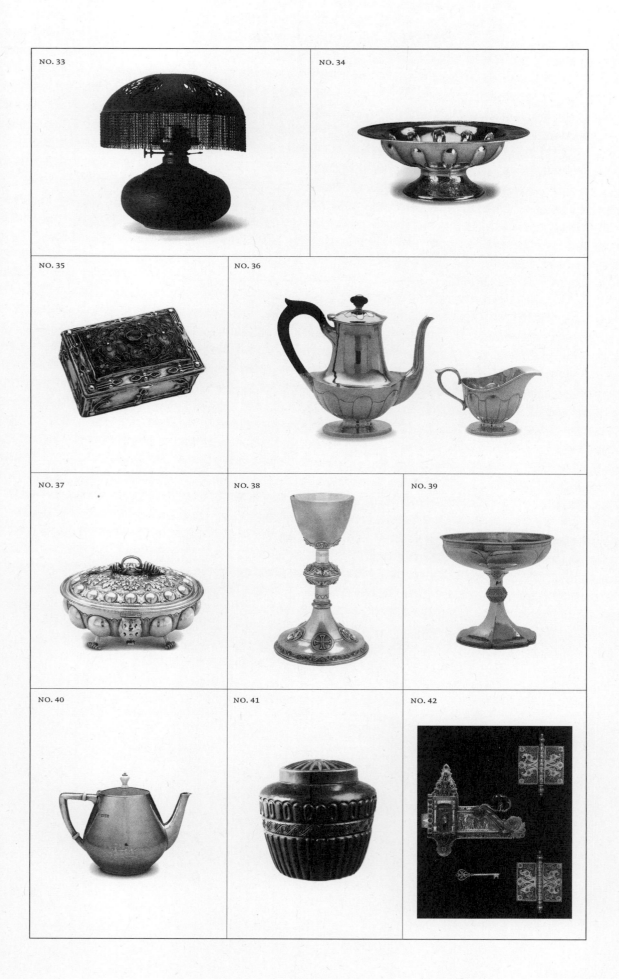

NO. 33

NO. 34

NO. 35

NO. 36

NO. 37

NO. 38

NO. 39

NO. 40

NO. 41

NO. 42

NO. 43
Frank J. Marshall
Covered box with peacock
medallion, ca. 1910
Silver with enamel
1 1/2 inches H x 4 1/4 inches W x
3 1/4 inches D
Marked on underside,
within a rectangle: "F.J.M."
Collection of Alexander
Yale Goriansky

NO. 44
Laurin Hovey Martin
Tazza, ca. 1902
Copper
13 1/4 inches H x
7 1/4 inches diameter
Collection of the
artist's family

NO. 45
Unknown maker
(possibly British)
Address book, ca. 1901
Embossed, gilt, and
painted leather cover
4 inches H x 3 1/8 inches W
Private Collection

NO. 46
H. Stuart Michie
Charger, ca. 1905
Copper and enamel
15 1/2 inches diameter
Private Collection

NO. 47
Katharine Pratt
Teapot, sugar bowl,
and creamer, ca. 1917–37
Silver, with ebony–handled teapot
Teapot: 3 1/2 inches H x
5 inches W
Sugar bowl: 2 1/2 inches H x
3 1/2 inches W
Creamer: 3 inches H x
3 1/2 inches W
Each marked, incuse:
"STERLING/PRATT"
Dedham Historical
Society Collection,
Dedham, Massachusetts

NO. 48
Augustus F. Rose
Covered box with chased
and repousséd lid,
ca. 1910
Silver
1 1/2 inches H x
3 inches diameter
Private Collection

NO. 49
Augustus F. Rose
Landscape, 1902
Enamel on copper in original oak frame
2 inches H x 1 1/8 inches W
(unframed); 7 inches H x
6 inches W (framed)
Private Collection

NO. 50
Augustus F. Rose
Vase, ca. 1900–01
Copper
12 inches H x 6 inches
diameter
Private Collection

NO. 51
Arthur J. Stone and
Herbert Taylor
Pair of altar vases, 1915
Silver with gold
9 7/8 inches H x 8 1/4 inches
diameter at shoulder
Chased on necks:
"Enter into his gates
with thanksgiving" and
"Come before his
presence with a song"
Marked on bottom: "Stone T"
Collection of the Pomfret School

NO. 52
Gertrude Twichell
Covered box, ca. 1915–20
Copper and enamel
2 1/4 inches H x 5 1/2
inches diameter
Scratched on underside:
"Twichell"
Private Collection

NO. 53
Mary Peyton Winlock
Covered jam dish with
spoon, ca. 1910–30
Silver, enamel, and
pressed glass
Dish: 2 inches H x
3 7/8 inches diameter
Spoon: 4 1/2 inches L x
1 1/2 inches W
Stamped on spout and
lid: "STERLING"
Collection of the
Henry Ford Museum &
Greenfield Village

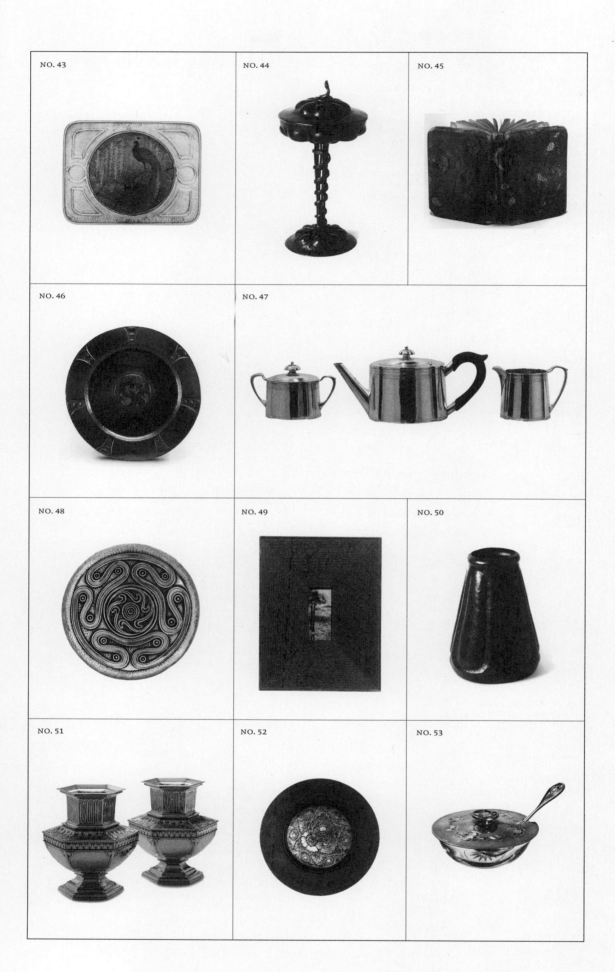

NO. 43

NO. 44

NO. 45

NO. 46

NO. 47

NO. 48

NO. 49

NO. 50

NO. 51

NO. 52

NO. 53

NO. 54
William E. Brigham
Cylindrical covered jar with
cabochons, ca. 1930s
Silver with lapis lazuli and
malachite, and gilt interior
3 7/8 inches H x 3 1/2 inches W x
2 3/4 inches D
Museum of Art, Rhode Island
School of Design, Providence;
Gift of the Estate of
William E. Brigham

NO. 57
Elizabeth Copeland
Oval pin with drop, ca. 1907
Gold and turquoise
with opal dangle
1 3/4 inches H x 1 1/8 inches W
Scratched: "EC"
Private Collection

NO. 55
William E. Brigham
*Design for Four Pendants
(suggested by Indian Jewelry).
Problem in Red and Green Balance,*
1918
Watercolor and pencil
13 5/8 inches H x
9 7/8 inches W
Signed and inscribed,
lower right: "W.E. Brigham"
Museum of Art, Rhode Island
School of Design, Providence;
Gift of the Estate of
William E. Brigham

NO. 56
William E. Brigham
Perfume bottle on
an elephant base,
ca. 1920–25
Carnelian, quartz crystal,
pearls, green quartz, gold,
enamel, and black onyx
6 inches H x 1 15/16 inches W
Museum of Art,
Rhode Island School
of Design, Providence;
Museum Appropriation Fund

NO. 58
Hazel Blake French
Pierced pin with cabochon
and bird design, ca. 1927
Silver with Sandwich
glass cabochon
3 1/2 inches L
Initialed, with fish insignia:
"HBF"
The Sandwich Historical
Society Glass Museum

NO. 59
Gorham Manufacturing Company
Handwrought silver link bracelet,
ca. 1910
Silver with cabochons
6 1/2 inches L x 3/4 inch W
Stamped: "Gorham Co.
HANDWROUGHT Sterling"
Collection of Yvonne Markowitz

NO. 60
Frank Gardner Hale
Jeweled scroll brooch, ca. 1920
Gold with zircons, diamonds,
sapphires, tourmalines,
and peridot
2 5/8 inches H x 1 1/2 inches W
Stamped on applied tab:
"F.G. Hale"
Private Collection

NO. 61
Frank Gardner Hale
Round grape leaf pin,
ca. 1910–15
Gold with tourmaline
1 1/2 inches H x
1 5/8 inches W
Stamped on reverse:
"F.G. Hale"
Private Collection

NO. 62
Frank Gardner Hale
Silver box with ship
plaque, ca. 1910–15
Silver with enamel
2 inches H x 4 inches W x
3 1/2 inches D
Stamped silver, signed
enamel: "F.G. Hale"
Private Collection

NO. 63
Frank Gardner Hale
Necklace with
chrysanthemum design,
ca. 1918
Gold with carved
jade pendant
Necklace: 41 inches L;
pendant: 3 1/2 inches H x
2 inches W
Stamped on applied tab
above jade, on reverse:
"F.G. Hale"
Collection of
Tazio Nuvolari

NO. 65A
Susan Leland Hill
Two jewelry studies
(necklace and cross), ca. 1915
Watercolor mounted
on black paper
12 inches H x 9 inches W
Signed and inscribed:
"Susan Leland Hill"
Society of Arts and Crafts,
Boston, Archives,
Fine Arts Department,
Boston Public Library;
courtesy of the Trustees of
the Boston Public Library
(DMCC venue only)

NO. 64
Frank Gardner Hale
Wirework necklace and
pendant with semiprecious
stones, ca. 1920
Gold and silver with peridots,
amethysts, tourmalines,
sapphires, and pearls
42 inches L
Stamped on applied tab,
on clasp: "F.G.Hale"
Collection of
Jacqueline Loewe Fowler
(DMCC venue only)

NO. 65B
Susan Leland Hill
Two jewelry studies
(pin and scroll pendant)
Watercolor mounted on black paper
12 3/16 inches H x 9 13/16 inches W
Insignia, lower right:
four–petaled flower
Society of Arts and Crafts, Boston,
Archives, Fine Arts Department,
Boston Public Library; courtesy of the
Trustees of the Boston Public Library
(NMAA venue only)

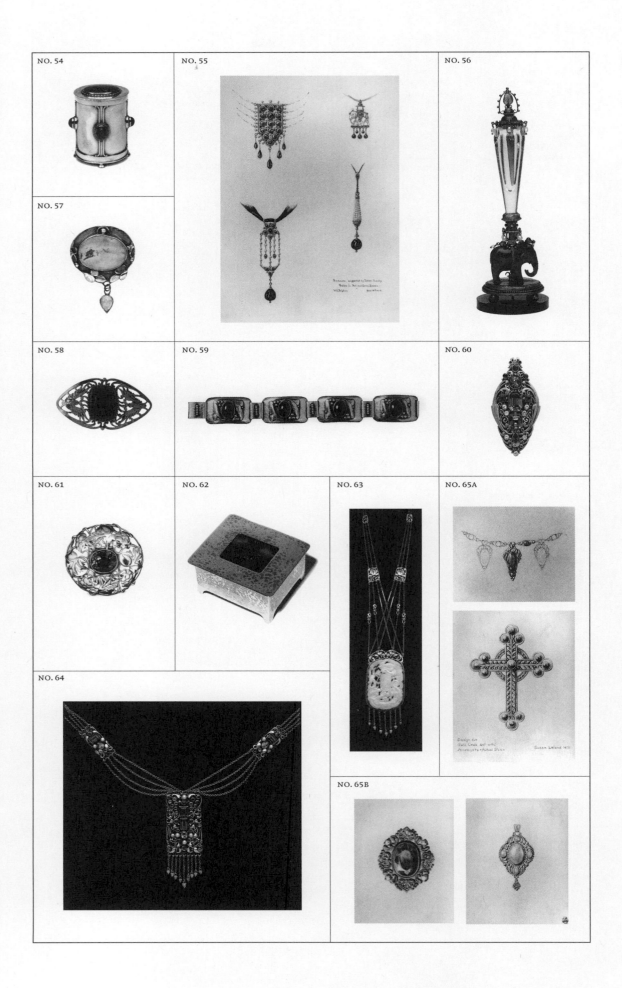

NO. 54

NO. 55

NO. 56

NO. 57

NO. 58

NO. 59

NO. 60

NO. 61

NO. 62

NO. 63

NO. 65A

NO. 64

NO. 65B

NO. 66
Edward Everett Oakes
Ball pendant on cord,
early 20th century
Gold mounted with
sapphires and pearls
28 inches L x
3 inches diameter
The Metropolitan Museum
of Art; Edward C. Moore Fund,
1923 (23.89)

NO. 67
Edward Everett Oakes
Jeweled casket, ca. 1929
Silver and green gold with
amethyst, black onyx, and
pearls, on a wooden base
4 1/8 inches H x 7 7/8 inches W x
6 3/8 inches D
Stamped on box underside,
with oak leaf insignia: "Oakes"
Collection of the Oakes family

NO. 68
Edward Everett Oakes
Rectangular pin with oak
leaf design, ca. 1925
Gold with pearls and
pale green beryl
7/8 inch H x 1 1/4 inches W
Stamped, with oak leaf
insignia: "Oakes"
Museum of Fine Arts,
Boston; Gift of Daniel and
Jessie Lie Farber

NO. 72A
Augustus F. Rose
Moorish style round pin,
ca. 1917
Silver with opal matrix
1 1/8 inches diameter
Private Collection

NO. 69
Edward Everett Oakes
Tooled filigree bracelet, ca. 1927
Gold
7 1/2 inches L x 5/8 inch W
Stamped on clasp,
with oak leaf insignia: "Oakes"
Private Collection

NO. 70
Margaret Rogers
Bar pin, ca. 1910–15
Gold with sapphires
and moonstones
Approx. 3 inches L
Collection of
Drucker Antiques

NO. 71
Margaret Rogers
Necklace with repeating
cabochon design,
ca. 1915–20
Gold with chrysoprase
and pearls
Approx. 16 inches L
Raised initials on applied
tabs: "MR" and "18K"
Private Collection

NO. 72B
Augustus F. Rose and
Antonio Cirino
Jewelry Making and Design
(Providence, R.I.:
Metal Crafts Publishing Co., 1917)
Cloth–bound book,
detail of page 81
9 inches H x 6 inches W
Private Collection

NO. 73
Josephine Hartwell Shaw
Cross and chain
(Renaissance–style necklace),
ca. 1914
Gold with amethyst
and pearls
Approx. 22 inches L
Incised in heart on pendant
back: "Shaw"
Museum of Fine Arts, Boston;
Gift of the maker in memory
of her husband, Frederick

NO. 74
Josephine Hartwell Shaw
Pendant necklace with
blister pearl, ca. 1907–12
Gold and silver with pearls
and blister pearl pendant
Approx. 19 1/2 inches L
with 2 5/8 inches L pendant
Incised on pendant back:
"J.H. Shaw"
Private Collection

NO. 75
Josephine Hartwell Shaw
Pendant necklace with
fire opal, ca. 1912–20
Gold with Mexican
jelly opal
Approx. 16 inches L
Incised on clasp: "Shaw"
Collection of
Gilbert Jonas

NO. 76
Society of Arts
and Crafts, Boston;
Bertram Grosvenor Goodhue,
designer
Medal of Excellence awarded to
Edward Everett Oakes in 1923
Bronze
2 inches diameter x 5/16 inch D
Inscribed in relief around edge
Collection of the Oakes family

NO. 77
Madeline Yale Wynne
Belt buckle, ca. 1900
Copper with
three pebble cabochons
3 inches H x
2 7/8 inches W x 1 inch D
Memorial Hall Museum,
Pocumtuck Valley
Memorial Association,
Deerfield, Massachusetts

NO. 78
Madeline Yale Wynne
Buckles for a pair of colonial
revival costume shoes,
ca. 1900–15
Silver on leather shoes
2 1/2 inches H x 2 inches W x
1/2 inch D (buckles);
3 3/4 inches H x 10 1/4 inches W x
3 1/8 inches D (shoes)
Memorial Hall Museum,
Pocumtuck Valley Memorial
Association, Deerfield,
Massachusetts

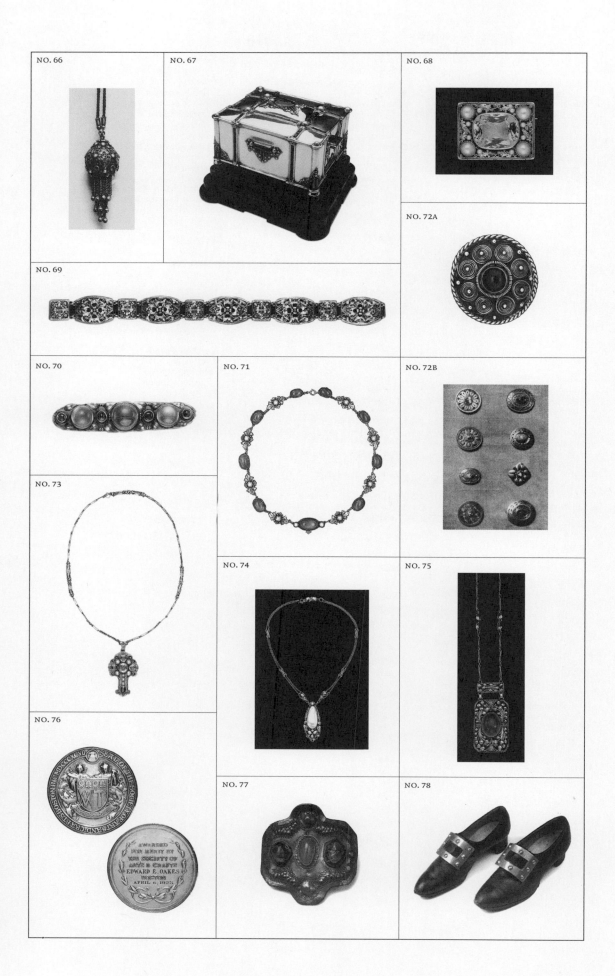

NO. 66

NO. 67

NO. 68

NO. 72A

NO. 69

NO. 70

NO. 71

NO. 72B

NO. 73

NO. 74

NO. 75

NO. 76

NO. 77

NO. 78

NO. 79
Lydia Bush–Brown
A Camp in Connecticut, 1919–26
Silk batik
wall hanging
64 1/2 inches H x
31 inches W
Insignia, lower right: "LBB"
with branch
Cooper–Hewitt,
National Design Museum,
Smithsonian Institution;
Gift of Lydia Bush–Brown Head

NO. 80
Various makers
Denison House lace sample book,
ca. 1915
Leather–bound book,
with cotton bobbin lace sample pieces
(display page worked by Teresa Pellegrini),
affixed to pages with
handwritten cost notations
12 inches H x 9 inches W x 2 1/2 inches D
Museum of Fine Arts, Boston;
Gift of Miss Florence Chase

NO. 81
George Fenety,
designer (attributed);
Frances Glessner
(Mrs. Blewett Lee), maker
Curtain panels with
embroidered rose design,
ca. 1910s
Linen with cotton thread
82 inches H x
44 inches W
Society for the Preservation
of New England Antiquities,
Boston, Massachusetts;
Gift of Mrs. Charles
Batchelder

NO. 82
Elwyn G. Gowen
Cushion with design of
stylized felines, ca. 1920s
Stenciled and printed cotton
15 inches H x 15 inches W
Private Collection

NO. 85
H. Stuart Michie
Old Books to Read, ca. 1905
Stenciled linen
wall hanging
101 1/4 inches H x
48 1/2 inches W
Private Collection

NO. 83
Elwyn G. Gowen
Wall hanging with grape
and vine motifs, ca. 1920s
Stenciled and printed
silk velvet
45 3/4 inches H x
33 inches W
Private Collection

NO. 84
Margaret Green,
embroiderer
Woman's ensemble
(skirt, vest, blouse) with
wheat design, ca. 1907
Embroidered cotton
with crocheted tassels
50 inches H (overall;
skirt 37 1/2 inches H) x
27 1/2 inches W (at waist)
Society for the Preservation
of New England
Antiquities, Boston,
Massachusetts; Gift of
Penelope Noyes

NO. 86
St. Margaret's
School of Embroidery, makers;
Bertram Grosvenor Goodhue,
possible designer
Embroidered hood (from a cope)
with Tudor rose and
pomegranate design, ca. 1900
Silk and metallic thread on velvet
18 1/2 inches H x
17 inches W (including fringe)
Private Collection

NO. 87
Society of Arts and Crafts,
Hingham
Woven rag rug, ca. 1905–10 (*detail*)
Plain–weave cotton
140 inches H x 123 inches W
Hingham Historical Society,
Hingham, Massachusetts

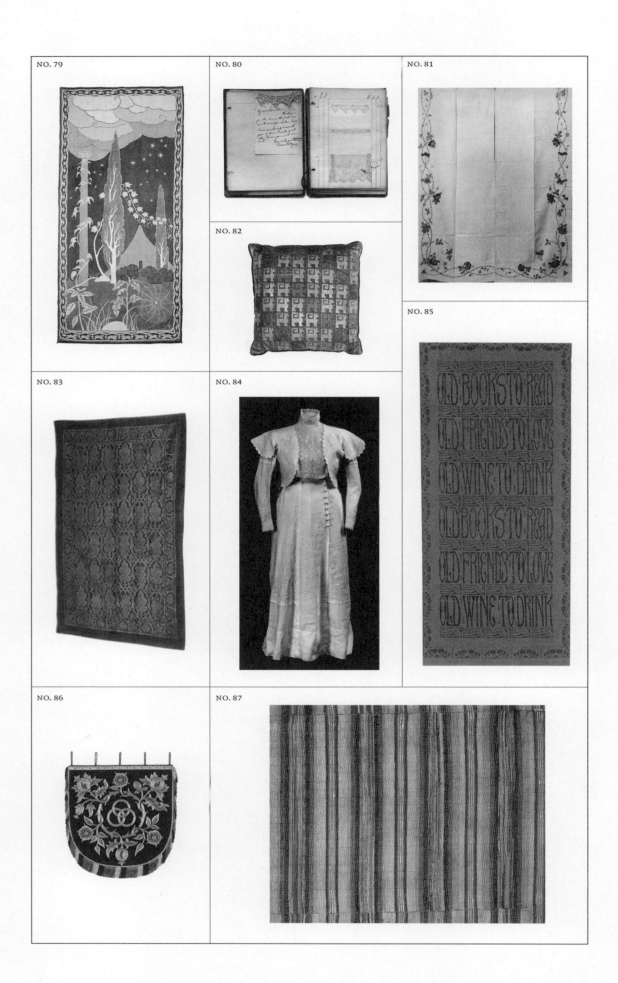

NO. 79

NO. 80

NO. 81

NO. 82

NO. 85

NO. 83

NO. 84

NO. 86

NO. 87

NO. 88A Society of Blue and White Needlework, Deerfield, makers; Margaret Whiting, probable designer Circular cover with floral design, ca. 1896–1926 Embroidered linen 23 3/8 inches diameter Insignia at bottom: "D" in spinning wheel Museum of Fine Arts, Boston; Gift by Special Contribution, 45.499 (DMCC venue only)	NO. 88B Society of Blue and White Needlework, Deerfield, makers Square cover with design of scrolling stems, ca. 1896–1926 Embroidered linen Insignia, lower right: "D" in spinning wheel 33 1/2 inches H x 33 inches W Museum of Fine Arts, Boston; Gift by Special Contribution, 45.407 (NMAA venue only)	NO. 89 Society of Blue and White Needlework, Deerfield, makers *Rose Tree*, ca. 1896–1926 Embroidered linen wall hanging 38 1/4 inches H x 13 1/2 inches W Insignia, lower left: "D" in spinning wheel Memorial Hall Museum, Pocumtuck Valley Memorial Association, Deerfield, Massachusetts
NO. 90 Society of Blue and White Needlework, Deerfield; Ellen Miller and Margaret Whiting *Textile Design Drawing* *(of bedspread designed and worked* *by Sarah Snell, East Bridgewater,* *Mass., 1760–80)*, ca. 1912 Colored pencil drawing 20 1/2 inches H x 20 1/2 inches W Museum of Art, Rhode Island School of Design, Providence; Gift of Margaret Whiting (DMCC venue only)		
NO. 91A Society of Blue and White Needlework, Deerfield; Ellen Miller and Margaret Whiting *Textile Design Drawing* *(of bedspread designed and* *worked by Elizabeth Reed,* *Deerfield, Mass.)*, ca. 1912 Colored pencil drawing 10 inches H x 8 1/4 inches W Museum of Art, Rhode Island School of Design, Providence; Gift of Margaret Whiting (NMAA venue only)	NO. 91B Society of Blue and White Needlework, Deerfield; Ellen Miller and Margaret Whiting *Textile Design Drawing* *(of bedspread designed and* *worked by Elizabeth Reed,* *Deerfield, Mass.)*, ca. 1912 Colored pencil drawing 10 inches H x 8 1/4 inches W Museum of Art, Rhode Island School of Design, Providence; Gift of Margaret Whiting (NMAA venue only)	
NO. 91C Margaret Whiting, author Description of bedspread, its maker and the designs, ca. 1912 Provenance document 5 1/2 inches H x 8 1/2 inches W (folded) Museum of Art, Rhode Island School of Design, Providence (NMAA venue only)	NO. 92 Unknown maker, Italy (Santa Margherita, Genoa) Lace pillow with bobbin lace in progress, ca. 1900–20 Cotton, cardboard, and wooden pillow; with 72 wooden bobbins and Genoese bobbin lace Pillow: 12 inches W x 8 5/8 inches diameter Lace: 5 5/16 inches H x 5 5/8 inches W x 9 5/16 inches D Museum of Fine Arts, Boston; Gift of Mrs. Teresa Pellegrini, 46.43 a-b	

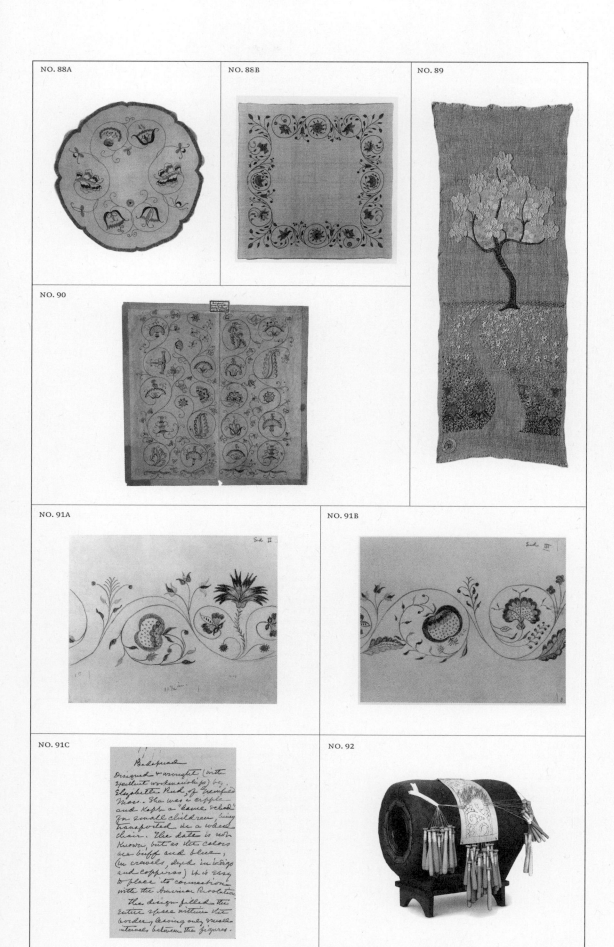

NO. 88A

NO. 88B

NO. 89

NO. 90

NO. 91A

NO. 91B

NO. 91C

Bedspread
Designed & wrought (with
spallant workmanship) by
Elizabeth Rush, of Trenfield
Mass. She was a cripple
and kept a "dame school"
for small children, being
transported in a wheel
chair. The date is not
known, but as the colors
are buff and blue,
(in crewels, dyed in indigo
and copperas) it is easy
to place its connection
with the American Revolution.
The design fills the
entire space within the
border, leaving only small
intervals between the figures.

NO. 92

NO. 93
Julia DeWolf Addison,
calligrapher and illuminator;
Julia DeWolf Addison,
Two pages from a
Life of Saint Barbara
Hand–illuminated manuscript on
vellum, ca. 1920s
16 3/4 inches H x
13 3/4 inches W (page one, shown);
8 inches H x 6 1/2 inches W
(page two)
Initialed, lower left:
"J.deW.A."
Department of Printing
& Graphic Arts,
The Houghton Library,
Harvard University;
Gift of Miss Alice B. Lovett
(DMCC venue only)

NO. 95
Will Bradley,
poster designer
Will Bradley,
Bradley: His Book, No. 30 [The Kiss]
(Springfield, Mass.:
The Wayside Press, 1896)
Lithograph and woodcut
39 7/8 inches H x
27 inches W (image)
The Metropolitan Museum
of Art, Leonard A. Lauder
Collection of American Posters;
Gift of Leonard A. Lauder, 1984
(DMCC venue only)

NO. 94
Cora Bailey, illuminator
Christ's Sermon in the Mount
(Boston: Edward F. Dellano, 1904)
Printed hand–lettered text
with hand–illumination
10 1/2 inches H x 8 7/8 inches W
Monogrammed, lower left: "CB"
Rare Books and Manuscripts
Division, The New York Public
Library; The Astor, Lenox, and
Tilden Foundations

NO. 96
William Addison Dwiggins,
title–page designer
*The Correspondence of
Philip Sidney and Hubert Languet*,
The Humanists' Library,
vol. V (Boston:
The Merrymount Press, 1912)
Printed book
9 3/4 inches H x
6 5/16 inches W
Wellesley College Library,
Special Collections

NO. 97
Bertram Grosvenor Goodhue,
type designer and decorator;
Daniel Berkeley Updike, printer;
Robert Anning Bell, illustrator
The Altar Book
(Boston: The Merrymount
Press, 1896)
Printed book with
photo–engraved illustrations
15 1/4 inches H x
11 1/2 inches W
Collection of
Martin W. Hutner

NO. 98
Bertram Grosvenor Goodhue,
type designer;
Daniel Berkeley Updike,
printer
Tacitus,
Vita et Moribus Julii Agricolae liber
(Boston: The Merrymount
Press, 1904)
Printed book
17 9/16 inches H x
12 3/8 inches W
Collection of Martin W. Hutner

NO. 99
Herbert Gregson,
calligrapher;
Anna Lessman, illuminator;
Carl H. Heintzemann, printer
Thomas Gray,
Elegy Written in a Country Churchyard
(Boston: The Craftsman's
Guild, 1901)
Printed hand–lettered text
with hand–illumination
11 1/4 inches H x 9 inches W
Collection of Richard Blacher

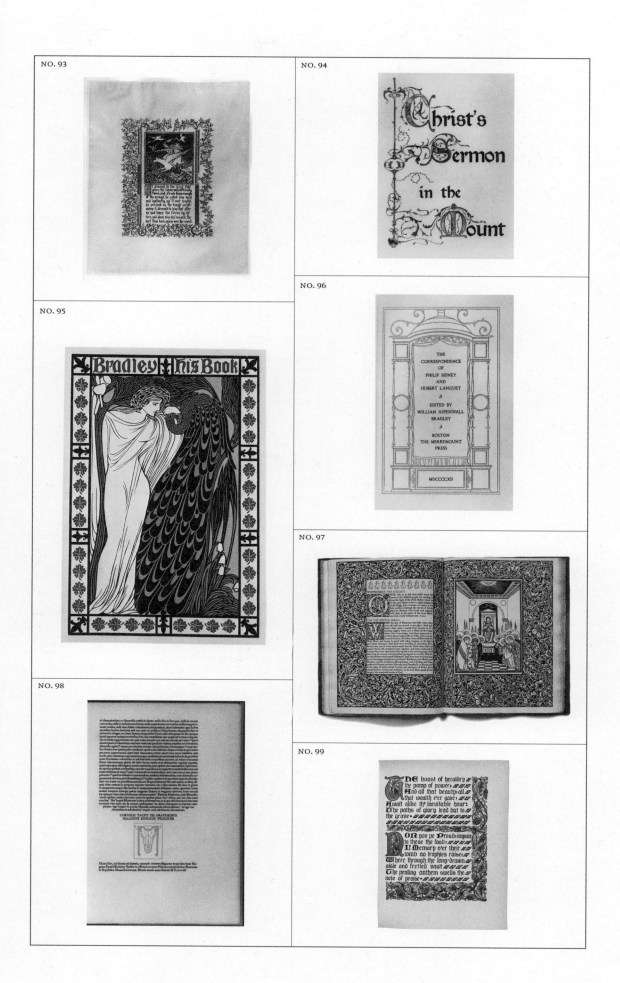

NO. 93

NO. 94

NO. 95

NO. 96

NO. 97

NO. 98

NO. 99

NO. 100A–F
Theodore Brown Hapgood, Jr.
Group of six bookplates, 1895–1910
Photo–engravings
Alfred Bartlett, 4 3/8 inches H x 2 5/8 inches W;
Elizabeth Briggs, 5 inches H x 2 5/8 inches W;
Ada Spencer Daggett, 4 5/8 inches H x 3 1/8 inches W;
Caroline Gertrude Ely, 4 5/8 inches H x 3 inches W;
Theodore Brown Hapgood, Jr., 3 7/8 inches H x 2 3/4 inches W;
A.F. Schenkelberger, 2 3/4 inches H x 2 inches W
Signed or monogrammed variously,
incl.: "TBH" and "HAPGOOD"
Collection of Thomas G. Boss Fine Books

NO. 101
Will B. Hunt,
poster designer
First Exhibition of the
Arts and Crafts, 1897
Commercial color lithograph
11 inches H x 15 3/8 inches W
Signed, lower left:
"·WILL·B·HUNT·INVT·"
Boston Public Library,
Print Department

NO. 102
Adrian J. Iorio,
designer (attributed)
Narrative of the Captivity
and Restoration of
Mrs. Mary Rowlandson
(Cambridge, Mass. and
London: 1682; reprinted
Lancaster, Mass.: 1903)
Printed book,
no. 10 of 250 copies
10 5/8 inches H x
8 3/8 inches W
Lancaster Town Library

NO. 103
Rosamond B. Loring,
papermaker
Sophocles, *Antigone*
(Boston and New York:
Houghton Mifflin
Company, 1930)
Printed book with paste
paper–covered boards
11 5/8 inches H x
8 1/4 inches W
The Houghton Library,
Harvard University;
Gift of Mrs. T.J. Newbold

NO. 104A
Ethel Reed,
cover designer
Gertrude Smith,
Arabella and Araminta Stories
(Boston: Copeland & Day, 1895)
Die–stamped cloth trade binding
8 7/8 inches H x 6 7/8 inches W
Wellesley College Library,
Special Collections

NO. 104B
Ethel Reed,
poster designer;
Copeland & Day,
publisher;
George H. Walker & Co., printers
Arabella and Araminta Stories
by Gertrude Smith with XV Pictures
by Ethel Reed, 1895
Commercial color lithograph
26 1/8 inches H x
14 1/2 inches W (image)
Signed, lower right: "·Ethel·Reed·"
Boston Public Library,
Print Department

NO. 105
Bruce Rogers,
type designer and typesetter;
Carl Purington Rollins,
printer
Maurice de Guérin,
The Centaur
(Montague, Mass.:
The Montague Press, 1915)
Printed book
12 3/16 inches H x
8 inches W
Inscribed on front fly–leaf:
"To Edith Diehl with
the compliments of
Bruce Rogers"
Wellesley College Library,
Special Collections

NO. 100 (A & D shown)

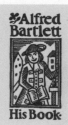 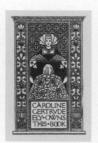

NO. 101

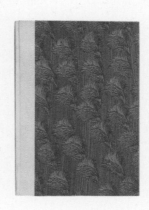

NO. 102

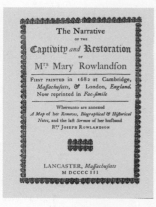

NO. 103

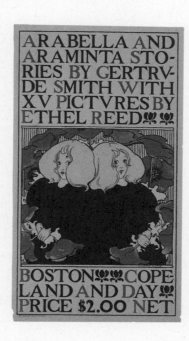

NO. 104A

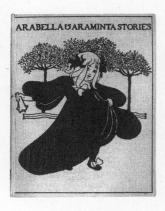

NO. 104B

NO. 105

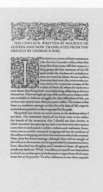

NO. 106
Amy Sacker,
cover designer
Théophile Gautier,
Captain Fracasse
(Boston: L.C. Page
& Company, 1900)
Die–stamped cloth
trade binding
8 1/4 inches H x
5 3/4 inches W
Monogrammed in ligature,
lower right: "AMS"
Arts of the Book Collection,
Yale University Library

NO. 107
Amy Sacker,
cover designer
Charles G.D. Roberts,
The Kindred of the Wild
(Boston: L.C. Page
& Company, 1902)
Die–stamped cloth
trade binding
8 1/2 inches H x
5 3/4 inches W
Monogrammed in ligature,
lower left: "AMS"
Collection of Sandra Adams

NO. 108
Mary Crease Sears,
cover designer;
Agnes Saint John, binder
Dante Gabriel Rossetti,
Hand and Soul
(Portland, Maine:
Thomas B. Mosher, 1899)
Book hand–bound in red
morocco with hand–tooling
6 1/16 inches H x
4 3/8 inches W
Stamped on spine:
"S & S/1899"
Department of Printing
& Graphic Arts,
The Houghton Library,
Harvard University;
Gift of Elizabeth Sears

NO. 109
Sarah Wyman Whitman,
cover designer
Nathaniel Hawthorne,
The Marble Faun vols. I & II
(Boston: Houghton Mifflin
and Company, 1899)
Die–stamped cloth
trade binding
6 3/4 inches H x
4 3/4 inches W each
Monogrammed on back cover,
center: "SW" in heart
Collection of Sandra Adams

NO. 110
Sarah Wyman Whitman,
cover designer
Tacitus, *Vita et Moribus
Julii Agricolae liber*
(Boston: Merrymount
Press, 1904)
Die–stamped cloth
trade binding
17 1/2 inches H x
12 3/8 inches W
Department of Printing
& Graphic Arts,
The Houghton Library,
Harvard University;
Gift of Philip Hofer

NO. 111
Sarah Wyman Whitman,
cover designer
Henry David Thoreau,
Cape Cod
(Boston and New York:
Houghton Mifflin and
Company, 1896)
Die–stamped cloth
trade binding
7 5/8 inches H x
5 1/4 inches W
The Houghton Library,
Harvard University;
Gift of W.B.O. Field,
1947

NO. 106

NO. 107

NO. 108

NO. 109

NO. 110

NO. 111

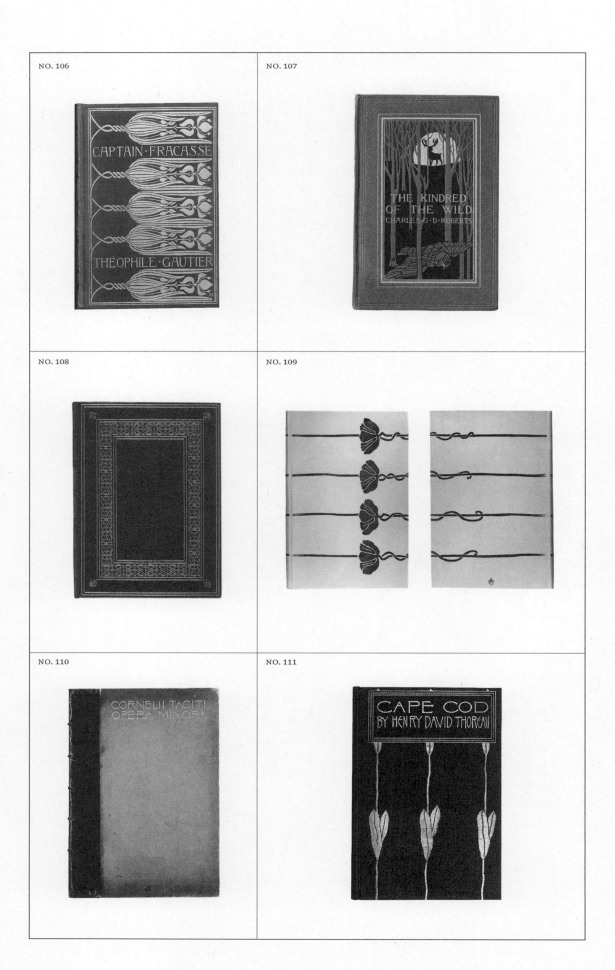

NO. 112
Frances and Mary Allen
The Minuet, ca. 1911
Platinum print
6 1/2 inches H x
8 1/2 inches W (sheet)
Stamped on reverse:
"Frances and Mary Allen,/
Deerfield, Mass./
All Rights Reserved."
Memorial Hall Museum,
Pocumtuck Valley
Memorial Association,
Deerfield, Massachusetts

NO. 113
Alvin Langdon Coburn
The Bridge, Ipswich, 1903
Multiple gum platinum
print, mounted to
cream wove paper
9 1/16 inches H x
7 1/16 inches W (image)
Collection of
George Eastman House

NO. 114
Alvin Langdon Coburn
The Dragon, 1903
Gum bichromate and
platinum print
7 5/8 inches H x
9 1/4 inches W (image)
Monogrammed: "ALC"
Collection of Manfred
Heiting, Amsterdam

NO. 115
Emma Coleman
*The Gleaner: Woman
Harvesting, York*, ca. 1883–86
Albumen print,
mounted to grey board
7 5/8 inches H x
4 9/16 inches W (image)
Old York Historical
Society, York, Maine

NO. 116
F. Holland Day
The Seven Last Words of Christ, 1898
Seven platinum prints in original frame
Approx. 5 1/16 inches H x 4 inches W (each);
8 1/2 inches H x 35 1/2 inches W (framed)
Norwood Historical Society, F. Holland Day
House, Norwood, Massachusetts

NO. 117
F. Holland Day
Untitled
(Nude Youth in Maine), 1905
Gum bichromate and
platinum print, in
two parts with black paper
mount visible in between
10 1/16 inches H x
7 1/2 inches W
Initialed, lower left: "FHD/1905"
Philadelphia Museum of Art;
Purchased with funds given by
Dorothy Norman

NO. 118
Arthur Wesley Dow
Salt Marsh, Ipswich River,
ca. 1904
Cyanotype
4 7/8 inches H x
6 7/8 inches W (image)
Museum of Fine Arts, Boston;
A. Shuman Collection,
1983.186

NO. 112

NO. 113

NO. 114

NO. 115

NO. 116

NO. 117

NO. 118

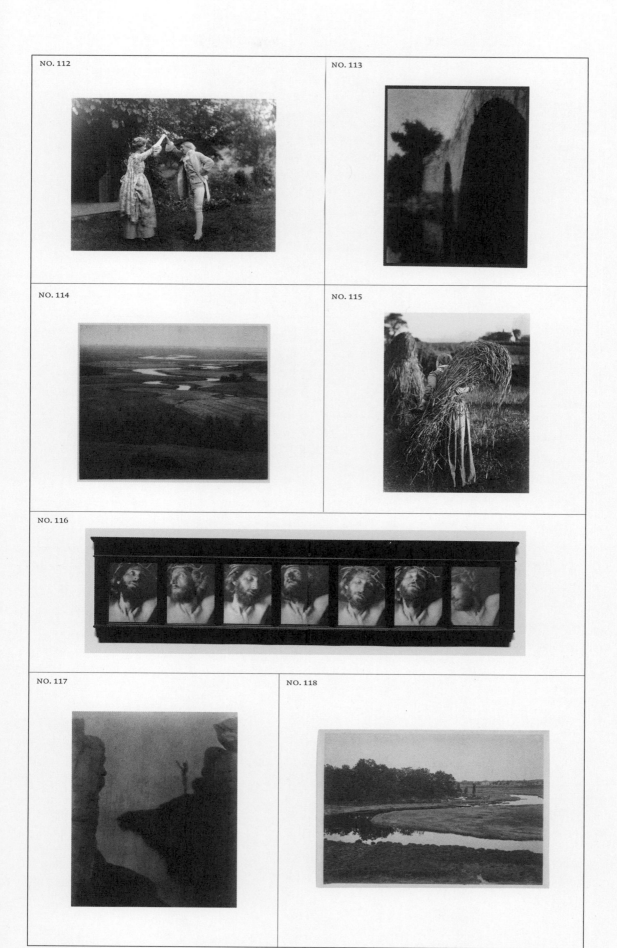

NO. 119A
Chansonetta Stanley Emmons
Children in Spring, Brighton,
Massachusetts, 1896
Silver print
7 11/16 inches H x
9 5/8 inches W (image)
Fogg Art Museum,
Harvard University Art Museums;
Purchased through the
generosity of Melvin R. Seiden
(DMCC venue only)

NO. 119B
Chansonetta Stanley Emmons
Haying, 1906
Silver print
4 3/8 inches H x 6 3/8 inches W
Signed and dated, lower left:
"CSEmmons/1906"
Museum of Fine Arts, Boston;
Gift of Mrs. Barbara Morss Marshall,
1985.728
(NMAA venue only)

NO. 120
Edwin Hale Lincoln
Trillium Grandiflorum (White Trillium), 1905
Platinum print
9 1/4 inches H x
7 3/8 inches W
Printed on mount at lower left:
"COPYRIGHTED 1905 BY
EDWIN HALE LINCOLN"
Collection of the Lee Gallery,
Winchester, Massachusetts

NO. 121
Wallace Nutting
Wallace Nutting's Place, Framingham,
1912
Platinum print,
hand–colored
9 5/8 inches H x
7 5/8 inches W
Signed, lower right:
"COPT 1912 by W. Nutting"
Society for the Preservation of
New England Antiquities,
Boston, Massachusetts;
Gift of Wallace Nutting,
1 December 1914

NO. 122
William B. Post
Landscape with Haystacks,
ca. 1900
Platinum print, mounted to
greenish–grey wove paper
3 1/8 inches H x
4 1/2 inches W (image)
Collection of the Lee Gallery,
Winchester, Massachusetts

NO. 123A
Sarah Choate Sears
Helen Sears,
ca. 1897
Platinum print
9 7/16 inches H x
7 3/4 inches W (image)
Fogg Art Museum,
Harvard University Art
Museums; Gift of
Montgomery S. Bradley
and Cameron Bradley
(DMCC venue only)

NO. 123B
Sarah Choate Sears
Helen Sears,
ca. 1897
Platinum print
8 7/8 inches H x
7 5/16 inches W (image)
Fogg Art Museum,
Harvard University Art
Museums; Gift of
Montgomery S. Bradley
and Cameron Bradley
(NMAA venue only)

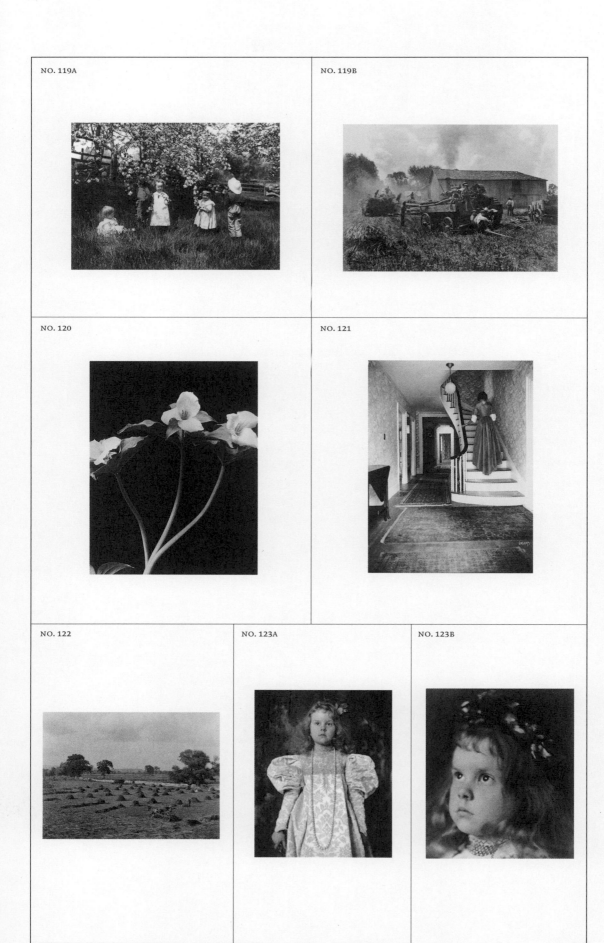

NO. 119A

NO. 119B

NO. 120

NO. 121

NO. 122

NO. 123A

NO. 123B

NO. 124A
Sarah Choate Sears
Untitled (Lily),
late 1890s
Silver print
9 3/8 inches H x
7 7/16 inches W (image)
Fogg Art Museum,
Harvard University Art Museums;
Gift of Montgomery S. Bradley
and Cameron Bradley
(DMCC venue only)

NO. 124B
Sarah Choate Sears
Untitled (Still Life),
late 1890s
Platinum print
8 inches H x
6 inches W (image)
Fogg Art Museum,
Harvard University Art Museums;
Gift of Montgomery S. Bradley
and Cameron Bradley
(NMAA venue only)

NO. 125
George H. Seeley
The Bowl of White Berries,
1909
Gum bichromate and
platinum print
17 3/8 inches H x
21 5/16 inches W
Incised, lower right:
"George H. Seeley/1909"
Gilman Paper Company
Collection

NO. 126A
George H. Seeley
Untitled (Abstract Winter
Landscape), 1909
Gum bichromate print
17 1/4 inches H x
21 inches W (image)
Signed, lower right:
"George H. Seeley 1909"
The Baltimore Museum of
Art; Purchase with ex-
change funds from the
Edward Joseph Gallagher III
Memorial Collection; and
Partial Gift of George H.
Dalsheimer, Baltimore
(DMCC venue only)

NO. 126B
George H. Seeley
Winter Landscape, 1909
Gum bichromate and
platinum print
17 1/4 inches H x
21 1/4 inches W
Signed, lower right:
"George H. Seeley/1909"
Gilman Paper Company
Collection
(NMAA venue only)

NO. 127
Clarence H. White
F. Holland Day and a Black Model,
ca. 1900–05
Platinum print mounted to
brown wove paper
9 1/4 inches H x
6 7/8 inches W (image)
Norwood Historical Society,
F. Holland Day House,
Norwood, Massachusetts

NO. 128
Clarence H. White
Rose Pastor Stokes,
Caritas Island,
Connecticut, 1909
Double–coated
platinum print
9 1/4 inches H x
7 3/16 inches W (image)
Initialed, lower right: "CHW"
Museum of Modern Art,
New York; Gift of Mr. & Mrs.
Clarence H. White, Jr.

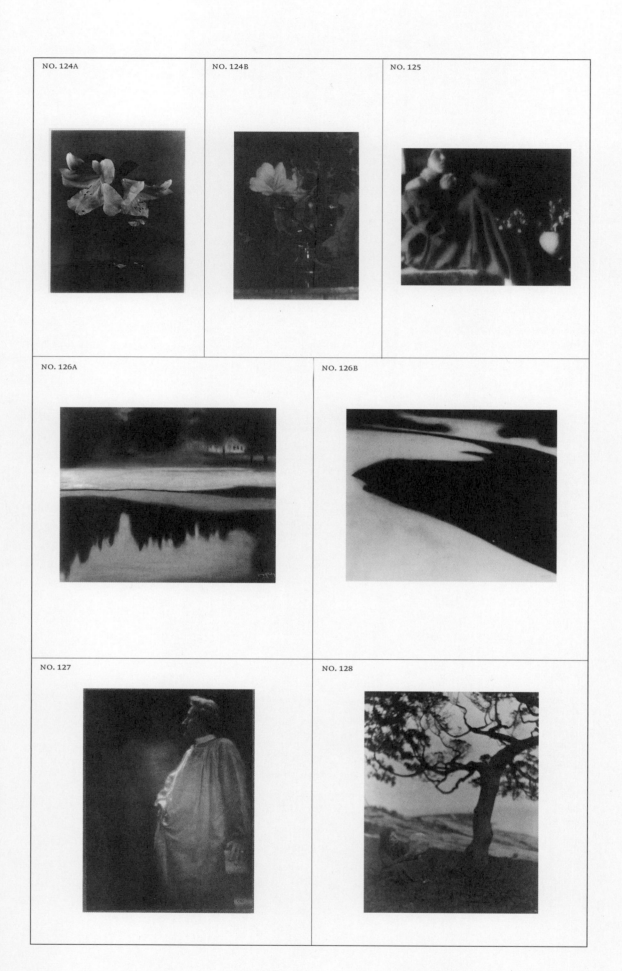

NO. 124A

NO. 124B

NO. 125

NO. 126A

NO. 126B

NO. 127

NO. 128

NO. 129A
Gustave Baumann
Tom a'Hunting, 1917
Color woodcut
11 inches H x 13 1/4 inches W (image)
Collection of Johanna and Leslie Garfield
(DMCC venue only)

NO. 129B
Gustave Baumann
Provincetcwn, 1917
Color woodcut
9 1/4 inches H x 11 inches W
Chop–mark insignia,
bottom center: hand in heart
Collection of Johanna and Leslie Garfield
(NMAA venue only)

NO. 130A
Ada Gilmore Chaffee
The Silva Sisters, 1917
Color woodcut
9 1/2 inches H x 11 1/4 inches W (image)
Ink signature, lower left
Collection of Johanna and Leslie Garfield
(DMCC venue only)

NO. 130B
Ada Gilmore Chaffee
Sail Loft, ca. 1916
Color woodcut
10 3/4 inches H x 11 1/8 inches W (image)
Ink signature, bottom center
Collection of Johanna and Leslie Garfield
(NMAA venue only)

NO. 131
Mary Jenks Coulter
From an Old Garden, ca. 1920
Color woodcut
7 inches H x 6 inches W
Monogrammed, lower left: "MJC"
Collection of Johanna and Leslie Garfield

NO. 132A
Arthur Wesley Dow
View in Ipswich, 1895
Color woodcut on Japanese tissue
5 inches H x 2 1/4 inches W (image)
Monogrammed, lower left: "A.W.D."
Museum of Fine Arts, Boston;
Gift of Mrs. Ethelyn H. Putnam,
41.710
(DMCC venue only)

NO. 132B
Arthur Wesley Dow
Bend of a River, 1895
Color woodcut
9 inches H x
2 3/8 inches W (block)
Museum of Fine Arts, Boston;
Gift of Mrs. Ethelyn H. Putnam,
41.716
(NMAA venue only)

NO. 133
Arthur Wesley Dow,
designer;
Louis Prang & Co.,
publisher and printer
Modern Art, 1895
Commercial color lithograph
17 7/8 inches H x
13 5/8 inches W (image)
Signed, lower left: "Arthur W. Dow"
Boston Public Library,
Print Department

NO. 134A
Edna Boies Hopkins
Iris, ca. 1915
Color woodcut
10 7/8 inches H x
7 1/4 inches W (image)
Museum of Fine Arts, Boston;
Bequest of John T. Spaulding,
48.906
(DMCC venue only)

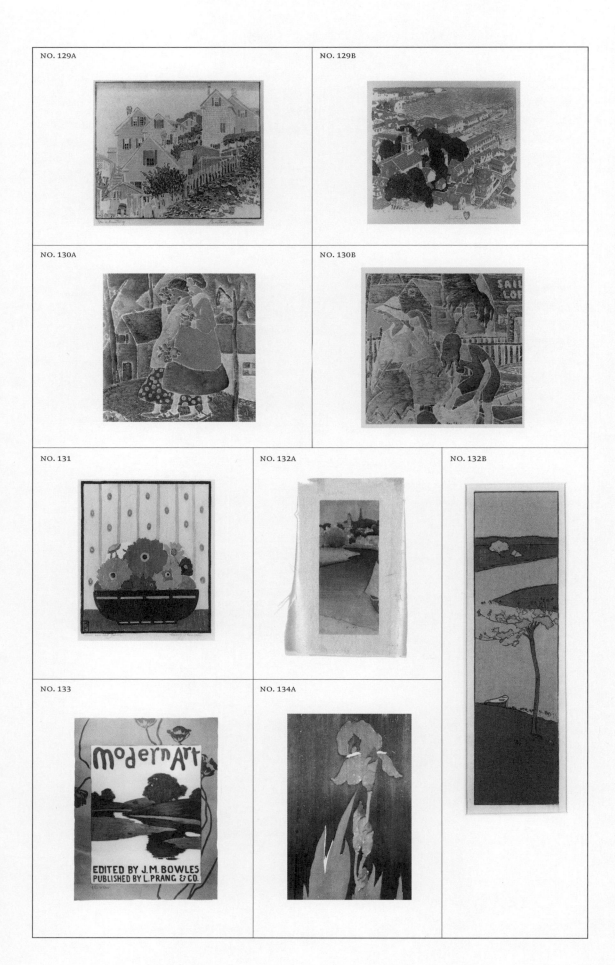

NO. 129A

NO. 129B

NO. 130A

NO. 130B

NO. 131

NO. 132A

NO. 132B

NO. 133

NO. 134A

NO. 134B
Edna Boies Hopkins
Untitled (Floral Still Life), ca. 1925
Color woodcut
9 inches H x
8 1/8 inches W (block)
Museum of Fine Arts, Boston;
Bequest of John T. Spaulding, 48.900
(NMAA venue only)

NO. 135A
Blanche Lazzell
Provincetown, 1925
Color woodcut
15 3/4 inches H x
13 1/16 inches W (image)
Collection of
Johanna and Leslie Garfield
(DMCC venue only)

NO. 135B
Blanche Lazzell
The Rose, ca. 1921
Color woodcut
9 1/2 inches H x
9 1/2 inches W (image)
Collection of
Johanna and Leslie Garfield
(NMAA venue only)

NO. 136A
Tod Lindenmuth
In Harbor, 1916–17
Color linocut
14 13/16 inches H x
15 7/8 inches W (image)
Collection of
Johanna and Leslie Garfield
(DMCC venue only)

NO. 136B
Tod Lindenmuth
The Runway, ca. 1925
Color linocut
14 1/4 inches H x 9 7/8 inches W (block)
Museum of Fine Arts, Boston;
Bequest of John T. Spaulding, 48.920
(NMAA venue only)

NO. 137
Mildred 'Dolly' McMillen
Christmas Greetings, 1918
Woodcut
10 1/2 inches H x
12 3/8 inches W (image)
National Museum of American Art,
Smithsonian Institution;
Gift of Helen Baltz

NO. 138A
Thomas Buford Meteyard
Moonrise (bookplate), 1896
Color woodcut
4 inches H x 2 3/4 inches W
Monogrammed at right, center: "M"
Collection of James and Alice Lyons
(DMCC venue only)

NO. 138B
Thomas Buford Meteyard
Marshes, ca. 1903
Color woodcut
5 1/8 inches H x 7 1/4 inches W
Collection of James and Alice Lyons
(NMAA venue only)

NO. 139
Juliette S. Nichols
The Bareback Rider
Color woodcut
9 1/2 inches H x
10 5/8 inches W (image)
Museum of Fine Arts, Boston;
Bequest of John T. Spaulding, 48.922
(DMCC venue only)

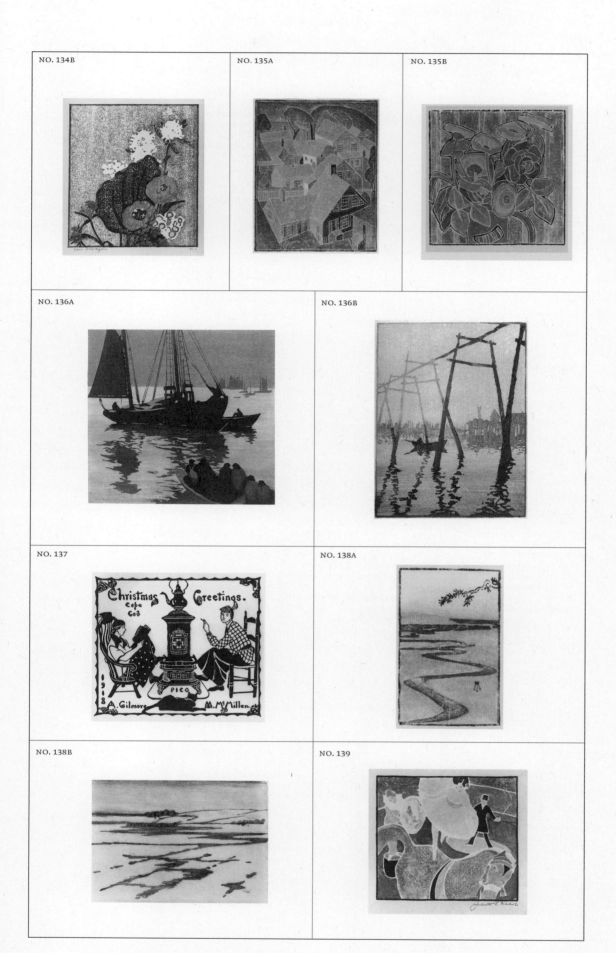

NO. 134B

NO. 135A

NO. 135B

NO. 136A

NO. 136B

NO. 137

NO. 138A

NO. 138B

NO. 139

NO. 140A
B.J.O. Nordfeldt
The Painting Class, 1915–16
Color woodcut
11 13/16 inches H x
10 13/16 inches W (image)
Philadelphia Museum of
Art; Gift of Mrs. Bror
Julius Olsson Nordfeldt
(DMCC venue only)

NO. 140B
B.J.O. Nordfeldt
The Schooner, 1915–16
Color woodcut
10 13/16 inches H x
11 13/16 inches W (image)
Philadelphia Museum of
Art; Gift of Mrs. Bror
Julius Olsson Nordfeldt
(NMAA venue only)

NO. 141A
Margaret Jordan Patterson
Morning Glories, ca. 1925
Color woodcut
10 inches H x 7 inches W
Worcester Art Museum,
Worcester, Massachusetts;
Thomas Hovey Gage Fund
(DMCC venue only)

NO. 141B
Margaret Jordan Patterson
Cape Cod, Cottage, 1914
Color woodcut
7 inches H x
10 inches W (image)
Inscribed at lower left:
"To AGATHA and TEDDY [?]"
Collection of John Rossetti
(NMAA venue only)

NO. 142
Vojtěch Preissig
The Bohemian Musician, 1916
Color linocut
6 5/16 inches H x
6 1/4 inches W (image)
Monogrammed, lower left: "V.P."
Worcester Art Museum,
Worcester, Massachusetts;
Sarah C. Garver Fund

NO. 143A
Rudolph Ruzicka
Tatiana & Veronica (Christmas),
ca. 1923
Color wood engraving
4 inches H x 2 7/8 inches W
Monogrammed in block,
lower right: "R"
Museum of Fine Arts, Boston;
Anonymous Gift, 36.391
(DMCC venue only)

NO. 143B
Rudolph Ruzicka
Persian Scene, ca. 1926
Color wood engraving
2 1/4 inches H x
3 1/8 inches W (block)
Monogrammed in block,
lower right: "R"
Museum of Fine Arts, Boston;
Gift of D.B. Updike, M31268
(NMAA venue only)

NO. 144
Maud Hunt Squire
Evening, ca. 1919
Color woodcut
11 1/4 inches H x
13 1/4 inches W (image)
Museum of Fine Arts, Boston;
Bequest of John T. Spaulding, 48.935
(DMCC venue only)

NO. 145
William Zorach
Fantastical Sea Scene,
ca. 1919
Color linocut
6 1/8 inches H x
7 1/2 inches W (image)
National Museum of American Art,
Smithsonian Institution;
Museum Purchase

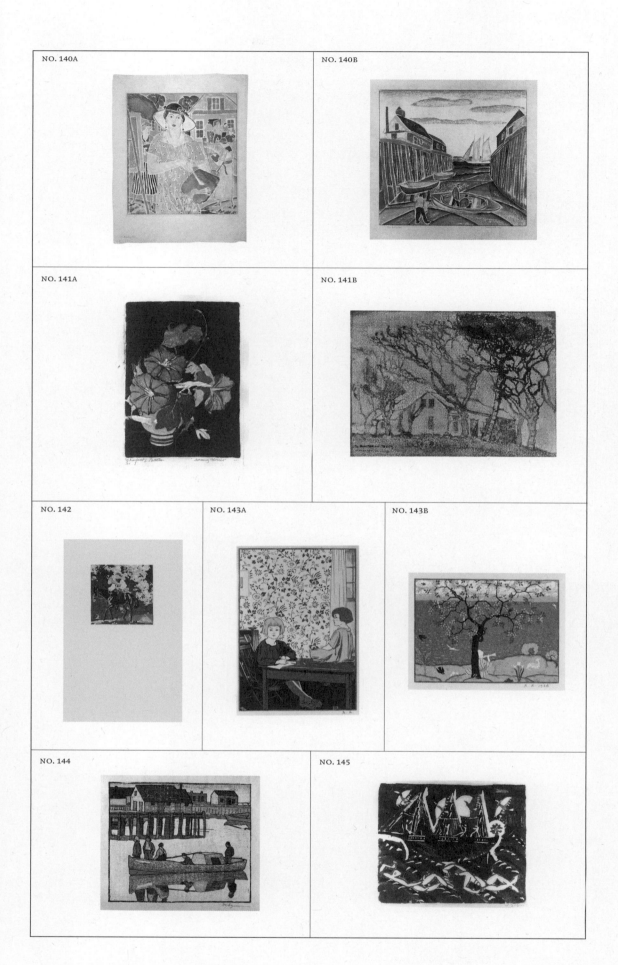

NO. 140A

NO. 140B

NO. 141A

NO. 141B

NO. 142

NO. 143A

NO. 143B

NO. 144

NO. 145

BIOGRAPHIES OF ARTISTS FEATURED IN THE EXHIBITION

Biographies of the artists whose works are included in the exhibition were prepared by David Acton (D.A.); Edward S. Cooke, Jr. (E.S.C.); Jeannine Falino (J.F.); Nancy Finlay (N.F.); Anne E. Havinga (A.E.H.); Marilee Boyd Meyer (M.B.M.); Susan J. Montgomery (S.J.M.); and Nicola J. Shilliam (N.J.S.).

RECURRING SOURCES AND ABBREVIATIONS

AAA : Archives of American Art

BPL : Boston Public Library

ca. : *circa*

CKAW : Chelsea Keramic Art Works

1897 exhib. catal. : *First Exhibition of the Society of Arts & Crafts, Copley Hall, Boston, 5–16 April 1897* (Boston: Heintzemann Press, 1897)

1899 exhib. catal. : *Exhibition of the Society of Arts & Crafts, Together with a Loan Collection of Applied Art: Copley and Allston Halls, Boston, 4–15 April 1899* (Boston: George H. Ellis, 1899)

Evans (1987) : Paul Evans, *Art Pottery of the United States: An Encyclopedia of Producers and their Marks*, 2nd ed. (New York: Feingold and Lewis, 1987)

Kaplan (1987) : Wendy Kaplan, ed., *"The Art that is Life": The Arts & Crafts Movement in America, 1875–1920* (Boston: Museum of Fine Arts, 1987)

MFA : Museum of Fine Arts, Boston

MS. : manuscript

Museum School : School of the Museum of Fine Arts, Boston

1907 exhib. catal. : *Exhibition of the Society of Arts & Crafts, Copley Hall* (Boston: Heintzemann Press, 1907)

1927 exhib. catal. : *Tricennial Exhibition of The Society of Arts & Crafts* (Boston: Museum of Fine Arts, 1927)

publ. : published

PVMA : Pocumtuck Valley Memorial Association (Deerfield)

repr. : reproduced

RISD : Rhode Island School of Design (Providence)

SACB : Society of Arts and Crafts, Boston

SI : Smithsonian Institution

SPNEA : Society for the Preservation of New England Antiquities (Boston)

Úlehla (1981) : Karen Evans Úlehla, ed., *The Society of Arts and Crafts, Boston: Exhibition Record 1897–1927* (Boston: Boston Public Library, 1981)

WEIU : Women's Educational and Industrial Union (Boston)

Who Was Who in American Art : Peter H. Falk, ed., *Who Was Who in American Art* (Madison, Conn.: Sound View Press, 1985)

Julia DeWolf Addison
(1866–after 1927)

Julia DeWolf Addison achieved an impressive reputation as an author, painter, illuminator, embroiderer, and ecclesiastical designer. After a childhood spent in England, she returned to Boston where she studied at MIT and subsequently at the School of Miss Amy Sacker. Her marriage to the Reverend Daniel Dulaney Addison took place in 1889. She exhibited in the first Exhibition of the Arts and Crafts in 1897 and in subsequent exhibitions in 1899, 1907, and 1927. She was a member of the Society of Arts and Crafts from its founding. In 1909 she became a member of Saint Dunstan's Guild, a group that evolved out of the Society's Committee on Ecclesiastical Work. The Guild was dissolved in 1910 due to legal impediments, but did mount one exhibition of its members' work. Addison did work for churches throughout the Boston area and also consigned items for sale to the SACB shop. Her publications include *The Art of the Pitti Palace, Classic Myths in Art, Arts and Crafts of the Middle Ages* and *Florestan the Troubadour*. (N.F.)

SOURCES

Papers, The Houghton Library, Harvard University; "Julia de Wolfe [sic] Addison: Author, Designer, Printer," *Town and Country Review*, London, n.d. (clipping in Archives of American Art); *Who Was Who in American Art*, p. 5.

The Allen Sisters:
Frances S. (1854–1941) and
Mary E. (1858–1941)

Initially trained as teachers, Frances and Mary Allen took up photography in 1890. Within a few years both sisters began to go deaf (perhaps as a result of a childhood illness), and by the end of the decade they had given up teaching careers and turned to photography to support themselves. They were familiar with the photographs of Emma Lewis Coleman (who had a residence in Deerfield in the 1890s), which may have influenced their naturalistic style and preservationist approach. In 1891 they published their work in Charles Warner's book, *Picturesque Franklin*. Until the early 1930s, they made portraits, genre studies, and scenic views of the Deerfield area, and produced a large group of photographs of "colonial life" which were quite popular and occasionally appeared in national magazines such as the *Ladies' Home Journal*. The Allen sisters sold their pictures through a series of catalogues

they had printed at the New Clairvaux Press in nearby Montague, Mass. While Mary joined the SACB as an intermittent member from 1911 to 1921, Frances did not join, although they exhibited together in the 1907 exhibition. (A.E.H.)

SOURCE

Naomi Rosenblum, *A History of Women Photographers* (New York: Abbeville Press, 1994), pp. 291–92.

Olof Althin
(1859–1922)

This Swedish–trained cabinetmaker produced custom mantelpieces and paneling for Back Bay residences, repaired antique furniture, and built colonial revival furniture. Among the great collections he worked on were those of Charles Hitchcock Tyler and Eugene Bolles, most of the former now at the Museum of Fine Arts, Boston, and most of the latter now at the Metropolitan Museum of Art. In the early twentieth century Althin had a shop at 537 Albany Street (at the corner of Wareham) and employed about five craftsmen, most of whom were of Swedish descent, but Althin also worked with Louis Knecht and F.W. Kulkmann, both members of the Society of Arts and Crafts. (E.S.C.)

SOURCE

Olof Althin papers, Winterthur Museum Library.

Cora Louise Bailey
(born 1870)

Following her studies at the School of the Museum of Fine Arts, Boston, Cora—sometimes known as "Corot"—Bailey was chiefly active as a designer of stained glass. She also illuminated at least one book, *Christ's Sermon in the Mount* [sic], published in Boston in 1904 by Edward F. Dellano, but never widely distributed (CAT. NO. 94). Examples of her work were included in the 1897 Exhibition of the Arts and Crafts, and she was a member of the SACB from 1907 to 1914. (N.F.)

SOURCE

Who Was Who in American Art, p. 27.

Mary Steere Batchelder
(active ca. 1907)

Little is known of metalsmith and jeweler Mary Batchelder. In the 1907 SACB exhibition, a Mrs. Mary A. Bachelder of Boston exhibited a silver pendant and chain with green tourmaline setting designed and executed by her. Other works which have appeared are a copper oil lamp (CAT. NO. 33), a covered box, and an enameled copper watch fob (private collection). She was listed in 1907 as a Craftsman in the SACB. (J.F.)

SOURCES

Úlehla (1981), pp. 22, 27; Skinner, sale 1348 (November 3, 1990), nos. 57, 182.

Gustave Baumann
(1881–1971)

Born on June 27, 1881 in Magdeburg, Germany, Baumann came with his family to Chicago in 1891. He became an apprentice in a printing shop in 1897 while attending evening classes at the Art Institute of Chicago. Three years later Baumann began working as an independent commercial artist. He went to Germany in 1905 for a year of study at the Kunstgewerbeschule in Munich. After returning to Chicago and commercial design, he made his first limited–edition color woodcuts in 1909. The following year he moved to the remote, picturesque village of Nashville, Indiana, where he seriously applied himself to color relief printmaking. ⁋ Baumann's first solo exhibition of prints was mounted by the Indianapolis Museum of Art in 1913. One of his eight color woodcuts shown at the Panama–Pacific International Exposition in San Francisco in 1915 won a gold medal. He made extended visits to Westport, Conn., Wyoming, New York, and Provincetown, Mass., producing prints in each location. Baumann moved to Santa Fe, New Mexico in 1918. He married and became a ubiquitous member of the artistic community there. In 1926 a solo exhibition of his prints was mounted at the Smithsonian Institution, in Washington, D.C. The most comprehensive collection of Baumann's prints is to be found at the Museum of Fine Arts in Santa Fe, where the artist died on October 8, 1971. (D.A.)

SOURCE

Martin Krause, Madeline Carol Yurtseven, and David Acton, Gustave Baumann: Nearer to Art (Santa Fe: Museum of New Mexico Press, 1993).

Will H. Bradley
(1868–1962)

Born in Boston, Bradley was raised in the Midwest and trained as a wood engraver in Chicago. By the time he returned to Massachusetts in 1894, he was already one of the most important American proponents of Art Nouveau. The magazine Bradley: His Book, which combined hand–set type with photomechanically reproduced illustrations and decorations, was published in Springfield from 1895 to 1896. Bradley's posters were one of the high points of the 1897 Arts and Crafts exhibition, though they, like most of his work, were photomechanically reproduced. From 1898 to 1901 Bradley's Wayside Press formed part of the University Press in Cambridge, analogous to Bruce Rogers's Department of Special Editions at the Riverside Press. At about this time Bradley discovered early American printing, contributing to a colonial revival style in book design, which in its most exaggerated form was sometimes known as "Bradleyism." Between 1901 and 1907 he designed a number of small books which were printed by Carl H. Heintzemann and issued with the imprint "The Sign of the Vine" from his home in Concord, Mass. After 1907, he left the Boston area to become the art editor of Colliers magazine. (N.F.)

SOURCES

E.G.G., "Sketches and impressions of an American printer," The American Printer (January 1924), pp. 42–46; Will Bradley, Picture of a Period, or Memoirs of the Gay Nineties and the Turn of the Century, also a Few of the Years that Followed (San Marino, Cal.: Rounce and Coffin Club, 1950); Anthony Bambace, Will H. Bradley: His Work: a Bibliographical Guide (New Castle, Del.: Oak Knoll Books; Boston: T.G. Boss Fine Books, 1995).

William Edgar Brigham
(1885–1962)

Brigham was born into a jeweler's family in North Attleboro, Mass., studied at the Rhode Island School of Design under Henry Hunt Clark, and attended Harvard's summer school under Denman Ross in 1905. He began his teaching career at RISD shortly after his graduation from that school in 1906. Brigham also spent time before or after his graduation in Boston working for an as yet unidentified jeweler. Around 1910 Brigham was hired to establish the crafts department at the Cleveland School of Art, returning to RISD in 1914 as head of the Department of Decorative Design, a post he held until his retirement in 1927. Brigham was a member of the Arts and Crafts societies of both Boston and Providence, receiving a medal from the SACB in 1936. He was also a member of the Rhode Island Ship Model Society. ⁋ Financially independent, Brigham maintained a studio in his home where he experimented with various materials. He produced many works in silver, enamel, and jewelry, and precious objets de vertu, many of which were notable for their historical references to both Western and Eastern cultures. Later in life, he and his wife (who had trained in Sweden) founded the Villa Handcrafts workshop, which excelled in tapestry weaving through the 1940s. (J.F. and M.B.M.)

SOURCES

Brigham files, Museum of Art, RISD; SACB papers, AAA/BPL; 1927 exhib. catal., nos. 66, 69–71, p. 6; Garrett D. Byrnes, "Brigham Creates Original Designs," *The Evening Bulletin*, November 13, 1930; *Craft Horizons* 3, no. 5 (May 1944), p. 17; Allen Hendershott Eaton, *Handicrafts of New England* (New York: Harper, 1949) pp. 95, 97; *Who Was Who in American Art*, p. 77; *Who's Who in Art* vol. 22 (New York: American Art Annual, 1925), p. 421.

Lydia Bush–Brown
(1887–1984)

The daughter of sculptor Henry Kirke Bush–Brown and painter Margaret Lesley Bush–Brown, Lydia Bush–Brown (Mrs. Francis Head) was born on November 5, 1887 in Florence, Italy and attended Milton Academy, just south of Boston. She trained at the Pratt Institute in Brooklyn, N.Y. and studied the science of dyeing with Charles Ernest Pellew, a chemist, in Washington, D.C. Listed as a SACB Craftsman (1920) and Master (1921), Bush–Brown was awarded an SACB Medal in 1924, and showed her textiles in Society exhibitions in 1921, 1924, and 1927. Based in New York for most of her career, Bush–Brown was celebrated for her batik resist–dyed silk murals, which appeared in many exhibitions, both in the United States and abroad (including the 1937 Paris Exposition). The artist's travels in Europe, Central America, and the Near East inspired many of her silk murals. (N.J.S.)

SOURCES

Art and Archeology (1922), pp. 188–190; Babette Becker, "The Silk Murals of Lydia Bush–Brown," *American Magazine of Art* (October 1928), pp. 556–60; SACB papers, AAA/BPL; Chris Petteys, *Dictionary of Women Artists* (Boston: G.K. Hall, 1985), p. 111; Gillian Moss, "Textiles of the American Arts and Crafts Movement," in Linda Parry, *William Morris and the Arts and Crafts Movement* (New York: Portland Books, 1989), pp. 21–22; *Who Was Who in American Art*, p. 93.

Sidney Thomas Callowhill
(1867–1939)

A prolific china and glass decorator, Sidney T. Callowhill was one of several china painters in his family, including his father James, brother James Clarence, uncle Thomas Scott, and daughter Dorothea V. Callowhill. Sidney probably learned his trade from his father or uncle, both china decorators at the Royal Worcester Porcelain Factory in England. Having immigrated to the Trenton, N.J. area around 1883, James Callowhill had moved his family to Boston by 1888 or 1889. James Sr. and James Clarence Callowhill pro-

duced the original watercolors for the lithographic plates Louis Prang used in *Oriental Ceramic Art* (Boston, 1897), and exhibited either those watercolors or the lithographs produced from them at the First Exhibition of Arts and Crafts in Boston, 1897 (see fig. 13). Sidney Callowhill and his father executed the original artwork for *The Golden Flower Chrysanthemum*, published by Prang in 1890. ❦ Callowhill lived or kept a studio in Boston and Roslindale before settling in Newton Centre, Mass. in 1911. He became a member of the SACB in 1907, and a Master in 1915. He exhibited frequently at the Society from 1897 to 1927, including solo shows in both the Boston showroom and the Society's New York gallery. Callowhill's work is marked "SIDNEY T. CALLOWHILL" in block letters, with the four "L"'s extending well below the rest of the word. (S.J.M.)

SOURCES

Ellen Paul Denker, *Lenox: Celebrating a Century of Quality, 1889–1989* (Trenton: Lenox and New Jersey State Museum, 1989); Alice Cooney Frelinghuysen, *American Porcelain, 1770–1920* (New York: Metropolitan Museum of Art, 1989); "Prominent Trenton Potters," *Crockery and Glass Journal* (December 17, 1903), p. 142; Ulehla (1981), p. 45.

Ada Gilmore Chaffee
(1883–1955)

Born in Kalamazoo, Mich. on June 17, 1883, Gilmore was the daughter of a prominent local merchant. Both her parents died by the time she was twelve years old, and along with her siblings she was sent to live with an aunt in Belfast, Ireland. There Gilmore began her art studies. She returned to Kalamazoo in 1900, and three years later moved to Chicago to study at the School of the Art Institute. She roomed with fellow student Dolly McMillen and the two women became fast friends. Together they studied briefly with Robert Henri on Long Island in 1912, and then went to Paris. Both learned the technique of color woodcut from American printmaker Ethel Mars. ❦ Gilmore was one of several artists who settled in Provincetown in 1915, and one of the first to embrace B.J.O. Nordfeldt's method for printing color woodcuts from a single block. In 1915 Gilmore's prints were shown at the Panama–Pacific International Exposition in San Francisco and the inaugural exhibition of the Provincetown Art Association. In 1923, while visiting Mars in France, Gilmore became close to the artist Oliver Newberry Chaffee, Jr., and within months they married. At this time Gilmore concentrated her activity on watercolor, and she became active in a circle of modernists that included Albert Gleizes, Chaim Soutine, and Jules Pascin. Gilmore and

Chaffee returned to the United States in 1928, and habitually summered in Provincetown, spending winters at Ormond Beach, Fla. After her husband died in 1944, she stayed on Cape Cod, continuing to paint and exhibit her watercolors until her death. (D.A.)

SOURCES

Ada Gilmore Chaffee, "Cape End Early Cradled Gifted Group of Print Makers Who Added to Art," The [Provincetown] Advocate, October 30, 1952, p. 5; David Acton, A Spectrum of Innovation: Color in American Printmaking, 1890–1960 (New York: W.W. Norton, 1990), pp. 70–71, 255.

Alvin Langdon Coburn
(1882–1966)

Boston–born Alvin Langdon Coburn became an enthusiastic and accomplished photographer at an early age. Introduced to the artistic possibilities of the medium by his cousin F. Holland Day, he traveled to London in 1899 and helped Day install the New School of American Photography exhibition there in 1900. A year later he helped Day bring the exhibition to Paris, where it was shown at the Photo–Club de Paris. On this trip he met Edward Steichen, Frederick Evans, Joseph Keiley, Constant Puyo, Robert Demachy, and Frank Eugene, and established himself among these leading photographers of the day. He moved to New York in 1902 and, at age twenty, joined Alfred Stieglitz as a founding member of the Photo–Secession. Seeking further training, he returned to New England to study with Arthur Wesley Dow, and apprenticed in New York with Gertrude Käsebier. ⟪ In 1903, he became a member of the English photographers' association known as the Brotherhood of the Linked Ring, and a one–man show of his work was held at the Camera Club of New York. Returning to Europe and photographing in London, Paris, Rome, and Venice, he learned the color autochrome process from Steichen and became accomplished in this new technique. In 1909, Stieglitz held a solo show of Coburn's work at Gallery 291 and in 1910, he included twenty–six Coburn photographs in the International Exhibition of Pictorial Photography at the Albright Art Gallery in Buffalo, N.Y. In 1912, Coburn settled in London, never returning to the U.S. His publications, which he illustrated with photogravures, included London (1909), New York (1910), and Men of Mark (1913). (A.E.H.)

SOURCES

Mike Weaver, Alvin Langdon Coburn: Symbolist Photographer, 1882–1966 (New York: Aperture Foundation, 1986); Helmut and Alison Gernsheim, eds., Alvin Langdon Coburn, Photographer: An Autobiography (New York: Dover Publications, 1978).

Emma Lewis Coleman
(1853–1942)

Emma Coleman studied in Paris in the 1860s, where she was exposed to Barbizon painting and, presumably, also to Barbizon photography. After returning to the United States in the 1870s, she began to make romanticized pastoral photographs that are clearly inspired by the Barbizon school. Susan Minot Lane, a painting student of Millet's disciple William Morris Hunt, posed for a number of photographs, and in turn used Coleman's photographs as models for her paintings. C. Alice Baker, a schoolteacher and preservationist, was also a frequent model. ⟪ From 1883 to 1886 Coleman executed a series of forty photographs showing people in colonial costume performing rural tasks, which later appeared in Sarah Orne Jewett's popular preservationist book, Deephaven, published in a limited edition in 1893. In the 1890s Coleman and Baker lived together in Boston, Kittery Point, Me., and in Deerfield — Baker's birthplace — where they were friends with photographers Frances and Mary Allen. Coleman frequently collaborated with Baker, taking photographs of colonial architecture in Deerfield and York and eventually producing several books relating to the preservation movement in New England, including Historic and Present Day Guide to Old Deerfield (1912) and New England Captives Carried to Canada (1925). (A.E.H.)

SOURCES

Sarah L. Giffen and Kevin D. Murphy, "A Noble and Dignified Stream": The Piscataqua Region in the Colonial Revival, 1860–1930 (York, Me.: Old York Historical Society, 1992), pp. 152–55; Ellie Reichlin, "Emma Lewis Coleman, 1853–1942: A Brief Biography," unpubl. MS. (Boston: SPNEA, 1981).

Sarah Ryel Comer
(active 1913–1927)

Little is known about Comer's career beyond what is documented in SACB records. She was a china and glass decorator, residing in Newton Centre while maintaining a studio in Dorchester. She became a member of the Society in 1913 and Master in 1915. Her husband Fred J. Comer, a glass decorator, became a member in 1918, the year they exhibited together at the Society. Comer exhibited regularly at the Society from 1916 to 1924, and signed her work with her full name. (S.J.M.)

SOURCE

Ulehla (1981), pp. 57, 279–83, 286.

Elizabeth Ethel Copeland
(1866–1957)

Born in Revere, Mass., Copeland attended the Cowles Art School in 1900 under Amy Sacker, the book designer and illustrator. While at Cowles, Copeland studied metalsmithing for the first time under Laurin Martin; her classmate was Sarah Choate Sears (see entry), who became her friend and patron. Copeland was sent by Sears in the winter of 1908 to Europe, where she visited museums and schools. It is possible that she studied in London with enamelist Alexander Fisher during this period. ⟨ Copeland's exhibitions and awards include the 1901 Arts and Crafts Exhibition, Providence Art Club; 1903 and 1910 annual arts and crafts exhibitions held at the Art Institute of Chicago; 1904 St. Louis Universal Exposition; 1907 SACB exhibition; 1915 bronze medal at the Panama–Pacific Exposition; 1915 Mrs. Albert H. Loch prize for original design, thirteenth annual Arts and Crafts exhibition at the Art Institute of Chicago; and the 1927 SACB exhibition. The SACB awarded Copeland a medal of honor in 1916, and she remained a member until 1937. Copeland died poor and unmarried at the age of ninety-two. (J.F.)

SOURCES
SACB papers, AAA/BPL; Henry W. Belknap, "Jewelry and Enamels," *Craftsman* 4 (June 1903), pp. 178–81; Irene Sargent, "The Worker in Enamel, with Special Reference to Miss Elizabeth Copeland," *The Keystone* 27 (Feb. 1906), pp. 193–96; Lillian Leslie Tower, "Rich Designs for Metal Jewelry Boxes," *Craftsman* 21 (Dec. 1911), pp. 321–32; Kaplan (1987), cat. no. 129, p. 268; Death Certificate, Massachusetts Department of Vital Statistics.

Mary Jenks Coulter
(1880–1966)

Born in Newport, Ky. on August 30, 1880, Mary Jenks studied at the Art Academy of Cincinnati with Frank Duveneck and Lewis Henry Meakin. She moved to Chicago and became a versatile artisan, working as a ceramist, watercolorist, book designer, jeweler, weaver, and fabric decorator, as well as a printmaker. She was married at this time, but nothing is known of her husband, or the circumstances or length of their marriage. Coulter was the first curator of prints at the Art Institute of Chicago. After travels in Europe in 1913, she earned a degree in philosophy from the University of Chicago. ⟨ In 1915 Coulter was in San Francisco, serving as jury chairman for the arts and crafts section of the Panama–Pacific International Exposition. Thereafter she frequently traveled between the American coasts. She was in Honolulu for two seasons studying with Lionel Walden, and she first went to Provincetown in 1918 to study with Charles W. Hawthorne. There she added color woodcut to her accomplishments as an intaglio printmaker. In 1926 Coulter became assistant director of the San Diego Fine Arts Gallery. She moved to Santa Barbara late in the decade, and lived there until the 1950s. The artist had married Orton Loring Clark by 1959 when she moved to Amherst, Mass. where she died on October 19, 1966. (D.A.)

SOURCE
Edan M. Hughes, *Artists in California, 1786–1940* (San Francisco: Hughes, 1986), p. 103.

Russell S. Crook
(active 1899–1927)

A multi–talented individual in the field of pottery, tiles, modeling, and sculpture, Crook received part of his education from the summer sessions of the New York School of Clayworking and Ceramics at Alfred University. He lived in Boston and Dorchester before settling in South Lincoln, Mass. in 1902. He worked as a plaster modeler for the architectural woodworking firm, John Evans and Company of Boston, and apparently freelanced as a modeler for other manufacturers, including Grueby Faience Company. ⟨ In 1900 he exhibited tiles at the Exposition Universelle in Paris. According to the SACB archives, Crook worked for "various potteries including Grueby's." In 1902 Crook modeled fireplaces for the Scituate estate called *Dreamwold*, a major commission for the Grueby Faience Company. He was an active member of the Wayland Arts and Crafts Society (1906–11), the National Society of Craftsmen (1906–07), and the SACB (1899–at least 1936). Crook occasionally signed his work in the glaze with a monogram of his initials in ligature. (S.J.M.)

SOURCES
"The Interesting Tile Work of 'Dreamwold'," *Brickbuilder* (October 1902), pp. 205–09; Ulehla (1981), p. 61; Linda J. Wesselman and Martha D. Hamilton, *Earliest Recollections: Furnishings from the Family of Edwin B. Sears* (Boston: SPNEA, 1984), p. 17.

Loring Cushing
(1840–1915)

Cushing joined the Tower Guild of toy–makers (later named the Tower Toy Company) in Hingham in 1861 and specialized in the making of doll furniture. He was a member of the Society of Arts and Crafts, Hingham, established in 1901, but never joined the SACB. (E.S.C.)

SOURCES

Marshall and Inez McClintock, *Toys in America* (Washington, D.C.: Public Affairs Press, 1961), pp. 83–84; *Handicraft* 5, no. 4 (July 1912), p. 49; broadside advertisement for Loring Cushing (Hingham Historical Society); letter to the author from Nancy Tiffin of the Hingham Historical Society, July 5, 1995.

Fred Holland Day
(1864–1933)

Affluent native of Norwood, Mass., F. Holland Day was an important contributor to both photography and fine book publishing at the turn of the century. Day took up photography in 1886 and by the early years of the next decade had become one of the most respected and influential Pictorialist photographers. He was a member of the Boston Camera Club in 1889 and participated in the early exhibitions of the SACB (of which he was a member for only one year, 1899–1900). He was one of the few Americans to exhibit in the salons of the Brotherhood of the Linked Ring, the prestigious photographic group in London, of which he became the third American Link in 1896. In February 1898 a major retrospective of 250 of his prints was shown at the New York Camera Club, and a month later at the Boston Camera Club. ❡ A rival of Stieglitz, Day's work was included in *Camera Notes* but was never featured in *Camera Work*, nor did he become a member of the Photo–Secession. In 1900 he organized the New School of American Photography exhibition, the first major exhibition of American Pictorialist photography, which was shown in London and Paris. In 1902 he bought the estate of his friend Louise Imogen Guiney in Five Islands, Me. and summered there until 1917. He exhibited the work of a number of American and European photographers in his Boston studio from 1902 until the building burned down in 1904, in a fire which destroyed many of his early prints and negatives. He became voluntarily bedridden at his Norwood home in 1917 and remained so until his death in 1933. (A.E.H.)

SOURCES

History of Photography, 18, no. 4 (Winter 1994), issue devoted to F. Holland Day, guest edited by Verna Posever Curtis; Estelle Jussim, *Slave to Beauty; The Eccentric Life and Controversial Career of F. Holland Day, Photographer, Publisher, Aesthete* (Boston: David R. Godine, 1981).

Dedham Pottery
(1895–1943)

The Dedham Pottery was established in Dedham, Mass., southwest of Boston, in 1895 with Hugh Cornwall Robertson (1844–1908) as its director. Robertson's family had been involved with potteries for generations. His father James, an accomplished potter, had brought the family to America from Scotland and England in 1853. After working at the East Boston Crockery Manufactory, James and his sons began to produce their own earthenware in nearby Chelsea. By 1872, the company was known as the Chelsea Keramic Art Works. Expanding production from flowerpots to art pottery and pressed tiles, CKAW developed a reputation for innovative decorative techniques and glazes, in direct competition with European and English ceramics. ❡ In 1884, after his father's death and his brothers' departures to other potteries, Hugh Robertson was left to manage the Chelsea factory alone. His obsessive experimentation with reproducing the lost Chinese oxblood or *sang–de–boeuf* glaze eventually bankrupted CKAW in 1889. Boston–area supporters of Robertson's efforts refinanced the pottery as Chelsea Pottery, U.S. in 1891. In 1895, production moved to a new site in Dedham. The classic crackle–glazed dinnerware with painted blue decoration was developed as a "tasteful" commercial product which could support the pottery and guarantee the patrons' investment while Robertson pursued his elusive glaze experiments. The directors of the new Dedham Pottery included Arthur Astor Carey (second president of the SACB); J. Templeman Coolidge; Joseph Lindon Smith; A. Wadsworth Longfellow, Jr.; and Sarah Wyman Whitman—all founding members of the SACB. Hugh Robertson joined the Society in 1901, receiving Master status in 1902. Several patrons, including Denman Ross and Joseph Linden Smith, designed some of the borders on the pottery. Dedham pottery was exhibited at the SACB in 1897, 1899, 1907, and 1919. After Hugh's death in 1908 he was succeeded by his son, William A. Robertson. Decorator Maud Davenport, who concealed her "O" mark in her hand–painted borders, worked for Dedham from 1904 to 1929. Her brother Charles became head of the decorating division. In 1929 William A. Robertson was succeeded by his son, J. Milton Robertson. The pottery closed in 1943. (S.J.M.)

SOURCES

Edwin Atlee Barber, "Recent Progress of American Potters," *The Clay–Worker* (May 1895), p. 580; "Dedham Pottery Formally Known as Chelsea Pottery, U.S., A Short History," pamphlet, 1898; Evans (1987), pp. 46–51, 82–86; Lloyd E. Hawes, *Dedham Pottery and the Earliest Robertson's Chelsea Pottery* (Dedham, Mass.: Dedham Historical Society, 1968); Úlehla (1981), pp. 67, 184.

Deerfield Society of Blue and White Needlework

see

Society of Blue and White Needlework, Deerfield

Denison House
(founded 1892)

Denison House was founded in 1892 by a group of college–educated women whose primary goal was to break down the barriers between workers of any kind and the so–called "leisure class." The founders stated that their ideal was democracy rather than philanthropy. Led by Helena Dudley and others (including Emily Balch, Helen Cheever, and Vida Scudder), the settlement house on Tyler Street created a program of activities, ranging from basket weaving to dancing, for the neighborhood population, which included European and Near Eastern immigrants. They also established relief programs for the same neighbors in times of financial hardship. ❧ Vida Scudder established the Circolo Italo–Americano in 1902, whose annual activities included a May Festa and a December Exhibition of Italian Arts and Crafts. Lace–making by recent Italian immigrants was a particular focus of this group, which in 1908 instituted classes in lace–making via the Denison House Women's Club. Around 1914–15 Denison House created the Folk Handicrafts Council which "brought yearly earnings of over $11,000 to 105 Italians, 36 Syrians, 4 Greeks, 2 Armenians, and 21 others." Envelopes used by the Folk Handicrafts group included the motto "*Per Pane e Piacere*" ("for bread and happiness"). ❧ Rather than Americanize their immigrant clientele, Denison House encouraged those who worked in the handicrafts workshops to develop traditional talents. The Denison House Folk Handicrafts sample book (CAT. NO. 80) includes the work of lace–making groups from far beyond Boston, including the Sybil Carter Indian Lace Association of the White Earth (Ojibwa) Reservation in Minnesota. (N.J.S.)

SOURCES

Denison House Archives, the Schlesinger Library, Radcliffe College; Eileen Boris, *Art and Labor: Ruskin, Morris, and the Craftsman Ideal in America* (Philadelphia: Temple University Press, 1986), pp. 133–34; Kaplan (1987), cat. no. 150, p. 308.

Arthur Wesley Dow
(1857–1922)

Born in Ipswich on April 6, 1857, Dow began his artistic activities as a boy. He went to Paris in 1884 to study at the Académie Julian, and then went to work at Pont Aven in Brittany. Back in Boston in 1889, where he worked as a painter and teacher, Dow became interested in Japanese prints. He was drawn to Ernest F. Fenollosa, curator of Oriental art at the MFA, who helped him to apply Japanese aesthetic principles to his own work. In 1891 Dow began to make color woodcuts based on traditional Japanese prints, and founded the Ipswich Summer School of Art. In 1895 he began to teach his new aesthetic and methods at the Pratt Institute in Brooklyn, N.Y. and in 1897 at the Art Students League in New York. Dow's instructional textbook *Composition*, first published in 1899, became immensely popular and the most influential aesthetic manual of its time. ❧ The artist visited Japan in 1903. On his return he became Director of Fine Arts at the Columbia University Teachers College, and the preeminent American art educator of the day. Dow also continued to produce his own oil paintings, prints, and photographs, and to write and illustrate books. He died suddenly in New York on December 13, 1922. (D.A.)

SOURCES

Arthur Wesley Dow, *Composition* (Boston: J.M. Bowles, 1899); Frederick C. Moffatt, *Arthur Wesley Dow, 1857–1922* (Washington, D.C.: Smithsonian Institution Press, 1977); Nancy E. Green, *Arthur Wesley Dow and His Influence* (Ithaca, N.Y.: Herbert F. Johnson Museum of Art, 1990).

William Addison Dwiggins
(1880–1956)

Dwiggins arrived in Boston from Ohio in 1904 and was soon designing title pages and illustrations for both Daniel Berkeley Updike and Alfred Bartlett. Although the influence of William Morris—which Dwiggins had absorbed from his teacher Frederick W. Goudy in Chicago—is strongly apparent in some of his earliest work, he soon abandoned this style, which was already out of date in Boston. With the encouragement of Updike, he explored other styles, notably those of the eighteenth century and the Italian Renaissance, which he always treated with a light and whimsical touch. He was a member of the SACB from 1906 to 1916 but does not appear to have played an active role in its activities, perhaps because he was more involved with the newly founded Society of Printers. Dwiggins's most characteristic work dates from the 1920s and 1930s, when he developed a highly personal version of art deco. (N.F.)

SOURCES

Papers, Boston Public Library; Dwight Agner, *The Books of WAD: A Bibliography of the Books Designed by W. A. Dwiggins* (Baton Rouge, La.: The Press of the Night Owl, 1974); Dorothy Abbe, "William Addison Dwiggins; A Talk Delivered to the Bookbuilders of Boston" (Boston: BPL, 1974).

Chansonetta Stanley Emmons
(1858–1937)

Chansonetta Emmons, who dabbled in painting, drawing, and photography, took up the camera as a serious occupation in 1898, after the premature death of her husband. Her prosperous brothers, who made their fortunes first by manufacturing dry–plate negatives and then by inventing and manufacturing the Stanley Steamer automobile, were the primary financial support for Emmons and her daughter Dorothy, which allowed her to specialize in her favorite subjects without having to seek commercial work. Emmons made most of her pictures shortly after 1900 in her rural hometown of Kingfield, Me.; in Chesham, N.H., where she took painting lessons from William Preston Phelps; and in Boston, where she spent the winters. Like many women photographers of her social standing, she focused her lens on family life and customs, themes she addressed with refreshing simplicity and directness. She was a member of the SACB from 1918 to 1927 and exhibited in the Society's 1927 exhibition. (A.E.H.)

SOURCES

Marius B. Péladeau, *Chansonetta: The Life and Photographs of Chansonetta Stanley Emmons, 1858–1937* (Waldoboro, Me.: Maine Antique Digest, 1977).

George Fenety
(1854–1933)

Fenety moved from Nova Scotia to Boston around 1878 and worked for several years as a potter at the Chelsea Keramic Art Works. However, he was listed as an embroidery designer and Craftsman in the SACB (1899–1902), exhibiting designs embroidered "by Miss Fenety" at the 1897 and 1899 exhibitions. Fenety's designs could be purchased either fully embroidered or outlined on fabric for customers to finish at home. His Boston residences are listed as 23 Studio Building (1897–1900), followed by 110 Tremont Street (1901–02), and as an "Art Embroiderer" at 120 Tremont Street, Room 419 (through 1933). (N.J.S.)

SOURCES

SACB papers, AAA/BPL; Kaplan (1987), pp. 380–81; *Polk's Boston City Directory* (1933).

Hazel Blake French
(1890–1972)

French was known for using Sandwich glass to emulate precious stones in her "interpretive jewelry." Born in Brockton, Mass., she spent her childhood summers in East Sandwich, Cape Cod, collecting glass chunks from the grounds of the old Sandwich Glass Factory and sketching. She entered the Museum School in 1909, studying design with C. Howard Walker and Huger Elliot, and jewelry and additional courses with George J. Hunt. French opened a studio in Sandwich after graduation in 1913, making period–style jewelry in silver and gold with twisted wire and precious stones. She married engineer Bertrand C. French, and had three children. French was proficient in many media — designing, painting, stenciling, decorating, leather, wood, basketry — but she focused on jewelry. Her pieces, named according to their romantic colors, became sought–after souvenirs for summer residents and visitors, including Russian and English royalty. French later taught jewelry and metalwork at the Sea Pines School and Cape Cod Institute of Music in Brewster, and in 1941 was featured in an MGM travelogue, *Picturesque Massachusetts*. Becoming a member of the SACB in 1925, French exhibited in Providence, at the Society's showroom in New York in 1925, in New Orleans, Philadelphia, and Chicago, as well as at the SACB's Tricennial Exhibition in 1927. Although the Jury found her work a little "too heavy," French exhibited at L'Exposition International, Paris, 1937. She became an SACB Master in 1936. (M.B.M.)

SOURCES

Questionnaire for *Allgemeines Lexikon*, SACB archives, AAA/BPL reel 2468:frame 247; Lavinia Walsh, "The Romance of Sandwich Glass," *Cape Cod Magazine* (December 15, 1927); *Cape Cod Times*, August 16, 1940; *Boston Globe*, October 23, 1923; *Wareham Courier*, September 2, 1967?; Allen Hendershott Eaton, *Handicrafts of New England* (New York: Harper, 1949), p. 246.

George Christian Gebelein
(1878–1945)

At the age of thirteen, Bavarian–born Gebelein was apprenticed to the Boston silversmithing firm Goodnow & Jenks. He later worked at Tiffany & Company in Forest Hills, N.J., and at William B. Durgin Company in Concord, N.H. In 1903, Gebelein left these larger enterprises for the Handicraft Shop, where he became well respected for his tea services and other table accoutrements made in a colonial revival style. In 1909 Gebelein opened a shop at 79 Chestnut Street, where he sold early American silver alongside his own. ❡ Gebelein established his identity as a maker of colonial revival style silver, remaining faithful to the spirit of the Revolutionary craftsman Paul Revere II throughout his own career. In advertisements, he emphasized his link to the colonial past through his apprenticeship with Goodnow & Jenks, which traced its history to Revere's shop. Forging a romantic link with the ideals and style of the Revolutionary era, Gebelein served a community that was closely tied to its heroic past. ❡ In the post–Depression era, Gebelein adapted his wares to suit more modest purses and sold copper bowls with silver electroplated interiors as popular wedding gifts. Just as Revere quickly made use of sheet silver when it became available, Gebelein utilized spun vessels and employed outside jobbers in order to produce attractive wares at a lower cost. Despite these innovations in his workshop, Gebelein's advertising continued to propound the virtues of hand craftsmanship that had first attracted his clientele. (J.F.)

SOURCES

Alexandra Deutsch, "George Christian Gebelein: Craftsman and Businessman," Symposium, Emerging Scholars in American Art, Museum of Fine Arts, Boston, April 28, 1995; Kaplan (1987), cat. no. 65, p. 178; Margaretha Gebelein Leighton et al., *George Christian Gebelein, Boston Silversmith, 1878–1945* (Boston: Stinehour Press, 1976).

George Ernest Germer
(1868–1936)

One of the greatest ecclesiastical metalworkers of the period was George E. Germer. Born the son of a jeweler in Berlin, Germer was apprenticed to the workshop of Otto Gerike, where he mastered chasing and modeling. In 1885, Germer won a medal at an annual apprentices' exhibition for his chased silver. He visited the major German cultural centers of Hanau, Cologne, and Dresden and worked at the Kunstgewerbe Museum in Berlin before emigrating to the United States about 1891. After working at silversmithing centers in Providence and New York, in 1912 he established an independent workshop at 26 Lime Street, Boston where he concentrated on ecclesiastical commissions. Germer purchased a farm in Mason, N.H. in 1917, but by 1927 had moved to Greenville, N.H. ❡ Germer fashioned ecclesiastical silver of his own design, as well as that designed by architects, for numerous churches. Among them are St. Peter's Church in Rochester, N.Y.; St. Mathias' and St. John's Churches in Detroit, Mich.; St. James', N.Y.; and King's Chapel, Boston. He also made silver for Grace Church, St. Peter's Church, Emmanuel Church, and the Cathedral of the Incarnation in Baltimore, Md. Germer received the Mrs. Albert Loeb prize at the Art Institute of Chicago in 1915. He was a member of the SACB and received the Society's medal of excellence in 1927. (J.F.)

SOURCES

SACB papers, AAA/BPL; Kaplan (1987), cat. no. 20, p. 136.

Bertram Grosvenor Goodhue
(1869–1924)

Bertram Grosvenor Goodhue was born on April 28, 1869 in Pomfret, Conn. From 1884 Goodhue trained in New York City as a draftsman with the architectural firm Renwick, Aspinall & Russell. He moved to Boston in 1889 to work with Ralph Adams Cram and Charles Francis Wentworth, who specialized in ecclesiastical architecture. Goodhue was made a partner in the firm of Cram, Wentworth, and Goodhue in 1892 (changed to Cram, Goodhue, and Ferguson in 1897). Although successful as an architect, Goodhue was one of the most creative and prolific Boston book artists of the 1890s. The influence of William Morris is clearly evident in his decorations for several Copeland & Day publications, including Dante Gabriel Rossetti's *House of Life* (1894) and Wilfred Scawen Blunt's *Esther: A Young Man's Tragedy* (1895). Together, Goodhue and Cram edited the *Knight Errant* between 1892 and 1894, and Goodhue designed the type as well as the lavish page borders of *The Altar Book* (1896), probably the most famous American Arts and Crafts book and Daniel Berkeley Updike's most significant publication in this style. ❡ Goodhue was an active member of the SACB (listed as Master 1897–1925) and designed the catalogue for the first Exhibition of Arts and Crafts held in Copley Hall in 1897. As the Arts and Crafts style he favored fell out of fashion, he produced fewer and fewer book designs, and became increasingly involved in his architectural work. Cram and Goodhue worked in the Gothic revival style for the architecture and interior decoration of such churches as All Saints', Ashmont (1892–1913), and Saint Thomas Church, N.Y. (1906–13). ❡ Goodhue taught decorative design at the Cowles Art School, then moved to New York in 1903 to oversee the Cram, Goodhue, and Ferguson commission for the United States Military Academy at West Point, never returning to Boston. After breaking with Cram in 1913, Goodhue undertook important architectural commissions, including the Cathedral of the Incarnation, Baltimore (1911–24) and the Nebraska State Capitol Building (1920–32). (N.F. and N.J.S.)

SOURCES

Letters, The Houghton Library, Harvard University; Norwood Historical Society; Bertram Grosvenor Goodhue, *Book Decorations* (New York: The Grolier Club, 1931); *Macmillan's Encyclopedia of Architects* vol. 2 (New York: The Free Press, 1982), pp. 229–31; Richard Oliver, *Bertram Grosvenor Goodhue* (New York: The Architectural History Foundation; Cambridge: MIT Press, 1983); James F. O'Gorman, "'Either in Books or [in] architecture': Bertram Grosvenor Goodhue in the Nineties," *Harvard Library Bulletin* 35, no. 2 (Spring 1987), pp. 165–83.

Elwyn George Gowen
(1895–1954)

Born January 19, 1895 in Sanford, Me., Gowen was a graduate of the School of the Museum of Fine Arts, Boston, where he studied with H.H. Clark, Denman W. Ross, C.H. Woodbury, and P. Hale. Gowen taught design, color, interior decoration, and the history of art at the Museum School until 1941, and at other institutions such as Scott Carbee and Charles II Woodbury School, as well as taking private pupils. He was elected a Craftsman of the SACB (1921), promoted to Master (1922), exhibited in the 1927 exhibition, and served as a juror (1928). Gowen is known for his work as a blockprinter, decorator, designer, etcher, and painter. He was also a member of the Ogunquit (Maine) Art Association and the American Federation of Arts. After leaving the Museum School, Gowen continued his art and his work as an interior designer until his death on December 28, 1954. (N.J.S.)

SOURCES

SACB papers, AAA/BPL; *Who Was Who in American Art*, p. 240; Obituary, *Boston Globe*, December 30, 1954; Obituary, *Boston Herald*, December 30, 1954.

Herbert Gregson
(born 1878)

Gregson appears to have been active chiefly as a commercial artist and a designer of book covers and bookplates. His masterpiece is the edition of Thomas Gray's *Elegy Written in a Country Churchyard* issued by the Craftsman's Guild in 1901 (CAT. NO. 99) with his hand–lettering and decorations. Gregson never joined the SACB or participated in the Society's exhibitions. (N.F.)

SOURCES

Ex–Libris: A Collection of Bookplate Designs by Herbert Gregson (Boston: W.P. Truesdell, 1907); *Herbert Gregson and his Book Plates* (Boston: printed at the Troutsdale Press and sold by C.E. Goodspeed, 1903).

Grueby Faience Company
(1894–1909)
Grueby Pottery Company
(1907–1909)
Grueby Faience and Tile Company
(1909–1919)

Grueby pottery functioned from 1894 to 1919 in three distinct phases. The original Grueby Company was founded by William Henry Grueby (1867–1925) in South Boston in 1894. Grueby had apprenticed at the Low Art Tile Works in Chelsea, Mass. in the late 1880s where he learned glaze chemistry from George Robertson, brother of Hugh Cornwall Robertson (see Dedham Pottery entry). In 1890 Grueby joined forces with Eugene R. Atwood, another Low employee, to found an architectural faience company. By 1894, Atwood and Grueby had separated, and Grueby Faience Company was established to produce glazed architectural terra cotta. ❡ Several important individuals were involved with the firm: Grueby himself, the glaze expert; William Hagerman Graves (1867–1943), who studied architecture at MIT before becoming Grueby's business manager from 1897 to 1909; George Prentiss Kendrick (1850–1919), designer, metalworker, and founding member of the SACB; and Addison Brayton Le Boutillier (1872–1951), an architect and graphic designer, who designed most of Grueby's tiles. All four were members of the SACB; Grueby and Graves were also members of the elite St. Botolph Club. Grueby pottery was influenced by the work of the late nineteenth–century French potters he saw at the 1893 Chicago exposition — especially Auguste Delaherche, Adrien–Pierre Dalpayrat, Alexandre Bigot, and Edmond Lachenal — along with Asian ceramics.

Grueby popularized opaque matte glazes, most notably in shades of green, but also available in yellow, blue, pink, mustard, and oatmeal. Floral decoration was applied by young modelers from the Massachusetts Normal Art School and the School of the Museum of Fine Arts, Boston. Grueby pottery was shown at SACB in 1897, 1899, and 1907. ❡ By 1900 the pottery had gained international recognition, winning gold medals at the Exposition Universelle, Paris; the Pan–American Exposition, Buffalo, 1901; and the Louisiana Purchase Exposition in St. Louis, Mo. in 1904. The firm's success spawned many imitators which contributed to the financial instability of the company. As part of a business reorganization, Grueby Pottery Company incorporated independently in 1907. The parent firm of Grueby Faience went into receivership in 1909, emerging as the Grueby Faience and Tile Company, devoted exclusively to tile production. The factory was rebuilt after a 1913 fire and was sold to Pardee Tile of Perth Amboy, N.J. in 1919. Grueby's operations used several impressed horizontal marks, including GRUEBY; GRUEBY/BOSTON. MASS; and GRUEBY POTTERY; and two circular marks, each with a lotus in the center: GRUEBY·POTTERY·BOSTON·U·S·A and GRUEBY·FAIENCE·Co·BOSTON·USA. (S.J.M.)

SOURCES
C. H. Blackall, "The Grueby Faience," *Brickbuilder* (August 1898), pp. 162–63; "Boston's Art Product—Grueby Ware," *Crockery and Glass Journal* (December 12, 1901), pp. 131–32, 135; W.G. Bowdoin, "The Grueby Pottery," *Art Interchange* (December 1900), pp. 136–37; Martin Eidelberg, "The Ceramic Art of William H. Grueby," *The American Connoisseur* (September 1973), pp. 47–54; Evans (1974), pp. 118–23; "Good Green Ware Gave Fame to Grueby Name," *Glass and Pottery World* (June 1908), pp. 13–14; *Grueby* (Syracuse: Everson Museum of Art, 1981); Annie Jones, "The Grueby Pottery," *Scrip* (March 1906), pp. 197–99; Susan J. Montgomery, *The Ceramics of William H. Grueby* (Lambertville, N.J.: Arts & Crafts Quarterly Press, 1993); Arthur Russell, "Grueby Pottery," *House Beautiful* (December 1898), pp. 3–9.

Frank Gardner Hale
(1876–1945)

Born in Norwich, Conn., Hale graduated from the Norwich Art School and the Museum School, under Henry Hunt Clark, in 1898. Initially a designer of book covers, book plates, and in particular, covers for published music, he exhibited in Minneapolis in 1901 before studying metalwork and jewelry–making in 1906 at C.R. Ashbee's Guild of the Handicraft, Chipping Campden, England, and jewelry and enamels with Fred Partridge in London. Upon his return in 1907, he became a member of the SACB. Living on Chestnut Street on Boston's Beacon Hill, he opened a studio at 2 Park Square. His apprentices included

Museum School graduate John Ballou, eighteen–year–old Edward Everett Oakes, and later Gertrude Rosendahl. An outspoken man, he was a member of the SACB Jury from 1910 to 1919, a member of the Council, and vice–president in 1926. He received many awards, including the Society's Medal of Excellence and a silver medal at the Panama–Pacific Exposition, San Francisco in 1915, and the Logan Award of the Art Institute of Chicago in 1917. In 1919, he established the Jewelers' Guild, becoming its dean. Hale lectured extensively around the country, often in conjunction with his many shows of jewelry and enamels. Hale married Julia Dwight in 1909 and later established the Marblehead Arts Association with his brother–in–law, New York portrait painter Orlando Roland. He was also a member of the Detroit Society of Arts and Crafts and the Copley Society. (M.B.M.)

SOURCES
Henry Hunt Clark, "Frank Gardner Hale, Jeweler," *American Magazine of Art* 14 (April 1923), p. 189; Questionnaire for *Allgemeines Lexikon*, SACB archives, AAA/BPL; *Who's Who in Massachusetts* vol. 1, 1940–41 (Boston: Larkin, Roosevelt and Larkin, 1940); SACB archives, AAA/BPL reels 300–20.

Theodore Brown Hapgood, Jr.
(1871–1938)

Hapgood studied at the Museum School and immediately embarked on a long and successful career as a designer. His work encompassed not only the bookplates and book covers for which he is chiefly known today, but also ecclesiastical vestments, tombstones, and architectural monuments. Calligraphy was a special interest, and he produced hand–illuminated manuscripts, the original hand–lettered text and decorations for the Craftsman's Guild edition of *Two Lyrics* by John Bannister Tabb, and the lettering for numerous title–pages. Hapgood was equally proficient in medieval, Renaissance, and American colonial ornament, switching easily from one style to the other depending on the nature of the commission. Though he is famous for his densely patterned medieval designs incorporating monks and scribes, he was also one of the chief popularizers of the colonial revival style. His involvement with the SACB began with the first exhibition in 1897 and continued until his death. (N.F.)

SOURCES
Archives, School of the Museum of Fine Arts, Boston; *Bookplates Designed by Theodore Brown Hapgood* (Boston: printed at the Troutsdale Press and sold by E.C. Goodspeed, 1907); Lewis Buddy III, "The Decorative Work of Theodore Brown Hapgood," *The Graphic Arts* 4, no. 6 (May 1913); William A. Kittredge, *Theodore Brown Hapgood* (Boston: Society of Printers, 1942).

Susan Leland Hill
(died 1961)

Hill's extensive training began at the School of the Worcester Art Museum in 1905 with Edmund B. Rolfe (who instructed her again in 1910 in metalwork and jewelry), with H. Gustave Rogers in 1906, and with George J. Hunt from 1907 to 1909. For the next two years, Hill attended design, modeling, and metalwork classes under Worcester's newly appointed Principal and Instructor of Design, H. Stuart Michie, to whom she sold several pieces. She attended summer school at RISD in 1909 under Henry Hunt Clark and Augustus Rose. Hill also attended pottery classes at Worcester in 1914, and the Berkshire Summer School of Art in 1915 and 1916. In 1923 she moved to Berkeley, Calif., but returned a year later for summer school at RISD. Maintaining a studio in California, Hill sold jewelry to metalsmith Harry Dixon. Hill became a member of the SACB in 1907, and exhibited in many specialized shows at its showrooms, as well as in the anniversary exhibition of 1927. A member of the New York Society of Craftsmen and San Francisco Society of Woman Artists, she exhibited extensively in Chicago, Cleveland, Minneapolis, Providence, St. Louis, and Washington. A single woman, Hill bequeathed her belongings to the Society, including her notebooks filled with drawings and ideas based on historical objects in museums. (M.B.M.)

SOURCES
Questionnaire for *Allgemeines Lexikon*, SACB archives, AAA/BPL reel 3468; Susan Leland Hill Papers, Boston Public Library; Annual Reports of the Worcester Art Museum, School of Drawing and Painting 1906–07, Library of the Museum of Fine Arts, Boston.

Society of Arts and Crafts, Hingham
(founded 1901)

Founded in November 1901, the Society was particularly renowned for basketry, vegetable–dyeing, toy–making, colonial revival embroidery, beadwork, metalwork, and rug–making. Around 1904 two–thirds of its members were women. Goods offered for sale were approved by a committee for each handicraft, supervised by a council of fifteen. Members who learned a craft at the Society forfeited their membership if they sold such craftwork other than through the Society, which had a permanent salesroom open three days a week at this period, and which held an annual exhibition every August. The seal of the Society featured the image of a bucket, since buckets had been a traditional local product since the eighteenth century. (N.J.S.)

SOURCES
Max West, "The Revival of Handicraft in America," U.S. Bureau of Labor Bulletin 55 (November 1904), pp. 1617–18; Susan Willard, "The Hingham Society of Arts and Crafts," in *Hingham* (Hingham, Mass.: Old Colony Chapter, Daughters of the American Revolution, 1911), pp. 120–21; C. Chester Lane, "Hingham Arts and Crafts: Their Aims and Objects," *Craftsman* 3 (December 1903), pp. 276–81.

Edna Boies Hopkins
(1872–1937)

Edna Bel Beachboard was the daughter of a prosperous banker in Hudson, Mich. In 1892 she married John Henry Boies and moved to Chicago, but her husband died two years later of tuberculosis. From 1895 to 1898 she attended the Art Academy of Cincinnati, where she met Ethel Mars, Maud Squire, and James R. Hopkins. Later, as a student of Arthur Wesley Dow at the Pratt Institute, she learned the fundamentals of Japanese color woodcut. ⁋After their marriage in 1904, Boies and Hopkins embarked on an unhurried journey around the world. An extended stay in Japan provided the opportunity for a methodical study of woodcut techniques. The couple settled in Paris and Edna devoted herself to color woodcut, exhibiting and selling her floral prints with great success. In 1914 they returned to Ohio, where James took a job teaching at the Art Academy of Cincinnati. Though they remained married and Edna regularly visited James, she did not stay in Ohio. In the summer of 1914 she was in Provincetown, and that fall in Manhattan. The first American solo exhibition of her prints was at the Berlin Photographic Company in New York in 1916. ⁋In 1920 Boies and Hopkins returned to Paris together. Edna made floral prints that reflected the influence in style and technique of the single–block white line method. Her printmaking waned after her return to the United States in 1923, and it seems that her career was cut short by disability. Hopkins died in New York in 1937. (D.A.)

SOURCES
Mary Ryan Gallery, *Edna Boies Hopkins: Color Woodcuts 1900–1923* (New York: The Gallery, 1986); Julia Meech–Pekarik and Gabriel P. Weisberg, *Japonisme Comes to America: The Japanese Impact on the Graphic Arts, 1876–1925* (New York: Abrams, 1990), pp. 180–89.

George Joseph Hunt
(1866–1947)

Born in Liverpool, England, George Hunt studied at the Liverpool Art Institute before moving to

London, where he apprenticed in the shop of Joseph Meyer from around 1880 to 1887. Hunt arrived in Boston shortly after his apprenticeship, and commenced work for various silver and jewelry manufacturers. In 1902 he was named a Craftsman in the SACB. Hunt returned to Liverpool briefly around 1903, registered his mark with the nearby Chester assay office, and produced a silver teapot (CAT. NO. 40). Upon his return to Boston around 1905, Hunt taught at the School of the Museum of Fine Arts, Boston, a position he retained until his retirement in 1942. In 1905, Hunt also opened a studio at 79 Chestnut Street, where he maintained a private School of Metalry. He was promoted to Mastership by the SACB in 1908. Evidence of his energy can be discerned from his demanding teaching schedule. In addition to his work at the Museum School, Hunt taught at the School of the Worcester Art Museum from 1906–09, at the Swain School in New Bedford from 1909–27, at the Minneapolis Summer School of Design, and in the summer of 1912 at the Chautauqua Institute in upstate New York. Although he did not exhibit widely, Hunt did receive prestigious secular and ecclesiastical commissions. Hunt's Nova Scotia–born wife, Emma Gates Wilson Hunt, was elected a Craftsman in the SACB in 1914, and worked as a jeweler from that time until about 1938. Hunt displayed his silver in the 1907 SACB exhibition. Both he and his wife, who showed filigree jewelry, were represented in the Society's 1927 exhibition. (J.F.)

SOURCES
Museum School Scrapbook, vol. 12, p. 112; SACB papers, AAA/BPL; "Jewelry and Silversmithing School at the Boston Museum of Fine Arts," The Jeweler's Circular (February 28, 1928), p. 247; Obituary, The Boston Daily Globe, March 10, 1947; Kaplan (1987), p. 136, fn. 3; Archives, Chautauqua Institute; Albert Nelson Marquis, ed., Who's Who in New England (Chicago: A.N. Marquis & Co., 1916), p. 583; correspondence, Robert B. Barker to the author, February 1, 1996.

Adrian J. Iorio
(1879–1957)

Iorio went to work for Will Bradley at his Wayside Press in Springfield. He accompanied Bradley to Cambridge after the Wayside Press was incorporated with the University Press and remained as head of the Wayside Department after Bradley departed. Bradley's influence is apparent in Iorio's early work. After leaving the Wayside Press, Iorio designed numerous book covers and decorations, many of them for Houghton Mifflin and Company. He also designed bookplates and advertisements. He was a member of the SACB from 1901 to 1903. (N.F.)

SOURCES
Adrian J. Iorio and his Book Plates (Boston: Charles E. Goodspeed, 1903); "An Exhibit of Designs by Adrian J. Iorio," The Graphic Arts 2 (1911), pp. 329–36; Who Was Who in American Art, p. 306.

George Prentiss Kendrick
(1850–1919)

Born in Natchez, Miss., Kendrick was living in Boston as early as 1869. Although his education and apprenticeship are not documented, Kendrick had garnered metalsmithing and design skills by the mid–1880s, when he produced a copper punch bowl for the Tavern Club in 1885, due in part to his association with Tavern Club member and architect Robert Day Andrews. Kendrick joined Andrews's firm Andrews, Jacques and Rantoul in Brookline, where he worked until he joined Grueby Faience as director in 1897. ⁋ At the first exhibition of arts and crafts held at Copley Hall that same year, Kendrick exhibited Grueby pottery, book designs, and ten examples of metalwork that were "designed and executed" by him. These included silver and copper bowls, inkstands, and a small silver jewel box. Evidence of Kendrick's involvement in the nascent society is the presence of his name among the twenty–one signers of the "Charter of the Society of Arts and Crafts" dated June 28, 1897. He later served as chairman of the Metalwork Department for the Society's 1907 exhibition and submitted metalwork which included a silver tankard, loving cup, and silver and copper tea caddies. Kendrick credited himself with having "designed and executed" the objects. The "smith work" was done by others, including Karl F. Leinonen of the Handicraft Shop, and S.D. Hicks, a coppersmith in Arlington. Whether such assistants were employed earlier in his career is unknown. (J.F.)

SOURCES
Susan J. Montgomery, The Ceramics of William H. Grueby (Lambertville, N.J.: Arts & Crafts Quarterly Press, 1993), pp. 21–23, 97, 111; 1907 exhib. catal., p. 40.

John Kirchmayer
(1860–1930)

Born and trained in Oberammergau in the Bavarian Alps of Germany, Johannes (also Ionannes, I.J.) Kirchmayer emigrated when he was around twenty years old, and probably worked in New York for A. Kimbel and Sons and then Herter Brothers, the two leading custom furniture and decorating shops in the East. By 1893, he was working for the firm of Irving & Casson of Cambridge as the lead carver on the interior woodwork and furniture for the James J. Hill house in St. Paul, Minn. Kirchmayer worked for Irving & Casson until about 1905, when he joined William F. Ross & Co., a Cambridge firm that specialized in custom domestic interiors and furniture. The impact of Kirchmayer on W.F. Ross can be seen in the advertisements in *The Boston Architectural Club Yearbook* and the Boston Directory for 1907. Before that time, Ross advertised as a "manufacturer of artistic furniture and interior woodwork," but after 1907 was billed as "modellers, carvers, interior work." As the head of a carving department that had as many as thirty–five carvers at one time, Kirchmayer became a partner in the Ross firm, where he worked until he retired in 1921 and began to work at home for special clients like George Booth. He was a charter member of the SACB in 1897, earned status as a Master that year, and served as vice–president of the Guild of Woodworkers that was established in 1907. Kirchmayer worked particularly closely with the two great American Gothic architects, Ralph Adams Cram and Henry Vaughn, both of whom were based in Boston. Examples of his work include the James J. Hill house in St. Paul, Minn.; the triptych at All Saints' Church in Ashmont, Mass.; various panels at St. Paul's Church in Chicago; reredos at St. Paul's Cathedral in Detroit; reredos at Christ Church, Pittsburgh; the main door and baptismal font at the Memorial Church in Fairhaven, Mass.; and much paneling at Cranbrook Academy (Bloomfield Hills, Mich). (E.S.C.)

SOURCES

Ralph Adams Cram, *My Life in Architecture* (Boston: Little, Brown and Co., 1936), pp. 187–88; F.W. Coburn, "Wood Carving and Architecture—Work by I. Kirchmayer and Others," *International Studio* (September 1910), pp. lxiv–lxv; Katherine Gibson, "A Wood–Carver of Today: I. Kirchmayer," in *The Goldsmith of Florence* (1929; repr. Freeport, N.Y.: Books for Libraries Press, 1967), pp. 171–85; letter from Craig Johnson, site manager of the James J. Hill House, to the author, October 3, 1994; Anne Webb Karnaghan, "Ecclesiastical Carvings in America," *International Studio* 85, no. 353 (October 1926), pp. 50–54; Ralph Bergengren, "I. Kirchmayer, Wood Carver," *House Beautiful* 37, no. 4 (March 1915), pp. 111–15, xvii; John Kirchmayer, "About Wood–carving," *American Magazine of Art* 14 (January 1923), pp. 19–21; audiotape, Andrew Dreselly interviewed by Robert Brown, June 26, 1981, AAA/SI; 1897 exhib. catal., p. 6; 1899 exhib. catal., pp. 18–21; 1907 exhib. catal., pp. 16 and 89; Ülehla (1981), p. 127.

Frank L. Koralewsky
(1872–1941)

Frank Koralewsky and his brother Gustav (1870–1954) were apprenticed to a master blacksmith near the town of Straslund, Germany. Gustav probably arrived in Boston around 1894, and his brother Frank shortly thereafter. By 1905 Gustav had begun working in Roxbury for Munich–trained Frederick Krasser (1870–1913), who collaborated with architects to produce ironwork, much of which can be seen on the grounds of Wellesley and Boston Colleges, and Harvard University. Krasser's firm was awarded a silver medal at the 1904 Louisiana Purchase Exposition. ¶ Frank Koralewsky joined Krasser's firm in 1906 and soon became chief designer, well–known for his medieval designs and for the quality of his workmanship. He was praised for the lock entitled "Schneewitchen" ("Snow White and the Seven Dwarfs," collection of the Art Institute of Chicago) — begun around 1905 and completed in 1911 — which won the gold medal at the 1915 Panama–Pacific Exposition. Detroit philanthropist George Booth purchased secular and ecclesiastical works from both men, including Koralewsky's cut steel lock depicting various craft activities (CAT. NO. 42). One year after Krasser's death in 1913, the Society jointly awarded its Medal of Excellence to Frank Koralewsky and Krasser. (J.F.)

SOURCES

SACB papers, AAA/BPL; Booth Papers, Archives, Cranbrook Academy; Ralph Bergengren, "An Adventure in the Medieval," *House Beautiful* 37 (January 1915), pp. 45–49; Anne Webb Karnaghan, "A Worker in Wrought Iron," *International Studio* 84 (August 1926), pp. 26–30; Obituary, *Boston Daily Globe*, November 7, 1941; *Arts and Crafts in Detroit 1906–1976: the Movement, the Society, the School* (Detroit: Detroit Institute of Arts, 1976), p. 56; Kaplan (1987), pp. 135–36, cat. no. 19.

Frederick W. Kulkmann
(active 1900–1920)

Kulkmann, a German–trained craftsman, maintained a shop with the carver Alfred Longuemere at 498 Harrison Avenue from 1902–06 and then moved to 537 Albany Street, where Olof Althin also had a shop. Kulkmann appears in several of Althin's accounts but the nature of their relationship is unclear. According to the 1907 exhibition catalogue of the SACB, Kulkmann, Longuemere, and Louis Knecht worked together in some capacity. Kulkmann seemed to be the Society's favored technician who executed work for architects and carvers. (E.S.C.)

SOURCES

Frederic Allen Whiting, "Modern Screens," in the SACB papers, AAA/BPL; Juried Craftspeople of 1934 to 1938, SACB papers, AAA/BPL; 1907 exhib. catal., pp. 16, 87–91; F.W. Coburn, "Wood Carving and Architecture—Work by I. Kirchmayer and Others," *International Studio* (September 1910), p. lxv; Ülehla (1981), p. 129; Boston City Directories.

Blanche Lazzell
(1878–1956)

Nettie Blanche Lazzell was born on October 9, 1878, near Maidsville, W. Va., the ninth of ten children. After completing a liberal arts degree at the West Virginia Conference Seminary in 1898, she continued her studies at the South Carolina Co-educational Institute and at West Virginia University. In 1908 she went to New York, where she studied with William Merritt Chase at the Art Students League. From 1912 to 1914 Lazzell was in Paris, a student at the Académie Moderne. ❨ At the outbreak of World War I, Lazzell came to Provincetown. After learning the white line color woodcut technique from Oliver Newberry Chaffee in 1916, she became a champion of the process. She made most of her 138 prints in her small wharfside studio, and taught the technique to many other artists. In 1923 she returned to Paris to study with Fernand Léger, Albert Gleizes, and André Lhote, and her style became more abstract. Lazzell was a member of the Société Anonyme, the international organization that promoted abstract art. ❨ After moving back to West Virginia in 1933, Lazzell made prints and painted murals for the Public Works of Art Project and the Works Progress Administration. For more than forty years she returned to Provincetown each summer to make prints and to teach. She died in Morgantown on June 1, 1956. (D.A.)

SOURCE
John Clarkson, *Blanche Lazzell* (Morgantown, W.Va.: Creative Arts Center Galleries, West Virginia University, 1979).

William Leavens & Company
(ca. 1896–1947)

William Leavens took over the direction of his father's firm in the mid-1890s and developed a specialty in cottage furniture. Leavens & Co. was the main manufacturer of Mission-style furniture in the Boston area. Located at 32 Canal Street and 31 Merrimac Street, they advertised extensively in *House Beautiful*, illustrating craftsman-style and colonial revival furniture—the latter referred to as "Old New England Furniture"—from 1902 until at least 1914. They considered the two styles mutually compatible. Much of the Leavens work is characterized by simple lines, white pine (often of poor quality) as a secondary wood, the use of rotary or gang dovetailing machines to construct drawers, and machined hardware made to look handmade. The firm was incorporated in 1915,

moved to 26 Franklin Street in 1943, and closed in 1947. (E.S.C.)

SOURCES
Boston City Directories; advertisements in *House Beautiful*.

Addison Brayton Le Boutillier
see Grueby Faience Company

Frances (Glessner) Lee
(1878–1962)

Mrs. Blewett Lee, née Frances Glessner, was the daughter of John Jacob and Frances Glessner of Chicago. Mrs. Lee grew up in Chicago in the house designed for her parents by the Boston architect Henry Hobson Richardson in 1885, and decorated with furniture and woodwork by Isaac E. Scott and William Morris textiles and wallpaper. In the 1910s, Mrs. Lee produced a great deal of embroidery. It was around this period that Mrs. Lee, assisted by her daughter Martha Lee Batchelder (1906–1994), embroidered the curtains designed by George Fenety of Boston. The curtains (CAT. NO. 81) were used in the Glessner summer home, *The Rocks*, in Bethlehem, N.H. Later in life, Mrs. Lee became a miniature-model maker. (N.J.S.)

SOURCES
Kaplan (1987), pp. 55, 65, and 625; Percy Maxim Lee and John Glessner Lee, *Family Reunion* (Hartford, Conn.: priv. printed, 1971).

Andrew Lees
(1844–1937)

Born in England of Scottish parents and trained by Scottish carvers in New Brunswick, Canada, Lees established a figurehead carving shop in Charlestown, Mass. in 1864. Around 1870 he moved his shop to Sudbury Street and began to advertise as an "architectural and artistic" wood carver and designer. He lived at 12 Maugus Avenue in Wellesley Hills and carved many fireplaces and built-in woodwork in the Wellesley area, but also sold small items such as bookends at the showroom of the Society of Arts and Crafts, which he joined in 1901. He gained Master status in that organization in 1914. (E.S.C.)

SOURCES
Margaret Urann, "Andrew Lees of This Town Noted as Boston's First Wood-Carver," *Wellesley Townsmen*, August 22, 1963; Barbara Gorely Teller, "Historical Exhibit Features Carvings of Andrew Lees," *Wellesley Townsmen*, February 17, 1983; files of the Wellesley Historical Society; Ulehla (1981), p. 134.

Anna Lessman
(active ca. 1901)

Lessman is unknown except as one of the illuminators of the edition of Thomas Gray's *Elegy Written in a Country Churchyard* issued by the Craftsman's Guild in 1901 (CAT. NO. 99). She may have been a student or an amateur who did little else in the way of book decoration. She was not a member of the SACB. (N.F.)

Edwin Hale Lincoln
(1848–1938)

Edwin Hale Lincoln took up photography in 1876 while living in Brockton, Mass. He first acquired a reputation in the 1880s for his photographs of yachts under full sail, but by the early 1890s Lincoln had started to photograph New England *botanica*, which became his lifelong passion. He also photographed estates in Newport, R.I., and Lenox, Mass. In 1893 he moved with his family to Dalton, Mass., and lived in nearby Pittsfield from 1902 until his death, when he was hit by a car at age ninety. ¶ Lincoln published his sensitive images of nature in several photographic series. His most extensive work, *Wild Flowers of New England* (1910–14), a survey of 400 platinum prints in eight volumes, won him the silver medal of commendation from the Massachusetts Horticultural Society in 1929. Two smaller, unbound editions of this work were issued in 1904 and 1907. In 1932, he received a gold medal from the American Orchid Society for *Orchids of the North Eastern United States Photographed from Nature* (1931). He also produced *New England Trees* (publication date unknown) and *Typical Wooden Vessels of the 19th Century* (from the photographs of yachts taken in 1883–89, published in 1929). (A.E.H.)

SOURCES
William B. Becker, "'Permanent Authentic Records': The Arts and Crafts Photographs of Edwin Hale Lincoln," *History of Photography* 13, no. 1 (January–March 1989), pp. 19–30; George Dimock, *A Persistence of Vision: Photographs of Edwin Hale Lincoln* (Lenox: Lenox Library Association; Pittsfield: Berkshire Museum, 1981).

Tod Lindenmuth
(1885–1976)

Born on May 4, 1885, in Allentown, Penn., Lindenmuth was the son of a photographer who taught him the techniques of his profession. He studied at William Merritt Chase's New York School of Art with Robert Henri, George Elmer Browne, and E. Ambrose Webster. As these artists had connections with Provincetown, Lindenmuth became a summer resident of Cape Cod. He developed an unusual specialty in multiple–block color linocuts printed on a press, that depicted the harbor and shore. Lindenmuth was among the founders of the Provincetown Printers group, and produced the covers for the annual catalogue of the Provincetown Art Association in 1916 and 1917. ¶ In the mid–1920s Lindenmuth married the Provincetown painter and printmaker Elizabeth Warren. During the Depression he worked for the Public Works Administration and the Works Progress Administration. Lindenmuth stopped making prints in 1940 to concentrate on painting. At that time he moved to Rockport, Mass. and spent his winters in Saint Augustine, Fla., where he died on November 6, 1976. (D.A.)

SOURCE
David Acton, *A Spectrum of Innovation: Color in American Printmaking, 1890–1960* (New York: W.W. Norton, 1990), pp. 96–97, 271–72.

Alfred F.J. Longuemere
(born 1856)

A French–trained carver and sculptor, Longuemere arrived in the United States in 1887. He first appeared in the 1904 Boston Directory at 498 Harrison Avenue and in 1907 formed a partnership with the carver William Hippler. Longuemere seemed to be one of the carvers favored by architects designing work for F.W. Kulkmann to fabricate. Throughout his time working in Boston, Longuemere lived in South Weymouth, but he moved to Grand Rapids, Mich. in 1913, and to Cleveland, Ohio in 1914. (E.S.C.)

SOURCES
U.S. Census 1910, vol. 96 E.D. 1168, sheet 17, line 20; 1907 exhib. catal., pp. 16 and 89; F.W. Coburn, "Wood Carving and Architecture — Work by I. Kirchmayer and Others," *International Studio* (September 1910), p. lxv; Úlehla (1981), p. 138; Boston City Directories.

Rosamond Bowditch Loring
(1889–1950)

Loring studied bookbinding at the school of Mary Crease Sears. After she set up her own studio, she had difficulty finding colored papers to go with the leathers she was using and decided to color her own, using as a guide the instructions in Zaehnsdorf's *The Art of Bookbinding*. Later she took lessons in marbling from Charles V. Safland of Fitchburg, Mass. She concentrated on paste papers and began making them professionally, selling them to students at the Sears School of Bookbinding. Her first large order was for the paste paper covers of *The Antigone of Sophocles*, published by Houghton Mifflin & Company in 1930 (CAT. NO. 103). She also designed and executed papers for several of Updike's Merrymount Press books. Loring joined the SACB in 1922. She gave demonstrations of marbling to the Society and to the Club of Odd Volumes. Her *Marbled Papers* (1933) and *Decorated Book Papers* (1942) remain standard works. Her collection of historical paper samples is in the Houghton Library at Harvard University. (N.F.)

SOURCES
Rosamond B. Loring Collection of Decorated Book Papers, The Houghton Library, Harvard University; *Who Was Who in American Art*, p. 380.

William B. Luce
(1861–1925)

Listed as a cabinetmaker in the records of the SACB, Luce made a wide variety of objects including doll houses, doll furniture, and burned reed baskets. (E.S.C.)

SOURCES
Ralph Bergengren, "Unusual American Toys," *House Beautiful* 39, no. 1 (December 1915), p. 19; *Handicraft* 5, no. 4 (July 1912), p. 49; Lorena and Francis Hart, *Not All Is Changed: A Life History of Hingham* (Hingham, Mass.: Hingham Historical Commission, 1993), pp. 270–75; letter to the author from Nancy Tiffin of the Hingham Historical Society, July 5, 1995.

Marblehead Pottery
(1904–1936)

Marblehead Pottery was established in 1904 along with workshops in weaving, metalwork, and woodwork to provide therapy for "nervous patients" at Dr. Herbert Hall's sanitarium in Marblehead, Mass. By 1908 the technical demands of the project were deemed too frustrating for patients and the pottery was converted to a commercial shop under the guidance of Arthur E. Baggs (1886–1947). Baggs had studied at the New York School of Clayworking and Ceramics, Alfred University under ceramicist Charles Fergus Binns. Baggs employed other designers, including the former metalsmith Arthur Irwin Hennessey, Maude Milner, Annie E. Aldrich and Rachel Grinwell. ❡ Marblehead pottery was exhibited at the SACB in 1907, 1924, and 1927. Baggs became a member of the Society in 1906 and received its Medal of Excellence in 1925. Baggs divided his time between running the pottery and teaching at the Ethical Culture School (1913–20), the School of Design and Liberal Arts in New York (1913–20), Cowan Pottery (1925), the Cleveland

School of Art (1925–28), and Ohio State University (1928–47). Both the pottery and tiles are marked with an impressed ship flanked by "M" and "P," and sometimes with the initials of designers, including Baggs's "AEB." A mark resembling a seagull seems to have been used in early pieces, including the Hollyhocks vase (CAT. NO. 26A). (S.J.M.)

SOURCES
Evans (1987), pp. 157–60; Herbert J. Hall, *Keramic Studio* (June 1908), pp. 30–31; *Handicraft* (June 1912), pp. 42–43; Ülehla (1981), p. 22.

Frank John Marshall
(1884–active until 1927)

At the age of seventeen, Marshall, from Jamaica Plain, Mass., although "not a high school graduate," was admitted to the Massachusetts Normal Art School. It is not known whether he graduated, but Marshall learned enough of enameling from metalsmithing professor Laurin Martin to become one of the more talented artists in the Boston area. He became a Craftsman in the Society in 1907, progressing to Master in 1913. In 1910 and 1911 Marshall participated in the Arts and Crafts exhibition at the Art Institute of Chicago, showing a variety of jewelry and brass, enameled copper, and silver boxes, and was favorably reviewed in the Fourth Annual Exhibition of the National Society of Craftsmen for his "enameled metal boxes, which create handsome color notes in the exhibition." His enamels varied from landscapes and peacocks to stylized floral designs. He also exhibited with Frank Gardner Hale and Elizabeth Copeland at the Little Gallery in New York in 1915. Throughout these years, Marshall's address was 12 Newbern Street, Jamaica Plain. (J.F.)

SOURCES
1907 exhib. catal., p. 43, nos. 731–32; Art Institute of Chicago exhibition catalogue (1910), cat. nos. 769–74; Art Institute of Chicago exhibition catalogue (1911), cat. nos. 447–55; Museum School Scrapbooks, vol. 7, p. 109; Archives, Massachusetts College of Art; J. William Fosdick, "The Fourth Annual Exhibition of the National Society of Craftsmen," *International Studio* 4, no. 2 (November 1910–February 1911), pp. lxxix –lxxxiii.

Laurin Hovey Martin
(1875–1939)

Martin was born in the Massachusetts textile mill town of Lowell, where he attended local schools and evening drawing classes. He enrolled in a three–year program at the Cowles Art School in Boston, from which he received two prizes in life drawing (1896). Martin continued his education at the Birmingham School of Art in England for three semesters, from fall 1897 to 1898. While there, he received a prize for excellence, and first prize for a chased plate. South Kensington School awarded him a medal in 1898. Martin then took private lessons from the enameler Alexander Fisher before returning to the United States around 1900. ❡ Martin became a teacher at the Massachusetts Normal Art School, where he taught from 1901 until his death in 1939. For a brief period in 1901, he taught at RISD, where Augustus Rose and Jessie Burbank (1905–27) came under his influence. In 1909 and 1913, he ran metal workshops in the summer Arts and Crafts program administered by art educator Henry Turner Bailey at the Chautauqua Institute in Lake Chautauqua, N.Y. (J.F.)

SOURCES
"Studio Talk," *The Studio* 16 (1899), pp. 199–200, ill. p. 200; Dora M. Morell, "The Arts and Crafts: Beauty in Common Things," *Brush and Pencil* 5, no. 5 (February 1900), pp. 222–32, ill. pp. 223, 228, 231; Eva Lovett, "The Exhibition of the Society of Arts and Crafts, Boston," *International Studio* 31 (1907), pp. xxvii–xxxii, ill. p. xxvii; correspondence, Glennys Wild, Keeper of Applied Art, Birmingham Museum and Art Galleries, to the author, October 31, 1995.

Mildred "Dolly" McMillen
(1884–ca. 1940)

McMillen was born and raised in Chicago, where she attended the School of the Art Institute from 1906. She went to Long Island in 1912, along with her fellow student Ada Gilmore, probably to continue her studies, and in the following year they traveled together in Europe. In Paris McMillen studied at the Académie Colarossi, and learned the techniques of woodcut from Ethel Mars. McMillen and Gilmore arrived in Provincetown in the spring of 1915, and were among the first artists to remain in the seasonal artists' colony year round. McMillen's prints were shown at the Panama–Pacific International Exposition in San Francisco in 1915. She was an original member of the Provincetown Printers group, and the only one among them to consistently print her woodcuts in black ink alone. She also exhibited in the annual shows of the Provincetown Art Association during the late teens. McMillen traveled to France in 1922, where she visited Mars and Maud Hunt Squire at Vence. Nothing is known of her life or artistic activities thereafter. (D.A.)

SOURCE
Chris Petteys, *Dictionary of Women Artists* (Boston: G.K. Hall, 1993), p. 465.

Merrimac Ceramic Company
(1897–1901)
Merrimac Pottery Company
(1902–1908)

Merrimac Ceramic Company was founded in Newburyport, Mass. by Thomas S. Nickerson in 1897, to produce florist ware and tiles. Nickerson began to produce art pottery around the turn of the century, and in 1902 changed the company name to Merrimac Pottery Company. Nickerson had studied with Sir William Crookes in England and experimented with glazes, including a green reminiscent of Grueby's matte green glaze. He also employed black, orange, brownish red, blues, and violet. In 1902 Nickerson introduced a line of garden pottery and "Arrelian" ware based on early Roman Empire redware. As a member of the SACB, Nickerson exhibited enameled tiles in 1899 and garden pottery in 1907. He was awarded a silver medal for art and garden pottery in 1904 at the St. Louis Exhibition. In 1908, the pottery was destroyed by fire and never reopened. Pottery produced after August 1901 has an impressed mark featuring the word "Merrimac" above a sturgeon, the fish known to local Native Americans as "merrimac." (S.J.M.)

SOURCES
Evans (1987), pp. 168–71; Henry Lewis Johnson, *House Beautiful* (February 1903), pp. 177–80; Ulehla (1981), p. 161.

Thomas Buford Meteyard
(1865–1928)

Born in Rock Island, Ill., Meteyard was the son of a Union army captain who died of his Civil War wounds in 1868. His mother returned with him to her family in Scituate, Mass. in 1881. He attended Phillips Academy in Andover, and became a special student at Harvard in 1885. Studies with Professor Charles Eliot Norton may have influenced his decision to become an artist. ❡ In 1888 Meteyard studied painting in London and in Paris, where he was the pupil of Léon Bonnat and Auguste–Joseph Delecluse. He was drawn to Impressionism, and the work of Claude Monet influenced his art. In 1891 he was at Giverny among a group gathered around Monet, including Theodore Robinson, Dawson Dawson–Watson, and Theodore Earl Butler, who became engaged to Monet's stepdaughter Suzanne the following spring. Together they produced five issues of the *Courrier Innocent*, an art and literary magazine for which Meteyard designed page layouts and illustrations. ❡ Returning to Scituate in 1893, Meteyard began producing magazine and book illustrations. His designs appeared in the Arts and Crafts periodical the *Knight Errant*, and in *Songs from Vagabondia*, a collection of poems by his college friends Bliss Carman and Richard Hovey. Meteyard's illustrations reflect the influences of English illustrator Aubrey Beardsley, as well as the *japonisme* and Symbolism he had encountered in Europe. Known to his friends as "the Tortoise," Meteyard marked his illustrations with a stylized monogram in the form of a tortoise. In 1895 the artist built a house in Scituate that he called "Testudo." He also made independent color woodcut landscapes that reflect European influences as well as that of Arthur Wesley Dow. Along with Dawson–Watson, by then director of the Hartford Art Society, Meteyard revived the *Courrier Innocent* for two issues in 1897. ❡ Meteyard moved to England in 1906, where he married and began a family. He experimented with a range of styles in his works of the World War I era. Thereafter, art seems to have become more a hobby than a profession. Meteyard died in Switzerland on March 17, 1928. (D.A.)

SOURCES
Nancy Finlay, "The Graphic Art of Thomas Buford Meteyard," *Harvard Library Bulletin*, new series, 1 (1990), pp. 50–66; Nicholas Kilmer, *Thomas Buford Meteyard, 1865–1928: Paintings and Watercolors* (New York: Berry–Hill Galleries, 1989).

Henry Stuart Michie
(1871–1943)

Born in Toronto, Canada, where he studied design and architecture, Michie came to the United States in 1898 to enter Pratt Institute, where he became a student and friend of Arthur Wesley Dow. Michie pursued additional studies in the prestigious Central and Camberwell Schools of Arts and Crafts in London from 1905 to 1906. ❡ Upon his return to the U.S., Michie traveled around the country, visiting and teaching at a number of Arts and Crafts schools and settlements, including the Minneapolis Guild of Handicraft and the Byrdcliffe colony in Woodstock, N.Y., and for Arthur Wesley Dow at Ipswich and Columbia University. Michie served as an instructor at the McKinley Manual Training School in Washington, D.C., and from 1907 to 1909 he served as head of the Arts and Crafts Department at George Washington University. ❡ By 1909 Michie had settled in Worcester, where he was appointed principal of the School of the Worcester Art Museum, a position he held until 1938.

Student work produced during his tenure at the museum demonstrates Michie's familiarity with printing, lettering, woodworking, metalworking, and textiles, a varied talent confirmed in his surviving works. Despite his involvement with many Arts and Crafts societies during the early part of his career, Michie became a member of the SACB only in 1926–27, long after he had settled in New England. Much of his work is informed by a Japanese aesthetic, fostered by his studies with Dow and by an art collection assembled during his formative years. Michie also collected textiles from many different cultures to use in his teaching, many of which were later donated to RISD. (J.F.)

SOURCES
Artist's papers, private collection; *Museum Notes* 76, no. 1 (Providence: Museum of Art, RISD, October 1989), p. 18; Ülehla (1981) p. 152.

Ellen Miller
see Society of Blue and White Needlework, Deerfield

Hermann Dudley Murphy
(1867–1945)

Murphy studied with Otto Grundmann and Joseph DeCamp at the Museum School in 1886, then studied painting in France from 1891 to 1896. Upon his return to the States in 1897, Murphy settled in Winchester, Mass. where he maintained a painting studio and frame–making shop. Although he had begun frame–making out of economic necessity when portrait commissions were few, the demand for his frames began to grow. In 1903 he named his shop Carrig–Rohane, after an ancestral home in Ireland, and in 1905 he moved the shop into Boston at 20 Grundmann Studios (Copley Hall at 194 Clarendon Street). As Murphy's painting career grew at the end of the first decade of the twentieth century, he became less active in the frame–making business; after 1910 reviews of his work do not mention frames at all. In 1911 his shop was incorporated as Thulin–Murphy, with leading craftsmen receiving shares in the company, and in 1915 was sold to Vose Gallery and moved to 162 Newbury Street. Among the craftsmen who worked for the Carrig–Rohane shop in the 1910s were Oscar Frank (a carver who had worked for John Evans), Robert Schmitt, Sidney Sargent (a gilder who worked for Carrig–Rohane until 1921 when he rejoined Walfred Thulin), James Maloy, and Adrian Eckberg. (E.S.C.)

SOURCES
Hermann Dudley Murphy papers, AAA/SI reel 4039; Carrig–Rohane Shop Records, AAA/SI; Frederick Coburn, "Individual Treatment of the Picture Frame," *International Studio* 30, no. 117 (November 1906), pp. 12–16; "Making Carved Frames Choice Work," *Christian Science Monitor*, November 22, 1913, p. 4; William Coles, *Hermann Dudley Murphy: 1867–1945* (New York: Graham Gallery, 1982); Suzanne Smeaton, "American Picture Frames of the Arts and Crafts Period, 1870–1920," *Antiques* 136, no. 5 (November 1989), pp. 1124–37; 1899 exhib. catal.; 1907 exhib. catal., p. 90; Ûlehla (1981), p. 158.

L.F. Nash
(dates unknown)

L.F. Nash, a china painter, may be related to Mrs. William B. (Maude) Nash of Brookline, Mass., who was listed as a designer and member of the SACB from 1920 to 1926. Nash's work is signed either "L.F.N." or "L.F. Nash." (S.J.M.)

SOURCE
Ûlehla (1981), p. 159.

Juliette S. Nichols
(ca. 1870–after 1957)

Very little is known about Juliette Nichols, who was among the color woodcut printmakers at work in Provincetown in the 1910s and 1920s. In the early teens she studied in Paris and associated with American women expatriates. The style and subjects of her prints suggest that she learned the technique of color woodcut in France from Ethel Mars. Nichols was among the artists who left Europe at the outset of World War I, and she settled on Cape Cod in the summer of 1915. She exhibited two works in the first Annual Exhibition of the Provincetown Art Association, and was also a member of the League of American Artists. In the early 1920s Nichols lived in Marietta, Ohio and in New York City, where she was active chiefly as a painter. However, she seems to have returned to France by 1924, and to have remained there throughout the rest of her life. (D.A.)

SOURCE
Jules and Nancy G. Heller, eds., *North American Women Artists of the Twentieth Century, A Biographical Dictionary* (New York: Garland, 1995), p. 522.

Thomas S. Nickerson
see Merrimac Pottery Company

B.J.O. Nordfeldt
(1878–1955)

Bror Julius Olsson was born in Tullstrop, Skane, Sweden on April 13, 1878. After moving with his family to Chicago in 1891, he was a printer's assistant for a Swedish–language newspaper while studying at the School of the Art Institute of Chicago. He returned to Europe in 1900, where he briefly attended the Académie Julian in Paris and learned the color woodcut technique from Charles Morley Fletcher in Reading, England. Back in Chicago in 1903, Nordfeldt began using his mother's maiden name to distinguish himself from another painter. ⟨The artist was in Europe from around 1908 to 1911 producing illustrations for travel articles for *Harper's Magazine*. In 1914 Nordfeldt spent the first of several summers in Provincetown on Cape Cod. He helped found the Provincetown Players and the Provincetown Theatre in New York. In 1915 it was Nordfeldt who originated the single–block, white–line color woodcut process, which became the hallmark of Provincetown printmaking. In 1915 one of the artist's color woodcuts won a silver medal at the Panama–Pacific International Exposition in San Francisco. He stayed there during World War I, working as a naval camouflager. Then the artist moved to Santa Fe, N. Mex., where he concentrated on painting in an Expressionist style; he also taught widely in the latter half of his career. Nordfeldt died on April 21, 1955, in Henderson, Tex. (D.A.)

SOURCE
Fiona Donovan, *The Woodblock Prints of B.J.O. Nordfeldt, A Catalogue Raisonné* (Minneapolis: University Art Museum, University of Minnesota, 1991).

Wallace Nutting
(1861–1941)

Minister, photographer, collector, author, preservationist, furniture manufacturer, lecturer, and student of colonial America, Nutting firmly believed in the power of historic artifacts to educate Americans about "the wonder of their land and the grace of old, forgotten things." For him, art could serve history by revitalizing the American character. Born in Massachusetts, Nutting left his career of sixteen years as a Congregational pastor (in Seattle, and Providence, R.I.) in 1904 because of ill health, and took up photography. In 1904 he established "Nuttinghame" at the old Obadiah Wheeler house in Southbury, Conn., where he oversaw "a genuine community of craftsmen and craftswomen." His platinum prints of rural landscapes and recreations of pre–Revolutionary interiors—available in sizes as large as 20 x 40 inches (5 x 8 inch and 8 x 10 inch prints being standard)—were hand–

colored by young women working in Nutting's homes (in Southbury and then Framingham, Mass.) and distributed to select dealers through catalogues published in 1912 and 1915. Their nostalgic view of an ideal time gone by appealed especially to American women of comfortable means. By 1930 Nutting had produced a series of books of photographs, collectively called the *States Beautiful*, of five New England states: Vermont, Connecticut, Massachusetts, Maine, and New Hampshire. The series was extended to include Pennsylvania, New York, Virginia, and even Ireland and England. ❡ As his photography business grew, Nutting moved back to the Boston area in 1912, settling in Framingham. Five years later, Nutting opened a furniture shop that employed about twenty–five men who initially made Windsor chairs and recreations of seventeenth–century joined and turned furniture. Only by 1928 (in Nutting's seventh catalogue) did the Nutting shop offer Georgian–style furniture in mahogany and walnut. In all, Nutting's shop is estimated to have made about a thousand pieces of furniture. Personally, Nutting favored the older "Furniture of the Pilgrim Century" for its rarity, its value as "the first artistic achievements of our early forefathers," and its "intrinsic merits" that included loving craftsmanship, distinctive architectural lines, and stately dignity. Through both his photography and furniture, Nutting was enormously influential as a popularizer of the colonial revival movement. (E.S.C. and A.E.H.)

SOURCES

Wallace Nutting, *Wallace Nutting's Biography* (Framingham, Mass.: Old America Company, 1936); Nutting, *Furniture of the Pilgrim Century, 1620–1720* (Boston: Marshall Jones, 1921); Nutting, "Notable Furniture of the Pilgrim Century," *Antiques* 18, no. 2 (August 1930), pp. 138–40; Walter Dyer, "The New Mission of an Old Farmhouse," *Country Life in America* 20, no. 11 (October 1, 1911), pp. 35–38; John Freeman, *Wallace Nutting Checklist of Early American Reproductions* (Watkins Glen, N.Y.: American Life Foundation, 1969); William Dulaney, "Wallace Nutting: Collector and Entrepreneur," *Winterthur Portfolio* 13 (1979), pp. 47–60; Beverly Seaton, "Beautiful Thoughts: The Wallace Nutting Platinum Prints," *History of Photography* 6, no. 3 (July 1982), pp. 273–79; Joyce Barendsen, "Wallace Nutting, an American Tastemaker: The Pictures and Beyond," *Winterthur Portfolio* 18 (1983), pp. 187–212.

Edward Everett Oakes
(1891–1960)

Born in Dorchester, Mass., Oakes attained a childhood reputation as a kite–maker and dreamed of studying engineering at MIT. At the age of eighteen, however, he went to work for jeweler Frank Gardner Hale, an apprenticeship and technical education which would last five years. Oakes then apprenticed with Josephine Hartwell Shaw for three years, also taking courses at Massachusetts

Normal Art School and the School of the Museum of Fine Arts, Boston. He married Irma Davenport in 1915. He opened his own studio at 44 Bromfield Street in 1918 with the help of fellow jeweler Elsie Parsons, who stayed on as bookkeeper and assistant. He became a member of the SACB in 1916, winning its Medal of Excellence in 1923. That same year, the Metropolitan Museum of Art purchased his ball pendant for its permanent collection, an unusual recognition for a contemporary artist. Oakes had many one–man shows around the country, lectured, was a member of the Jewelers' Guild, and served on the SACB Council from 1926 to 1929. He exhibited at the Society's 1927 anniversary exhibition, and in Detroit in 1930. At his summer school in New Hampshire in the 1930s and 1940s, he influenced many students with his style. A prolific worker, he was a member of the SACB for forty–four years, and apprenticed both his son Gilbert and granddaughter Susan Oakes Peabody, who is still active. (M.B.M.)

SOURCES

Anne Webb Karnaghan, "Edward Everett Oakes: Master Craftsman, Maker of Hand–Wrought Jewelry," *American Magazine of Art* (December 1926); Jewelers' Guild Reports, SACB Annual Reports (1916–32), AAA/BPL; Oakes papers, AAA/BPL; conversation with Susan Oakes Peabody, October 5, 1995.

Margaret Jordan Patterson
(1867–1950)

The daughter of a sea captain, Patterson was born on board ship in November 1867, near Surabaya, Java. She grew up in Maine and Boston, becoming a teacher in Massachusetts and New Hampshire public schools. In 1895 she attended the Pratt Institute, and was a student of Dow. Patterson made her first trip to Europe in 1899 and over the next decade she traveled abroad nearly every summer. She studied with Claudio Castellucho in Florence and with Ermengildo Anglada–Camrasa in Paris. Around 1910 Patterson learned the color woodcut process from Ethel Mars in Paris, who helped arrange her first solo exhibition of prints at the Galerie Lévesque in 1913. Her first American solo exhibition of color woodcuts was mounted at the Louis Katz Gallery in New York in 1914. At that time she became head of the art department at Dana Hall School for Girls in Wellesley. In the 1920s floral still life prints began to supplant her landscape woodcuts. Patterson exhibited and sold her work across the country, and received wide acclaim. She retired from teaching in 1940, but continued to paint and make prints

until her death in Boston on February 7, 1950.
(D.A.)

SOURCE

Feay Shellman Coleman, *Margaret J. Patterson, 1867–1950* (Cambridge: J.R. Bakker Gallery, 1988).

Paul Revere Pottery
(1908–1942)
(also known as the Bowl Shop and
the Saturday Evening Girls)

The Paul Revere Pottery evolved from a library club which provided educational, cultural, and social resources for Jewish and Italian immigrant girls of Boston's North End. The eldest girls met on Saturdays and became known as the Saturday Evening Girls. Librarian Edith Guerrier (1870–1958), designer Edith Brown (1870–1932), and patron Helen Osborne Storrow (1864–1944) established pottery as a vocational workshop in which unmarried women could learn artistic and income–producing skills. ❡ Guerrier and Brown met at the School of the Museum of Fine Arts, Boston. Guerrier also attended Massachusetts Normal Art School in 1897, and Brown (along with Arthur Baggs of Marblehead) attended Harvard extension school classes under Denman Ross in 1906–07. In 1908 the Bowl Shop moved to 18 Hull Street, Boston, "in the shadow of the Old North Church," and soon became known as Paul Revere Pottery. Over the next seven years, a steady stream of young decorators created dinnerware with stylized floral and animal motifs, and moralistic mottoes. The incised designs were outlined in black and filled in with flat color. In 1915 the operation moved to a new site in Brighton, built by Mrs. Storrow. Although Edith Brown became a member of the SACB in 1909, Paul Revere Pottery was not exhibited until 1916. It sold in the SACB showrooms and through department stores, including Filene's and Marshall Field's, through the 1920s, but remained heavily subsidized by Mrs. Storrow. In 1932 director Edith Brown died, and though it lingered on, the pottery finally closed in 1942. Paul Revere Pottery is sometimes marked "S.E.G." or "P.R.P.," along with the decorator's initials. An impressed circular mark of Paul Revere on horseback was frequently used. (S.J.M.)

SOURCES

[Edith Brown], "The Story of Paul Revere Pottery," *Craftsman* (November 1913), pp. 50, 70; Evans (1987), pp. 213–16; "The Paul Revere Pottery," *House Beautiful* (January 1922), p. 50; Margaret Pendleton, "Paul Revere Pottery," *House Beautiful* (August 1912), p. 74; Ulehla (1981) pp. 37, 169.

Teresa A. Pellegrini
(active ca. 1906–1952)

Pellegrini began her training at the age of five at a special lace school in her native Italy. She created original work, repaired antique laces for American museums and private collectors, and taught lace–making. She was elected an SACB Craftsman (1907–12), promoted to Master (1913–27), participated in the 1907 SACB exhibition, and was also a member of the Needleworkers Guild. Pellegrini demonstrated lace–making at Craftsman shows at Horticultural Hall, and was an active member of Denison House's Circolo Italo–Americano. Married to Antonio Pellegrini, her Boston residences included 33 Carver Street (1907–08); 69 Carver Street (1908–12); 384A Boylston Street (1913); 248 Boylston Street, Garden Building, Room 502 (1914–15); 46 Falmouth Street (1915–22); and 161 St. Botolph Street (1923–52). She died in Boston on August 3, 1952. (N.J.S.)

SOURCES

SACB papers, AAA/BPL; Denison House Archives, the Schlesinger Library, Radcliffe College; Allen Hendershott Eaton, *Handicrafts of New England* (New York: Bonanza Books, 1939), pp. 110–11; *Polk's Boston City Directory* (1952).

Molly Coolidge Perkins
(1881–1962)

Daughter of amateur painter/preservationist/antique collector J. Templeman Coolidge III, Perkins was an accomplished photographer of the idealized rural life enjoyed by Boston's privileged class when only fourteen years old. She studied modeling with Bela Pratt at the Museum School in 1899, and learned design from Joseph Lindon Smith, who had taught decorative drawing and design at the Museum School from 1887 to 1891. She showed carved, painted, and gilded candlesticks at the 1897 SACB exhibition and a bracket, frame, and panel at the 1899 exhibition. She married John Forbes Perkins in 1905, and continued to carve, although she did not show at the 1907 exhibition. She carved numerous panels, cornices, and pieces of furniture for the house that Addison Le Boutillier designed for Molly and her husband in 1912, and continued carving in the 1920s. (E.S.C.)

SOURCES

1897 exhib. catal., p. 6; 1899 exhib. catal., p. 18; Ulehla (1981), pp. 58 and 171; Sarah Giffen and Kevin Murphy, eds., "A Noble and Dignified Stream": The Piscataqua Region in the Colonial Revival, 1860–1930 (York, Me.: Old York Historical Society, 1992), esp. pp. 129–31. Interviews with family members in the summer of 1995 also provided invaluable insight into Coolidge's artistic training.

Leander Plummer
(1857–1914)

A Harvard–trained mining engineer (class of 1879), Plummer left that profession to take painting classes at the Académie Julian in Paris from 1883 to 1887, and enrolled in carving classes taught by Karl von Rydingsvärd in the early 1890s. At his home in New Bedford, Plummer first carved furniture and at the turn of the century began to carve panels depicting fish. His first significant panel of two codfish, carved and stained in 1902, was installed at the Eastern Yacht Club in Marblehead. Plummer carved about forty or fifty panels during the next five years. He worked on commissions and also showed at Doll & Richards. (E.S.C.)

SOURCES

Leander Plummer papers, AAA/SI reel 634; R.W. Wooley, "Some Remarkable Piscatorial Wood Carvings," *Country Life in America* 14, no. 6 (October 1908), p. 592; *The New Bedford Evening Standard*, April 21, 1906, pp. 5–6.

William B. Post
(1857–1925)

A stockbroker and amateur photographer in New York City, Post summered in Fryeburg, Me., where he began photographing the rural landscape around 1889. He was a collector of pictorial photographs, an active member of the Society of Amateur Photographers of New York and the New York Camera Club, and a frequent exhibitor at national exhibitions. In 1901 Post moved permanently to Maine, and was a member of the SACB from 1915 to 1921. A friend of Alfred Stieglitz, he joined the Photo–Secession in 1903 and his photographs were included in *Camera Notes* and *Camera Work*. Although Post was not among those invited to exhibit at the International Exhibition of Pictorial Photography at the Albright Art Gallery in Buffalo, N.Y., his work was submitted and approved by the judges for inclusion in the open section of the show. (A.E.H.)

SOURCE

Weston J. Naef, *The Collection of Alfred Stieglitz: Fifty Pioneers of Modern Photography* (New York: Metropolitan Museum of Art, 1978), pp. 416–17.

Katharine Pratt
(1891–1978)

Pratt entered the School of the Museum of Fine Arts, Boston in 1910 and received her diploma in 1914. In 1915 she held an exhibit of her silver at the Women's Educational and Industrial Union in Boston, and received an experimental scholarship from the WEIU that enabled her to study silversmithing under George C. Gebelein. Pratt was elected a Craftsman in the SACB in 1916, promoted to Master in 1918, and made a Medalist in 1931. In further recognition of her achievements, she served the Society as a member of the Jury and on the Council and Craftsman Advisory Boards. She also exhibited a variety of works in silver, enamel, and precious stones at the Society's 1927 exhibition. Pratt exhibited her work at the Paris Exposition des Arts et des Techniques in 1937, where she received the *diplome de médaille d'or*. ❡ The daughter of the superintendent of the Massachusetts General Hospital, Pratt taught therapists at the Boston School of Occupational Therapy to bind books, work with silver and leather, and make jewelry. She also taught silversmithing at Beaver Country Day School for Girls in Chestnut Hill. Pratt lived in St. Paul's Square, Dedham from 1917 to 1921, and at 41 School Street, Dedham from 1922 to 1927. She moved to Santa Barbara, Calif. in 1962, where she died in 1978. (J.F.)

SOURCES

Museum School Scrapbook, vol. 8, p. 25; 1927 exhib. catal., p. 9, nos. 115–19; Jenny Perry, "Woman Silversmith Continues to Learn," *Santa Barbara News–Press*, July 4, 1967, p. B–1; Kaplan (1987), cat. no. 66, p. 180.

Vojtěch Preissig
(1873–1944)

Born in the village of Svetec, near Teplitz, Bohemia on July 31, 1873, Preissig was a student of Friederich Ohmann at the Art Academy in Prague. In 1898 he went to Paris to continue his studies with Franz Kupka and Alphonse Mucha. Back in Prague in 1903 he studied intaglio at the Graphic Academy and relief printmaking with August Schmid. The following year he opened his own workshop which, like the Wiener Werkstätte, produced a wide range of original printed materials. Preissig became a versatile craftsman and an expert in color etching, but his business failed. ❡ Preissig moved to New York in 1910 and worked as a commercial artist until he began teaching at the Art Students League. In 1914 Dow engaged him to teach at Columbia Teachers' College, and the two artists exhibited together at the Montclair Museum. During World War I Preissig made propaganda posters for distribution in Czechoslovakia. He moved to Boston in 1916 to join the faculty of the Wentworth Institute of Technology, where he headed the graphic arts department until 1924, and became one of the most influential designers and teachers in Boston. Preissig returned to Czechoslovakia in the late 1920s, and died in the Nazi concentration camp at Dachau on June 1, 1944. (D.A.)

SOURCES

Irena Goldscheider, *Czechoslovak Prints from 1900 to 1970* (London: British Museum Publications, 1986), pp. 21–22; Tomáš Vlček and Jiri Zantofsky, *Vojtěch Preissig, 1873–1944* (Prague: Narodni Galleri, 1968).

Charles Prendergast
(1863–1948)

Prendergast, who worked for a custom manufacturer of interior woodwork in the 1890s, began to make frames in about 1897 while living in Winchester, Mass. He worked with his brother, Maurice Prendergast, and formed a loose cooperative venture with his fellow Winchester artist Hermann Dudley Murphy in 1903. Prendergast's role in that partnership remains unclear for he was not a shareholder when the company was incorporated in 1911, but he did continue to make frames and mirrors until he moved to New York in 1914. (E.S.C.)

SOURCES

Carol Derby, "Charles Prendergast's Frames: Reuniting Design & Craftsmanship," in *The Prendergasts & The Arts & Crafts Movement: The Art of American Decoration & Design, 1890–1920* (Williamstown, Mass.: Williams College Museum of Art, 1989), pp. 28–43; Nancy Mowll Mathews, *The Art of Charles Prendergast from the Collections of the Williams College Museum of Art & Mrs. Charles Prendergast* (Williamstown, Mass.: Williams College Museum of Art, 1993), esp. pp. 10–15.

Ethel Reed
(1874–before 1925)

Reed was born and raised in Newburyport, Mass., where she received her first training in art from Laura Coombs Hills. She later studied at the Cowles School in Boston, where Bertram Grosvenor Goodhue was one of her teachers. While a student, she began designing posters and book decorations in a distinctive Art Nouveau style, first for the *Boston Herald* and later for the small literary presses Copeland & Day and Lamson, Wolfe and Co. For a short period in 1895 and 1896, she was the most celebrated of the Boston book artists. Her brilliant though eccentric work may be an example of the sort of "specious originality" which the Society of Arts and Crafts sought to discourage. She left for Europe in May 1896 and subsequently contributed a few designs to the British publisher John Lane. She died sometime before 1925, when Richard Le Gallienne, in *The Romantic Nineties*, recalled "the noble silent beauty of Ethel Reed, whose early death robbed the world of a great decorative artist." (N.F.)

SOURCES

Letters, American Antiquarian Society, AAA; St. Elmo Lewis, "Ethel Reed, an Appreciation and a Prophecy," *Poster Lore* book 11, part 1 (September 1896), pp. 2–10; "Ethel Reed, Artist," *Bradley: His Book* 1, no. 3 (1896), pp. 74–76; "The Work of Miss Ethel Reed," *The Studio* 10 (1897), pp. 230–36; Richard Le Gallienne, *The Romantic Nineties* (New York: Doubleday Page, 1925); Nancy Finlay, *Artists of the Book in Boston, 1890–1910* (Cambridge: Houghton Library, 1985), pp. 100–02.

Hugh Cornwall Robertson
see Dedham Pottery

Bruce Rogers
(1870–1957)

Rogers's early designs for the Indianapolis periodical *Modern Art* clearly reflect the influence of William Morris. When *Modern Art* moved to Boston in 1895, Rogers moved with it; by that year he was supervising the production of trade books for Houghton Mifflin and Company. In 1900 he was placed in charge of the newly created Riverside Press Special Editions, Houghton Mifflin's venture into limited edition publishing, in which paper, type, decorations, and format were carefully selected to complement the literary content of the text. By this time, Rogers was experimenting with a variety of historical styles; although only his books in Gothic styles are usually considered Arts and Crafts books, this seems an arbitrary distinction. Rogers was a member of the SACB from 1899 to 1912, by which time he had left Boston. In 1915 he designed and printed a small edition of *The Centaur* by Maurice de Guérin, using his own Centaur type, on a hand–press in Carl Purington Rollins's Dyke Mill in Montague, Mass. (CAT. NO. 105). He later worked with Emery Walker in England, with William Edwin Rudge in New York, and as an advisor to Harvard University Press. (N.F.)

SOURCES

Ralph Bergengren, "Art and Craftsmanship in the Printing of Books," *The Outlook* 90, no. 4 (September 26, 1908), pp. 202–09; Frederic Warde, *Bruce Rogers, Designer of Books* (Cambridge: Harvard University Press, 1925); J.M. Bowles, "On the Early Works of Bruce Rogers," *The Colophon* part eleven (1932), pp. 1–10; John Dreyfus, *Bruce Rogers and American Typography* (New York: Cambridge University Press, 1959); Irvin Haas, *Bruce Rogers: A Bibliography* (Port Washington, N.Y.: Kennikat Press, 1968); Joseph Blumenthal, *Bruce Rogers: A Life in Letters* (Austin, Tex.: W. Thomas Taylor, 1989).

Margaret Rogers
(1868–1949)

Born in Boston, Rogers studied design at Massachusetts Normal Art School in 1890, and received private instruction from Albert Munsell (inventor of the Munsell Color System), and muralist Vesper L. George. She traveled to England, Italy, Holland, and France as part of her education. Although not much is known about her life, she was recognized as an important and prolific art jeweler. Unmarried, she supported herself with her work, retailing through several stores, including McAuliffe and Hadley, Boston. Rogers's work was featured in several magazines, including *House Beautiful* (1906), *Good Housekeeping* (1911), and the *Magazine of American Art* (1916). She maintained her jewelry bench in the Silversmiths' Cooperative at 79 Chestnut Street and later at 26 Lime Street. A member of the SACB since 1904, Rogers was awarded the Society's Medal of Excellence in 1915. She exhibited in Detroit in 1905, Boston in 1907 and 1927, and also in Chicago, where she won two medals. A prominent figure, she was dean of the Jewelers' Guild for four years. In her later years, Rogers summered in Barnstable, on Cape Cod. (M.B.M.)

SOURCES
Questionnaire for *Allgemeines Lexikon*, SACB archives, AAA/BPL; *Who's Who in Massachusetts* vol. 1 (Boston: Larkin, Roosevelt and Larkin, 1940); *Who Was Who in American Art*.

Carl Purington Rollins
(1880–1960)

Rollins went to work for the Boston printer Carl Heintzemann in 1900, shortly after leaving Harvard College, where he had first been exposed to the work of the Kelmscott Press. While working with Heintzemann, he met Daniel Berkeley Updike and Henry Lewis Johnson. He joined the SACB in 1903 and remained a member for many years. In 1903 he left Boston to operate the printing office at the Reverend Edward Pressey's utopian community, New Clairvaux, in rural Montague, Mass. In 1908 he moved his press into an old mill in Montague and set up the Dyke Mill Industries, which for a time included rug–making, dyeing, candle–making, and a cabinet shop. It was here that Bruce Rogers visited him in 1915 and printed *The Centaur*. Rollins continued to operate the Montague Press until 1918, when he left Montague to become the printer to Yale University. (N.F.)

SOURCES
Carl Purington Rollins, "Fifty Years of Work and Play with Type," *Yale University Library Gazette* 23, no. 1 (1948), pp. 19–24; Margaret Rollins, *Carl Rollins at Montague, 1903–1918* (New Haven: Yale University Press, ca. 1963); *Who Was Who in American Art* vol. 4, pp. 807–08.

Augustus Foster Rose
(1873–1946)

Born in Nova Scotia, Canada, Rose moved to Massachusetts as a youth and in 1896 graduated from the Massachusetts Normal Art School. Rose later studied architectural design, wood–turning, and pattern–making at MIT, and attended Denman Ross's course at Harvard. Rose also attended an evening course in metalwork at RISD that was taught by Laurin Martin, whom Rose credited with sparking his great interest in the medium. A brief period in England followed, where he studied pottery at the Royal College of Art, took private classes in jewelry and enameling with Alexander Fisher, and studied silversmithing with John Williams and A.H. Howe at the Northampton Institute. ⟨Upon his return to the United States, Rose taught drawing and manual arts at the Providence Manual Training High School (later called Technical High School) and at East Boston High School, while also teaching Saturday children's classes at RISD. In 1906 he published *Copper Work*, a textbook for metalworkers, and in 1910 was appointed head of the Normal Art, Jewelry, and Silversmithing programs at RISD. In 1917, with Antonio Cirino, who later succeeded Rose in his position, he published *Jewelry Making and Design*. Rose was appointed director of Manual Arts in the Providence public schools in 1925, a position he held until his retirement in 1943. ⟨In addition to his teaching career, Rose established a mail order company called the Metal Crafts Supply Company (1917–57) for the metals enthusiast. In 1925 he purchased the Gorham Manufacturing Company's collection of fine works in silver, copper, brass, porcelain, bronze, and ivory, which the silver firm had used to provide inspiration for their designers. With these goods, Rose opened the Metal Crafts Shop in the same year. Shortly thereafter, he published a brochure series called *The Metal Crafts, Things In and About Metal* (1927–42) for teachers and hobbyists. (J.F.)

SOURCES
Arts and Crafts Exhibition, Providence Art Club, 1901, p. 15, cat. no. 30; Augustus F. Rose, *Copper Work, A Text Book for Teachers and Students in the Manual Arts* (Worcester: Davis Press, 1906); Augustus Rose and Antonio Cirino, *Jewelry Making and Design* (Worcester: Davis Press, 1917); Obituary, *Providence Journal*, July 20, 1946.

William F. Ross & Company
(ca. 1904–21)

William F. Ross, the founder of this firm, was a cabinetmaker from Nova Scotia who specialized in high–end domestic paneling and architecture. He originally worked out of a small shop at 81 Bristol Street, Cambridge, Mass. but in 1904 moved to a larger space at 201–205 Bridge Street in East Cambridge and advertised as William F. Ross & Co. Within two years, Ross had brought in the carver John Kirchmayer (see entry) and the cabinetmaker Otis T. Lockhart as partners and expanded the shops to 193–207 Bridge Street. The company employed about thirty–five carvers, the most prominent being Kirchmayer and his apprentice Andrew Dreselly. (E.S.C.)

SOURCES
Boston City Directories; *Boston Architectural Club Yearbook*; audiotape, Andrew Dreselly interviewed by Robert Brown, June 26, 1981, AAA/SI.

Rudolph Ruzicka
(1883–1978)

Ruzicka was born on June 27, 1883, the son of a tailor in the village of Kourim in central Bohemia. After emigrating with his family to Chicago in 1894, he left school at age fourteen to take a job with the Franklin Engraving Company. In 1903 Ruzicka moved to New York to work at the American Banknote Company, and later became an independent commercial designer. ❡ The artist came under the spell of Auguste Lepère, and began to make wood engravings. In 1916 he moved to Dobbs Ferry, N.Y. He was engaged by Daniel Berkeley Updike to create wood–engraved views of Boston landmarks as "keepsakes" for customers and associates of Updike's Merrymount Press, prints that were very influential in New England. Afterwards he produced similar suites of views of New York, and Newark, N.J., featured in his first solo exhibition of prints at the Newark Public Library in 1917. Ruzicka was also a distinguished typographer, who designed three different type styles. During the 1940s he undertook major design projects for the *Encyclopædia Britannica* and *Reader's Digest*. Late in the 1940s he moved to the Boston area, and was retained as a designer by Charles Scribner and Company. In this phase of his career he often worked for colleges and universities, designing diplomas and awards. In 1962 Ruzicka moved to Hanover, N.H., where he died on July 10, 1978. (D.A.)

SOURCE
Edward Connery Lathem, *Rudolph Ruzicka, Speaking Reminiscently: Informal Recollections* (New York: Grolier Club, 1986).

Amy Sacker
(1876–1965)

Following studies at the School of the Museum of Fine Arts, Boston, Sacker quickly achieved success as a cover designer, illustrator, and designer of bookplates. Today she is remembered for her trade bindings, which are in a variety of styles, ranging from purely decorative patterns to figurative compositions resembling contemporary poster designs. Although her work is uneven, at her best she was the equal of the better–known designers Sarah Wyman Whitman and Margaret Armstrong. Examples of her work were included in the first Exhibition of the Arts and Crafts in 1897 and in subsequent exhibitions in 1899, 1907, and 1927. She was also an influential and beloved teacher, first at the Cowles School and afterwards at her own School of Miss Amy Sacker, where she taught decorative design, including metal, wood, and fabric design, bookbinding, and interior decoration. She served on numerous committees of the SACB and was Chairman of the Salesroom Committee. In 1930 she was awarded a bronze medal, the Society's highest honor. (N.F.)

SOURCES
Archives, School of the Museum of Fine Arts, Boston; SACB papers, AAA/BPL; *The Book Plates of Amy M. Sacker* (Boston: printed at the Troutsdale Press and sold by Charles E. Goodspeed, 1903); *Who Was Who in American Art*, p. 537.

Saturday Evening Girls
see Paul Revere Pottery

Mary Crease Sears
(died 1938)

Like many Boston book artists, Sears began her studies at the Museum School, but she was obliged to go to France for the instruction she sought in hand–bookbinding. While in Paris, she met Agnes St. John, who returned to Boston with her and collaborated on many of her projects. Although a Parisian influence may be detected in an elaborate mosaic binding executed by Sears and St. John for a copy of the Merrymount Press edition of *Flowers of Song from Many Lands*, simpler bindings in gold–tooled morocco, which they considered suitable for books intended for use as well as for beauty, are more typical of their work. Sears first exhibited with the SACB in 1899 and continued to be involved with the Society until her death, serving as a member of the Council, the Nominating Committee, and the Jury. She was awarded the Society's bronze medal in 1914. Always interested in education, Sears was instrumental in having bookbinding introduced into the school curriculum in Haverhill, Mass. Her own Sears School of Bookbinding operated for many years and was continued after her retirement by Margaret Danforth, one of her students. (N.F.)

SOURCES
SACB papers, AAA/BPL; Joseph Newman, Northeast Document Center, Andover, Mass.; Claire Coburn Swift, "The Fine Art of Bookbinding," *The Outlook* vol. 90 (October 24, 1908), pp. 433–40.

Sarah Choate Sears
(1858–1935)

Sarah Choate Sears (Mrs. J. Montgomery Sears) was a wealthy Bostonian from the prominent Sears family, and an active member of the Boston art scene as a photographer, painter, silversmith, and philanthropist. She was a life member of the SACB and contributed to the Society's 1897 and 1899 exhibitions. For the latter, she served on the exhibition, illustration, printing, bookbinding, engraving, and photography committees. She also contributed two embroidery panels and eight photographs, and loaned examples of English and European silver, missals, and sixteenth–century Italian furniture. ❧ Sears won prizes for her watercolors at the 1893 World's Columbian Exposition in Chicago, the 1900 Paris Exposition Universelle, the 1901 Buffalo Pan–American Exposition, and the 1904 Louisiana Purchase Exposition in St. Louis. Also exhibited in St. Louis were four examples of her metalwork and jewelry, and a cushion cover embroidered after a design by William Morris. Sears took up photography with the help of F. Holland Day, with whom she campaigned for a national association of photography and a major exhibition at the Museum of Fine Arts, Boston. She joined the Boston Camera Club in 1897; a one–person show of her platinum photographs was held at the club in 1899. She became a member of the Photo–Secession and the English photographic organization the Brotherhood of the Linked Ring in 1904. (J.F. and A.E.H.)

SOURCES
Official Catalogue of Exhibitors, Universal Exposition, St. Louis, U.S.A., Department B, Art (St. Louis, Mo.: Official Catalogue Company, Inc., 1904), p. 87; Stephanie Mary Buck, "Sarah Choate Sears: Artist, Photographer, and Art Patron" (Master's thesis, Syracuse University, 1985); Naomi

Rosenblum, *A History of Women Photographers* (New York: Abbeville Press, 1994), pp. 99, 320; Erica E. Hirschler, "Sarah Choate Sears," in Trevor Fairbrother et al., *The Bostonians: Painters of an Elegant Age, 1870–1930* (Boston: MFA, 1986), p. 225.

George H. Seeley
(1880–1955)

Born in Stockbridge, Mass., George Seeley moved to Boston in 1897 to study painting and drawing at the Massachusetts Normal Art School. While in Boston he met F. Holland Day and became interested in photography. Shortly after returning to Stockbridge in 1902 he became an art teacher in the town's public schools, a position he held for several years. Seeley contributed to the *Photo–Era* magazine competition in 1903, and gained significant recognition in December 1904, when his work was included in the First American Photographic Salon in New York. At that exhibition, his photographs were admired by Stieglitz and he was invited to join the Photo–Secession. Stieglitz published two of his prints as photogravures in the July 1906 issue of *Camera Work*, six in the October 1907 issue, and ten in the January 1910 issue. In 1908 Stieglitz held a solo show of Seeley's work at the Little Galleries of the Photo–Secession, and in 1910 he exhibited twenty–three large gum–bichromate prints in the International Exhibition of Pictorial Photography organized by Stieglitz at the Albright Art Gallery in Buffalo, N.Y. Seeley continued to take pictures until the 1920s but exhibited them less frequently. His main subjects included his sisters Lillian and Laura, and the landscape around his hometown of Stockbridge. (A.E.H.)

SOURCE
George Dimock and Joanne Hardy, *Imitations and Imaginings: The Photographs of George H. Seeley* (Pittsfield: The Berkshire Museum, 1986).

Josephine Hartwell Shaw
(1865–1941)

Shaw attended Massachusetts Normal Art School in the late 1890s, and the Pratt Institute under several instructors, including Arthur Wesley Dow. She was a teacher at the William Penn Charter School, Philadelphia, and taught drawing in Providence before turning her attention to jewelry. In 1901 and 1902 Shaw attended Harvard's summer school in the theory of design under Denman Ross and Henry Hunt Clark. After becoming a member of the SACB in 1905, she married silversmith Frederick Shaw and by 1906 was receiving national attention in magazines such as

House Beautiful and *Good Housekeeping*. Shaw exhibited in Boston's tenth anniversary exhibition in 1907, and beginning in 1908 was a regular exhibitor in Chicago, winning medals in 1912 and 1918. A brooch and ring were purchased for the MFA's collection in 1913, a rare event for a contemporary artist. Awarded the SACB's Medal of Excellence in 1914, Shaw took on Edward Everett Oakes as an apprentice. Later she would refer customers to him for jewelry repairs. Also in 1914, two years after her husband's death, Shaw moved from Brookline to Duxbury. In the 1920s she maintained a well-known tearoom in her historic house during the summer, making jewelry during the winter. She made jewelry for Julia Marlow Southern, a prominent actress and Arts and Crafts patron, as well as for members of Boston's elite. Hard hit by the depression, Shaw resigned from the Society in 1939. (M.B.M.)

SOURCES

Questionnaire for *Allgemeines Lexikon*, SACB archives, AAA/BPL; Kaplan (1987), cat. no. 128, p. 267; Student rosters for the Harvard summer school course, "Principles of Design: Symmetry, Rhythm, and Harmony," 1901 and 1902, Harvard University Archives; Margery L. MacMullan, *Stopping Along Duxbury Roads* (Duxbury, Mass.: Duxbury Rural and Historical Society, 1991), p. 75.

Sisters of the Society of St. Margaret
(1871 to present)

Although the first Sister of the Society of St. Margaret came to Boston from England in 1871 to take charge of the Children's Hospital, the order was not established until 1873 as a branch of the Anglican order based in East Grinstead, Sussex. In addition to superintending the hospital work, Sister Teresa, assisted by Sister Jessie, also developed the Embroidery Rooms, which became St. Margaret's School of Embroidery, located first at the Louisburg Square building and later at 23 Chestnut Street, Boston. ⁋As well as creating embroidered banners and vestments in the English Arts and Crafts style for their own convent, the School received commissions from many prominent churches, including the Church of St. James the Less in Philadelphia in 1878; Grace Church, Newark, N.J.; and for All Saints', Ashmont (for which Bertram Grosvenor Goodhue designed a celebrated purple and gold altar frontal in 1895); St. John the Evangelist, Bowdoin Street; and the Church of the Advent, Brimmer Street—all Anglo–Catholic Episcopalian churches in Boston. The School's vestments were exhibited at the church's General Conventions in Boston (1877) and New York (1880) and at the

1897 exhibition of SACB. After the death of Sister Teresa in 1915, Sister Mary Elisabeth supervised the needlework until 1932, when the work ceased. (N.J.S.)

SOURCES

Sister Catherine Louise, S.S.M., *The House of My Pilgrimage: History of the American House of the Society of St. Margaret, 1873–1973* (Boston: publ. Sisters of the Society of St. Margaret, ca. 1973), pp. 26–27; Sister Mary Elisabeth, "St. Margaret's School of Embroidery," *The Church Militant* (May 1955), pp. 9–10.

Society of Blue and White Needlework, Deerfield
(1896–ca. 1926)

The Society was founded at the Godfrey Nims Homestead, Deerfield, Mass. in 1896 by Margaret Whiting (1860–1946) and Ellen Miller (1854–1929), who trained as artists in New York. Initially established to record examples of eighteenth–century needlework preserved in the Deerfield Historical Society, the Society recruited local women as the project expanded to encompass similar textiles surviving in collections in the Connecticut River Valley. Traditional skills, such as dyeing and embroidery, were revived to make reproduction textiles. The group also began to create original designs inspired by colonial examples, and shared in the profits from sales of their work proportionally to their labor. Finished pieces were signed with an embroidered "D" within a spinning wheel, and were exhibited at Arts and Crafts society exhibitions throughout the country, including the SACB 1899 and 1907 exhibitions. (N.J.S.)

SOURCES

Georgiana Brown Harbeson, *American Needlework* (New York: Bonanza Books, 1938), pp. 152–55; Margery Burnham Howe, *Deerfield Embroidery* (New York: Scribner, 1976); Kaplan (1987), pp. 174–75.

Maud Hunt Squire
(1873–ca. 1955)

Born on January 30, 1873, Squire grew up in Cincinnati, Ohio, where she attended the Art Academy from 1894 to 1898. There she met fellow student Ethel Mars, and they remained close companions throughout their lives. Squire exhibited a portrait of Mars at the Cincinnati Art Museum in 1899, and within a few months the two artists had moved to New York. Late in 1903 they went to Europe and settled in Paris. Squire and Mars became active in bohemian art circles, regularly attending Gertrude Stein's salon. They are mentioned in *The Autobiography of Alice B.*

Toklas, and Stein used them as the models for her short story, "Miss Furr and Miss Skeene." Their works at this time reflected the influence of the Nabis and *japonisme.* Both artists learned to make color woodcuts from Edna Boies Hopkins, an old friend from Cincinnati. They exhibited their prints at the Salon d'Automne from 1907 to 1913. Squire and Mars returned to United States in the spring of 1915 and settled with several of their friends in Provincetown. Squire's prints were shown at the Panama–Pacific International Exposition in 1915, and at the Provincetown Art Association from 1917 to 1920. At that time she was at work as an illustrator of children's books by such authors as Robert Louis Stevenson, Charles Kingsley, and T.P. Williston. The two artists had moved to Vence, France by 1921, and Squire exhibited her paintings at the Salon d'Automne in 1923 and 1925. Her membership in the Société des Dessinateurs des Humoristes suggests that she continued her work as an illustrator. The two artists visited Wiesbaden in 1923, and for the next two years divided their time between France and Germany. They returned to Vence in 1925, where Squire remained until her death in about 1955. (D.A.)

SOURCE
Jules and Nancy G. Heller, eds., *North American Women Artists of the Twentieth Century, A Biographical Dictionary* (New York: Garland, 1995), p. 522.

Arthur J. Stone
(1847–1938)

Because of his seniority among the early Arts and Crafts practitioners in America, and his consummate skill, Arthur Stone became one of the first New England silversmiths of the era to achieve national recognition. Born in Sheffield, England, Stone was apprenticed at the age of fourteen to master silversmith Edwin Eagle. He attended evening classes at the National School of Design in Sheffield and continued his studies at the nearby Ruskin Museum. After a brief period in Edinburgh, where he worked as a chaser and designer, Stone returned to Sheffield to work for James Dixon and Sons as a designer, modeler, and chaser. He emigrated to the United States in 1884 and first worked for the William B. Durgin Company in Concord, N.H. In 1887 he became chief designer of hollowware for the F.W. Smith Silver Company of Gardner, Mass. In 1895–96, he briefly worked for the J.P. Howard and Company of New York City. Stone returned to Gardner in 1896 to marry Elizabeth Bent Eaton, and by 1901 had established his own workshop there. ❡ Stone joined the SACB in 1901 as a Craftsman. By 1903, he was awarded Master status. Stone exhibited his work in the Arts and Crafts exhibition at the Art Institute of Chicago in 1903, and at the Universal Exposition in St. Louis in 1904, where he won a silver medal for his copper and silver jardinière, silver plaque, and tea caddy. He also exhibited in the 1907 and 1927 SACB exhibitions, and held numerous solo exhibitions at the Arts and Crafts societies in Boston and Detroit. (J.F.)

SOURCES
Elenita Chickering, *Arthur J. Stone, 1847–1938: Designer and Silversmith* (Boston: Boston Athenaeum, 1994), p. 26; (see pp. 180–81 for a full list of metalsmiths in Stone's workshop, omitting George W. Fisher); Elenita Chickering to the author, April 7, 1995; SACB papers, AAA/BPL.

Gertrude S. Twichell
(ca. 1889–after 1937)

Twichell was the daughter of Milan G. Twichell, Superintendent of Practical Arts in Framingham. In 1916 she enrolled at Massachusetts Normal Art School, where she studied with Laurin Martin, receiving her diploma in 1920 in applied design. A member of the SACB, Twichell was elected a Craftsman in 1916, and promoted to Master in 1927. At the Society's 1927 exhibition, she presented hollowware and boxes made of silver or copper decorated in cloisonné and plique–à–jour enamel. She also produced jewelry set with enamels and precious stones for that exhibition. Some of her enamels were more representational in nature, with such titles as *Garden O' Dreams* and *The Princess.* ❡ In 1929 Twichell wrote a two–part series on enameling for *The Handicrafter,* a Jamaica Plain (Mass.) publication, in which she reviewed the history of the craft, illustrated with medieval examples and with works of her own making, including one made jointly with her father. She submitted a silver dish with blue enamel to the Paris Exposition of 1937. At about the same time, she began to experiment with aluminum and copper jewelry, which was criticized by the Society for being "too gift shop in effect." ❡ Twichell lived at 15 Fayette Street in Boston; Whalom Road in Fitchburg (1917–26); Franklin Square House, Boston (1927); and 44 Bromfield Street. Later in her career, she lived in St. Petersburg, Fla. (J.F.)

SOURCES
Archives, Massachusetts College of Art; 1927 exhib. catal., nos. 151–53, 188, 266–68; SACB archives, AAA/BPL; Gertrude S. Twichell, "Enameling," *The Handicrafter* 2 (November–December 1929), no. 1, pp. 3–7, and no. 2 (January–February 1930), pp. 36–40.

Daniel Berkeley Updike
(1860–1941)

Updike began his career as an office boy for Houghton Mifflin and Company, learning the various operations of a printing plant and a publishing company. In 1893 he left to found the Merrymount Press. The earliest books to issue from this press, such as *The Altar Book* (1896), reveal a strong Arts and Crafts influence and are directly derived from the work of William Morris. Updike played an active role in the 1897 Exhibition of the Society of Arts and Crafts and the subsequent founding of the SACB; his involvement continued well after the turn of the century. An interest in period decoration and in pure typography is increasingly evident in later Merrymount Press books. While rejecting the excesses of Morris's style, Updike remained committed to basic Arts and Crafts principles: the appropriateness of form to content, the importance of good design and good craftsmanship, and the production of works for a broad general public, not an elite few. From 1911 to 1917 he was one of the instructors at the influential Course in Printing offered by the Harvard Business School. In 1926 he was awarded a bronze medal by the SACB, their highest honor. (N.F.)

SOURCES
Archives of American Art; Daniel Berkeley Updike Collection, The Providence Public Library, Providence, R.I.; Peter Beilenson, ed., *Updike: American Printer and his Merrymount Press* (New York: American Institute of Graphic Arts, 1947); George Parker Winship, *Daniel Berkeley Updike and the Merrymount Press* (Rochester, N.Y.: The Printing House of Leo Hart, 1947).

William Joseph Walley
(1852–1919)

Walley was born in East Liverpool, Ohio, where his father was a potter. He was apprenticed at the Minton Factory in England before he was ten years old and spent eleven years learning the operation of a pottery. In 1873 Walley returned to Portland, Me. where he attempted to establish his own art pottery. Having no success, Walley moved to Worcester, Mass. in 1885, to revive a pottery established by Frank B. Norton, grandson of the founder of Bennington Works. In 1898 Walley began his own pottery on the site of the old Wachusett Pottery in West Sterling, Mass. He was a one–man company, producing candlesticks, tiles, vases, bowls, lamps, and his famous "devil mugs" from the local red clay. Walley became a member of the SACB in 1904 and a Master four years later, exhibiting at the Society in 1907.

His pieces are marked with an impressed "W.J.W." (S.J.M.)

SOURCES
Evans (1987), pp. 316–17; Lura Woodside Watkins, *Early New England Potters and Their Wares* (Cambridge: Harvard University Press, 1950; repr. Archon, 1968), pp. 95–97, 231–32; Ruth Ann Penka, *A Village Potter: William J. Walley*, (Fitchburg, Mass.: Fitchburg Art Museum, 1992).

Clarence H. White
(1871–1925)

Originally from Newark, Ohio, Clarence White began to make photographs in 1894 while working as a bookkeeper. His quiet images of family and friends soon attracted the attention of Alfred Stieglitz and F. Holland Day; in 1899 Stieglitz arranged a solo exhibition of White's work at the New York Camera Club, and Day organized a similar exhibition at the Boston Camera Club. White was also represented in the 1899 exhibition of the SACB, although he was not a member. In 1902 he joined the Photo–Secession when it was first organized. In 1906 White moved with his family to New York City, where he was hired by Arthur Wesley Dow to teach photography at Teachers College of Columbia University. His work was included repeatedly in *Camera Work*; he was the featured artist in the twenty–third issue, published in July 1908. ⸪White and his family were frequent visitors to F. Holland Day's estates in Norwood, Mass., and Georgetown, Me. In 1910 he opened a summer school named the Seguinland School of Photography, in an old hotel near Day's home in Maine, and established the Clarence White School of Photography in New York in 1914. In 1916 he became the first president of the Pictorial Photographers of America. White was an influential teacher for the next generation of photographers including Karl Strauss, Margaret Bourke–White, Dorothea Lange, Doris Ulmann, Laura Gilpin, Ralph Steiner, Paul Outerbridge, and Anton Bruehl. (A.E.H.)

SOURCES
Symbolism of Light: The Photographs of Clarence H. White (Wilmington: Delaware Art Museum, 1977); *A Collective Vision: Clarence H. White and His Students* (Long Beach: University Art Museum, California State University, 1985).

Margaret Whiting
see Society of Blue and White Needlework, Deerfield

Sarah Wyman Whitman
(1842–1904)

Whitman was a major figure in the Arts and Crafts movement in Boston, even though her most significant work was the trade bindings she designed for the large commercial publishing house Houghton Mifflin and Company. As early as the 1880s she revolutionized trade binding design in Boston, introducing light colors and simplified patterns in place of the typical Victorian brightly colored and heavily gilt bindings. Whitman also painted in oils and worked in stained glass, and her Beacon Hill home served as a meeting place for many of the artists and writers of the 1880s and 1890s. Whitman's trade bindings were well–represented in the 1897 Exhibition of the Arts and Crafts in Copley Hall. She greeted the formation of the SACB with enthusiasm and played an active role during its formative years. Her last published work is the cover of the 1904 Merrymount Press *Tacitus*. (N.F.)

SOURCES
Letters, Houghton Mifflin archives, The Houghton Library; "Memorial to Mrs. Whitman," *Cambridge Tribune*, February 11, 1905, p. 4; John Jay Chapman, *Memories and Milestones* (New York: Moffat, Yard and Company, 1915), pp. 103–12; Charles Gullens and John Espey, "American Trade Bindings and their Designers," in Jean Peters, ed., *Collectible Books* (New York: R.R. Bowker Co., 1979), pp. 36–38; *Who Was Who in American Art*, p. 676.

Mary Peyton Winlock
(active 1888–1927)

Winlock entered the School of the Museum of Fine Arts, Boston in 1888, and received an award from the Department of Decorative Design in 1891. She attended Ross and Clark's class in the Principles of Design and Symmetry, Rhythm and Harmony at Harvard University in the summer of 1899. ❛Winlock became a member of the SACB in 1901, where she was listed as a jewelry and metalwork designer. She was ranked as a Craftsman in the Society from 1901 to 1919, and as a Master from 1920 to 1927. She exhibited a book cover design for *Bobby McDuff* at the 1901 Providence Art Club. In 1903 she displayed an enameled belt buckle and an enameled matchbox in the Arts and Crafts exhibition at the Art Institute of Chicago. At that time, her workshop was listed at the Handicraft Shop, 1 Somerset Street, Boston. In 1904 Winlock participated in the St. Louis Universal Exposition, where she exhibited an enameled silver matchbox holder. In 1904 and 1905 she contributed hollowware and jewelry to the first and second exhibitions of Arts and Crafts at the Detroit Museum of Art, and participated in the 1907 SACB exhibition. Her home address was listed in 1888 as 35 Concord Avenue, and soon after as 59 Langdon Street, Cambridge. By about 1920, Winlock had moved to 15 Craigie Street in Cambridge. (J.F.)

SOURCES
Museum School Scrapbook, vol. 1; *Boston Herald*, May 31, 1891; Úlehla (1981), p. 234; *Arts and Crafts Exhibition*, Providence Art Club, March 19–April 9, 1901, p. 10, cat. no. 103; *Official Catalogue of Exhibitors, Universal Exposition, St. Louis, U.S.A.*, Department B, Art (St. Louis, Mo.: Official Catalogue Company, Inc., 1904), cat. no. 900; *Catalogue of the Second Annual Exhibition of Original Designs for Decorations and Examples of Art Crafts having Distinct Artistic Merit* (Chicago: Art Institute of Chicago, December 3–20, 1903), p. 41, cat. nos. 459–460; *First Annual Exhibition of Arts and Crafts* (Detroit: Detroit Museum of Art, 1904), p. 12, cat. nos. 190–92; *Second Annual Exhibition of Applied Arts* (Detroit: Detroit Museum of Art, 1905), p. 14; 1907 exhib. catal., p. 47, cat. nos. 817–19.

Madeline Yale Wynne
(1847–1918)

Born in Newport, N.Y., multi–talented Wynne was encouraged by her artistic father and liberal mother to pursue the arts. Daughter of Linus Yale, Jr. (the inventor of the Yale lock), Wynne experimented with tools and metalwork, developing her "own line of metalwork and enamels without instruction." Wynne studied painting in 1877 at the School of the Museum of Fine Arts, Boston, where she taught for several years. She also trained at the Art Students League in New York. Throughout her career, Wynne applied herself to a variety of media—creating paintings, painted furniture, and etched and enameled hollowware—although she is best known today for her jewelry. ❛In 1885 Wynne and her widowed mother bought an historic house, the "Old Manse" in Deerfield, Mass. where they summered, prompting her interest in preservation and colonial revival handicrafts—including needlework, leather, basketry, furniture, and pyrography. A stimulating leader, Wynne helped found the Society of Deerfield Industries in 1901 and the League of Handicraft in 1907. In 1893 she and her mother joined her brother Julian—also an avocational metalworker—in Chicago for the winter, thus starting a yearly routine of travel between Deerfield and Chicago. Wynne also established a studio in Chicago in 1896 and helped found the Chicago Arts and Crafts Society in October 1897. Wynne exhibited at Chicago's first exhibition in 1898 and again in 1899, in Springfield, Mass. in 1902, and in Minneapolis in 1903, among others. (J.F. and M.B.M.)

SOURCES
Questionnaire for *Allgemeines Lexikon*, SACB archives, AAA/BPL; "Necrology: Madeline Yale Wynne; Annual Meeting 1918," *History and Proceed-*

ings of the Pocumtuck Valley Memorial Association 9 (Deerfield: PVMA, 1912–1920), p. 420; Maribeth Bernardy, "Crafting a Life: Biography of Madeline Yale Wynne," unpubl. MS. (Deerfield: PVMA, n.d.); Sharon Darling, *Chicago Silversmiths* (Chicago: Chicago Historical Society, 1977), p. 63; Kaplan (1987), p. 264.

William Zorach
(1887–1966)

Born in Eurburg, Lithuania on February 28, 1887, William Zorach emigrated with his family to Ohio in 1891. He took evening classes at the Cleveland School of Art from 1902 to 1905, while working in a commercial lithography shop. In 1907 he went to New York to study at the National Academy of Design with George Maynard and Edgar Melville Ward. Zorach was in Paris in 1910, where he attended the Académie de la Palette as the pupil of Jacques–Emile Blanche and John Duncan Fergusson, and was deeply influenced by the Fauves. The artist's first solo exhibition of paintings was mounted at Taylor Galleries in Cleveland in 1912, the year in which Zorach married the artist Marguerite Thompson. In 1916 the Zorachs began to summer in Provincetown, and showed paintings and prints at the second Provincetown Art Association. They were also active members of the Provincetown Players, on the Cape and in New York. Zorach returned yearly to Provincetown through 1923, by which time he had ceased painting and printmaking to concentrate on sculpture. He taught at the Art Students League from 1929 to 1958, and during the 1930s was a lecturer at Columbia University. Retrospective exhibitions of his work were shown at the Art Students League in 1950 and at the Whitney Museum in 1959. Zorach died in Bath, Me. on November 15, 1966. (D.A.)

SOURCES
William Zorach, *Art is My Life* (Cleveland: World Publishing Co., 1967); John I.H. Baur, *William Zorach* (New York: Whitney Museum of American Art, 1959).

INDEX

text references | [figure references]

A

Académie Julian, 155, 212, 225, 228
Adams, Sandra (lender), 5, 190
Addison, Julia DeWolf, 103, 120, 131, 132, 206
   Life of St. Barbara produced by, [130], 186, [187]
Adriatic Sea, the (Murphy), [52], 166, [167]
After the Storm, photograph (Harvey), [148]
Ainslie, Maud, 162
Albee, Helen, 114
Aldrich, Thomas Bailey, 118
Alfred University. *See* New York School of
   Clayworking and Ceramics
Allen, Frances S. and Mary E., 149, 206, 209
   The Minuet (photograph) by, 149, 192, [193]
Alpers, Edith (lender), 5
Altar Book, the (Updike), 118, 131
   pages from, [124-25], 186, [187]
   Sears's binding for, 131
Althin, Olof, 45, 206, 219
   oak chest by, 166, [167]
Andrews, Robert D., 18, 22, 218
Antigone (Sophocles), Riverside Press edition with Loring's boards,
   132, 188, [189], 222
Appleton, William Sumner, 21
apprenticeship, traditional, 48, 52, 75, 97, 214, 226
Aquidneck Cottage Industries, 104
architects, 23, 41, 56, 214, 219, 220, 224
   influence of, 22, 27, 37, 47-48, 75, 103, 120
   in SACB, 22, 35, 36
architecture, 15, 18, 24-25, 38
   periodicals and yearbooks, 29, 43, 44, 48
Argosy, the (Brigham), [96], 98
Art Nouveau, 47, 95, 103, 145, 153, 161
Arts & Crafts Exhibition Society, English, 33
Arts and Crafts movement, 15, 117
   aristocracy and, 19, 21-23
   in Boston, 9, 14-19, 28-31
   definitions of, 38-39
   English, 30, 33, 87, 101, 103, 131, 153
Arts and Crafts of the Homeland (exhibition)
   poster for, [155], 161
"Art that is Life, the": The Arts & Crafts Movement
   in America, 14
Ashbee, Charles Robert, 17, 29, 36, 73, 75, 84, 88,
   95, 129, 216
Ashbee, Janet, 129

B

Bacon, Francis, 22, 27
Baggs, Arthur, 62, 69
Bailey, Cora Louise, 206
   Christ's Sermon in the Mount illuminated by, 186,[187]
Bailey, Henry Turner, 83
Ballou, John, [94]
Baltimore Museum of Art (lender), 5, 196
baptismal font (Woolley and Copeland), [76], 81
Bareback Rider, the, woodcut (Nichols), 200, [201]
Barr, Charles H., 75, 75n.9
Bartlett, Alfred, bookplate designed for, 130, 188, [189]
basket making, 16, 28, 114, 114n.35
Batchelder, Ernest, 29
Batchelder, Mary Steere, 206-07
   table lamp by, 174, [175]
Bates, Kenneth, 82, 85
batik, 114-15
   Bush-Brown wall hanging, [106], 115, 182, [183]
Baumann, Gustave, 162, 207
   Provincetown, woodcut by, 198, [199]
   Tom a' Hunting, woodcut by, 198, [199]
Baxter, Sylvester, 113
beadwork, 38
Beardsley, Aubrey, 118
Beaux-Arts training, 24, 25, 26, 29, 36
Bell, Robert Anning, illustrator of *The Altar Book*,
   118, [124-25], 186, [187]
Bend of a River, woodcut (Dow), 198, [199]
Benson, Frank W., 22, 54, 56

Berberian, Rosalie (lender), 5, 170
Berenson, Bernard, 21
Berlin Woolwork, 102
Bertoia, Arrieto (Harry), 83, 85
Bigelow, Francis Hill, 45
Bigelow, Kennard & Company, 30, 54
Bigelow, William Sturgis, 21, 102
Binns, Charles Fergus, 37, 62
Bird, E.B., 119
Birmingham School of Art, 81, 222
Blacher, Richard (lender), 5, 186
Blair, William, 81, 85
Blanchard, Porter, 22
Blaney, Dwight, 45
Blunt, Wilfred Scawen, 118
bobbin lace, 182, [183], 184, [185]
Bohemian Musician, the, linocut (Preissig), [160], 202, [203]
Bolles, H. Eugene, 45
book covers
   embossed gilt and painted leather (English), 176, [177]
   for Gautier's *Captain Fracasse* (Sacker), 190, [191]
   Goodhue's, for SACB catalogue, [120]
   for Hawthorne's *Marble Faun* (Whitman), 117, 190, [191]
   for Prang and Co.'s *Modern Art* (Rogers), [119]
   for Roberts's *Kindred of the Wild* (Sacker), [128], 190, [191]
   for Rossetti's *Hand and Soul* (Sears), [128], 190, [191]
   for Smith's *Arabella and Araminta Stories* (Reed), 188, [189]
   for Tacitus's *Agricola* (Whitman), 190, [191]
   for Thoreau's *Cape Cod* (Whitman), 190, [191]
   Updike's, for SACB exhibitions, 131, [132]
bookends, wooden
   by Lees, 166, [167]
   by Morse, [54], 56
book pages
   from *The Altar Book* (Updike), [124-25], 186, [187]
   from *A Day at Laguerre's* (title page), 118, [118]
   from de Guérin's *The Centaur* (Rogers and Rollins), [127], [130],
      188, [189]
   from Tacitus's *Agricola* (Goodhue and Updike), 186, [187]
   title page of Rowlandson capitivity narrative, 188, [189]
   title page to Sidney-Languet letters (Cleland and Dwiggins),
      130, 186, [187]
bookplates
   by Hapgood, 130, 188, [189]
   Moonrise (Meteyard), 200, [201]
   photo engravings of, 130, 188, [189]
books and bookbinding, 16, 22-23, 81, 117, 131-32
   See also printers and printing
   and calligraphy, 120, 131
   revival styles in, 129
   training for, 130, [130]
Booth, George G., 48, 73, 81, 166
Boris, Eileen, 104
Boston
   Arts and Crafts movement in, 9, 14-19, 28-31
   as center for printmaking, 153
   as publishing center, 117
Boston Consolidated Gas model dining room, 44, [45]
Bostonians, the: Painters of an Elegant Age, 1870-1930, 15
Boston Public Library (lender), 5, 178, 188, 198
Bowles, Janet Payne, 75, 75n.10, 85
Bowl of White Berries, the, photograph (Seeley), [142], 143, 196, [197]
Bowl Shop. *See* Paul Revere Pottery
bowls
   copper and enamel (Cauman, Hay, and
      Macomber), [82]
   copper, silver (Wynne), 72
   silver footed (Copeland), 174, [175]
   sugar, silver (Pratt), 176, [177]
boxes
   copper and enamel (Twitchell), 176, [177]
   jewelry (Eckberg), 53, 166, [167]
   powder, silver (Little), [76]
   silver with chased lid (Rose), 176, [177]
   silver with enamel (Copeland), 72, [77], 174, [175]
   silver with peacock medallion (Marshall), [80], 176, [177]
   silver with ship plaque (Hale), 97, 178, [179]
   sugar, silver (Gebelein), 76, 174, [175]

239